The
Making of
Psychology

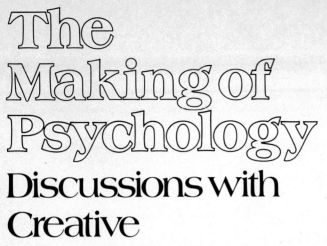

The Making of Psychology

Discussions with Creative Contributors

Richard I. Evans
University of Houston

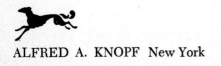
ALFRED A. KNOPF New York

To my lovely wife and children

THIS IS A BORZOI BOOK PUBLISHED BY ALFRED A. KNOPF, INC.

First Edition

9 8 7 6 5 4 3 2 1

Library of Congress Cataloging in Publication Data

Evans, Richard Isadore, 1922–
    The making of psychology.

    A series of interviews with 28 psychologists.
    1. Psychologists—Interviews. 2. Psychology.
I. Title. [DNLM: 1. Psychology—History.
2. Psychology—Biography. BF109.A1 E93m]
BF109.A1E9   150   75-46518
ISBN 0-394-31153-1

Manufactured in the United States of America

COVER PHOTOS

FRONT COVER: *Left to right, top row*: Konrad Lorenz, Harry F. Harlow; *center row*: Carl Rogers, B. F. Skinner, Neal Miller; *bottom row*: Erik Erikson, Albert Bandura, David McClelland. BACK COVER: *Top to bottom, left column*: Philip Zimbardo, Stanley Schachter, Ernest Hilgard, R. D. Laing; *right column*: Stanley Milgram, Jean Piaget, Donald Norman.

Preface

For the help received during the long process of planning and completing the discussions presented in this volume, I am indebted to a great many individuals. Though space prohibits mentioning everyone who so kindly assisted me in this venture, I wish to express my appreciation to at least some of these persons.

I am grateful for the support of the National Science Foundation, without which this project could not have been implemented.

Thanks are accorded my secretary, Ms. Jan Prevatt, who assisted me in many chores involved in completing this volume, and to Ms. Jeanne Seward for transcribing the original tapes of some of the discussions.

Special thanks go to psychology graduate student Bettye Earle Raines, who made valuable contributions in every phase of this book, transcribing tapes of most of the discussions, providing extensive editorial assistance, checking relevant bibliographical sources, and collating the final manuscript. Ms. Kay Murray also contributed much to this volume in her extensive editorial work on a great number of the discussions during their early, unedited stage.

For permission to utilize sections of previously published discussions, thanks are accorded E. P. Dutton and Company, Inc., Harper and Row, Publishers, and Ziff-Davis Publishing Company, publisher of *Psychology Today*.

Finally, the wonderful cooperation of the various participants cannot be emphasized enough. Not only were they willing to participate in the taping sessions involved in this project, but were willing to make a number of excellent suggestions in their reactions to the final form of the manuscript, which reflect my discussions with them.

Richard I. Evans
Professor of Psychology
UNIVERSITY OF HOUSTON

Contents

Section Two
Learning/Cognition/
Altered States of Consciousness   69

Section Three
Physiological Psychology/Motivation/ Emotion

Section Four
Personality: Behavioral/Social/Existential 197

Introduction:
A Perspective
on the Discussion
Style and Content

This book is the eleventh in a series based on discussions with outstanding contributors to the field of psychology; this is the first book in the series to include discussions with a number of contributors and to represent a diverse range of areas in psychology. To assist in understanding the goals of the discussion style used here, as well as its content, some perspective may be of value. This series was launched in 1957 with completion of recorded conversations with the late Carl Jung and the late Ernest Jones (Evans 1964, 1976), supported by a grant from the Fund for the Advancement of Education. Continued support for the series has been provided under a grant from the National Science Foundation. The basic purpose of the project is to produce, for teaching purposes, a series of films and books that introduce the student to significant contributors in the field of psychology. It is hoped that these films and books may also serve as documents of increasing value in the history of the behavioral sciences.*

The interviews presented in this book are designed to introduce the reader to the contributor's major ideas and points of view, hopefully conveying through the extemporaneous discussion a feeling of the personality of the contributor. The contributors included in this volume were selected to represent the major areas of psychology reflected in current introductory psychology textbooks. However, no effort was made to provide a complete coverage of the field. Many of the individuals included here have produced significant ideas in more than one area of psychology. One of the characteristics of creative contributors may be that their work cannot be easily pigeonholed into any one field in psychology.

The sample of contributors included in this volume, although not exhaustive, is at least representative. In looking over the field, it is obvious that there are many other contributors who might just as easily have been included here. And, in fact, they may be included in a second volume.

When we completed the first book in the series based on discussions with Jung and Jones (Evans 1964), we thought the word *conversation* best described the process and content of the material. We soon learned that this implied to some potential readers something a bit more casual

---

* The films are distributed by Macmillan Films, Inc., 34 MacQuesten Parkway, South, Mt. Vernon, New York 10550.

and superficial than we had intended. Even though we emphasize spontaneity in the discussions with our participants, this should not detract from the significance of the content. A relatively informal discussion with an outstanding contributor to a discipline, as he seriously examines his own work, should not be less significant by virtue of its informality. A more detailed description of the philosophy and techniques of this project is reported elsewhere (Evans 1969c).

A few additional points bearing on the contents of this particular volume should be made. The questions I use are intended to generate discussion of the ideas found in many of the published writings of the interviewees, but it is not expected that a comprehensive summary of their work could be evoked. For one thing, the selectivity necessary in completing the discussion within a limited time interval made such an inclusive summary impossible. But we are hoping that we have produced material that offers a pleasant alternative to those students today who have become increasingly dependent upon and satisfied with only secondary sources to learn about the major contributors to psychology. The content developed through these discussions provides "original source" exposure to the ideas of creative psychologists, which in turn may encourage the reader to go back to the original writings that develop these ideas more fully. At least, used in conjunction with introductory textbooks, I would hope that such original statements by significant contributors would be more stimulating to the student than many of the the books of "readings" appear to be.

It might be in order to explain my role in these discussions. As codiscussant or interviewer I saw my role as that of a medium through which the interviewees could express their views. Extensive critical examination of the views of the participants must be left to another type of project. In a limited space it would be impossible both to introduce the contributor's views and to criticize them as well. Also, I expect that some people who worked with us on this project would not have done so if they had sensed primarily a critical attack on their work.

It should also be pointed out that in their writings, these individuals can rewrite and polish until they deem the product satisfactory. In the spontaneity of our discussion, they are often called upon to develop ideas extemporaneously. As mentioned earlier, I hope that this element of spontaneity presents a feel for the "men behind the ideas" as well as the ideas themselves. Because preservation of this naturalness of communication is essential, few liberties have been taken with the basic content of the responses to my questions, although some editorial license was exercised in the interest of readability and clarity. So the discussions presented here duplicate, insofar as possible, the tenor of the exchange between the interviewees and myself.

Let me outline the overall format of the questions that I posed in the discussions. In almost all the discussions, I attempted to evoke a statement of the most important work of the participant, and also to elicit information on the research leading to this work. In this respect, it was interesting to record, in their own words, how many of these contributors moved from one area to another, say from an interest primarily in social or clinical psychology to an interest in a different field such as physiological psychology. The interviewees were also provided an opportunity to evaluate their own work in terms of its importance, and to react to some criticism.

Although most of these discussions were completed in the past year, some were extracted from earlier books or transcriptions of films, and they were not updated. References are made to the published dates of the books or films from which such discussions were extracted.

It has been exciting for me, as a social psychologist, to have an opportunity to interview such a unique sample of creative individuals. Even in those instances where the persons were previously known to me only through their published works, their genuine interest in communicating their work to students in this less didactic manner, and their willingness to trust me in mediating this process, is greatly appreciated.

REFERENCES

Evans, R. I. 1964. *Conversations with Carl Jung and reactions from Ernest Jones.* New York: Van Nostrand.

———. 1966. *Dialogue with Erich Fromm.* New York: Harper.

———. 1968. *B. F. Skinner: the man and his ideas.* New York: Dutton.

———. 1969a. *Dialogue with Erik Erikson.* New York: Dutton.

———. 1969b. *Psychology and Arthur Miller.* New York: Dutton.

———. 1969c. Contributions to the history of psychology: ten filmed dialogues with notable contributors to psychology. *Psychol. Reports* 25:159–164.

———. 1971. *Gordon Allport: the man and his ideas.* New York: Dutton.

———. 1973. *Jean Piaget: the man and his ideas.* New York: Dutton

———. 1975a. *Carl Rogers: the man and his ideas.* New York: Dutton.

———. 1975b. *Konrad Lorenz: the man and his ideas.* New York: Harcourt.

———. 1976a. *R. D. Laing: the man and his ideas.* New York: Dutton.

———. 1976b. *Jung on elementary psychology.* New York: Dutton.

Section One
Ethology
Development
Intelligence

This section includes contributors whose work is related to the impact of the genetic-developmental process on the individual. In contemporary psychology, as the nature-nurture controversy is explored, increasing emphasis is being given to the importance of some aspects of biological determinism. The introductory psychology book of several years ago almost inevitably focused on the importance of cultural–environmental–social influences in shaping individual development. The work of the persons represented in this section undoubtedly contributed to the modification of emphasis.

When Konrad Lorenz and Nikolaas Tinbergen became the first behavioral scientists to be awarded the Nobel Prize, the work of the ethologists, already beginning to influence many psychologists, was highlighted. Lorenz's concept of evolutionary epistemology—suggesting that in the evolution of the species, genetically preprogrammed "knowledge" aids in coping with the environment—presented many possibilities for the study of behavior. Tinbergen's elegant discussion of the methodology of the ethologist certainly geared the psychologist to study behavior in its natural setting, and to explore the effects of genetic programming on individual behavior.

In an extraordinarily innovative line of research, Harry Harlow provides some experimental substance for the ideas of the ethologists, as he observes "mother love" in monkeys, in its unfolding, identifying the stimuli involved in this affectional process.

After many years of neglect, particularly by American psychology, Jean Piaget's concept of genetic epistemology finally became influential in the thinking of psychologists. Piaget's theories of development include a progression of naturally developing cognitive "sets" toward the environment that even precede language; "constructions" result from the interaction of these sets with the environment. Piaget's work should remind behavioral scientists that it is important to consider the "givens" in the analysis of experience and behavior.

Arthur Jensen has stressed the importance of genetic determination in individual development. Because he has focused on a possible hereditary relationship between intelligence and race, his work, perhaps more than that of any others, has aroused tremendous controversy.

1

It should be emphasized that both the heading for this section and the selection of individual contributors to it are entirely arbitrary. Any one of these individuals might easily have been included in another section, or several sections. In fact, it seems characteristic of most of them that their work is not easily confined to the limits and definitions of one area. An arbitrary assignment to a more traditional niche serves primarily as a guide for teachers and students in relating these discussions to contemporary introductory textbooks.

1

Konrad Lorenz

(1903–   )

Nobel laureate Konrad Lorenz, now retired, continues research at his home in Altenberg near Vienna. He received his M.D. degree from the University of Vienna in 1928, and in 1933 his PhD. His distinguished academic career includes appointments to the University of Vienna, the University of Königsberg, and the Institute for the Physiology of Behavior (Max Planck Society for the Advancement of Science). Professor Lorenz pioneered in the field of ethology, where his unique contributions include the discovery of imprinting, his highly provocative work on aggression, and the development of the concept of evolutionary epistemology.

Ethology is Nothing New/The Organism and Its Environment/One System//
Imprinting/And Some Interesting Analogies//The Ethological Approach
to Motivation//Some Dangerous Tendencies/Aggressivity/Aggression/
Violence//Pornography and the Disappearance of Love//Looking for Trouble/
The Need for Aggression?//Some Comments on "Popular" Ethology//

Professor Lorenz and I discuss the evolution of his contributions to ethology
for which he received the Nobel Prize. He defines ethology and tells how he
first became interested in this approach to the study of organisms. We also
discuss his observations on imprinting, and he suggests possible analogies to
human behavior. We compare the ethological approach to motivation to the
more traditional psychological interpretations and discuss the sources of social
motivation such as social approval. Professor Lorenz comments on his theory of
aggression, or aggressivity, as he prefers to call it, and reacts to misinterpretations of his book, ON AGGRESSION. He offers his analysis of the presidential
commission reports on pornography and violence and some reasons for the limited
impact of peace versus war models. "You cannot teach a person not to be enthusiastic," he explains, "but you can teach him what to be enthusiastic about." He
reacts to Skinner's behavioristic model, and comments on various popular generalizations from his work in ethology, such as Ardrey's THE TERRITORIAL
IMPERATIVE and Morris' THE NAKED APE. In conclusion, he describes some
of his current writing and some plans for the future.

EVANS: Dr. Lorenz, have your observations of animals produced
any data that could throw light on the relations between man and
woman? For example, the late Abraham Maslow (1954) studied married
couples and discovered that the source of most conflict between husbands
and wives was the question of which mate was to dominate the other.
Is it possible that marital, sexual or economic problems are merely surface
manifestations of a fundamental battle for dominance?

LORENZ: It could be. In many fishes and birds, there is no great
external difference between the sexes, and each can potentially dominate
the other. When my daughter-in-law (Oehlert-Lorenz 1958) did her
doctoral research, she found that when you put two sexually mature fish
[cichlid fish of the species Cichlasoma biocellatum] of the same size
together, both are sexually aroused. In addition, each is aggressively
aroused against the other and slightly afraid of it. Now aggression and
fear mix the same in males and females. But aggression and sex, and
fear and sex, mix differently in the two sexes. The male can be highly
aggressive, and at the same time sexually aroused. He can beat the
female until the scales fly and the next moment engage in sexual movements. But if he's even a little afraid of her, his sexuality flops. Exactly
the opposite is true in the female. She can be deathly afraid of the male
and still be aroused. But if the male fish is so weak that she dares be
aggressive, he becomes an uninteresting sexual partner. She kills him,
even if she must then die of spawn retention. The same mechanism works
in many birds. Being dominated suppresses male sexuality; being domi-
nating suppresses female sexuality.

EVANS: Do you think that dominance is that clear in human sex?

LORENZ: No, among human beings there is no such thing as a pure
male or a pure female. There are female elements in every man and
male elements in every woman. The relationship in human married
couples is not so simple. In some respects I submit to my wife. Her
assessment of strange people, for example, is much better than mine.
In other respects she submits to me. To what extent maleness objects
to being dominated is an open question.

EVANS: Women are becoming increasingly concerned about the
belief of some men that they should be dominant and that women should
be submissive. Among animals, is the male always dominant?

LORENZ: I'm sorry to have to disappoint the ladies, but in most cases
there is clear male dominance. In those fish I just spoke of, the female
becomes frigid with a non-dominant male. But there are a few exceptions. In one species of turnicidae, which are quail-like birds, for example, the female is more beautiful than the male, she dominates him, and
he sits on the eggs. This is also true among a few species of fish.

EVANS: Woman's liberation is not the only movement to question
human sexual roles. The gay liberation movement objects strongly to
the idea that homosexuality is deviant. What has your observation of
animal pairings led you to think about homosexual behavior?

LORENZ: That's an interesting question. The capacity for homosexual behavior is part of the normal makeup of many animals. Any two male pigeons—or female pigeons—put together will engage in homosexual activities. The dominant bird will play the male role, the dominated bird will play the female role. You don't know that you're studying a homosexual pair until you observe that the nest is empty or that it contains twice as many eggs. You see, a pair of lesbian pigeons may produce double the normal number of eggs—and the eggs may be fertile because both lesbians are having affairs with a male pigeon.

In geese, falling in love and pair-bonding can be as dissociated from copulation as it can in man. You may find a very strong homosexual bond between two male geese who behave like a pair though they cannot copulate. They never do—they always forget that the other refuses to be mounted and they try again every spring. Each goose behaves in a perfectly normal male way and if he could speak, he would say, "I love my wife very much but she's definitely frigid."

EVANS: What happens to such a pair in the goose world?

LORENZ: Homosexual male pairs rise very high in the rank order of a goose colony, because the fighting potential of two males is superior to that of a heterosexual pair. Therefore, they are admired by unmarried females. Often when they fail to copulate because each wants to mount and neither will crouch, a loving female will crouch between them and is copulated by one or by both. This female is gradually accepted by the two males, but she gets no respect. Nobody offers her a "triumph ceremony." If she succeeds in getting a nest and laying, she may awaken the parental response in both males and they may guard the nest and accept the babies. Then you have a *menage à trois* in which two males love each other and the female loves one of them.

EVANS: But can you consider that normal goose behavior?

LORENZ: It can't be considered deviant or errant because Peter Scott has shown a large incidence of such triangular marriages among the wild, pink-footed geese of Iceland. They are particularly successful in defending and rearing goslings, because two males can defend babies better against dangers such as gerfalcons. Goose homosexual behavior turns out to have survival value. There should be no moral objection to homosexuality. Many people, however, have an esthetic, emotional aversion to homosexual behavior. I once saw two boys embrace in a bathroom. The sight was slightly repulsive to me, but in moral terms, why shouldn't they kiss? In an overpopulated world, it would be a good thing if there were more homosexuality.

EVANS: It has been argued that, at the current rate of reproduction, man will soon surpass the population that the world can support. Have you seen animal groups in which overpopulation was followed by some solution to the problem?

LORENZ: Certainly. Overpopulation is bad economics. If you overexploit the animal or plant on which you depend, you destroy your own means of sustenance. Territorial behavior, in which animals defend their own turf, has the survival value of limiting the number of animals and of distributing them equally over the available habitat. Some animals lack such limiting mechanisms: there is a population-limiting factor in lions, but none in jackals or hunting dogs.

EVANS: But those concerned with human overpopulation argue that it's a question of total available energy and food resources and that dispersion is no answer. When dispersion can no longer provide food for animal groups, do the animals simply perish?

LORENZ: Cases in which lack of food directly regulates animal populations are rare. Usually other mechanisms step in long before lack of food becomes a limiting factor. Our planet can feed many more people than it can support in dignity and freedom. The spatial requirements for a mentally healthy life are much larger than the requirements set by food production.

EVANS: Some theorists say that as crowding increases, leadership patterns shift from participatory to autocratic forms. Does that make any sense to you?

LORENZ: This happens in monkeys; the mechanism of it is clearly understandable, and it is justifiable to conclude that it might be the same in man. When you have an uncrowded rhesus monkey or baboon population, then the capacity to claim leadership depends on the individual's ability to form alliances, in other words, to form friendships. The leaders in the baboon group studied by Ivan DeVore (Washburn and DeVore 1961) were very old, but they maintained their primacy because they kept together and defended each other. Experiments have shown similar results in a normal rhesus colony. If you crowd the animals, they get irritable, and this snappishness breaks up friendships. Old leaders cease to be friends. From the moment when irritability becomes stronger than bond behavior, the strongest, most violent, most aggressive individual will rule. You get a single, strong ruler.

EVANS: So in a crowded society, you would get enmity, hostility and aggression.

LORENZ: The most crowded place I know is the bus terminal on 42nd street in New York City. The people are irritable and snappish. If you ask a person for directions, he snaps at you because he's irritated by the lack of elbow-room. The same consequences of crowding can be found among cats. They show elevated blood-pressure and all the other symptoms of stress.

EVANS: How far can you generalize from animals to man? Isn't there a point at which you jump too far in translating such effects of crowding?

LORENZ: Man is a very conditionable animal, and we don't know just how far you can train man to fit another environment. But I strongly doubt whether you can condition man so that he does not become nervous and neurotic when he is crowded. My experience has been that people who live miles from their nearest neighbors and are not over-whelmed by social contacts show the greatest human kindness. I once had an experience that has remained fresh in my memory. When I lived in Munich, I was over-fed with human contacts; we had as houseguests an American couple who lived in the wilds of Wisconsin. Just as we sat down to dinner, the doorbell rang and I said, "Who the hell's that again?" The most indecent thing I could have said would not have shocked these two people more profoundly. To be less than overjoyed when the doorbell rang was incomprehensible to these people who lived deep in the country. This made me realize how much I had become a victim of crowding.

EVANS: Do animal groups ever engage in family planning, on the "unconscious" level, of course?

LORENZ: A lot of mechanisms act that way. Let me cite one example. If food is so short that wolves have to kill big game to survive, as they do on Lake Superior, then a large pack must come together. In a large pack of wolves, only the alpha female—the dominant female—breeds. She prevents all other females from copulating. If big game is not necessary for food, then the pack dissolves into single pairs and every single female breeds. To be more precise, if it takes a pack of 40 wolves to kill a moose, then only one female out of 20 breeds. So there is a mechanism that accommodates the rate of reproduction to the available food.

EVANS: Do you think we must use drastic methods to curtail human population?

LORENZ: You speak of drastic measures. We *cannot* take drastic measures, even though every single problem that presses on humanity ultimately stems from overpopulation. If we attempt to solve the problem by any means other than education, we're back in the wildest kind of authoritarianism. If we cannot curtail population voluntarily, we cannot curtail it at all. The main danger of voluntary limitation, of course, is that intelligent, responsible people plan their families, while irresponsible fools do not. Then you get the wrong kind of selection.

EVANS: William Shockley, a Nobel prize winning physicist, argues that people with low IQs should be given economic incentives for sterilization. He believes that black people are genetically inferior to whites in at least one kind of intellectual potential. Arthur Jensen (1969) has found that blacks do not perform as well as whites on tests that supposedly measure an abstract type of intelligence. How do you perceive the black-white IQ argument?

LORENZ: The IQ test is an intelligence test developed in terms of white, middle-class culture and very possibly unfair to those of a different race and culture. No man can deny that the races are different, but it is stupid to contend that this difference necessarily implies a difference in value. The pintail duck is genetically different from the mallard, but one is not more valuable than the other. According to my friend

John Garcia, R. C. Tryon (1940) tried to create intelligent rats by breeding those that were particularly bright. His rat IQ test was a maze, and he chose the rats that learned to run through the maze fastest. In Tryon's maze, a trap door shut whenever a rat took the correct turn. After selecting breeding stock for many generations, Tryon finally learned that he was not selecting intelligent rats, but rats that were insensitive to trap doors shutting behind them. Garcia argues that there's exactly the same kind of danger with intelligence tests (Garcia 1972). To claim that one subspecies is better biologically than another is to take an absurd position.

EVANS: One of the things that I have observed about you in the last few days is that you are concerned about over-enthusiastic generalizations derived from ethological studies. Do such popular books as Desmond Morris' (1967) *The Naked Ape* and Robert Ardrey's (1966) *The Territorial Imperative* trouble you? Morris, for example, seems to feel we should get rid of all social customs that do not have biological roots in the earlier primates.

LORENZ: First, may I say that both Morris and Ardrey are good friends of mine. I agree with some aspects of *The Naked Ape*, because Morris treats man as if his important characteristic is his culture. But I do not agree with his view that every cumulative social tradition in the human species was a side issue, to be deplored rather than admired. Furthermore, if I were to give a name to any species, I would choose the function by which the species survived. For example, I would call a woodpecker, "woodpecker" because it lives by pecking wood. If I were forced to call the human species apes, the name I chose should at least show that they are the culture apes, the cumulating-tradition apes, the ideal conception of all apes. That man is naked is inessential; he might just as well be furry.

EVANS: And Ardrey's *Territorial Imperative?*

LORENZ: Robert Ardrey has become a very good ethologist in his own right; he has learned a lot. But *The Territorial Imperative* is overgeneralized. I feel it's a bit too daring. While reading it, I suffered all the agonies one feels when sitting in a car beside a driver who takes a stretch of road much faster than you feel is safe, but you're helpless to slow him down. In other words, Ardrey was sticking *my* neck out. I emphasize that this is *not* the case with his later work. I'm fully in agreement with that.

EVANS: What criticisms of your own work have troubled you the most?

LORENZ: Criticism troubles you because through it you may discover something is wrong with your own position. The mere defense of one's position does not necessarily require any strong involvement. The criticisms that troubled me most are the criticisms to which I reacted most completely and which changed my attitudes. Daniel Lehrman's (1953) paper, "Critique of Konrad Lorenz's Theories," is an example of such criticism. He expounded a behavioristic attitude, saying that all the behavior I attributed to genetic programming could be learned. In that his criticism more than slightly over-simplified my views, it was unjust. But Lehrman quoted experiments of Z. Y. Kuo (1932), who concluded that the heartbeat moving passively by the chick's head before hatching teaches the chick to peck.

I answered this criticism later in a paper that I prepared for a congress on instinct. To state it simply, I pointed out that in order to avoid the concept of innate behavior, Kuo postulated an innate school marm, the heartbeat, teaching the chick *how* to peck. Of course, this teacher cannot teach the chick *what* to peck at. It took me 10 years to find out that the innate school marm is, indeed, the problem of what all learning is, because as learning improved the survival value of behavior, the learning apparatus had to contain information about what ought to be learned and what ought to be extinguished. There must be a teacher who pats you on the shoulder and says, "That's right, do it again," or, "No, no, don't do that again, it causes a bellyache." In other words, during evolution the neural structures develop in ways that prepare the organism to associate certain stimuli and prevent it from associating other stimuli. So in the long run, Lehrman's paper proved to be the most constructive and most helpful of all the criticisms I have received.

Let me say here, however, that there is still a widespread fallacy among psychologists and sociologists that everything social in the human organism is cultural, therefore learned. If I am convinced of anything, it is that this is absolutely untrue and that our ancestors were social animals, highly social animals.

EVANS: But the environment has a profound influence.

LORENZ: Nothing, of course, is entirely innate, because however fixed the genetic program of behavior, it needs the environment to be realized. Only information is innate. The genes provide a blueprint for development, but the organism, even before birth, is constantly affected by the environment.

EVANS: Another behaviorist, B. F. Skinner (Evans 1968), has increasingly questioned the value of motivational terms like aggression. He feels that this kind of concept is irrelevant and that we can shape and modify behavior simply by arranging the contingencies in the environment. Do you agree that forgetting about terms like aggression might make a better science of behavior?

LORENZ: For Skinner and the other operant conditioners, only one approach is scientifically legitimate—to alter the situation with a reinforcer, which certainly increases the probability of a behavior occurring more often. But practically *all* organisms with a higher developed nervous system have a learning apparatus that feeds back the results of successive behavior to antecedent behavior. The learning apparatus is pretty much the same in cephalopods, in crustaceans, in insects, and in vertebrates. If you study nothing but this learning apparatus, you fail to consider the things that are different among species. In other words, you leave out everything that makes a pigeon a pigeon, a rat a rat, a man a man, and most of all, a healthy man healthy and an ill man ill. The Skinnerian has no right to comment on innate behavior or on aggression, because he cuts it from consideration. You never hear Skinnerians admit that they are unable to condition a female pigeon or a female rat to lie on her back during copulation. This is phylogenetically programmed behavior and you cannot condition it by the Skinnerian technique.

EVANS: Natural selection has resulted in receptive female rats that will not lie on their backs, no matter how many food pellets drop in the tray.

LORENZ: Look at John Garcia's work. He showed that if you feed a rat a certain food and then punish it by electric shock or dropping ·it in water or inflicting some kind of pain, there is no effect. It keeps on eating the food. But if you make it nauseated after it eats the food, it will refuse to eat that food again. And if it's eaten an extensive menu of 10 or 12 dishes, it will refuse the single new food in the group, no matter what sequence the dishes were fed in. This shows you how "intelligent" such an innate program is (Seligman 1972).

EVANS: Some behaviorists would argue that their interest lies in modifying, controlling, and predicting behavior, so that your work has no interest for them.

LORENZ: But you cannot control behavior until you know what the reinforcers are. You have to know the innate behavior patterns in order to know what situations act as reinforcement. Garcia can control his rats in a way that Skinner cannot, because he knows which reinforcements work—and which do not. I defy anybody using Skinnerian methods to settle a gray-lag goose colony in a new locality.

EVANS: But Skinnerians would look at your work and say that you're using operant conditioning without specifying the contingencies in Skinnerian language.

LORENZ: I do use operant methods, but I use other methods, too, particularly other sources of information. I do not reject anything that Skinnerians *do*, but I reproach them for a number of things they *don't* do—for instance, simple observation of an animal's adaptation to his natural environment. I don't think many behaviorists have ever studied a wild rat in the field just to see what it does. They might get some valuable information as to effective reinforcers, if they'd do it.

EVANS: From your observations, you could give Skinnerians ideas for reinforcers that laboratory experiments would never reveal. Professor Lorenz, you are best known among laymen for your book, *On Aggression* (Lorenz 1966). Aggression is a highly loaded term. When they hear the title of your book, many people automatically assume that you are talking about violence.

LORENZ: This explains why many people think that I have written an apology for violence. Most of the book deals with the question of how animals *avoid* violence and killing. In German, the words aggression and aggressivity are synonymous; in English and in French they are not. So my book should have been titled *On Aggressivity* not *On Aggression,* and certainly not *On Violence.* Now let's forget that word and refer to it as "I-can-lick-you" behavior.

If you put together two little boys, two fish of one species, two roosters, two monkeys, they will behave exactly as Mark Twain describes a meeting between Tom Sawyer and a new boy. The first words Tom says are, "I can lick you," and the inevitable fight ends just as soon as one boy hollers, "Nuff!" It's not a drive to kill another person, but the drive to lick him into submission. It has to do with rank order or territory, and not with a killing instinct.

EVANS: Then is killing always an accident?

LORENZ: More or less. In only two species does fighting between two rivals continue to the death of one adversary: one species of lizard and the Indian elephant. In territorial fights, only the loon, a waterbird, actually kills a fellowbird in defense of its territory. The very scarcity of such examples demonstrates how rare this behavior is.

EVANS: Would you say that genetic programming is present in man's aggressivity?

LORENZ: If I were to write *On Aggression* again, I would make a much stricter distinction between individual aggressivity within a society and the collective aggressivity of one ethnic group against another. These may well be two different programs. They appear to be different in animals. The behavior patterns of animals seeking status and fighting for rank order are entirely different from the behavior patterns of the whole group fighting another group. I may have been wrong in not distinguishing precisely enough between these two factors. They are of a very different nature and have a different value.

EVANS: That's true. A gentle civilian can become a fierce killer with the declaration of war. Do both kinds of aggressivity have survival value?

LORENZ: Yes, they do. If you lack personal aggressivity, you are not an individual. You have no pride in yourself and are everyone else's man. And collective, militant enthusiasm, which is the prerequisite for war, is also the prerequisite for all higher human endeavor. Without the instinct of collective enthusiasm, a man is an emotional cripple; he cannot get involved in anything. One must educate people so that collective enthusiasm is not misdirected. Extreme nationalism is so dangerous because a man can be whole-heartedly French or English or German. But man can be broader than this. One can be a biologist at the same time that he is an enthusiastic musician or philanthropist.

EVANS: Even if individual and group aggressivity are different programs, aren't both directed by social reinforcement?

LORENZ: It's always there. There's nothing in human behavior—

down to our way of moving our lips when talking—that is not ritualized. Entirely unritualized behavior is obscene. Scratching, picking one's nose, yawning, stretching, not to mention more improper acts, are unritualized behavior. If a person fails to conform to normal social rituals, he's obviously hostile. If your friend enters the room without smiling, speaking, or noticing you, your first thought is, "My God, I've offended him." Man is a creature of culture, so if I say that there are innate programs underlying all our social behavior, this does not mean that there's not a culturally determined superstructure on it.

EVANS: You're saying that *all* social behavior, not just aggressivity, has been innately programmed by natural selection. In writing *On Aggression,* you chose aggressivity, but you could have chosen any one of a number of behaviors.

LORENZ: Of course. Anxiety is also dangerous and threatening. Somebody who knows more about it than I do ought to write a parallel volume *On Anxiety.* I chose to write on aggressivity because with the prevalence of nuclear weapons, aggressivity seems to be one of man's most dangerous motivations.

EVANS: Some readers are troubled because you appear to believe that aggressive behavior can be spontaneous, that aggression will appear without actual provocation.

LORENZ: I'm convinced of it. I cannot prove it in man. I can prove that in certain animals, aggressivity follows all the rules of threshold-lowering and appetitive behavior. You can see an animal looking for trouble, and a man can do that too. I'm quite sure that human societies are coercive mechanisms that turn aggression into prescribed channels. The same relationship holds between the internal drive welling up and the higher centers sitting on it to restrict aggressivity as in other instinctive behavior patterns.

EVANS: In the United States, two drives have been singled out: sex and violence. The President's Commission on Pornography (1970) concluded that any sexual excitation aroused by pornography is relatively harmless, and that pornography should not be banned. But the Commission on Violence (1969) found that the portrayal of violence can be a destructive model and recommended that we attempt to eliminate film and television violence. Can you reconcile these conclusions?

LORENZ: I agree that the depiction of sex and violence have two effects. Nearly seventy years ago, Julian Huxley wrote that all these activities are at the same time self-stimulating and self-exhausting. Of course, aggressivity is self-rewarding. It's a very real question whether encouraging people to feel a vicarious destructive aggressivity increases the probability of such aggressivity, or whether the vicarious aggression acts as a catharsis. I think that the possible danger of removing inhibitions is much more important. If children are accustomed to seeing wars, murders and fights on TV, their inhibitions against committing these violent acts may lessen. It's not that you're increasing the potential for aggressivity, but that you're lowering the inhibitions by creating a social climate that tolerates aggressive acts.

If you're a sexual sadist, you may also engage in violence. But the main danger of pornography is that it de-romanticizes all sexual behavior. It does away with falling in love, with all the beauty and ceremony of pair formation. This is quite as dangerous to our culture as violence is.

EVANS: What do you mean here by dangerous? It's dangerous in a different sense from violence, isn't it?

LORENZ: Yes. The destruction of people sounds very cruel, but our culture can tolerate a certain amount of it and still survive. But the destruction of the higher emotions, the disappearance of love and the finely adapted bond behavior, may present more danger to the survival of our culture than violence.

EVANS: Are you saying that pornography may reinforce nonselective, instant sex, and may gradually extinguish what we call love responses?

LORENZ: Yes. I think pornography may extinguish the finer, more sensitive and socially more important superstructure of sexual behavior. For example, the Kinsey Report (Kinsey et al. 1948, 1953) and Masters and Johnson (1966) talk about copulation as if copulation were the only type of sexual behavior. As I see it, sexual behavior begins with becoming conscious of the opposite sex, with falling in love, with elaborate forms of courtship that are partly innate and partly cultural.

EVANS: Do you find courtship behavior in animals?

LORENZ: Of course. But all these finer superstructures of sexual behavior tend to disappear in domestic animals very much as they do in urbanized man. If you compare the domestic animal with the wild species, you find that the unselective eating and the unselective instant copulation we consider bestial are largely confined to domestic animals.

There's another danger in pornography: instead of doing things, you resign yourself to watching things. That's a general trend in our culture, not to do but to be content with watching, and from that point of view, even watching violence might be beneficial. All these things are two-edged swords; they work both ways.

EVANS: I'd like to talk more about aggression. Mallick and Mc-Candless (1966) set up an experiment in which children played very aggressive games. Afterwards, they were allowed to play other games, and they were more aggressive than ever. This work suggests that aggressive activity doesn't necessarily discharge the need for aggression; it may reinforce it.

LORENZ: I think there may be a misunderstanding of my view. I never intended to imply that you cannot reinforce aggression. Of course you can. We know that fish can be trained to be more aggressive than they usually are. But that same fish, deprived of the possibility to discharge any aggression, will become spontaneously aggressive. If you withhold all aggression-eliciting environmental situations, you cannot hope that the need to discharge cumulative, built-up aggression will atrophy. Teaching a child to discharge aggression more successfully could certainly enhance aggression, and it may also lessen the inhibitions against aggression. The process is more complicated than it appears.

EVANS: So the results of these studies do not surprise you.

LORENZ: I'm not surprised that the children become more aggressive, but I should be surprised if cutting off all aggression-eliciting factors produced a nonaggressive child. You see the difference? Many studies show that children in a totally permissive, nonfrustrating environment are very aggressive. On the other hand, you can encourage aggression by reinforcing it with social approval. One study compared a tribe of Indians with Bushmen. The Indians are highly aggressive, and they encourage their children to be aggressive toward others by ritualizing the aggression. They take a stick and beat the other chap on the head in a very expressive, but not a strong, manner, while the Bushmen, who are less aggressive than the Indians, intentionally and directly channel aggression into innocuous paths. Exposed to aggression as children in two different ways, the adults of the two tribes are strikingly different. However, the early aggressive behavior of children in both tribes is much the same in magnitude.

EVANS: The study that you mentioned describes a form of social learning that we call modeling (Bandura 1973). Now, applying this to televised violence, it is possible that such violence becomes a model that reinforces violent patterns. I gather that you agree.

LORENZ: Yes, indeed. When a model's violence is rewarded, the child is much more likely to imitate it. The highly dangerous models are figures like James Bond, professional killers who are glamorized as heroes. There's no beneficial discharge in such cases.

In *On Aggression* I wrote another thing that I would qualify if I wrote it again. Nowadays, I have strong doubts whether watching aggressive behavior even in the guise of sport has any cathartic effect at all.

EVANS: Suppose we could do a reasonably good job of banishing violence from TV and eliminating war toys. Suppose we eliminated most models of violence in our culture. Would this reduce the overt violence in our society?

LORENZ: It would at least reduce the enthusiasm for war. You cannot teach a person *not* to be enthusiastic, but you can teach him what to be enthusiastic about. I may not get enthusiastic over Napoleon, but I get highly enthusiastic about Charles Darwin (1859) and he represents constructive aspects of our culture. You can teach a person what causes are worthy of embracing, even though the act of embracing is emotional and highly genetically programmed. But that is what I mean when I say that war is institutional: wars in general are still regarded as worthy causes. We must get accustomed to the idea that

war is no longer functional. Nuclear weapons have made war a form
of suicide. The elimination of war should be the major task of social
education.

EVANS: Let's look at the developments that led to World War II.
How do you assess the rise of aggression in Germany that led to the
kind of fanaticism we found in the Hitler *Jugend*?

LORENZ: I have a very arrogant theory about that. When young
people in Germany nowadays are disillusioned and blase and grasping
at straws, embracing wrong causes, becoming violent, it's often said
that their actions come from the disappointment they suffered to the
national ideals put forth by Hitler. I believe that the success of National
Socialism was symptomatic of a dearth of real ideals. The musical *West
Side Story* shows how the same patterns emerge in New York street
gangs. Genetically perfect, decent, good, young men create an adversary
just in order to be collectively enthusiastic in fighting him. That is the
Nazi spirit. If you realize that these young men in *West Side Story*
created their own fighting company, you can realize how susceptible
young people are to the demagogue who proffers dummy ideals, much
as we use a dummy model to make our stickleback fish fight. The success
of Hitler in Germany is evidence of the danger that arises when there
are no real ideals to embrace. Youth is perfectly right about rebelling
against the rat race of commercial competition and against the destruction and pollution of the environment. But the question is what ideals
to give them instead. We need something like a new ethic.

EVANS: Peace models always seem to be less attractive than war
models.

LORENZ: Yes, because man is collectively enthusiastic, militarily
enthusiastic, and it's a complicated demand on him to be enthusiastic
about peace. But I think we can get people there. Today we can be
enthusiastic about saving the environment. Here in Austria the youth
movement to protect the environment is gaining ground rapidly. There
are enough obstacles to overcome if we are to save humanity. There are
truly magnificent causes about which youth can become enthusiastic.
It's a shame that we don't communicate this to them convincingly enough.

EVANS: Do you feel that symbols of aggressivity like Hitler could
rise again? Do you think the groundwork is still there?

LORENZ: I have a deep-rooted fear that it might be so. I believe,
considering the high danger of collective aggressivity in the *West Side
Story* sort of enthusiasm, that the scientist has the duty to deviate from
his general rationale of saying only things that he can prove. When the
danger is serious enough, as I believe it is, it is the duty of the scientist
to call attention to that danger. Man must know that the horse he is
riding may be wild and should be bridled before it's too late.

REFERENCES

Ardrey, R. 1966. *The territorial imperative*. New York: Athenum.

Bandura, A. 1973. *Aggression: a social learning analysis*. Englewood Cliffs, N.J.: Prentice-Hall.

Darwin, C. 1859. *On the origin of species by means of natural selection or the preservation of favored races in the struggle for life*. London: Murray.

Evans, R. I. 1968. *B. F. Skinner: the man and his ideas*. New York: Dutton.

——. 1975. *Konrad Lorenz: the man and his ideas*. New York: Harcourt.

Garcia, J. 1972. IQ: the conspiracy. *Psychol. Today* 6: (4) 40–43.

Jensen, A. 1969. How much can we boost IQ and scholastic achievement? *Harvard Educational Review* 39: 1–123.

Kinsey, A. C., Pomeroy, W. B., and Martin, C. E. 1948. *Sexual behavior in the human male*. Philadelphia: Saunders.

——, and Gebhard, P. H. 1953. *Sexual behavior in the human female*. Philadelphia: Saunders.

Kuo, Z. Y. 1932. Ontogeny of embryonic behavior in aves, I and II. *J. Exper. Zool.* 61: 395–430; 62: 453–489.

——. 1932. Ontogeny of embryonic behavior in aves, III and IV. *J. Comp. Psychol.* 13: 245–272; 14: 109–122.

Lehrman, D. 1953. A critique of Konrad Lorenz's theory of instinctive behavior. *Quarterly Review of Biology* 28: 337–363.

Lorenz, K. 1966. *On aggression*. New York: Harcourt.

Mallick, S. K., and McCandless, B. R. 1966. A study of catharsis of aggression. *J. Pers. Soc. Psychol.* 4: 591–596.

Maslow, A. 1954. *Motivation and personality*. New York: Harper.

Masters, W. H., and Johnson, V. E. 1966. *Human sexual response*. Boston: Little, Brown.

Morris, D. 1967. *The naked ape*. London: Jonathan Cape.

National Commission on the Causes and Prevention of Violence. 1969. *To establish justice, to insure domestic tranquility*. New York: Award Books.

Oehlert-Lorenz, B. 1958. Kampf und Paarbildung Eineger Cichliden. *Zeitschrift für Tierpsychologie* 15: (2) 141–174.

The Report of the Commission on Obscenity and Pornography. 1970. New York: Bantam.

Seligman, M. 1972. Biological boundaries of learning. *Psychol. Today* 6: (3) 59–61.

Tryon, R. C. 1940. Genetic differences in maze-learning abilities in rats. *Yearbook of Natural Social Studies Education* 39: 111–119.

Washburn, S. L., and DeVore, I. 1961. The social life of baboons. *Sci. Amer.* 204: 62–71.

Nikolaas Tinbergen

(1907–   )

Nikolaas Tinbergen's outstanding contributions to the field of ethology have brought him the Nobel Prize as well as the prestigious Dutch Swammerdam Medal which is awarded only once each decade. He received his Ph.D. from Leiden University in 1932, later becoming a professor there and organizing a teaching course in animal behavior. A postwar series of lecture tours brought his work to the attention of American and British scientists, and he accepted a position at Oxford University where he became professor of zoology. His research in the field of ethology emphasized the importance of the unobtrusive experiment involving the interaction of the animal with its natural environment. Now retired from the university, Professor Tinbergen continues his research both at his home near Oxford and at his retreat in northern England.

The Ideas That Led to the Nobel Prize/von Frisch's Bees/Lorenz's Observations/Developing the Unobtrusive Measurement/Ethology/An Application of Methods//Heredity versus Environment/An Overreaction to Learning/Genetic Programming/Part Nature-Part Nurture/The First Phase of Cooperative Interaction//Innate/Learned/Interacting with the Environment/The Human Young Is Less Precisely Programmed/Motivation/Predispositions to Learn//Aggression/Animal and Man/Cultural Traditions/Male-Female Roles//Innovative Concepts/Innate Releasing Mechanisms/Social Signals/Nonverbal Communication/Autism/Concentrating More and More on Man/Some Contemporary Social Problems and Ethological Applications//

Professor Tinbergen and I discuss the work that led to his Nobel Prize. He tells how he came to work with von Frisch and Lorenz in the field of ethology, defines ethology in a very precise manner, and traces both its evolution and his involvement in it over four decades of research and study. He describes the development of naturalistic observation as an important and reliable technique for studying behavior in both animals and humans. We discuss genetic programming, learning, the interaction of the organism with its environment, and the development of motivational systems. Professor Tinbergen presents the ethologist's view of such issues as aggression, war, and male-female roles in family and career relationships. He then explains the development of such concepts as the "innate releasing mechanism," and describes his interest in nonverbal communication, an outgrowth of naturalistic observation, and its applications to the treatment of autistic children. We conclude the discussion with his comments on some contemporary social problems, as he remarks: "Apart from pursuing our animal studies, we should concentrate more and more on man. The human species is in a perilous situation since man, as a consequence of his cultural evolution, has changed his environment so much —pollution, depletion of natural resources, mental stresses. The ethologist could help the study of human behavior with a new approach. We wouldn't claim that our approach is the approach, but we could be of assistance."

EVANS: Professor Tinbergen, when you, Karl von Frisch (1955), and Konrad Lorenz (Evans 1975b) received the Nobel Prize, in 1973, for your work in ethology, it was a landmark because it was the first time a Nobel Prize was given to any of the behavioral disciplines. How did you, Lorenz, and von Frisch begin developing the ideas that led to this award?

TINBERGEN: Von Frisch's approach was a very typical one for a biologist. He started from what we call a functional question: What is this for? It so happened that in his time, a senior physiologist had pronounced, on the basis of quite good experiments, that honeybees were color-blind. He had honeybees with clipped wings walk toward two lights of different colors, of which he could vary the intensity, and he found that quite independent of wavelength and color, the bees always went for the brightest light. And on the basis of that, he pronounced that bees are color-blind. Von Frisch couldn't believe that. Why? He knew that many flowering plants go to great lengths to produce flowers, beautifully colored flowers. He also saw that bees pollinated these flowers. He thought the colors of the flowers could not be there for nothing; therefore, the bees probably respond to colors. He turned to experiments in the field and found that bees did indeed respond differently to different colors.

EVANS: How did von Frisch become involved with Lorenz?

TINBERGEN: They were both Austrians, so Lorenz knew of von Frisch. But, Lorenz himself was primarily the observer, discerning patterns in what he observed. He was not in the field at all. He's not an experimenter, and he has a tremendous admiration for the man who can experiment. He has often said he felt that what he needed, so to speak, were experimenters who could test his ideas.

EVANS: You were more precisely influenced by von Frisch; is that correct?

TINBERGEN: Well, yes. In my earlier work on the homing of the digger wasp (1935), I was really applying von Frisch's method to a new subject. Then later, my experimentation moved more in the direction of social interaction between animals. That was done independently of

Lorenz, but we soon got together, and from then on we worked together.

EVANS: Could you describe von Frisch's experimental methodology a bit more precisely because obviously the fact that he influenced you so strongly led to a key development in ethology.

TINBERGEN: Well, von Frisch, working in the natural environment, obviously always had to do with less-controlled situations than usually exist in the lab. So, when he was faced with an animal responding to the environment, he had to tease out, to disentangle, what it was in the environment that the animal actually responded to.

EVANS: Wouldn't it be very difficult to do much manipulation in the environment without affecting it? How do you preserve the naturalness?

TINBERGEN: The essence of an experiment is that you manipulate the situation, and therefore, that you take something away from the naturalness. But you disturb as little as possible.

EVANS: Wasn't biology up to this point more likely to manipulate much more obtrusively?

TINBERGEN: In a certain sense, that is true. For instance, by the very act of taking an animal into the laboratory, you manipulate the environment in an unknown way. You may elicit behavior patterns other than the ones you are investigating at the moment.

EVANS: In fact, one of the important developments in psychology has been greater focus on the whole matter of unobtrusive measurement, the theory being that the measurements we use themselves become obtrusive, and therefore affect the naturalness of the situation. This is precisely the issue that confronted you as pioneers in the field of ethology.

TINBERGEN: That's a fair description of what happened. The basic difference was, I think, that we were interested in the whole behavior repertoire of any animal prior to experimentation, so we saw a number of phenomena that the laboratory worker just hadn't seen. And we observed any interesting animal that we happened to meet outside; American psychologists in particular had very early selected the white rat as a model animal for the study of general problems—problems that were, incidentally, derived from human behavior. That's another difference between psychology and ethology. Psychology really started with problems of human behavior and became involved with learning of all kinds. We were all zoologists and therefore were faced with a variety of animal species, each behaving in a specific characteristic way. We only gradually worked our way up from insects, fish, and birds to mammals, and then finally, in later years, we began to have a look at man, whom we hadn't dared touch in the beginning.

EVANS: One of the problems of some of the very early empirical studies in animal behavior was that the researchers tended to base their conclusions on the observations of only one individual. Isn't there a built-in bias here?

TINBERGEN: Well, that was one of the weaknesses in the beginning, of course. There were only a few of us; so what you call inter-observer reliability could not easily be established in that stage of the game. Until the film and videotape came onto the scene, we could not really observe what had happened and preserve it for repeated scrutiny.

EVANS: Professor Tinbergen, what exactly is ethology?

TINBERGEN: I like to define ethology as no more than the application of certain biological methods to the phenomenon of behavior, which had for a long time escaped rigorous observation, and certainly experimentation, because it seemed so intangible. And I think the great thing that Lorenz and his followers did was that they considered behavior the function of just another organ—of course, a very special organ—the brain. It is very different from any other organ, after all, in its function and machinery. You can discover something about how that machinery works and what it does for the survival of the animal by observing and recording its behavior as objectively as possible.

EVANS: Of course, what you've been saying already suggests the always-present nature-nurture problem—heredity versus environment. Were you, von Frisch, and Lorenz always concerned about how to resolve this problem?

TINBERGEN: Yes. One could say that in the early stages of ethology, in a primitive way, we were reacting, and in a sense, overreacting to the prevalent notion in psychology that everything in behavior was learned. We were struck most by the fact that so many different individuals of the same species do behave in very similar ways, almost identical ways, even in situations where they could not possibly have learned it; for instance, when they were raised in isolation and couldn't have learned by example. So we had concluded that not everything is learned; the programming of behavior is part nature, part nurture, and we over-emphasized nature—i.e., genetic programming. The lower down you go on the scale, the more behavior is internally programmed and the less is left to learning. But all animals can learn to a certain extent and supplement genetically preprogrammed behavior by interaction with the environment, which involves a number of types of learning. Gradually we came together. The psychologist criticized us vigorously and we criticized the psychologist vigorously, and that was the first phase of cooperative interaction. It always begins, not by ignoring each other, but by criticizing each other.

EVANS: So on the one hand, at first you felt that genetic programming was, perhaps, almost entirely responsible for behavior, and then you gradually began to modify your position; is that what you're saying?

TINBERGEN: That's what I'm trying to say. Ethologists began to turn more and more to the interaction of the environment with what is genetically provided as a blueprint for growth and later functioning, and the extent to which this interaction supplements programming for effective behavior. We discovered, of course, in doing that, that many animals learn a great deal more than we actually suspected.

EVANS: In the early history of psychology, we had a great many problems with the term "instinct," because it was rather ambiguous; it could mean so many different things. In your field, didn't you have the same problems of definition with the term "innate"?

TINBERGEN: Well, to a certain extent. It's not so much the word "innate" as coupling it with a noun. Innate behavior exists to just as little extent as, say, purely factory-made or purely homemade pieces of equipment. I like to use an analogy: When you build a little toy car at home, you buy a number of components that are factory-made; let's equate that for the moment with genetically programmed, innate behavior. Then you may buy a sheet of metal, again factory-made. To work it into your car you have to cut it, you have to bend it; that I equate with interaction with the environment—i.e., learning, in the case of the animal. Now you can't say of this sheet metal, and certainly not of the whole car, that it is entirely factory-made or entirely homemade. It's both in one. To bring the analogy back to behavior, the emphasis now is not on classification between innate and learned behavior, because most behavior is both in one or neither. How is the animal programmed? Well, partly by starting with simple, really innate instructions, but from the moment the embryo begins to develop, it begins to interact with the environment.

EVANS: Some years ago, Harvard psychologist Henry Murray (1938) made the statement that one of the problems in understanding behavior is that in some respects, every individual is different from every other individual; in some respects every individual is like some other individual; and in some respects every individual is like every other individual. Now I gather, at the animal level, uniqueness is not as extensive as at the human level; is that correct?

TINBERGEN: That's a fair statement. First of all, of course, we have learned from the geneticist that even within a species, no two individuals are genetically exactly alike; they are all slightly different. That is true of man perhaps even in a larger sense. People have compared man, in that respect, with domesticated animals, where natural selection has been relaxed in certain ways so that aberrant individuals are not discriminated against so much. So probably the human population, even within one race, is more variable than that of most wild animals. On top of that, of course, the human species is, as Jerome Bruner (1968) says, very immature at birth. The human young is less precisely genetically programmed than any animal. Much more is left to interaction with the environment.

EVANS: Now how do you verify that? You would have to take infants, observe them longitudinally, as well as lower animals.

TINBERGEN: It brings us to a real, crucial difference between our work with animals and with man. For ethical reasons, we cannot carry out the really crucial experiments about the development of behavior that would answer this question. You cannot deliberately raise a thousand children of a representative pool in one way and another thousand children in another way. But the difference between man and any other animal is so extreme that nobody will doubt that the human being has to learn an enormously greater amount than any other animal. When the difference is that large, there is consensus of opinion, and, after all, scientific conclusions are no more than consensus of opinion.

EVANS: Professor Tinbergen, you wrote a book in 1951, *The Study of Instinct* (Tinbergen 1951) dealing with instincts, the nature of instincts, and it was very interesting to me that in this book you attempt to deal with the underlying mechanisms that more or less trigger off what we in psychology have called "motivation"—that is, all conditions that arouse, direct, and sustain the organism. We, at least historically, have tended to look at drives such as the need for food or water, or for, perhaps, some form of avoidance of pain, as primary drives. Then, as learning begins to override primary drives, it leads to what we call secondary drives.

TINBERGEN: Well, let me first say that the book didn't appear until 1951, but I wrote it largely in 1948; so it represents the very early stages in our thinking. It was actually the first attempt at a summary of where we stood. It is grossly outdated now. I still like the approach, and I think that there is a certain link of the kind that you indicated. We began to discover that most animals are equipped with what we would call a number of functional systems, say the feeding system, or the reproductive system. And I would say that we were not thinking so much in terms of secondary drives incorporating more learning, but rather that these major functional systems were subdivided into subsystems. For instance, a reproductive system begins in many animals with the phase of aggression—a dominant male driving off other males. In some animals that is followed by preparation of a nest or something else for the young, then you will get the actual mating. After that you get a parental phase. We know now a little bit about how this is controlled internally, for instance, by changing hormone balances in the body. Of course, in the course of further work, we also discovered that in all these systems and subsystems, interaction with the environment was more important than we had thought.

EVANS: If you were to rewrite this book today then, you would perhaps focus a bit more on the effects of the environment and learning?

TINBERGEN: There is one thing that I would certainly change. I would not speak of innate behavior anymore. You can speak of innate genetic differences between individuals or between species, but a product as such, in the form of behavior, could not often be called totally innate or totally learned. Approaching the same problem from the other side, we also began to see more and more (and this is already indicated in *The Study of Instinct*) that different species have what we call different predispositions to learn. Nowadays, we would say that learning in the widest sense is ultimately genetically programmed; you do not just "learn" anything. Certain things are not learned by one species that are easily learned by another species.

EVANS: In describing your systems concepts, you refer to territoriality and also to aggression.

TINBERGEN: We were very impressed with the fact that so many of the higher animals, at least in the reproductive season, are territorial. They are attached to a particular area and they have learned its layout. This helps them a great deal in finding hiding places in case of a predator attack, in finding food, in knowing where to build the nest, etc. We also found that in the beginning of the breeding season, the males will concentrate entirely on antagonistic interaction, mainly with other males, to the exclusion of anything else. While engaged in aggressive encounters they will not feed, for instance. On the question of to what extent primitive man had a system of aggressive interaction, there are methods by which one can conclude that it is very likely that ancestral man must have had systems of hostile interaction of various kinds. Living in small groups, there hadn't only to be cooperation between socially hunting males, for instance, but also a kind of complicated dominance order. That involves a certain amount of hostile interaction in status seeking. Of course, war is a phenomenon which we don't know in animals—war within the species. It doesn't happen in the wholesale and really killing way in which we wage it. If there is any link with our old genetic programming, which we still carry in us, so to speak, that could be related to war, I think it would be intergroup aggression.

EVANS: The territoriality and aggressivity, which you describe as being part of your motivational systems theory, might be pragmatic, serve a purpose in animals, might allow the species to survive. And yet, animals do not have wars. What accounts for the fact that these same drives persist at the human level?

TINBERGEN: An animal ethologist can only speculate, and I go way outside my field of competence, of course. I have some ideas about this. I do think that we still drag with us a part of our old genetic programming. I have an idea that as communities of man grew larger, and nation-states became more sharply defined, it was easier to consider a man belonging to another nation as not just another fellow man, but as an enemy, in the fullest sense of the word. Actual warfare has the character of desperate defense, and demagogues who want to prepare nations for war, tell the people that they are threatened by the other man. In the ultimate, desperate defense by any animal, whether it's against a predator or whether it's against a fellow animal of the same species, there are no inhibitions. Now, there are many different functional systems in which violence is used, of course, in any animal, and also in man. We have not only man-to-man hostile interaction, but we also have defense against predators. We have defense against parasites. I have an idea, from what I know of the preparation of individual soldiers for warfare, that man somehow has the ability to fuse all these different motivations so that the overall motivation with which he meets the enemy, combined with his organizational abilities, has made it easier to go all out for killing other people. In the individual who does the fighting, most warfare is really not motivated by aggression, but by desperate fear.

EVANS: Pursuing the subject of motivation in a slightly different direction, as you know we have this great preoccupation with differences between men and women, that has been culturally reinforced, and has put women in a kind of submissive position. Have you observed motivational differences between male and female at the animal level?

TINBERGEN: In most animals there's just not any doubt; it's just a matter of fact that males and females are differently programmed behaviorally, and that there is a division of labor. Take a very simple example, mating. In man, it has been demonstrated that we are genetically different. Bodily development, including the development of the brain, which is ultimately responsible for behavior, runs a different course in males than in females, and therefore it is to be expected that males and females are slightly differently programmed. But that, of course, has nothing to do with the fact that we drag with us cultural tradition. Apart from the mother doing the mothering in the early phases of education and the father having another role, in society there are typically male and typically female occupations. Our western society is a very masculine society, and women are quite right when they say that they have been discriminated against in many ways. When they go whole hog and demand absolute equality in occupation, rather than equality in opportunity according to their capabilities, then, I think, they exaggerate things.

EVANS: Another widely discussed concept of yours is what you originally called "innate releasing mechanisms," and later simply "releasing mechanisms." Would you explain what you meant by this?

TINBERGEN: Well, we began to notice that animals in different situations react specifically to different aspects of the environment. We postulated, therefore, that they must have machinery which switches on or off selectively the perception apparatus, depending on the motivation—whether an animal is feeding or mating, for instance. We called this the "innate releasing mechanism," because we were mainly occupied with what elicits behavior. Very soon, we realized that it is not always unlearned, and therefore, we dropped the term "innate." It links up with what the neurophysiologists call "gating," namely, screening off part of the potentially available input.

EVANS: Another very important book that you wrote was *Social Behavior of Animals* (Tinbergen 1953). What were you essentially dealing with in that book?

TINBERGEN: Well, again, this book is very much outdated. It is a sketch of the state of knowledge as it was then, the emphasis being mainly on the mechanism of social interaction. At that time, we saw it as being based on signal and response to signal, neither of which need be learned and, therefore, can be constant throughout the species. Later, of course, we saw that particularly on the recipient side, there's a great deal of learning. This little book concentrates on that concept, how animals communicate with each other without using words.

EVANS: And how do they communicate with each other?

TINBERGEN: By what we nowadays would call social signals. What I did not incorporate in that book, and it's a definite gap, was that so very often signals come on top of a relationship that is gradually built up between two animals.

EVANS: At the human level, we might find an analog for this in "body language"; isn't that correct?

TINBERGEN: Yes, that's what we still think, that the human species, particularly when very young, relies for a great deal of communication on nonverbal signs and responses to signs, including facial expressions, body stance, and so on.

EVANS: So you feel that this is another example of genetically programmed behavior that is carried over from the lower organism to the higher organism?

TINBERGEN: Well that is very much under investigation now, to what extent nonverbal communication in man is learned. The method of study, of course, is cross-cultural comparison, to see to what extent different cultures influence this type of interaction.

EVANS: But you do feel it's unlearned at the animal level?

TINBERGEN: The giving of the signal is very often unlearned and very often even the response is unlearned, although there more learning takes place. In cross-cultural comparison, the simple elements of nonverbal communication turn out to be relatively constant. For instance, I don't think there is any human population known that doesn't smile and in which the smile doesn't express a friendly motivation, to use a colloquial word.

EVANS: Could you give a specific example of a communication pattern you've observed in one of the species you were studying?

TINBERGEN: In gulls, for instance, both the staking out of territories, which means repelling intruders, and pair formation are done by means of very specific signs, in which each gives its specific calls and specific postures, which are appropriately responded to by the others. Another example, taken from gulls, is signalling by color. When the newly hatched chick, even when hatched in an incubator, faces an adult for the first time and is hungry, it begins to peck at the red patch on the yellow bill of the parent. That is a normal response to a signal, but the signal in this case is not a movement, but a patch of color, like a flag.

Although we do have a very rich repertoire of nonverbal communication, far less is known about this in humans than in some of the better-studied animal species. We think that this is because we are programmed (not by learning) to respond intuitively to the slightest facial expression so that we find it difficult to study this form of communication objectively.

EVANS: A book that you published in 1958, *Curious Naturalists* (Tinbergen 1958), is enjoying a rebirth of interest. It is rather autobiographical, isn't it?

TINBERGEN: Well, that is really my favorite book. It's semiautobiographical, and it describes what I myself and the people I worked with did in the course of some twenty years. It's full of little pictures of how we went about our work, how we went from one question to the next.

EVANS: One of your more recent major efforts is your book called *The Animal and Its World: Forty Years of Exploratory Behavior By An Ethologist* (Tinbergen 1972). I gather that it is a collection of some of your most important papers.

TINBERGEN: That's right. I would have never done it on my own initiative. My friend Desmond Morris prodded me. I selected papers partly because they had originally been published in German and were not really known in the English-speaking world, and partly because I thought they were representative of my development and the development of my research group.

EVANS: Are there other things, looking back on your work, that you might want to cite as important contributions?

TINBERGEN: Yes, there is one thing which, curiously enough, I was made aware of by the comments of colleagues on the Nobel Prize. They pointed out that in the last ten years or so, my work had moved in an ecological direction, in an understanding of how different animal species, although closely related, occupied different niches to which they were behaviorally adapted. We showed, so to speak, how an evolutionary decision, selection of a new niche for a species, reverberated through the whole behavioral system of that species. That is a direction which our investigations took as soon as we began to switch from the study of one particular species to comparative studies of a number of closely related species.

EVANS: Being a bold departure from the traditional laboratory research, it is natural that the field of ethology, and even you in particular, would have been the subject of considerable criticism. What are some of the criticisms, over the years, that have bothered you the most, Professor Tinbergen?

TINBERGEN: Well, it's true, of course, we stuck out our necks. We were overconfident and overcritical of other behavioral sciences. I think the criticism that has influenced me most was the American criticism of our rigid distinction between innate and learned behavior. In other cases, the criticism was a basic misunderstanding. For instance, when we coined the term "releasing mechanisms," we meant to characterize an achievement of an unknown mechanism, knowing quite well that the mechanisms would be different in different species, even in different behavioral patterns in the same species. This was misunderstood. It was thought that we meant that the mechanism had to be always the same.

EVANS: Another recent publication of yours is *Early Childhood Autism: An Ethological Approach* (1972). Here you took a methodology that ethology developed over the years, dealing with animals, and applied it at the human level. Is that not correct, Professor Tinbergen?

TINBERGEN: Yes. We felt very strongly that where ethologists moved into the human realm, they were too easily extrapolating facts found with animals and trying to apply them to humans. But we thought that we might apply certain methods that we have learned with animals to human situations that are similarly limited, and that is the way in which we happened to stumble on this problem of early childhood autism. The method we applied was, so to speak, dictated by the subject, since these children do not develop speech. We were forced to study them in the same way as we study nonverbal expressions of motivations in animals. And what we found by studying these expressions in the really autistic children, mildly autistic children, and normal children, was that the expressions of the autistic children revealed strong motivational conflict, an emotional conflict, in which fear or apprehension of other persons and also of strange environments was overriding. That was important because it showed that overriding apprehension and withdrawal blocked two main channels by which children learn. One is through social interaction, with all its various elaborations, and the other is by exploring the external world. We considered that it was wrong to think, for instance, that the speech defect was primary. We felt that nondevelopment or regression in speech was a secondary consequence of the children not wanting to socialize, and this has supported other opinions about the nature of this mental aberration. It has important consequences for possible therapy because if we were correct, it would mean that speech therapy alone would be symptom treatment, and that the main therapy would have to concentrate on restoring emotional balance. This is being tried out in various places, and we have to wait and see whether it really will fulfill that promise.

EVANS: How do you go about observing these autistic children?

TINBERGEN: You cannot observe them in large groups; you have to observe intently one or, at the most, two children and their interaction with situations and with people. You can't experiment with them, so the next best you can do, since these children fluctuate in the severity of the symptoms, (and even normal children show bouts of autistic behavior) is try to find correlations with the situations that bring on such bouts of deterioration. We found that these were invariably unfamiliar situations in the social sphere. These children become so oversensitive to anything another person, particularly an adult does, that even if you smile in a friendly way at them, they shrink back in horror.

EVANS: Observational methods in this area are not entirely new.

Is there something unique about what you are doing that your background in ethology prepared you for?

TINBERGEN: The main new thing that we bring is this systematic reading of subtle expressions in the children and connecting them with the situations that bring on these bouts of more severe autistic behavior. As a sideline, we come more and more to the conclusion that there is no evidence really showing that these children are irreparably, perhaps genetically damaged.

EVANS: Do you believe that this may lead to other significant applications of ethological methodology in dealing with human problems?

TINBERGEN: Yes, I think, really, that apart from pursuing our animal studies with all kinds of new techniques and approaches, at least some of us should concentrate more on man. I feel that time is running out for us; the human species as a whole is in a very perilous situation. What we derived from our original studies was how an animal fits into its environment. Since man, as a consequence of his cultural evolution, has changed his environment so much, it begins now to backfire in all kinds of ways. We wouldn't claim that our approach is *the* approach to apply, but we could be of assistance.

EVANS: Let's take a really serious problem in our society right now. We are moving rapidly to a society of aggression, fear on the streets, people owning guns. A lot of people attribute this to the complex, congested life, the crowding of the city. Do you feel that perhaps the field of ethology could develop some solutions to problems like this?

TINBERGEN: Well, I see possibilities. I don't think much of a beginning has yet been made by the ethologist. Maybe we can contribute something new. For instance, we know man is originally programmed for living in small communities where everybody knows everybody else, where there is both cooperation and competitiveness. Compare that with the way people live now, not only densely crowded, but also in what we call an anonymous society, where you meet strangers all the time. The increased stresses of society, particularly modern Western society, may well lead to situations of frustration where you get increased irritability, increased inclination toward violence or anarchy in the widest sense. Of course, we know already that large cities do breed criminality. One of the factors there, which might or might not prove later to be of relevance, is that it is so easy to hide in a large city. The very notion of an anonymous society is that you can disappear; you can lose your identity, in the sense of being identified by police, or whoever has to cope with criminality.

EVANS: Do you think that perhaps ethology might provide some ground rules for more effective city planning?

TINBERGEN: Well, I can see this coming. One of the things we have noticed is, for instance, that the mixed-age play group of children, which was very common in our time, even in cities, is now breaking up. In addition, as Bronfenbrenner (1958, 1961) has said, family life is virtually breaking up, particularly in America. Even where parents and children live together, the children sit in front of the goggle box—the television set—while the parents may be upstairs having cocktails. The amount of time in which parents are together with the children where they don't interact at all, is, I think Brofenbrenner mentioned, something like twenty-eight hours a week, which is the major part of the time they would normally be together. That, combined with the disappearance of the opportunity for mixed-age play groups, worries us a great deal. New evidence about child development shows that interaction between children of different ages and sexes and interaction between adults and children in close communities where people know each other contribute a great deal, not only to normal adult behavior, but even to such things as mothering, parental behavior. There is more and more evidence, not only in man, but also in monkeys, that the young females learn a great deal from mothering the younger members of the group, and that if they are deprived of this opportunity, they may grow up into less efficient mothers themselves. You could get a kind of deculturation process. Fortunately, we have enough genetic programming inside us to hope for resilience which may reverse this trend. But those are only loose thoughts derived from incidental observations, just an illustration of how I think that the typical ethological method of watching and wondering and putting two and two together might lead at least to hypotheses that then can be more rigorously checked.

REFERENCES

Bronfenbrenner, U. 1958. Socialization and social class through time and space. In *Readings in social psychology*, 3rd ed., eds. E. Maccoby, T. Newcomb, and E. Hartley, pp. 400–24. New York: Holt.

———. 1961. Some familial antecedents of responsibility and leadership in adolescents. In *Leadership and interpersonal behavior*, eds. L. Petrullo and B. Bass. New York: Holt.

Bruner, J. 1968. *Processes of cognitive growth: infancy*. Worcester, Mass.: Clark University Press.

Evans, R. I. 1975. *Konrad Lorenz: the man and his ideas*. New York: Harcourt.

Frisch, K. von. 1955. *The dancing bees*. New York: Harcourt.

Murray, H., et al. 1938. *Explorations in personality*. New York: Oxford.

Tinbergen, N. 1935. Ueber die orientierung des bienenwolfes. *Zeitsch. Tierphysiol.* 21: 699–716.

———. 1951. *The study of instinct*. Oxford: Clarendon Press.

———. 1953. *Social behavior of animals*. London: Methuen.

———. 1958. *Curious naturalists*. London: Country Life.

———. 1972. *The animal and its world*. London: Allen & Unwin.

———, and Tinbergen, E. A. 1972. *Early childhood autism: an ethological approach*. Berlin: Parey.

Harry F. Harlow

(1905–   )

Harry Harlow became an assistant professor of psychology at the University of Wisconsin in 1930, shortly after receiving his Ph.D. from Stanford University. With the exception of a two-year tour as chief psychologist for the United States Army (1950–1952) he has remained at the University of Wisconsin, becoming George Cary Comstock Research Professor of Psychology. He established the university's world-renowned Primate Laboratory and directed its landmark research activities in primate affectional systems, learning abilities, the effects of social isolation, and the induction and therapeutic treatment of depression in monkeys. Professor Harlow served as editor of the Journal of Comparative and Physiological Psychology (1951– 1963) and as president of the American Psychological Association (1958). He is now associated with the University of Arizona.

You Start to Think of Human Problems/Primate Research/Creating the Model//Contact/Comfort/Curiosity/The Surrogate Mother//It's Both Genetic and Learned/Behavior and Socialization//These Unhappy Little Monkeys/Induced Psychopathology and Therapeutic Techniques//You Have Only One Environment/Laboratory versus Natural Setting Research//

As we begin the discussion, Dr. Harlow describes the thinking and processes that led him into the area of primate research. "If you work with monkeys," he said, "you start to think of human problems, and for most of our major research programs, we created models out of human models. We were very successful within the limits of the fact that a monkey is not quite human." He discusses the surrogate-mother studies and the evolvement and development of the concept of the affectional systems. He comments on the effects of both learning and genetic programming in basic behavioral patterns and socialization, and reacts to contemporary problems concerning the heritability of intelligence, primate genetic research, and modeling as a form of social learning. Dr. Harlow and I discuss the continuing research involving induced psychopathology in monkeys and the therapeutic techniques used in its treatment. We conclude the discussion as he reacts to some criticisms of his work and offers some interesting comments on the problem of laboratory studies compared with research in the natural environment.

EVANS: Dr. Harlow, in looking over your illustrious career as a creative investigator, one is struck by the fact that you often were asking big questions. One of the big questions that you dealt with was the relative roles of biological maturational development and the environment. I wonder if you'd like to comment on how you happened to get interested in this fundamental problem.

HARLOW: I think probably that working with primates led me to become interested in the problem, because the variables that control primate behavior are complex and they are also obviously both genetic and experiential. I entered into primate research in Wisconsin and after working with monkeys for a year, I lost interest in other animals, although I have used other animals for research purposes. But to me, monkeys are obviously so much more capable, so much more of an intellectual challenge, than anything else.

EVANS: Of course, the area of comparative psychology has always presented very serious problems to the investigator. One is the problem of anthropomorphism, and this is, in fact, one of the problems that ethologists like Lorenz (Evans 1975b) have repeatedly been accused of having. Another problem is not so much a matter of reading human motives into the animal's behavior as it is generalizing from animal studies to the human level. I know, as one of the pioneers in comparative psychology, you must have faced that from the start. How did you think about that problem?

HARLOW: Well, this happened gradually, but if you work with monkeys, you start to think of human problems. You read about human problems, and you must believe that they can be translated into monkey research. Also, if you have human-type problems in monkeys, like the psychopathologies, you find that people will pay more attention to them if you call them human-type names. Actually, for most of our major research programs, we created models out of human models. That is, we took human types of capabilities, like thinking, and tried to see if we could translate them to monkeys. We were very successful within the limits of the fact that a monkey is not quite human. The social behavior problems in which we became interested we called the "love systems." The love systems in the monkey are not as subtle as in the human, but the basic systems are all the same, and probably most of the variables that control, say, infant love in the monkey, are the same as in a human being. Eventually, we came to the conclusion that whether or not monkey data generalizes to human beings, human data generalizes to monkeys very effectively. As a matter of fact, I did the definitive paper on that, published in the *American Psychologist* (Harlow 1958; Harlow and Suomi 1970).

EVANS: Dr. Harlow, there's a very difficult problem in contemporary psychology. It began to some degree with Freud (1953), but I think it also now relates to the work of Lorenz and the other ethologists, and in a very strange way to the work of Arthur Jensen (1969). It is the whole issue of what role genetic programming plays in the development of human behavior. To what degree is man an ultimate victim of biological determinism? To what degree can man shake loose from this, even in the area of intellectual development? Now certainly, way before these issues became the center of a lot of our thinking, you had been thinking about them. I wonder if you'd like to comment.

HARLOW: Well, there are many aspects to it. In the first place, I probably have more faith in genetic components, genetic variables, than most psychologists today. If you simply compare a monkey with a human being, for example, you realize this is the best possible measure of genetic components. A monkey can do anything a human being can do, intellectually, until the normal human being attains about three years of age. From that point on, it's obvious that the learning components transcend the genetic.

EVANS: It would be interesting to hear you trace the development of the line of research that began with "love" or "affection" or "proximity" and the attempt to determine the roots, or bases, of this kind of behavior.

HARLOW: Now, I was not a very strong "internal drive" man, and I thought that the theory behind "drive" was probably nonsense. I thought the most important motives of the human being and his associated cousins were due to external stimuli, not to internal stimuli. I was flying once from Washington to Madison, and on the plane were only four or five people, and five or six hostesses, each trying to be the most friendly. Right over Detroit—I had lots of background on this, I should have caught on some years before—I saw sitting right beside me the cloth-surrogate mother, and I thought, "My God, this can be turned into research." I liked it; one reason I liked it was that it fitted in with my theoretical position that the internal drives are relatively unimportant compared with the external incentives. Now take one of the love systems, the love of the infant for the mother; the interesting thing is that it is the only love system on which for many years the behaviorists like Miller and Dollard (Miller and Dollard 1941) and the psychiatrists, Anna Freud, et al., were in total agreement. Both schools thought, and described, and assumed that the love of the infant for the mother was a derived drive, dependent upon the association of the sight of the face and body with nursing. So I thought that with the surrogate preparations one could test this. When it was tested, the results were absolutely the opposite; they overwhelmingly favored what we called "contact comfort," bodily comfort.

EVANS: Your research on surrogate mothers went through an evolution. As you began studying the organism in much later stages of development, you found certain by-products of the surrogate-mother experience. Could you describe that for us?

HARLOW: The data that we obtained when we first used these combinations of nursing and nonnursing surrogates was simply overwhelming. Perhaps there's nothing more dangerous than to do something that's overwhelming, because you can't believe it yourself. You look at the data and it would appear that nursing is a variable of no importance whatsover—that contact comfort was the only variable.

EVANS: So here you were finding, in effect, that contact with a kind of wire and terry cloth mother seemed to serve about the same purpose as contact with the real mother.

HARLOW: That is right. I've taught elementary psychology for many years, and I've always told the students that they must never try to find *the* variable that produces an important fact of behavior, because there is never *a* variable; there are always multiple variables. And if that were true, then it had to be true of our mother-love, love-for-mother system. So that led us to a series of studies to try to find out if there were variables other than body comfort, and the data demonstrated it. Nursing was a variable of statistically significant importance up to 110 days of age; it wasn't as important as the contact comfort, but it was there. Rocking motion, as any father who has tried to calm a yappity child should know, is a variable. The other enormously important variable is temperature; temperature is undoubtedly a variable in all the affectional systems.

EVANS: The psychoanalysts were particularly interested in the finding that lack of contact with the real mother somehow had an effect on the sexual performance of the monkey. I wonder if you'd like to comment on that.

HARLOW: You see, in classifying the kinds of love—although nobody's ever really bought my classification and I don't think anyone ever will—first, you have the love of the mother for the infant, and contemporaneously, you have the love of the infant for the mother. Then it gradually dawned on us that love between infants, infant affection, was of enormous importance in the animal's subsequent life. Indeed, if you raise babies with a mother and take away all infant affection, they're going to have a hell of a hard time. Infant affection does many things. In the first place, the love of the infant for the mother is an enormously specific love. It's not a kind of love that generalizes, and it's not, therefore, the kind of social love that we usually mean when we use the term "love." Playmates, however, give infants a wide variety of the same and different sexes in all kinds of situations, and this is where a generalized affection can develop. Also, assuming we understand it, the primary mechanism for the production of age-mate affection is play. And I don't think anyone else ever saw that relationship before. So this infant affectional system of play is of enormous importance to the individual, and it leads to patterns that can generalize into sexual patterns. You find fragments of sex in the play of the monkey infants, but it's not until they approach puberty that these things become very well coordinated into the total effective sexual pattern.

EVANS: Now to me, the thing that's particularly powerful about your work, and of course the work of Tinbergen, Lorenz, von Frisch,

Hinde, and many others, is the fact that it has begun to challenge a kind of cherished notion of social psychology: that what we call social motives, or those derived from primary motives, are learned. For example, Lorenz argues that the need for social approval is well recognized and observed in primates, and in other lower animals. As a matter of fact, a lot of social behaviors are genetically transmitted. How do you react to that?

HARLOW: Well, I think there are any number of basic behavioral patterns that are unlearned. Now, if you have a basic "unlearned" pattern that's going to lead to socialization, it has to be a very persisting pattern. During the times it persists, it will be modified by learning. There's just no other way. Whether you want to call it genetic or learned, I don't care. It's *both* genetic and learned. For example, in play, there are certain relatively specific responses which, when the animal is at an appropriate age, will elicit play in age mates. I don't think we really understand it. We know also that total social deprivation before the animal is old enough to play—that's about ninety days of age—will enormously inhibit the pattern of play. We know that being raised by a terry cloth mother until this time will inhibit it also, much more than being raised by a single real mother. A single real mother is much more efficient, much more subtle, much more variable.

EVANS: I see. Now, let's go a step further. On the basis of a great deal of statistical data with various measurements, Arthur Jensen argues that racial differences in IQ persist, and that genetic components account for 80 percent of the variance. Does that make any sense to you? You said perhaps it doesn't make any difference whether you're talking about environmental influence or genetic determination. What about such speculations?

HARLOW: Well, I think it's rather meaningless because, for example, what is meant by "social deprivation"? You'll never raise monkeys as human children would be raised in real social deprivation. There are so many different kinds of deprivation. I once talked to Shockley, who started off the whole IQ thing, at a meeting of the National Academy. Shockley was a kindly man, an idealistic man, a very fine person. He told me he was going to do this—to show that intelligence was primarily genetic. And I said, "Well, if you want to go search the literature you'll find that this is true, insofar as the literature is true." Jensen's study hadn't come out yet, but I knew some of the earlier work. "But," I said, "who's going to believe you? No one. People are going to believe exactly what they want to believe, and in a sense, that's their right, because you'll find it impossible to set up an adequate experimental design controlling all the variables unless you can get research support of a hundred million dollars a year for a hundred years." Is is really possible to lay out the whole range of environments that you would like to consider? I still think that, basically, Jensen is probably right, but it's essentially impossible to test.

EVANS: Now what about the next step? If we argue that genetics determine "certain desirable human characteristics," perhaps we should begin working toward some form of eugenics, or selective breeding. How do you feel about that?

HARLOW: To do selective breeding, you have to have at least eleven generations. That would mean 330 years of human effort, and the experimenter wouldn't get very much credit; he'd have to be a very old man. I don't think an effective primate genetic study will ever be done.

EVANS: In the area of child development, whether you wished it or not, there have been constant interpretations of your work as it reflects on the work of Bowlby (1960), Spitz (1950), et al.—the whole group that argues for the importance of affection to the infant, focusing on the importance of mother love. The indication is that without such affection, the infant deteriorates physiologically. The investigators looking at this problem have attempted to make inferences from your work that either validate it or challenge it. I think it might be interesting to see how you resolve that.

HARLOW: Well, there were criticisms of Bowlby, and a lot of the criticism was legitimate. But I thought that one thing our research might do was show that basically Bowlby was right, basically Spitz was right. I don't think it influenced the way we did the experiments at all, but again this was patterning an animal problem after an established human area of research. Human research cannot be done entirely at an elegant level of precision. The monkey data really add nothing, but they indicate that the Bowlby and Spitz interpretations were true.

EVANS: In a good deal of your early work you were certainly aware of Hull (1943) and Spence (1956), who were the "radical" behaviorists of that day. Skinner (Evans 1968) is today wearing that mantle. Skinnerian theory generally attempts to arrange the contingencies in the environment to increase the probability that certain responses occur, and does not deal with some of the subtleties of developmental models that you have looked at in your career. A Skinnerian would say that although interesting, such subtleties don't contribute a great deal to predicting or controlling behavior. I wonder how you'd react to that.

HARLOW: Well, I was a very close friend of both Hull and Spence, but I didn't like the behavioral theory. Hull was a "derived-drive" man. A drive is a highly precise unconditioned response. Then, supposedly conditioned on to it were all other behaviors. I didn't think they gave enough credit to other kinds of motivation, such as incentive motivation. Spence was not as anti-incentive as Hull was. This reductionism bothers me at a certain point. No one can possibly question the intellectual competence of both Hull and Spence, but eventually I think they ran themselves into a hole.

EVANS: And Skinner?

HARLOW: Skinner's a genius. Someone has said he's an intellectual solipsist and that's the only way to understand him, and that's probably true. That's taking nothing away from Skinner. Now Skinner did an interesting thing. He completely changed the concept of unlearned behavior. Unlearned behavior ceases to be a reflex, a specific response (though sometimes it may look that way), but is to be thought of more as a complicated, ongoing kind of behavior. I'm not sure but Skinner would also translate it this way.

EVANS: Now, how would you see that in juxtaposition to your work?

HARLOW: Well, a lot of people have taken the kind of learning problems in which we were interested, at least at one time, utilized Skinnerian techniques, and had very, very great success.

EVANS: There's a social learning paradigm Bandura (1971) is looking at now, which is using such things as modeling. It seems to me that your work is replete with what could be called "social learning theory."

HARLOW: I think that one of the great lacunae in the research that we've turned out is any semidefinitive or definitive study of modeling. For example, I laid out the variables producing infant-mother affection; another variable is a variable based upon modeling—that is, the infant modeling from the mother. Now, we didn't catch on to this soon enough. I'm sure it can be done, and I'm sure it will be done. I think Bandura is one of the new, really interesting, creative investigators.

EVANS: Moving to another area, I think that your work certainly challenges the traditional models of motivation that are being taught. The basic model is the biocentric model: the organism is born with a number of primary drives; these are unlearned. They are part of the inherited nature of the organism; they are universal; their satisfaction is necessary for the survival of the organism.

HARLOW: Now, the number of drives that are inborn, given at birth, are few and unimportant. These are not the kinds of motivating forces that really influence and determine complex social or learning behaviors. They are reflexes; they can condition to some things and not to others. Many of these behaviors disappear fairly soon.

EVANS: So in this model, for example, one would cite hunger, thirst, avoidance of pain, and so on.

HARLOW: The so-called homeostatic model.

EVANS: Right. Do you feel that the homeostatic model might be subject to some scrutiny?

HARLOW: I think it should be scrutinized carefully to see if *anything* about it is true. For example, we still have trouble with "curiosity." The studies that Butler and I (Butler and Harlow 1957) did together clearly show that curiosity, in the right situation, is a totally predictive, long-persisting motive. We've tried to find the unlearned bases for social play, and we hit upon curiosity and manipulation, but these two are simply not the real answer. I spent years trying to find the real answer and did not find it. But my wife has just completed this research on self-motion play—primarily individual play whose development reaches a significant height prior to the development of social play—and I think that this probably is the most important, most primitive, basically unlearned motive that there is. Any motive that persists for a considerable number of months isn't going to end up totally unlearned, and you probably are never going to fragment the learned and unlearned components. I think if there is any single thing for people to think about when they do research, it is that every complex item of behavior has beneath it multiple variables.

EVANS: Another area in which you've been interested and have pioneered is the whole area of brain and behavior. Now, this is going in many, many directions. There is the exotic work of Joe Kamiya, in the area of biofeedback, studying the possibility of willful control of brain rhythms and how it affects the organism.

HARLOW: I don't think it will be willful. . . .

EVANS: You're following this biofeedback work; does it make any sense to you?

HARLOW: Kamiya's research is simply pretty; it's cute. It's good and I think he's the first person really to do a very brilliant research study which had a large payoff. In my own case, we started off with an interest in cortical localization in intellectual functioning, and when we started work, we found there were no adequate measures of intellectual function for monkeys. In a sense, that led us to other kinds of research. But we've always maintained interest; we have ongoing studies at the present time.

EVANS: In looking over your work, what do you, yourself, believe to be some of your most important contributions?

HARLOW: I think some of the area studies on differential functions, differential parts of the cortex (Harlow, Meyer, and Settlage 1951; Harlow et al. 1970) was adequate research, and I think our success in getting the monkey to do high-level, human-type learning problems (Harlow 1949, 1953, 1959) was a real contribution because then you could manipulate the variables. For example, you could study the effects of different kinds of horrible environmental experiences on their intellectual processes. There isn't very much loss. These capabilities are not dependent on early, happy environments. I think there's no question that the fortunate semiaccident of the surrogate mother (Harlow and Harlow 1966; Harlow and Suomi 1970) was the best, probably my most important contribution because it led to so many things; it led to all the affectional systems (Harlow 1962, 1969; Harlow and Harlow 1965). At the present time, we're getting into a systematic program on induced psychopathologies in monkeys (Harlow and Harlow 1971; Harlow, Harlow, and Suomi 1971; Harlow and Suomi 1970, 1971, 1974).

EVANS: Could you describe the methodology? This is very intriguing.

HARLOW: The methodology is perfectly simple. You take a human psychopathology as a model and see how far you can induce it in monkeys. We started off with childhood, or anaclitic, depression. We translated that from the human infant to the monkey, and the transition was just perfect. It just about led me to say that I didn't know whether monkey data generalizes to man, but I know damn well that human data generalizes to monkeys.

EVANS: Are you continuing this work right now, at the University of Arizona?

HARLOW: In part, but the research is going on mainly at the University of Wisconsin. For the last two years there have been very effective studies made on rehabilitation, the theory being that if you turn these unhappy little monkeys into masses of protoplasm, unthinking and unfeeling, you ought to try to bring them back out of it. We started off with a depression. Suomi (Harlow and Suomi 1971) achieved the first real success with therapy. The technique that was used was the simplest technique. You're taking animals out of total social isolation. Now, if you take monkeys out of social isolation, say, at a year of age, and put them with a year-old normal animal, you're lost because the isolate is so scared, it doesn't know what to do. However, if you have the "therapist" younger than the isolate, then you have an excellent therapeutic situation, because an emotionally destroyed animal is not afraid of an infant half its age. Also, the therapeutic infant provides a basis for modeling behavior, if I may use this recondite term. The isolate animal soon adapted and felt at ease with the normal animal, and then it followed and learned, probably primarily by modeling and sharing various activities of play, and then, lo and behold, it was recovering. We know that the recovery is essentially complete when the isolates have engaged in sex behavior; that's the best criterion of all for normalcy.

EVANS: You have a long history of brilliant, fascinating, creative work; nevertheless, there have been a lot of criticisms of your work. Which of these criticisms have you thought were particularly unfair?

HARLOW: Well, I don't think I'm thick-skinned, but it's my theory that if somebody wants to do some other research, that's his right. Let him go ahead and do it, and let him interpret it any way he wants. I think we're often criticized for acting as if the monkey were a small human being.

EVANS: Yes, the criticism of anthropomorphism.

HARLOW: Now I know the taxonomy of the primate order better than almost anyone else in the world. That is the truth. After all, I taught the damn course for twenty years and no one can do that and come out with the belief that monkeys are just little men.

EVANS: Would there be others?

HARLOW: My guess is people don't like the fact that I've put little value on the primary drives, that I don't rate them as a basic motivating mechanism because Hull and Spence did such a good job of selling this theory.

EVANS: If you were just to speculate, where do you think we might be going in the field of psychology? What do you think would be the most profitable thing; what would you tell a group of young graduate students?

HARLOW: Well, I once had a graduate student come up after I lectured, who said, "Dr. Harlow, there's one thing I'd like to ask you. How do you become famous, fast?" And I said, "That's a simple and easily answered question. All you do is outlive all of the bastards. Someone is going to become famous and if the others are gone, you'll be it." The research interests of the ethologists, at least to begin with, are very narrow. They're interested primarily in submammalian forms while psychology has drifted at least to mammalian forms. This makes quite a difference in the way you're going to see these things, because the so-called instincts of the lower forms appear to be relatively simple. It seems to me that the kind of behavior that is the basis for learning—I'm perfectly happy to call it either unconditioned response, which is too precise, or instinct, which is too vague—differentiates the schools.

EVANS: Do you think the naturalistic methodology is going to have a very big payoff? In social psychology, we're moving out into the field, into the environment, looking at the organism in its natural setting. Do you think that this is a healthy trend?

HARLOW: What do you mean by "natural setting"? What is a natural human environment? It is the most totally artificial setting that was ever created. You put the human being into his natural environment and all his problems will be solved. There won't be any human beings. I think it's been found, by and large, that monkeys do better in a naturalistic environment, but in many ways they don't. Even animals that are sub-human often do far better in a laboratory environment than outside. You have to have them in a laboratory where you can control antecedent conditions before you can understand their behavior, and I think that will hold true for a long time.

EVANS: So the kind of simple empiricism of Lorenz and his studies of imprinting, which seem to show a kind of natural process, is really a lot more experimental than I guess we see.

HARLOW: Oh, a lot of their research was totally experimental.

EVANS: And so, making inferences from this for studying social phenomena, one must keep in mind that the purely natural environment can't be replicated.

HARLOW: Well, let's say it this way. The only natural environment of any animal is the one he has. If you take him out of the one he has, it doesn't matter whether it is feral or not, he'll be in a hell of a spot. You have only one natural environment. You can't change it.

REFERENCES

Bandura, A. 1971. *Social learning theory.* New York: General Learning Press.

Bowlby, J. 1960. Separation anxiety. *Int. J. Psychoanal.* 41: 89–113.

Butler, R. A., and Harlow, H. F. 1957. Discrimination learning and learning sets to visual exploration incentives. *J. Genet. Psychol.* 57: 257–85.

Evans, R. I. 1968. *B. F. Skinner: the man and his ideas.* New York: Dutton.

———. 1975. *Konrad Lorenz: the man and his ideas.* New York: Harcourt.

Freud, S. 1953. *The standard edition of the complete psychological works,* ed. J. Strachey. London: Hogarth Press.

Harlow, H. F. 1949. The formation of learning sets. *Psychol. Rev.* 56: 51–65.

———. 1953. Mice, monkeys, men and motives. *Psychol. Rev.* 60: 23–32.

———. 1958. The nature of love. *Amer. Psychol.* 13: 673–85.

———. 1959. The development of learning in the rhesus monkey. *Amer. Scientist* 47: 459–79.

———. 1962. The heterosexual affectional system in monkeys. *Amer. Psychol.* 17: 1–9.

———. 1969. Age-mate or peer affectional systems. *Advances in the study of behavior,* vol. 2, eds. D. S. Lehrman, R. A. Hinde, and E. Shaw, pp. 333–83. New York: Academic Press.

———. Ethology. In *Comprehensive textbook of psychiatry,* 2nd ed. Eds. A. M. Freedman, H. I. Kaplan, and B. J. Sadock. Baltimore: Williams & Wilkins, in press.

———, and Harlow, M. K. 1965. The affectional systems. In *Behavior of nonhuman primates,* vol. 2, eds. A. M. Schrier, H. F. Harlow, and F. Stollnitz, pp. 287–334. New York: Academic Press.

———, and Harlow, M. K. 1966. Learning to love. *Amer. Scientist* 54: 244–72.

———, and Harlow, M. K. 1971. Psychopathology in monkeys. In *Experimental Psychopathology,* ed. H. O. Kimmel, pp. 203–29, New York: Academic Press.

———, Harlow, M. K., and Suomi, S. J. 1971. From thought to therapy: lessons from a primate laboratory. *Amer. Scientist* 59: 538–49.

———, Meyer, D. R., and Settlage, P. H. 1951. The effects of large cortical lesions on the solution of oddity problems by monkeys. *J. Comp. Physiol. Psychol.* 44: 320–26.

———, and Suomi, S. J. 1970. The nature of love—simplified. *Amer. Psychol.* 25: 161–68.

———, and Suomi, S. J. 1971. Social recovery of isolation-reared monkeys. *Proc. Nat. Acad. Sci.* 68: 1534–38.

———, and Suomi, S. J. 1974. Induced depression in monkeys. *Behav. Biol.* 12: 273–96.

———, and Suomi, S. J. Reaction and cure of anaclitic depression in monkeys. *J. Child. Med Ctr.* (In press).

———, et al. 1970. Effects of combined frontal and temporal lesions on learned behaviors in rhesus monkeys. *Proc. Nat. Acad. Sci.* 66: 577–82.

Hull, C. 1943. *Principles of behavior.* New York: Appleton.

Jensen, A. 1969. How much can we boost IQ and scholastic achievement? *Harvard Educational Review* 39: (1) 1–123.

Miller, N., and Dollard, J. 1941. *Social learning and imitation.* New Haven: Yale University Press.

Spence, K. 1956. *Behavior theory and conditioning.* New Haven: Yale University Press.

Spitz, R. 1950. Anxiety in infancy: a study of its manifestations in the first year of life. *Int. J. Psychoanal.* 21: 138–43.

Jean Piaget

(1896–   )

Jean Piaget has won international acclaim for his revolutionary ideas about human development and the ways in which children learn. After completing his Ph.D. in the natural sciences at the University of Neuchâtel in 1918, he studied psychology and psychiatry in Zurich and worked with Dr. Simon in Binet's laboratory in Paris. His distinguished academic career includes appointments to the J. J. Rousseau Institute, the University of Neuchâtel, the University of Lausanne, and the University of Geneva where he established the International Center for Genetic Epistemology in 1956. In 1969 he became the first European to receive the American Psychological Association Distinguished Scientific Contribution Award, in part because ". . . he has approached heretofore exclusive philosophical questions in a resolutely empirical fashion and created epistemology as a science, separate from philosophy, but interrelated with all human sciences."

The Future of Psychoanalytic Theory and Some Reactions/Freud/ Erikson/Homeostatic Model of Motivation/Cognitive versus Behavioral Models//Learning or Development: Which is More Fundamental?/Internal and External Reinforcers//All Our Mental Structures Must Be Constructed/ Developmental Levels of the Child: Sensory-Motor; Preoperational; Operational; Formal Operational/Intelligence/Genetic Components/ Measurements//Looking for New Things/Causality/Interdisciplinary Research/Some Comments on Montessori/Redefining Learning//

Dr. Piaget and I begin our discussion with his reactions to psychoanalytic theory, Freud's psychosexual development, and Erikson's psychosocial development. He states, "A phenomenon is always biological in its roots, and social at its end point. But we must not forget, also, that between the two it is mental." He expresses his views concerning the traditional homeostatic model of motivation, learning, and perception. Dr. Piaget then traces his vitally important stages of cognitive development from the beginning sensory-motor period (to two years) to the preoperational period (two to seven years) to the concrete operational period (seven to eleven years) and finally to the formal operational period (eleven to fifteen years). His discussion of such notions as imitation and awareness of self and the different rates of the child's development during the periods is particularly interesting. We discuss the controversy centering on Jensen's position on racial differences and Dr. Piaget comments on both the genetic components of intelligence and the effective measurement that is possible. In conclusion, he gives us an account of the work in progress at the International Center for Genetic Epistemology, emphasizing the interdisciplinary nature of the research, and answers a final question concerning the great difficulty many epistemologists and psychologists express in understanding his work. I ask what he does in such a situation. "I wait," he says.

EVANS: To begin our discussion, Dr. Piaget, we have always thought it rather interesting to get the reaction of our distinguished interviewees to psychoanalytic theory. We know, of course, that you have had contact with several aspects of the psychoanalytic movement.

PIAGET: In fact, I have learned a lot from psychoanalysis. This psychodynamic point of view completely renovated psychology. But I think that the future of psychoanalysis will be the day it becomes experimental, as Rapaport and his students such as Wolfe have already started to do. Until it becomes experimental, as long as it simply remains at the level of discussion of clinical cases, it is not entirely convincing in all of its detail.

EVANS: How do you feel about Freud's concept of the unconscious?

PIAGET: I think that the concept of the unconscious itself is completely general; it is not at all restricted to the emotional life. In any area of cognitive functioning, all the processes are unconscious. We are conscious of the result, not of the mechanism. When we take cognizance of our processes, we start from the periphery and go from there towards the heart of the mechanism, but we never get there entirely. The emotional unconscious is therefore a special case of the unconscious in general; and this is whatever cannot be made clearly explicit, because of an absence of reflective abstraction, conceptualization, etc. The unconscious is whatever is not conceptualized.

EVANS: Erikson (Evans 1969) tried to parallel Freud's *psychosexual* development with a process of *psychosocial* development, feeling that at the same time that we have a series of biological developments in the individual there are also some very important psychosocial developments which have to do with the development of values and character and personality.

PIAGET: Oh, I am convinced that is fundamental. It is impossible to disassociate the biological and the social aspects when you are dealing with psychological development. A phenomenon is always biological in its roots, and social at its end point. But we must not forget, also, that between the two it is mental.

EVANS: How do you view the homeostatic model of motivation, which is pretty much the kind of model you see in psychoanalysis and is reflected in most of our introductory psychology textbooks in the United States? This model, borrowed from physiology, represents the organism as continually responding to needs which create tensions which "demand" reduction.

PIAGET: I think this is a basic model, and it is not only in psychoanalysis and in American psychology that we find this kind of regulatory model. For instance, Pierre Janet had a theory of affectivity, of which we know all too little, in which he speaks of regulations among what he calls the elementary feelings. He is not speaking here of feelings which govern conduct between one individual and another, but of elementary feelings like effort, fatigue, the joys of success, the sadness of failures, etc. In his theory, all such feelings are regulations, and homeostasis is basic.

In cognition, as well, homeostasis is a basic model. Right throughout cognitive development, every progress is the result of a self-regulation. Moreover, I think that the notion of homeostasis, which marks the end state, must be completed by Waddington's notion of homeorhesis, or the dynamic equilibrium which characterizes the path of the development. When there is deviation from the path, self-regulations come into play to bring about a return to the path.

EVANS: Of the two general orientations to learning, cognitive versus behavioral, which would you lean toward the most, the cognitive model of Tolman (1932), which emphasized the role of experiential organization in learning, or behavioral models such as Skinner's (Evans 1968)? Also, how would you relate learning to development?

PIAGET: Oh, there is no question that I feel closest to Tolman, with his meaningful indices, etc. It seems to me that there are two central questions in the problem of learning in relation to development. The first one is whether development is simply a matter of a series of learnings, or whether learning depends on what embryologists call competence: the organism's possibilities. That is, is learning the fundamental thing, or is development the fundamental thing? Well this is the very problem that B. Inhelder is currently studying, and I think we already have every proof that development is more fundamental than learning. The same learning situation has a different effect according to the stage of development of the subject.

The second question is this: Is learning simply a matter of associations which are confirmed by external reinforcements? External reinforcements do play a role, of course, but they are not at all the whole story. Internal reinforcements play their role, too. All of the homeostatic and self-regulatory models that we were talking about a moment ago demonstrate that external reinforcement is insufficient.

EVANS: What approach to perception would be most compatible with your own views?

PIAGET: Our central emphasis is to distinguish between perception as a resultant, or stabilized totality, and perceptual activity. Perceptual activities are our own active efforts to explore a figure, or to explore the relationship between figures. Perceptual activity like this has a great deal in common with intelligence. Similar mechanisms come into play. For instance, there are mechanisms in common between perceptual constancies on the one hand and operational conservations[1] or higher applications of reasoning on the other, even though the latter appear seven or eight years later. One problem is to try to get at what is the common mechanism, but we also want to try to understand why this same mechanism comes into play so much later in the case of intelligence than in the case of perception.

EVANS: Dr. Piaget, as I understand your own developmental model, you appear to believe that the process of knowing begins to take place before the child acquires language, and this prelanguage stage you called the sensory-motor period. Is this correct?

PIAGET: It is entirely correct. The sensory-motor period is extremely remarkable in development, because it is during this period, from birth to the middle of the second year, that the most fundamental and the most rapid changes take place. At birth, there are only isolated actions like sucking, touching things by accident, listening, etc. And furthermore everything is centered on the infant's own body. For the infant, objects do not exist in themselves and the infant is not conscious of itself as a subject, as Baldwin (1955) showed a long time ago. But during the first year and a half or so, a Copernican revolution takes place, in the sense that now the child's own body is no longer the center, but has become an object among other objects, and objects now are related to each other either by causal relationships or spatial relationships in a coherent space that englobes them all. All of these basic changes take place before there is any language, which demonstrates to what an extent knowledge is tied to actions, and not only to verbalizations.

EVANS: What would be some specific things that we would observe in this infant as it progresses from the very beginning to the end of this sensory-motor period?

PIAGET: There are six substages, but as an example, let us look at one type of conduct which is one of the first clear-cut examples of sensory-motor intelligence. A child wants an object which is out of his reach, but which is resting on a blanket, and he pulls the object to him by pulling the blanket that the object is resting on. This may seem rather simple on the face of it, but it assumes a lot of relationships, and we can follow the progressive construction of each of these relationships.

---

[1] Although Piaget seldom uses the exact phrase "operational conservations" in his works, he probably intends to denote higher-order mental acts which have the property of remaining structurally invariant across symbolic transformations.

For example, the relationship "resting upon." This relationship is not at all obvious to an infant; to carry out the more complicated conduct, the child first had to construct that relationship. Another relationship involved here is that of moving the distant object from one place to another. The idea that it is possible to move an object with some consistency from one place to another also had to be constructed by this child. Then there is the matter of coordinating these two relationships together, by using the blanket, not quite as a tool, but as an intermediary between the child itself and the distant object. That is one example of an act of sensory-motor intelligence in which we were able to follow all the steps in the construction of the various relationships involved.

EVANS: Here, Dr. Piaget, you are postulating that there is understanding without language. Since we use language to communicate, it is rather difficult to visualize what understanding without language must be like. Is there any way that you can describe what this must be like?

PIAGET: When there is no language there is no concept in the sense of a name for a collection of objects, let us say. But there are already what I call schemes, which are another kind of instrument of generalization. The scheme is what there is in common among several different and analogous actions. For example, in the case that I was just talking about, once it has constructed the relationship "pull closer by means of an intermediary object," it can generalize this to another situation where a different object may be resting on a different support. This is a generalization in action; it is a scheme. The coordination among schemes is the equivalence, in a simpler form, of the coordination of concepts which we do by means of language. Schemes do not require language because the scheme is designated by perceptual indices—"resting upon," "distance," and so forth. Schemes are instruments of action. But they are generalizing instruments; we could think of them as practical concepts. The main difference is that a concept designates many things at the same time, whereas a scheme is what is common among different actions carried out at different times; but a scheme does tie actions together, just as a concept ties things together.

EVANS: In discussing the six substages, you point out that toward the end, the child begins to have a concept of itself. Relating object to scheme with respect to the child's self, how could we show this interrelationship? In other words, how can you relate subject and object and the scheme in between?

PIAGET: At the beginning of the sensory-motor period there is no subject. There is a complete lack of differentiation, which Baldwin (1955) called the dualism between the subject and the object. Gradually the subject's actions are differentiated, diversified, and coordinated together. To the extent that they are coordinated, the relationships among objects become specialized, and causal relationships among objects are recognized as being independent of the subject's own actions, and the external world takes on some order. The scheme is the fundamental instrument of this coordination which gives rise to this double-faceted construction of the subject on the one hand and permanent objects on the other. As long as there is no subject, that is, as long as the child does not recognize itself as the origin of its own actions, it also does not recognize the permanency of objects other than itself. At the end of this sensory-motor evolution, there are permanent objects, constituting a universe within which the child's own body exists also. The relationship between the two is progressive coordination.

EVANS: As you know, the concept of imitation in early childhood has been of increasing interest to the social-learning researchers in American psychology (e.g., Bandura and Walters 1963). In your view, how does imitation function within the sensory-motor period?

PIAGET: Yes, of course. A scheme in the sense that we were talking about earlier is above all an instrument of assimilation, not of imitation. An object is assimilated into a possible action. But at the same time, the action must be accommodated to the particular characteristics of the object, or of the present situation. Sometimes this accommodation takes precedence over assimilation and becomes an end in itself. To the extent that this happens, we can speak of imitation. There is a very close relationship between the development of imitation and the development of intelligence in general, because imitation depends upon schemes, which of course are sensory-motor intelligence in action. But imitation becomes a separate function to the extent that these actions are carried out in the interests of accommodation for its own sake.

EVANS: Now, moving from this sensory-motor period, which is a prelanguage stage, you begin the preoperational period at about age two and carry it through to about seven. Would you care to comment about this period?

PIAGET: The period from two to about seven years of age is characterized by two things. First, the appearance of the semiotic function, that is, the representational, or symbolic, function. This includes language, of course. But not only language. It also includes mental imagery, deferred imitation, drawing—none of which was present before this age. The semiotic function is due to the interiorizing of imitation, and the important aspect here is that the child can now represent to itself an object when it is absent. Now this ability permits the development of a new level of intelligence—intelligence in representation and thought. It is no longer restricted to action. But on this new level, the child must reconstruct everything that it has acquired at the level of actions; it has to reconstruct in conceptual terms everything that it has constructed so far in terms of schemes. This whole period, then, is a preparation for the construction of concrete operations. Since the reconstruction of what has been acquired at the sensory-motor level takes a long time, the concrete operations don't appear immediately as soon as the semiotic function appears. Furthermore, in the sensory-motor level, actions take place in immediate space and in the present time, while with the appearance of the semiotic function actions can project in the future.

EVANS: Now, from this preoperational level apparently you see the organism moving to an operational level which now becomes increasingly complex. Could you briefly discuss the mechanisms in this operational level, which occurs from seven to eleven years of age?

PIAGET: The essence of an operation at this level is that it is the interiorization of coordinations which exist already on the plane of actions, but now since they are interiorized, there is the possibility of reversibility—one can return to the past in thought. And furthermore, operations are always coordinated into total structures, for example, the system of classification, or an ordered series, or the series of natural numbers, or one-to-one correspondences, and so forth. Total structures like these constitute a very new field, now, and constitute instruments which are much more powerful than the sensory-motor instruments. But there is a form of limitation here, in that these instruments apply only to objects themselves. We do not yet have operations which apply to hypotheses, as we will find in an older child.

EVANS: The next stage to which you refer is the formal operational period, estimated to appear between the ages of eleven and fifteen. This, of course, is a highly sophisticated level. Could you comment briefly on this period?

PIAGET: The main thing is that we now have the possibility of applying operations not only to objects, but to hypotheses, formulated in words. To work with hypotheses, one must be capable of carrying out operations on operations. The content of any hypothesis is already a form of concrete operations; and then to make some relationship between the hypothesis and the conclusion, this is a new operation. Operations on operations now open up a much broader field of possibilities. In particular, we now have the possibility of the combinatorial, by means of which we can relate any proposition to any other proposition, or any operation to any other operation. In addition, the combinatorial analysis[2] makes it possible to establish sets of subsets which bring together the two types of reversibility which, in concrete operations, always remain separated. These two types of reversibility are negation, on the one hand, and reciprocity on the other. The group of four transformations, as it is called by mathematicians, is one example of a structure in which negation and reciprocity are related to one another.

EVANS: Looking at this entire developmental process, from the sensory-motor all the way through to the higher operational levels, there is quite a bit of flexibility and individual differences, is there not?

PIAGET: Oh yes, of course, there can be fixations at certain stages; there can be delays and accelerations. But I would even go further.

---

[2] Combinatorial analysis refers to a method which guarantees that all possible combinations of variables will be exhaustively inventoried (Flavell 1963).

Within the formal operational level, it is entirely possible that some people, for instance those in manual professions, specialized laborers of various sorts, may reach the formal operational level in their particular professional domain, but not right across the board.

EVANS: To move to a different area, there is a very interesting controversy in the United States involving a report by Dr. Arthur Jensen (1969) of the University of California. This report appears in the *Harvard Educational Review*. Dr. Jensen suggested that there might be genetic deficiencies in the black child; that although in one type of intelligence, a fairly concrete type of intelligence, there may be no differences, there may be a type of abstract intelligence in which the Negro child is genetically inferior. I wonder how you feel about this, Dr. Piaget.

PIAGET: I think there are two remarks to be made. First, obviously genetic factors play a role in the development of intelligence. But they can do no more than to open certain possibilities. They cannot do anything about actualizing these possibilities. That is, there are no innate structures in the human mind which simply come into being; as I have been pointing out throughout this discussion, all our mental structures must be constructed. So genetic factors or maturational aspects are not adequate for explaining what really takes place at any given stage.

My second comment would be this, how is Jensen measuring intelligence? Is intelligence measured only on the basis of some performance, or are we really getting at the competence, the internal structure? I am afraid that in studies of this sort people have always measured performance, and it is quite obvious that performance will vary according to the social environment. For my part, I have no faith in measures that are based on intelligence quotients or on any other performance measure. So in general, Jensen's conclusion seems to be debatable.

EVANS: Dr. Piaget, looking at the general problems that you have dealt with in your work, I think it would be very interesting to hear your own estimate of what you consider your most important contribution. Now I understand that this question is complicated because we could say contributions to philosophy, contributions to mathematics, contributions to psychology, but looking at your work as a whole which would you consider to be most significant?

PIAGET: Well, I think my role has been above all to raise problems —problems which other people were not seeing, because they were not looking at things from this interdisciplinary point of view. When you look at development from an epistemological perspective, a whole host of problems becomes very clear, so clear that it seems astonishing that nobody had seen them before.

EVANS: One of the difficulties I believe you have encountered in the transition from the philosophical system to the psychological system has been criticism of your research approach. The "experimental design" traditionally used in psychology involves the stating of a hypothesis and the testing of this hypothesis, which can be done in many ways. Your own research has not often followed this traditional pattern which makes your approach subject to criticism. How would you answer the critics of your research approach?

PIAGET: I answer this in the simplest way possible. If you start out with a plan, you necessarily falsify everything. Everything that is really interesting to you necessarily must fall outside any plan you have in advance. The reason I don't have experimental plans is that I am looking for new things. For me, an experiment is successful when I find something unexpected, totally unanticipated. That's when things become interesting.

EVANS: Dr. Piaget, what are you working on now? What are your dreams for the future?

PIAGET: Oo la. New projects always follow unforeseen problems as they come up. During the past few years we have been studying causality. It's a point of view that is very different from the point of view we had had previously. Up to that point, we had always been studying the subject's operations. But in studying causality, we deal instead with objects, and with the resistance that objects present to the subject's understanding. And yet we have found that the development of causality goes through stages which are very comparable to the stages of operational development, except that in this case the operations are attributed to the objects. That is, an object itself is thought to be an operator, and to operate on other objects, and so forth. Now if operations are attributed to objects, this raises the whole problem of the role of one's own actions, and of taking cognizance of one's own actions. How does a child discover in his own actions causal relationships among objects, on the one hand, and the operations of his own thinking on the other hand? So here is a whole new problem—the relationship between two kinds of abstractions, those based on objects and those based on actions. We are deep into the problem of these two types of abstractions, and we do not know yet what will come from it.

EVANS: A unique and important aspect of your Institute is its interdisciplinary nature. Obviously you want to bring together such disciplines as cybernetics, mathematics, biology, philosophy, cultural anthropology, sociology, and psychology to investigate the development of "knowing" in man. It would be interesting to learn how some of these other disciplines relate to the problems in development of knowing and knowledge. For example, how would cultural anthropology relate to this problem?

PIAGET: Cultural anthropology teaches us two things. First, it can shed light on the generality of the mechanisms that we find. Are these mechanisms specific to our Western societies, or are they universal? So far, the comparisons that people have made seem to show that these mechanisms are common ones, and are to be found in each of the several societies that have been studied from this point of view with some accelerations or retardations, of course, according to the social mechanisms.

But secondly, what we study here is the ontogenetic development. We study individuals. Of course, they are individuals within the context of society, but still it is individuals that we focus on. But what cultural anthropology can give us—to the extent that it has an historical dimension, which I realize is difficult—what it can give us is the sociogenesis as well as the psychogenesis. The comparison of the two is indispensable.

EVANS: I noticed a very interesting observation in your Columbia University lecture on "Genetic Epistemology." You stated that you were most fundamentally interested in the matter of how primitive man began to think, how knowledge evolves, and that you became interested in cognitive development in children because this was the only available way of looking at the whole historical development of cognitive processes in man in general. Is this still your fundamental interest?

PIAGET: Yes. Of course, that is quite right. My problem is the development of knowledge in general. Unfortunately, this history is very incomplete—especially at its primitive beginnings, which are actually the most important. So I am doing what biologists do when they cannot constitute a philogenetic series, they study ontogenesis.

EVANS: Another part of the interdisciplinary team at the Institute is the mathematicians. Why do you think that mathematics is so important in the study of the development of knowledge?

PIAGET: Because, along with formal logic, mathematics is the only entirely deductive discipline. Everything in it stems from the subject's activity. It is manmade. What is interesting about physics is the relationship between the subject's activity and reality. What is interesting about mathematics is that it is the totality of what is possible. And of course the totality of what is possible is the subject's own creation. That is, unless one is a Platonist.

EVANS: Now, pursuing the application of your work to education, one of the most interesting movements that we've had in the United States as well as in Europe results from the teachings of the Italian, Maria Montessori (1964). Montessori and some of her followers refer to your work at various points.

PIAGET: I think that Montessori's idea of focusing on activity is excellent, but the materials are disastrous, I think. With a standardized material, one doesn't dare try to change it. And yet the really important thing is for the child to construct his own materal.

EVANS: I see. In other words, Montessori has not gone far enough in allowing independence.

PIAGET: Yes, that's it. But no, it's above all the standardized material that is the mistake.

EVANS: What would be your hope with respect to the future influence of your work on the field of education? Would you think the time will come when it will really revolutionize our entire educational system?

PIAGET: Oh, I hope so very much, especially in educating for an experimental frame of mind. For instance, a lot of the mathematics which is being taught now is modern math, but it is often still taught with very archaic methods. And, at least in Europe, nothing at all is done to develop an experimental frame of mind. Experiments are performed in front of the child, but the child is not the experimenter.

EVANS: If I can see the thrust of what you would hope for, Dr. Piaget, concerning education, particularly in the lower grades, it would be a greater opportunity for the child to direct his or her own behavior and experiences, to modify curricula allowing him or her more freedom to develop as an individual at his or her own level. Is this correct?

PIAGET: Yes, but it is important that teachers present children with materials and situations and occasions that allow them to move forward. It is not a matter of just allowing children to do anything. It is a matter of presenting to the children situations which offer new problems, problems that follow on from one another. You need a mixture of direction and freedom.

EVANS: Dr. Piaget, in American psychology we find learning and learning theory of great interest to us, particularly in learning as a function of external reinforcement as Skinner has emphasized. Now, it's very clear that you do not focus on learning in that way. Is it a question of your system redefining learning?

PIAGET: We have to redefine learning. We have to think of it differently. First of all, learning depends upon the stage of development, or on the competence, as the embryologists put it. And development is not simply the sum total of what the individual has learned. Secondly, in thinking of reinforcements, we must think not only of external reinforcements, but of internal reinforcements, through self-regulation.

I think there has to be a new approach in learning research, and that is just what Barbel Inhelder and Madame Sinclair and Magali Bovet are working on now. They are looking for the learning processes which are based on the developmental factors that our psychogenetic studies have revealed.

EVANS: Your approach appears to view the child as experimenter. A parallel for this child-experimenter notion can be found in earlier psychological literature. The term "curiosity" was generally discussed as a pervasive motive. Would you say that this natural curiosity is in fact the important thing in the process of human development?

PIAGET: Yes, yes. But it is a curiosity which goes through various steps in the sense that whenever one problem is solved, new problems are opened up. These are new avenues for curiosity. We have to follow this development of problems. We should not allow children a completely free rein on the one hand, nor channel them too narrowly on the other.

EVANS: Well, to draw the parallel here, Freud may see the organism born an animal, seeking primarily to satisfy biological, often unconscious needs. You also see the organism as seeking primarily to satisfy a need, but in focusing on curiosity you are dealing with a seemingly more rational need.

PIAGET: Yes, but I think that there is a transition between biological satisfaction and intellectual satisfaction. As sense organs and motoricity widen an organism's field of activity, then biological needs take on an aspect of implicit curiosity which keeps growing and flourishing. We see it already in primates, for example. Chimpanzees demonstrate intellectual curiosity. For example, once when one of my children was in his playpen—this was when he was at the sensory-motor level, well before any language—I held out an object to him horizontally, so that if he simply tried to pull it towards himself, it was blocked by the rails of the playpen. He tried various positions, and finally got it in, but he got it in by chance, and he wasn't satisfied. He put it back outside the playpen and tried to do it again, and continued until he understood how he had to turn it to get it through the rails. He wasn't satisfied just to succeed. He wasn't satisfied until he understood how it worked.

EVANS: Looking back at the very beginning of your experiences, what were some of the things that you did wrong when you first started working with children?

PIAGET: Oh, my errors. I believed in language too much. I had the children talk instead of experiment.

EVANS: Suppose we could stimulate the evolvement of the cognitive stages maximally to achieve an ideal development process, would this be a means of developing highly creative individuals? In other words, we don't know very much about creativity. Could we intervene into the system of cognitive development with some of the insights from your research as a means of increasing the probability that we will produce a highly creative individual?

PIAGET: Oh, I think so. Oh, I think so.

EVANS: In this sense, what would you define as a creative individual?

PIAGET: It is to build a structure that is not preformed, neither in hereditary nor in social environment, nor in the physical environment.

EVANS: Finally, Dr. Piaget, I was wondering what is your reaction to the fact that you're sort of caught between two disciplines. On the one hand, the philosophers and epistemologists don't really understand the direction of your work and on the other hand, many psychologists have great difficulty fully understanding your work. What do you do in a situation like this?

PIAGET: I wait.

REFERENCES

Baldwin, A. L. 1955. *Behavior and development in childhood.* New York: Dryden Press.

Bandura, A., and Walters, R. H. 1963. *Social learning and personality development.* New York: Holt.

Evans, R. I. 1968. *B. F. Skinner: The man and his ideas.* New York: Dutton.

———. 1969. *Dialogue with Erik Erikson.* New York: Dutton.

———. 1973. *Jean Piaget: The man and his ideas.* New York: Dutton.

Flavell, John H. 1963. *The developmental psychology of Jean Piaget.* Princeton, N.J.: Van Nostrand.

Jensen, A. 1969. How much can we boost IQ and scholastic achievement? *Harvard Educational Review* 39: (1) 1–123.

Montessori, M. 1964. *The Montessori method.* Translated by A. E. George. New York: Schocken.

Piaget, Jean. 1951. *Play, dreams and imitation.* New York: Norton.

———. 1960. *Psychology of intelligence.* Totowa, N.J.: Littlefield, Adams.

———. 1968. *Six psychological studies.* New York: Vintage Books.

———. 1969. *The child's conception of physical causality.* Totowa, N.J.: Littlefield, Adams.

———. 1950. *The language and thought of the child.* London: Routledge & Kegan Paul.

Tolman, E. C. 1932. *Purposive behavior in animals and men.* New York: Century.

Arthur Jensen

(1923–   )

*Arthur Jensen became highly visible with the
publication in 1969 of research suggesting that
IQ differences between black and white children may be genetically based. He has done
extensive research in the area of genetic bases
for intelligence, and has made significant contributions to learning theory. Professor Jensen
trained in psychology at the University of California at Berkeley and at San Diego State
College. He received his Ph.D. from Columbia University Teachers College in 1956
and spent two years in postdoctoral research with Dr. Hans Eysenck at the University of London. Currently professor of educational psychology at the University of
California at Berkeley, he was instrumental in establishing the Institute of Human
Learning and serves as an advisory editor to the* Journal of Educational Psychology.

Learning/Pavlov-Thorndike-Hull-Eysenck/Reactive Inhibition/Serial Rote
Learning/Looking Around for a Testable Hypothesis//IQ/Terman/IQ
Constancy/Twin Studies/Testing/Culture-Fair/Culture Loading/Test Bias/
Environment/Enrichment/Experience/Head Start/It's Very Much Like the
Curve for Physical Height//The Controversy/Environment/Heredity/
Educability/Group Differences/A Product of Evolution/It Shouldn't Be
Surprising to Find Variations/Prejudice/Ideological Bias/A Test of
Psychology's Capabilities//Dysgenics/Meritocracy/Reactions to Shockley and
Herrnstein/A Summing Up/Think of Yourself in Terms of What *You* Are//

Dr. Jensen and I discuss the beginning of his career, as he worked in learning
theory in the tradition of Hull. Influenced by the work of Eysenck, he investigated the ways in which personality differences relate to "work inhibitions"
and then moved into the area of learning and intelligence measurement. Dr.
Jensen describes his studies of intelligence, its determinants, and the methods
available for measuring intelligence. Challenged by a problem encountered by
a graduate student working with minority children, he attempted to develop a
culture-fair method of measuring intelligence. This work led to a growing
interest in the crucial problems of society today with its varying socioeconomic levels, and Dr. Jensen describes some of his efforts to understand and
correct these inequities. We talk about the controversial HARVARD EDUCA-

TIONAL REVIEW article which suggested the possibility of genetic differences in intelligence between blacks and whites, and the repercussions of that work. In summarizing the issue, he comments: "I have felt that unless psychology could face this particular problem without prejudice and without ideological and political biases, it's unlikely that it could face other really important social issues. It's a kind of test of the capability of psychology to behave in a scientific way." He reacts to the work of Shockley and Herrnstein and presents some interesting ideas for improving education and opportunity. Asked how black students might respond to his work, he concludes, "You have to think of yourself in terms of what you are, and not in terms of your origins."

EVANS: Dr. Jensen, in your earlier work, you were very heavily involved in learning theory, and were really a follower of some of the hypotheses of the late Clark Hull (1943, 1952). What were the basic ingredients of Hull's learning theory, as you would describe it?

JENSEN: What Hull tried to do, really, was to combine the work and findings of Pavlov (1927) and Thorndike (1932) into a hypothetico-deductive system, a formalized system that could be called a reinforcement theory of learning. In this theory he tried to subsume all of the then-known facts of conditioning and learning, both classical and instrumental learning, under a set of seventeen basic postulates having to do with stimulus reception, reinforcement, generalization, discrimination, and so on. The whole system can be summarized in one very elaborate equation that Hull gave for reaction strength or reaction potential. This is the strength of the acquisition of a given habit as a function of the number of reinforcements, drive strength, the delay between response and reinforcement, stimulus intensity, and a number of other such variables.

EVANS: It seems that you were most interested in what Hull called "reactive inhibition," or "work inhibition." What, precisely, did Hull mean by these terms?

JENSEN: Hull postulated that any reaction would leave behind a trace of inhibition that would oppose the recurrence of that action, and that this inhibitory potential would dissipate in time. He called this inhibitory potential "reactive inhibition." One can see evidence of this, for example, in pursuit rotor learning, where, with continued practice, the task becomes increasingly difficult. This is not due just to muscular fatigue, but to an actual inhibition in the brain, a cortical inhibition of some kind, which opposes the actions so that the performance deteriorates. I was interested in it because I was, at that time, about 1955 and 1956, working with Eysenck (1947, 1960), and reactive inhibition was one of the important constructs in Eysenck's theory of personality.

EVANS: Eysenck, as I recall, analyzed personality through his very elaborate factor analysis and came up with a couple of factors that seemed very important that he called neuroticism and introversion/ extroversion. Did Eysenck see in Hull's conception of reactive inhibition a greater brain-inhibiting mechanism operating with the introvert than would be the case with the extrovert?

JENSEN: He hypothesized that the underlying physiological basis for the dimension of extroversion/introversion was individual differences in reactive inhibition, in a tendency to build up and dissipate what he called cortical inhibition. He believed that the extrovert built up cortical inhibition more rapidly than the introvert and also dissipated it more fully; so that one would predict, for example, that introverts would be better at repetitious tasks that build up inhibition, because it doesn't build up as fast in them. Extroverts need more variety and change, and the basis of their sociability, of their rhathymia, to use Guilford's (Guilford and Zimmerman 1949) term, is this tendency to build up reactive inhibition and the need to get away from it, to make it dissipate. Hull actually perceived of reactive inhibition as being a noxious internal stimulus.

EVANS: How did your own early work fit into all this?

JENSEN: I was interested in making some contribution to Eysenck's program of research, and looked around for testable hypotheses that could be derived from the Eysenckian theory. I did an experiment on work inhibition and devised a gadget for measuring it that involved tapping telegraph keys that were differentially weighted so that some would require more work, more pressure, to tap. I wanted to see if there were personality differences in the tendency to gravitate away from the keys that involved more work. I also became involved in research on serial rote learning.

EVANS: What do you mean by serial rote learning?

JENSEN: This is a form of learning in which the subject learns the sequence of a number of stimuli, say nonsense sentences or words, or any kind of responses. The subject has to learn to anticipate what's coming next and next in a series that's presented in a constant order, over and over, maybe twelve or fifteen stimuli. It's well known that the middle items are the most difficult to learn, so you have a bow-shaped curve of errors up until mastery of the complete list. Hull explained this bow-shaped serial position curve in terms of inhibition accruing to items in the list, and accruing more to items in the middle. If this were a form of inhibition, then one would predict from Eysenck's theory that extroverts should have a more bowed serial position curve than introverts, but we found out it was not the case. There was no difference between introverts and extroverts in serial rote learning, and that raised a question of whether Eysenck's theory was wrong, or whether Hull's theory was wrong. So I began investigating individual differences in serial learning and in the bowing of the serial position curve, and that became one of my major interests for a few years.

EVANS: Dr. Jensen, from the very beginnings of philosophic thought, there has been a major issue over the relative importance of heredity and environment in shaping the individual. The implications of this are vast, of course. In psychology this nature-nurture issue is manifested in the area of intelligence and intelligence testing. We have the masterful work of Lewis Terman (1916) who developed a series of ideas concerning the role of heredity. For example, there are his famous genetic studies of genius (Terman and Oden 1947) in which he suggested that measured IQ would be a factor that would be related to the entire life styles of people.

JENSEN: I think it's one of the landmark researches in the history of psychology. Certainly Terman was the first person to systematically study children who today would be called gifted, with IQs over one hundred forty, and follow them into adulthood. They're still being followed by some of Terman's successors at Stanford (Oden 1968). What Terman found with these fifteen hundred or so gifted children, was that they had much more distinguished adult accomplishments than the general run of the population. Many more of them graduated from college; a large percentage of them went into the professions or high-level managerial positions. Their income levels are much higher than the average; they have a lower divorce rate, lower rates of neuroticism and mental illness, greater satisfaction in life.

EVANS: Now Terman compared these people with what group?

JENSEN: Well, he just compared them with the statistics of the general population on all these variables. He did not have a control group and therefore some people criticized this study.

EVANS: There are other types of research studies that have dealt with the constancy of IQ. They have demonstrated that IQ is surprisingly constant.

JENSEN: Well, the question of IQ constancy was based on the notion that mental age increased at a fairly constant linear rate between the ages of about four or five and about twelve, and this seems to be pretty much the case. Growth periods are not perfectly linear for individuals; they are for the average within that age range. After age twelve, the curve becomes quite negatively accelerated and levels off somewhere around sixteen years of age or so.

EVANS: In other words, it's not unlike the curve for physical height?

JENSEN: It's very much like the curve for physical height, very much like the curve for the growth of vocabulary. The most important studies of the importance of IQ are the studies done by Nancy Bayley (Bayley 1968) at Berkeley and various people at Harvard, where they correlate IQ at a given age with IQ at age eighteen to see how much of the variance at age eighteen—young adulthood—is predictable from various younger ages. And we know that below one year of age, the prediction, the correlation, is about zero. It's not until you get up to about three or four years of age that the prediction becomes substantial. By four years of age, about 50 percent of the variability in persons at age eighteen is predictable. By age nine or ten, the prediction is quite high, something like 60 to 70 percent. It appears that the variables that affect physical development, the hormonal changes that affect physical changes at puberty, are not very important factors in mental development. It seems to go on at a very steady rate right through puberty.

EVANS: Now the fact that the prediction rate is not perfect raises the question of what accounts for these variances. There is the possibility that it is environmental differences. There were the famous Iowa studies that looked at this problem in great detail. What results did they have and how do you feel about them?

JENSEN: Yes, the Iowa studies were largely concerned with the effects of early influences on mental development. One in particular was concerned with the effects of the nursery school experience on later development. These people drew the conclusion that these early experiences were extremely influential, and that even children who might be expected to grow up to be mentally subnormal in some way were brought up to normal levels by highly stimulating nursery school experiences, etc. These studies were subjected to a great deal of critical scrutiny when they were first published back in the 1930s, and were found to have all kinds of statistical, methodological deficiencies. I don't believe that anyone today regards those studies as having proved their point, which doesn't necessarily disprove their thesis; it simply means that their evidence did not support it.

EVANS: Looking at other facets of this nature-nurture problem, one of the most widely cited older studies was one by Newman, Freeman, and Holzinger (1937). Do you recall that particular study?

JENSEN: Yes, that was probably the first really well done twin study. They had nineteen pairs of monozygotic—identical—twins, who had been separated fairly early in life, most of them in infancy, and reared in different homes. Holzinger found these twins when most of them were teen-agers or young adults, and tested them all on the Stanford-Binet Test and a number of other tests to see how much they differed. It turned out that the identical twins reared apart were more alike in IQ than even fraternal twins who were reared together, which is very strong evidence for a hereditary component in intelligence.

EVANS: Dr. Jensen, the measurement-oriented psychologist who looks at problems of individual differences is one who tends to be very precise, very data-bound. Am I correct in seeing you as part of this group?

JENSEN: I think so, yes.

EVANS: How did you happen to move into that area?

JENSEN: Well, I was teaching courses on learning theory at Berkeley, and one of my students came to me with a problem. The student was a school psychologist in a school with many Mexican-American students. He pointed out to me that many of these students tested very low on the usual IQ tests and were being placed in classes for the educationally retarded, mentally retarded, but did not seem to be retarded in other ways. Socially, on the playground and so forth, they seemed to be quite normal children. I suggested he test them on a Spanish version of the Wechsler Intelligence Scale (Wechsler 1940), but they still got low scores. It was almost as if the tests were culturally biased, and for this particular group I think that was largely the case. He asked me if I could come up with anything better, and since I was a learning man at the time, I said, "Why don't you give these children something to learn and see if they're retarded in pure learning abilities." And so we set about to devise some experimental serial learning tasks. We administered a battery of these learning tests to these children and found that most of them were in the average range. So I thought I had invented a culture-free or culture-fair method of mental assessment. I began trying this on other children, on black children, on white children of different socioeconomic levels, and this got me interested in the culturally disadvantaged child.

EVANS: Your interest in so-called culture-fair or culture-free intelligence tests was, of course, precipitated by the continuing concern that the whole series of widely used individual intelligence tests was, to some degree, culture-bound.

JENSEN: Right. No matter what the measurement is, it is a measurement of the phenotype, which is a product of the interaction of the genotype and environmental influences, all environmental influences from the moment of conception on. So you can never measure the genotype directly. All tests are, in a sense, culture-loaded. The vehicle for the expression of intelligence is cultural, but one has to distinguish between culture loading and test bias with respect to a particular group. To the extent that groups differ in their exposure to whatever sets of skills or knowledge the test is sampling, the test is biased.

EVANS: There were classic studies on racial intelligence and IQ in the 1930s that Klineberg (1935, 1963, 1971) reports on; these studies found that on almost any measure, the black scored lower than the white in the South. When they moved to the North, on the whole, both groups would be a little higher. But there would always be the suggestion that the tests were unfair to the black because given an opportunity to function in a "more stimulating" environment in the North, on an average the IQ would move up.

JENSEN: Of course, in those days the schools in the South were far below those in the North, and many of the blacks in the South were not even going to school. Their first introduction to school was in the North, and particular tests used there were language-bound tests like the Stanford-Binet and some group tests that depend upon scholastic skills, reading and writing; so those results were not surprising. If the child is deprived of all kinds of experiences that are prerequisite for even beginning to perform on a test, then you can bring him up quite readily several IQ points, maybe more than that. But if the environmental deficiencies are not that great, then it's harder to make a gain. Environmental enrichment programs for a middle-class child would make practically no difference at all. It's like taking more vitamins when you're already having an adequate diet.

EVANS: In the Head Start program, the government theory was that since children from "deprived" environments had to compete in school with white, middle-class children, they should be given exposure to a more stimulating kind of environment to prepare them to function better in school.

JENSEN: I think it was believed that the main reason for the scholastic differences between the lower-class black and the middle-class white was in the kinds of experiences these children had had at home before beginning school. The idea was to give them several weeks of large doses of verbalization experiences, experiences in listening to an adult tell stories and give directions, etc., so these children would have some kind of experience that would prepare them for school. I think the idea was that if you got both groups up to about the same level in these kinds of experiences or in the ability to respond to the demands of kindergarten, that they would then stay on the same track, and that of course, proved not to be the case. Within six months or a year, both were on the tracks they would have been on if they had not had this previous experience. So then they invented Project Follow-Through to keep the enrichment program going for another couple of years, and that didn't have very much effect.

EVANS: What seems to be happening is that you're using a measure of intelligence, and the dependent variable, the criterion that is almost always measured, seems to be performance in school. It doesn't seem to be related to other types of life experiences. At the very beginning of your thinking, were you limiting it primarily to the school environment?

JENSEN: I was, but that doesn't mean I don't believe that the abilities measured by IQ tests are not important outside the school environment. I think they are; although I don't think they are as highly correlated with nonscholastic criteria. There are important correlations, we know, on the job. The armed forces find a lot of use for these tests as predictors for trainability for different kinds of occupations, etc.

EVANS: You were given a very interesting invitation by the *Harvard Educational Review* to try to write something about this. Is that correct?

JENSEN: Yes. I'd already written a few things about this, and the *Harvard Educational Review* wanted me to synthesize these various ideas.

EVANS: I wonder if you might mention a few of those shorter articles.

JENSEN: Yes, the first important one was in the *American Education Research Journal,* the January, 1968, issue, called "Race, Social Class and Implications for Education" (Jensen 1968a). I did another paper on culture-fair testing (1968b) in which I brought out my notion of two levels of mental ability: Level I, which is rote-learning ability, memory, etc., and Level II, which is cognitive intelligence. One I did was on twin studies of intelligence (1968c), heritability of intelligence, and one was a paper presented to the National Academy of Sciences, "Patterns of Mental Ability and Socioeconomic Status" (1968b).

EVANS: So you had already become rather visible from a perspective that interested the *Harvard Educational Review* (Jensen 1969a, 1969b), which solicited this paper, which in turn became the center of all the controversy and discussion. As I recall, the editors recognized that there was a controversy brewing, and so they invited a number of people to respond to your original paper.

JENSEN: They were invited at the same time I was invited to do this paper.

EVANS: Who were those in the group of original respondents?

JENSEN: J. McV. Hunt (1969), Jerome Kagan (1969), Lee Cronbach (1969), Carl Beireter (1969), James Crow (1969), a genetics professor at Wisconsin, David Elkind (1969), a developmental psychologist—that was the original group. Then a man named Brazziel (1969), a black educator wrote an irate letter to the *Harvard Educational Review* after the article came out, and so they asked him to expand it into an article and that was included. They should have included these commentaries on my article in the same issue, but they didn't because of deadline problems.

EVANS: As I recall, in none of the three papers that preceded this one had you actually stated categorically that you felt that blacks, or for that matter any other minority, were inferior to whites in intelligence, but you were simply hypothesizing the possibility.

JENSEN: I said nothing about any other minority groups. I was just talking about blacks, and there's never been any argument, for a long time before I came on the scene, that blacks are about one standard deviation below whites, on the average, in IQ. And I really did not go beyond that in my *Harvard Educational Review* article. I didn't say in any definite way that I thought blacks were genetically lower in IQ; I said this was a reasonable hypothesis.

EVANS: Going back to Klineberg's study (1963), and others since then, there is at least some differential data that you could upgrade IQ as a result of environmental stimulation. But by and large, this work is not complete. It has not demonstrated either (1) that with the ultimate stimulation, the IQ of the minority will necessarily reach parity with the IQ of whatever the majority group happens to be in these studies, or (2) that changes that are noticed in the individual will persist over time.

JENSEN: In my own examination of all of the evidence I've been able to find, I have not been able to satisfy myself that all of the differences observed between blacks and whites will be explained in terms of any of the environmental factors that have been mentioned by psychologists and sociologists as being important in IQ. I'm not saying that IQ is not affected by environmental factors; I'm just saying that the difference between environments of whites and blacks on the average does not seem to me to be large enough to account for the magnitude of the IQ difference.

EVANS: Obviously there's a tremendous heterogeneity among blacks. There's a tremendous range of coloration, and a tremendous number of backgrounds—tribes, environments, and so on. Would it be safe to say that most of these studies don't make any effort to delineate heritage?

JENSEN: That's true. Most studies have simply used the social definition of black. If a person calls himself black, or identifies with that group, or is called black in the census or in the school records, he's black, despite the fact that the black population, like any human population, is very heterogenous. The American black population is racially hybrid, and the amount of admixture differs considerably in different parts of the country. There have been studies that have tried to classify blacks in terms of Caucasian admixture, using various physical indices—skin color, interpupillary distance, nasal width, all of these things—to see if any of these indices correlate with measures of mental ability, IQ, etc. They are all flawed in one way or another, which I've pointed out in my book, *Educability and Group Differences* (Jensen 1973). I have a section that deals with correlations between physical indices of racial mixture and IQ. There are correlations in the predicted direction, but their meaning is somewhat ambiguous. If there's been selective mating in the black population for physical traits that are on the Caucasian side, then it could be that these traits become associated with mental ability because the more able blacks will be able to pick wives, let's say, who have more of these Caucasoid traits; so you'll get a correlation between intelligence and Caucasian features from that, not from the Caucasian ancestry, per se.

EVANS: You surveyed, I gather, all the available studies you could find relating mental ability to race. Is that correct?

JENSEN: Yes.

EVANS: And in this study, you looked at other ethnic groups as well. Is that right?

JENSEN: Well, I've looked at Japanese-Americans and Chinese-Americans and Mexican-Americans. Those are the only people I've studied. Other people have studied American Indians, and I've looked at the results of those studies, but I haven't done them myself.

EVANS: And of course there's a limited data base on the differences in IQ between Protestants and Jews and so on.

JENSEN: I mention this in my book, *Educability and Group Differences* (Jensen 1973); there have been studies that have found Jews to average around 110 in IQ as compared with about 100 in the general population, but no one has studied Jewish intelligence very systematically. The data are really quite skimpy, and one would have a hard time drawing any very strong conclusions.

EVANS: Would you begin making some genetic interpretations of this difference or do you think this could be environmental difference?

JENSEN: Well, it could be either one, but it wouldn't surprise me in the least if there were genetic factors involved in this.

EVANS: Is there any other group that the data indicate would be superior?

JENSEN: Well, the Orientals in this country. There's little doubt about it, especially those in California. They come out as the top group in California on IQ and scholastic tests. Now, one can't generalize from migrant populations like that to their home populations, because they're undoubtedly a selective group, for whatever reason.

EVANS: What about some of the earlier studies that compared urban and rural differences? These were often introduced as some demonstration of how important environmental factors were.

JENSEN: Right. Well, this is found throughout the world. It's been found over a period of many years, and I think it probably represents some real differences, in that the average IQ of a community will be governed somewhat by employment opportunities, which affect the kinds of persons who are attracted to the community and the persons who can make a go of it. So that even in California we find large differences in average IQ among the white population from one community to another.

EVANS: You're really supporting a selective migration hypothesis?

JENSEN: Yes.

EVANS: With the advent, intensification, and broadening of the woman's movement, I see a number of people reexamining the data on the difference in intelligence of men and women. Could you talk a little bit about the differences as you see them?

JENSEN: Well, the most clear-cut difference, which I think is very well established, is in spatial visualization ability. That's the only one of Thurstone's Primary Mental Abilities Tests that shows a pronounced sex difference. On good tests of spatial visualization ability, only about one-fourth of the females exceed the male median. Now there's recent work at the University of Chicago which I think demonstrates quite convincingly that spatial ability is attributable to a single recessive sex-linked gene, a gene carried on the X chromosome (Bock and Kolakowski 1973).

EVANS: It's clear that by and large the model of genetic versus environmental as a determination of intelligence in your own mind goes far beyond the black and white issue.

JENSEN: Oh yes, that's a minor part of the issue.

EVANS: What conclusions did you reach in the *Harvard Educational Review* paper (which you've articulated in several other situations since—in *Psychology Today* [1969c] and other articles, and in an Academic Press book, edited by Ebling, *Racial Variation in Man* [Jensen 1975]).

JENSEN: Well, to put this simply, in the broadest context, I see man as a product of evolution, as are all other living organisms. Part of the process of evolution depends upon a variation in all kinds of traits. One of the things that insures the survival of the species is the variation of the species for biological adaptation. One has to study man from this standpoint and take account of his genetic heritage, which is a product of evolution, and which evolved in somewhat different ways for different populations to adapt to the demands of their environments, both physical and cultural. It shouldn't be surprising, therefore, to find variations in mental abilities which have some genetic and biological basis. I believe that the research, based on the study of twins and adopted children, of correlations between different degrees of kinship, and so on, establishes a strong genetic factor in individual differences in intelligence, and we shouldn't be surprised that different human groups that have been isolated breeding populations for centuries differ in mental as well as physical traits. We know that they differ in the physical; this is obvious, and there's evidence that they differ in mental abilities. I think that some of this difference is traceable to genetic differences. Now, I've focused on the black population of the United States for two reasons; one is that their educational plight has been of national concern; we've looked for explanations of their educational problems, and ways of remedying them, and the other is that we have more data on American Negroes than on any other racial group. I have also felt that unless psychology could face this particular problem without prejudice and without ideological and political biases, it's unlikely that it could face other really important social issues. It's a kind of test of the capability of psychology to behave in a scientific way.

EVANS: Despite the fact that we are very concerned in our society about humanistic values, with all of our religious traditions directed toward tolerance and acceptance of our fellow man, there has been a consistent tendency to see the black as an inferior. After a long and hard struggle, there is perhaps now some opportunity for the black to have something approaching equal opportunity. The black has been championed by many liberal whites, and has even been reluctantly accepted by some of the more conservative elements of society, and then data like yours comes along which *seems* to reinforce the inferiority hypothesis. Now before your work, William Shockley (1972) of Stanford had been saying the same thing, in a somewhat cruder way. And since then there's been Herrnstein (1973) at Harvard with his paper on so-called meritocracy. It's been said that you three have now given a scientific basis to bigotry, which will diminish this important social change. But there's no evidence of you being a racist in any sense. You probably would be very supportive of the movement to give greater equality and opportunity to blacks.

JENSEN: Absolutely, yes. I'm a strong advocate, and always have been, of equal opportunity, of civil rights. I've been opposed to racial or social class segregation. I believe in treating people in terms of their own individual characteristics, rather than in terms of their group membership. My motivations have nothing to do with racist thinking in that sense, at all, but I was very much put off by what I call the ideological-ism of the 1950s and 1960s that I saw in psychology. There was a great taboo against even raising questions about genetic or biological influence on individual differences and especially on group differences of any kind. This doctrinaire taboo seemed to me to be a corruption of behavioral science by ideological thinking, even though I agreed with the democratic ideals of this ideology.

EVANS: What about Shockley?

JENSEN: Well, he and I know very much the same kind of evidence, but I think his interest and concerns are quite different from mine. Mine have had more to do with ways of changing the educational system to make it more profitable for the entire population. Shockley's been more concerned with what he calls dysgenics—that is, the genetic downbreeding of the population, be it black or white, or whatever. He's concerned with the relatively rapid increase, as he sees it, of the less able elements in society, who cannot take their productive place in a technological society. Now whether it should be a concern, I don't know, because I haven't investigated this myself, but I do think that we should be able to look at this, and in this, I support Shockley.

EVANS: What about the morality of a program in eugenics?

JENSEN: Well, that's one of those loaded questions, really, because almost anything one says will get one in some kind of hot water, or misrepresent one's real thoughts about these matters. Now, of course, we're practicing eugenics, in a sense, already. Every large medical center today has medical geneticists, who engage in genetic counseling, and I'm certainly in favor of making genetic counseling available to everyone.

EVANS: What is your understanding of what Herrnstein (1973) was trying to say about meritocracy?

JENSEN: Well, Herrnstein pointed out that variability in intelligence, as we understand it, has a genetic component, and that intelligence is correlated with educability. He believes that if you have no social barriers to occupational mobility, if it's based purely on merit, on free competition among individuals for the best jobs, then occupational level and social class level will be ultimately determined by the genes; the more you equalize opportunity, the larger the percentage of the variance that will be due just to the genetic variability. So eventually you will have a meritocracy, a class structure of occupations and social classes that is almost a hereditary hierarchy brought about by a complete equalitarian philosophy of society. And I think his prediction there is quite right. It's sometimes misinterpreted, because people forget the extent to which the genetic system is a kind of lottery. The average IQ difference between siblings in the same family is about thirteen or fourteen IQ points; that's a big difference. It's about the same difference as the average difference between whites and blacks. And we make no fuss about this difference. The bright child in the family, more often than not, will have a higher-level occupation than the less bright child in a given family, even though they're from the same social background, the same family background. So in every generation, in Herrnstein's meritocracy, you will have a reshuffling of genotypes—children inherit their genes, not their genotypes, from their parents. In every new generation, the genes are reshuffled and redistributed throughout the social hierarchy, so that a person born into the lowest class can end up in the top class in the next generation. I think that we're fairly close to that situation now; Herrnstein and I see very much eye to eye on this. But he stays out of the question of racial differences.

EVANS: Today, there are a surprising number of our college students who do not look askance at the possibility of moving into some of the more "menial" forms of activity, activities that may not require a high level of intellectual capacity. So perhaps it's increasingly no longer the case that the result of higher IQ is a higher status in society.

JENSEN: If everyone received the same monetary rewards, could have the same style of life, so to speak, there may still be other bases for preferring one kind of occupation to another, but there wouldn't be any social stigma attached to having one rather than another. Everyone would be able to have the "good life" in terms of having access to all the necessities and to leisure time and so forth. And I think that the world is going to have to come to that. I think that's a desirable kind of thing to work toward. There are many differences between persons other than mental ability, of course. They just don't happen to be as salient in our particular kind of society, which is highly geared to the educational system, which is geared to the occupational structure. I think that a lot of our problems are going to have to be solved by changing our values, changing our notions about what education for the total population is all about, what its purposes are.

EVANS: Dr. Jensen, suppose you have in your class a black student who reads your research and in his mind it raises nagging doubts concerning his own competence?

JENSEN: In the preface to my book, *Educability and Group Differences*, I have something to say about this—that every person is a unique combination of genes. Your genetic background can produce so many different combinations even within one family, as I've pointed out, that you have to think of yourself in terms of what you, yourself, are, and not in terms of your origins. I think it's racist thinking, to think of yourself in terms of your group or your ancestry. What about a Japanese fellow, say, who's six feet three inches. Should he worry about the fact that the Japanese population as a whole is shorter than, say, the Scandinavian population as a whole? He's six feet three inches which is tall enough to be a basketball star. Now if he were five feet four inches he'd never make it as a basketball star, not because he's Japanese, but because he's five feet four inches. Its the same thing in the intellectual realm.

REFERENCES

Bayley, N. 1968. Behavioral correlates in mental growth: birth to thirty-six years. *Amer. Psychol.* 23: 1–17.

Beireter, C. 1969. The future of individual differences. *Harvard Educational Review* 39: (2) 310–18.

Bock, D., and Kolakowski, D. 1973. Further evidence of sex-linked major gene influence on human spatial visualizing ability. *Amer. J. Hum. Genet.* 25: 1–14.

Brazziel, W. 1969. A letter from the south. *Harvard Educational Review,* 39: (2) 348–56.

Cronbach, L. 1969. Heredity, environment and educational policy. *Harvard Educational Review* 39: (2) 338–47.

Crow, J. 1969. Genetic theories and influences: comments on the value of diversity. *Harvard Educational Review* 39: (2) 301–09.

Elkind, D. 1969. Piagetian and psychometric conceptions of intelligence. *Harvard Educational Review* 39: (2) 309–37.

Eysenck, H. 1947. *Dimensions of personality.* London: Routledge & Kegan Paul.

———. 1960. *The structure of human personality.* London: Methuen.

Guilford, J., and Zimmerman, W. 1949. *The Guilford-Zimmerman temperament survey: manual of instructions and interpretations.* Beverly Hills, Calif.: Sheridan Supply Company.

Herrnstein, R. 1973. *I.Q. in the meritocracy.* Boston: Little, Brown.

Hull, C. 1943. *Principles of behavior: an introduction to behavior theory.* New York: Appleton.

———. 1952. *A behavior system: an introduction to behavior theory concerning the individual organism.* New Haven: Yale University Press.

Hunt, J. 1969. Has contemporary education failed? Has it been attempted? *Harvard Educational Review* 39: (2) 278–300.

Jensen, A. 1968a. Race, social class and implications for education. *Amer. Educ. Research Journal.* January 1968.

———. 1968b. Patterns of mental ability and socioeconomic status. Paper presented at the National Academy of Sciences, Washington, D.C. April 1968.

———. 1968c. Uses of twin and sibling data. Paper presented at the meeting of the American Psychological Association, San Francisco, California, August 1968.

———. 1969a. How much can we boost IQ and scholastic achievement? *Harvard Educational Review* 39: (1) 1–123.

———. 1969b. Reducing the heredity-environment uncertainty: a reply. *Harvard Educational Review* 39: (3) 449–83.

———. 1969c. Input: Arthur Jensen replies. *Psychol. Today* 3: (5) 4–6.

———. 1973. *Educability and group differences.* New York: Harper.

———. Another look at culture-fair testing. In *Western Regional Conference on Testing Problems, Proceedings for 1968,* Educational Testing Service. (Reprinted in Jensen, A. 1973. *Educational differences.* pp. 167–222. London: Methuen.)

———. 1975. Race and mental ability. In *Racial variation in man,* ed. J. Ebling. New York: Academic Press.

Kagan, J. 1969. Inadequate evidence and illogical conclusions. *Harvard Educational Review* 39: (2) 274–77.

Klineberg, O. 1971. Black and white in international perspective. *Amer. Psychol.* 26: 119–28.

———. 1963. Negro-white differences in intelligence test performance: a new look at an old problem. *Amer. Psychol.* 18: 198–203.

———. 1935. *Negro intelligence and selective migration.* New York: Columbia University Press.

Newman, H., Freeman, F., and Holzinger, K. 1937. *Twins: a study of heredity and environment.* Chicago: University of Chicago Press.

Oden, M. 1968. The fulfillment of promise: 40-year follow-up of the Terman gifted group. *Genet. Psychol. Monogr.* 77: 3–93.

Pavlov, I. 1927. *Conditioned reflexes.* New York: Oxford.

Shockley, W. 1972. Dysgenics, geneticity, raceology: a challenge to the intellectual responsibility of educators. *Phi Delta Kappan* Jan. 1972, 297–307.

Terman, L. 1916. *The measurement of intelligence.* Boston: Houghton Mifflin.

———, and Oden, M. 1947. *The gifted child grows up.* Stanford, Calif.: Stanford University Press.

Thorndike, E. 1932. *The fundamentals of learning.* New York: Teachers College.

Wechsler, D. 1949. *Wechsler intelligence scale for children.* New York: Psychological Corporation.

Section Two
Learning
Cognition
Altered States
of Consciousness

In recent years in psychology the distinction between cognition, or mental processes, and behavior has been blurred by important new directions of research. The work on information processing and short- and long-term memory, for example, has made it less fruitful to study learning from the simpler stimulus-response (S-R) or stimulus-organism-response (S-O-R) models. Even the determination of internal versus external stimulation as related to the modification of behavior is now far from clear-cut in terms of the "new" cognitive psychology. Added to this, the more exotic areas of research, including biofeedback and extrasensory perception, have challenged the development of behavior control by simply arranging the contingencies of the environment. One has the feeling that the proverbial nighttime search under the street lamp for an object that has been lost in the darkness may be applicable here; that perhaps we are beginning to look for answers where they exist, rather than where it is easiest to look.

In this section, Ernest Hilgard, first a straightforward behaviorist, then a synthesizer of theories of learning, who interacted with some of the early cognitive psychologists and who then moved into a previously taboo area of research, hypnosis, is typical of the flexibility found in many creative contributors.

B. F. Skinner represents one extreme of this issue as he brilliantly revolutionizes an entire field with his dramatic demonstrations of behavior modification based on imaginative strategies of environmental control. Skinner prefers to keep the "blurred" areas of cognition and experience in the background as much as possible, concentrating on specific behaviors and environmental contingencies.

At the forefront of the new cognitive approach, Donald Norman now pursues information-processing models after establishing influential distinctions between short-term and long-term memory, and the subsequent modifications of these processes. His work seriously challenges the attempts to modify behavior by simply controlling the environment of the individual.

A pioneer and a veteran in research in taboo areas, J. B. Rhine describes the utilization of rigorous experimental methodology in the attempted validation of parapsychological phenomena. Certainly, the whole concept of extrasensory perception challenges learning and cognitive psychologists alike, skeptical though many of them may be.

Finally, Joe Kamiya introduces the concept of biological control by feedback—biofeedback—creating an awareness of the physiological processes as a means of controlling those autonomic processes once considered not subject to conditioning or self-control. The entire biofeedback area, further discussed later in this book by Neal Miller and others, calls for an open mind to areas in the modification of human behavior and experience previously unexplored.

Ernest Hilgard

(1904–   )

Ernest Hilgard completed his undergraduate work in chemical engineering and studied at Yale Divinity School before focusing on psychology in which he earned his Ph.D. from Yale in 1930. He was associated with Yale's highly creative Institute of Human Relations, and has made significant contributions to the areas of learning as a researcher, analyzer, and synthesizer of the field. A past president of the American Psychological Association (1949), he is a professor emeritus of psychology at Stanford, where he continues his innovative research into hypnotic phenomena, his primary field for the past decade.

Pavlov's Book/Functionalism/Gestalt Psychology/Developing an Eclectic Point of View//Learning Theory/Human Learning/Genuinely Relevant Problems/A Healthy Trend/Ingenuity Beyond Conditioning Theory/Utilizing What We Learn//Humanistic Psychology/Methodological Problems/A Common Framework of Values/Whether It Is Psychology or Not/Solving the Problems/Interdisciplinary Training//A Problem Loaded with Psychology/Hypnosis/A Convenient Approach/History/Research and Methodology/Applications/Hypnosis and Drugs/Use and Misuse/A Psychologist First and a Hypnotist Second/Our Methods and Our Tools//

As Dr. Hilgard and I discuss the convergence of ideas that led him to become an outstanding researcher in the area of learning and an analyzer and synthesizer of the field, he defends the eclectic point of view, both for its open-mindedness and its mediating qualities. He then calls attention to several trends in learning that he considers important, including the increased emphasis on human learning and ingenious applications of what has been learned. He speculates on methodological problems in humanistic approaches to psychology, and distinguishes between value-free and value-neutral positions in research. Dr. Hilgard offers some interesting ideas for graduate training, including the development of a "nose for the problem" and the interdisciplinary approach: "You don't care whether it's psychology or not; you solve the problems of our cities, the problems of race relations, the problems of international bitterness; those problems don't belong to any one discipline." He then traces the background of his work, going back to his graduate training, which sparked his interest in hypnosis as a field of exploration. He presents a brief history of hypnosis, describes some of his research, and connects the findings to important and practical applications in solving human problems. He comments on hypnosis and drugs, the possible misuses of hypnosis, and some of the problems that face the serious researcher in the field. He maintains that such a researcher must be a psychologist first and a hypnotist second. In conclusion, Dr. Hilgard and I discuss the importance of an effective introduction to psychology for students, and he suggests that the best method is to make it relevant to the student's own life.

EVANS: Dr. Hilgard, although you have devoted a large part of your research for the past decade to one of the most intriguing and perhaps most controversial areas of psychology, hypnotic phenomena, you have obviously remained active in other areas as well. For example, your book, *Theories of Learning* (Hilgard and Bower 1975), which was first published in 1948, I believe, has become a classic in the field. It might be interesting to begin our discussion by asking how you happened to move into the area of learning, not only as a researcher, but as an analyzer and a synthesizer of this field.

HILGARD: As one becomes autobiographical, he usually says things that aren't so, but looking back, I suppose it had something to do with the time I happened to come on the scene. The problems of learning were very much in the fore; Pavlov's (1927) book had just appeared in English, for example. The people with whom I was trained were broad-minded people—people like E. S. Robinson, who represented a functionalist position, and J. F. Brown, a graduate student at Yale who had just come back from studying with the Gestalt psychologists. So I was in a cross-discussion of functionalism and Gestalt psychology. My own professor was Raymond Dodge, who was essentially a functionalist, though he worked with very objective methods. Yerkes was there, working with chimpanzees and talking about insight. These were behaviorists who were objectivists in method but not in theory. The one who really introduced the arch-behavioristic method at Yale, of course, was Clark Hull (1943). I was an instructor in the department, and had completed the investigatory work for my dissertation although I hadn't published it, when Hull arrived. I had some limited contact with Hull, so when Marquis and I wrote *Conditioning and Learning* (Hilgard and Marquis 1940) I had already acquired a broad background. We included Tolman's (1932) point of view, and even had a little work on psychopathology; so even though the title included the term "conditioning," it wasn't merely a conditioning book. It was in the 1930s when I came on the scene—at a time when Thorndike (1932) was developing his notion of spread of effect; Guthrie's (1935) book came out in 1935, and Skinner's (1938) first important book came out in 1938. The Gestalt psychologists were getting settled in this country; there was Wertheimer

(1945) and Lewin (1935) and I guess the only one I didn't know well whose views were treated in the book was Thorndike, who was a somewhat older man. But I had met him and his work was familiar. When you know these people you see their earnestness, and you see how some of the things they are saying are very sensible things; when you take the background of my own teachers and the people I knew and perhaps something in my own personal history—all this made me somewhat eclectic and that put me in a good position to be a kind of expositor of other views.

EVANS: Philosophically, of course, eclecticism is sometimes described as a weak position, and it appears you were willing to be an integrator of theories at a time when it was probably more fashionable to accept a point of view, learn it, and stick to it. Do you feel that you paid a price for your eclecticism?

HILGARD: I don't like eclecticism, either. I have fantasies about a position, and a lot of disciples and followers defending it against all comers—it's fun to do that—but something within me holds back from it. I like to keep a sense of wonder about the complex problems we haven't yet solved, and I'm impatient with the person who thinks he has the pat answer. I'm glad there are people who have fixed positions; I'm not against that. But you have some gains and some losses. I wouldn't recommend eclecticism for everybody, but maybe the field as a whole needs some kind of mediator to keep people tolerant towards each other.

EVANS: Looking at the current status of learning theory, which you are always reevaluating as successive editions of your book come out, is there a significant trend, something happening to solidify our thinking about learning in one direction or another, as you see it?

HILGARD: There are a number of things happening, many of them continuous with what has happened in the past, but there are a couple of things I would point to. There is much greater attention to human learning—for a while the attention was almost exclusively on animal learning. The recognition that we have a kind of code book which we bring to a learning situation, verbal learning particularly, and the linguistic material entering into our study of learning, has brought into fresh focus problems of memory, short-term memory, long-term storage. So one trend is this much greater attention to human learning. The second thing is a healthier integration with the practical problems of instruction, which has come about in a sort of back-handed way, perhaps. Skinner's development of programmed learning is one side of it, and computer-based instruction that draws on a high level of technical competence is another. This use of learning theory in relation to genuinely relevant problems is a very important contemporary development.

EVANS: Considering your very basic work in conditioning, let's look at a movement that is attempting to take conditioning theory into the next cycle, therapy. In our discussions, Skinner (Evans 1968) made the very interesting statement that the danger of this is pretty much like trying to build a bridge when you know only a few simple principles of stress and strain. Do you think this should be encouraged or do you see some pitfalls here?

HILGARD: I'm a strong believer that you can go to the basic theory for hunches and ideas, but you don't just pin the theory on the practical situation. Those from other disciplines—psychoanalysis, for example—can use operant conditioning, but the ingenuity that is actually involved in the sessions goes beyond conditioning theory. I have seen some very skilled work with psychotic patients, using token rewards, so I think that these are very hopeful things, but I take a kind of research and development view. You start with your basic thing, and you modify it, you show ingenuity and inventiveness, and you evaluate it to see if it is really working in that situation. And if it works, it still may work for some other reason.

EVANS: In a sense, you're saying that some of these people may be bringing strategies to bear which go far beyond the simple paradigm they are supposed to be working within. That's a very interesting observation.

HILGARD: For instance, there is imitation included in the social learning that Bandura (1961) is doing. He's objective, but he is finding enormous help through modeling. This has been little represented in Skinnerian theory or any others.

EVANS: There still seems to be a great preoccupation with learning theory that is involved in all of our training, and there are those people who believe that this may even be what psychology is; that perhaps it isn't much more.

HILGARD: I thought that idea was already over the hump. People aren't as deferential in giving an explanation in formal learning terms as they once were. We are aware of social interaction, of cognitive disciplines, of linguistics and generative grammar, all things that were very poorly handled in learning theory. It's settling down a bit, but these ideas almost captured the field, prematurely, I think. Performance is important—much of Skinner's theory is performance theory, not learning theory—but how we utilize what we learn is more important. Psychology is in a better place now I would think.

EVANS: Another movement may be putting learning in a different perspective; what has been described as the "Third Force," the group that says that as psychologists involved with human beings, we must make some kind of commitment about the ultimate humanness of the individual; that we can't limit ourselves to a biological deterministic view or a social deterministic view. They see an ultimate drive toward being, toward individuation. There are those, of course, who think this would be stripping away the rigor, the precision, all the science that we have worked so hard to build up in this field. How do you feel about the importance of this movement?

HILGARD: It is certainly something to be reckoned with. After all, the American Psychological Association elected Abraham Maslow as its president. But the main point, I think, is that psychology has to adopt some kind of value orientation. If you are going to serve human welfare, you have to define it some way, in terms of what's noble in life, what's courageous, what's worth living for, what human ideals you are ready to defend, and one certainly can't be against reflection on these matters. The question of the role of science is a puzzling one. These ideas sometimes come as a breath of fresh air and make us examine what we are doing, but when the cards are down, you have to find some way to do the job. The humanistic psychologist who wants to discover something about experience has to turn to the kinds of devices that we have used right along in the study of attitudes and motivation, and so on.

EVANS: You are saying that this so-called Third Force hasn't really developed a methodology that is any different from the more traditional type of psychological research?

HILGARD: We're trying to improve them all along. One has to distinguish, I think, between value-*free* and value-*neutral* research positions, but values are inherent in a civilized community (we'll call it that). Many values are so common—not universal, but so common—that you have no trouble getting agreement. Health is better than illness; it is better to live long than to die; it's good if you have a place for art and music, and have open parks and public areas. These are the same things that the humanistic people talk about, but since there is such agreement, you can go ahead and do your scientific work within that framework of values without getting into any trouble. Nobody has trouble as a scientist because he tries to reduce people's agony and pain, even though that has some value orientation. You might say that Job had boils for his own good, and to give him penicillin would have been the worst thing you could do.

EVANS: Of course, this does present a dilemma when we consider what will best equip the student of psychology for what will be happening in the field. Some are trained in a very knowledgeable, disciplinarian paradigm, and they consider such questions irrelevant. Others are following the broader, more philosophical course you just described. If you could see ideal training for graduate students, how would you resolve this?

HILGARD: I have always felt that the main problem of science is not criticism—that's just a technical problem—but how to initiate inquiry and discover problems and then how to work them down into a manageable form. After that you can bring in your statistical tests to see if you have found anything. But sometimes we turn it around and teach experimental design before we teach how to have a "nose for the problem." One way to get a nose for problems is to thrust right into them, so I feel that some kind of naturalistic exposure to the problems of society is needed—observing children, or observing riots, or whatever it may be—in the community where many of our psychological problems begin. Instead of protecting students from these things, we would sensitize them, and then bring them back to get a little distance and say, "Now, look, we can't just stand in awe of this. How can we bring our science to bear on it?" Another problem is where you think of all the problems as arising essentially out of your discipline. The counterpart to that, or the supplement, is to have a problem-solving approach. You don't care whether it is psychology or not—you solve the problems of our cities, the problems of race relations, the problems of international bitterness—those problems don't belong any one discipline. How are we going to train our students to face them? What I fear in the disciplinary approach is that the student has to win his spurs, do a lot of tool-sharpening, to gain the respect of his fellows within the discipline, before he feels free to move out into other areas, and by that time you've lost a good many years. I think interdisciplinary training might assemble the abilities necessary to attack the problem. You can put it all in the person so the psychologist is, himself, a sociologist, a political scientist, and so on, or you can learn to work with a task force, where you feel comfortable with sociologists, economists, and others.

EVANS: You're saying then, that the student of the future will have to think in terms of these complex problems, that our culture will demand this kind of confidence. And if the student doesn't get this in his formal training, he will have to learn it after he graduates.

HILGARD: It's not too early to start, you know.

EVANS: Dr. Hilgard, in recent years you have become interested in the area of hypnosis. In the history of psychology, there have been ups and downs in the acceptance of this particular phenomenon as a legitimate area of inquiry for the psychologist, so our students might like to hear how you happened to get interested in hypnosis at this stage of your career.

HILGARD: Sometimes these discontinuities look more discontinuous than they are. As a matter of fact, I have been interested in the problem of control and loss of control, voluntary and involuntary action, right from the start. My doctoral dissertation compared conditioned responses and voluntary responses, their latency characteristics and so on, so this is something that had been of interest to me all along. Later I did some work on conditioned discrimination, control through instructions and through efforts to resist. These are the same kinds of questions one asks with hypnosis. My first experiment on suggestion was published in 1936 (Berreman and Hilgard 1936). I just never got around to it full steam. It's partly a matter of getting a little confidence; we do tend to work where the light is brightest, where we have techniques. I had been dean for awhile, and when I got back to the lab, I thought, "Why don't I pick a problem that is just loaded with psychology, whether I can get the psychology out of it or not." That's a little facetious, but there is a lot of psychology in hypnosis, and I figured it followed the problem of control, loss of control, motivation, psychodynamics, my interest in psychoanalytic theory—it would serve as a very convenient approach to some of these problems.

EVANS: This might have come up, too, in your association with Clark Hull during your student years. Many of us forget that Hull also pursued research in this field.

HILGARD: Of course I was acquainted with his work; it was going on while I was there, but I never participated in it. That may have been in the background, that I did know some of the problems that were amenable to experimental attack. That 1936 study was from a list of topics suggested by Hull, but there was no direct line there.

EVANS: You moved into the area of research on voluntary control, saying that maybe hypnosis was involved. Other investigators have worked in similar areas, but there is no doubt that many people shy away from this; it almost might be described as a taboo area. Why do you feel that people have become suspicious of involvement and concerned over research in it?

HILGARD: There are all sorts of historical reasons. The old Mesmer period was all mixed up, and later some of the experiences in England were unpleasant—it would take a long time to go over the whole history—but one of the striking things was Freud, for he was very much interested in it. He worked with Breuer, and translated both Charcot and Bernheim, who were the two poles at the time, into German. Since Freud was the man who was doing most at developing an interest in the functional basis in neurosis, the people who might have been most scientifically interested in hypnosis were the people who followed Freud. Then he put a kind of a taboo on it after his work with Breuer and never again used hypnosis, even though the culture of psychoanalysis is a direct inheritance from hypnosis. But this set it back. Hull might have made hypnosis more attractive to American psychologists, but he rejected it, talked about it as a very messy field, in a way, and this could have set it back. Behaviorism is another thing. At the height of behaviorism, we were uneasy about dreams, hallucinations, or regressions, and while it may have been possible to work on them within the behavioristic setting, people just didn't, and I think that is another reason. We are much freer now. In fact the dream research, the study of rapid eye movements and EEGs and so on, have made it respectable to work in this field. The psychological and physiological studies of sleep, for example, include several papers on hypnosis because this is such a convenient way into the control of dreams.

EVANS: When you look at the literature on hypnosis, you see two directions: clinical reports and clinical research, much of it anecdotal (and this is probably the kind of thing most often under serious indictment by the experimentalist and the researcher), and then the research that is really experimental. In the sense that the hypnotic process is an interactive one, is a clinical process, can these things be separate?

Wouldn't the problems of controlling any interactive clinical situation transfer over when you are using a technique of this sort in an experimental situation?

HILGARD: You have to be sensitive to the fact that this is a kind of intrusive technique. It is highly personal, and there must be respect for personality and for clinical methods. I wouldn't like to carry out experimental research in this field without clinical control. My wife, Dr. Josephine Hilgard, who is a psychiatrist, works with us on this and we don't have any trouble. Now and then there are minor things, headaches or sleep disturbances that need to be cleared up, to find out if they are related to the hypnosis. I think the main difference is not a difference in the sensitivities, it is a difference in the choice of problems. In a fully clinical situation, you give service to people who knock on the door. In that sense we don't do it, but we do have clinical dissertations on phobias, for example, and the bearing of hypnosis on it. We are not a clinic, but the problems intertwine.

EVANS: One area I know you are interested in is the problem of pain. Traditionally, medicine and dentistry have used hypnosis clinically as a valuable tool, but you have started some much-needed research on pain, experimentally. How have you proceeded in this research?

HILGARD: This is a good illustration of our not going out and picking people who are in pain, but producing the pain in the laboratory with normal people and studying the psychophysics of it, the physiological consequences, just the way we might study hearing or any other sensory phenomena. We are using two methods. One is the hand in ice water—the so-called cold pressor response—and the other is tourniquet pain sometimes called ischemic pain—you put a tourniquet on the arm, exercise a little, and the pain mounts. We had to do these first without hypnosis because they hadn't been done in the quantitative way we wanted. That is just straight experimental psychology. Then we reduce the pain under hypnosis, having established the parameters, and we can show, for example, that the blood pressure rises in the normal response to pain, but in the hypnotized subject, who is not responding to pain, the blood pressure may not rise. It gives you a feel for the reality of what you are working with. It is nonclinical, but it is clinically relevant, because it can be applied in childbirth and painful burns and terminal cancer. It doesn't take our work to show that it can be done, but the more we find out about it, the more sensibly the conditions can be stated with respect to its use and its practical applications.

EVANS: An area of concern to psychology at the moment is the use of human subjects, the ethics of manipulating human subjects. Of course, you mentioned that your wife, Dr. Josephine Hilgard, who is a physician, is working with you, and this obviously meets the most stringent controls that anyone could have, but would you go so far as to say that in experimental research using hypnosis, that a physician should be present, or at least sitting in on the project?

HILGARD: Well, physicians are available in college health services, and they don't have to be sitting right in your laboratory. Certainly, I would want the university health service to know what I was doing; it just protects you against complaints. It's not a dangerous thing, but there are some people who have a thin hold on reality, and they might blame hypnosis for something that had nothing to do with it. We are also very clear in having the subject know what he is going to do. He isn't suddenly thrown into a pain experiment without knowing what to expect.

EVANS: This eliminates any deceptive element.

HILGARD: Yes, but there's a curious thing about the relationship of deception in hypnosis and ordinary deception. It is not interpreted as deception by the subject, for example, to have a hallucination that he is waking up with a rabbit in his lap. That is part of the contract in hypnosis, that strange things happen. When it is all over, of course, we are very careful to be sure that he doesn't think of it as a real rabbit. We take a number of precautions of this sort. And telling a person that a rod is hot, when it is just an ordinary pencil, is different from some of the sociopsychological experiments in which you tell a person that he is applying for a job and then at the end you tell him there wasn't really a job there. We have had no complaints, and we have very good public relations with our subjects. Our experiments are quite popular with the Stanford students.

EVANS: In terms of using hypnosis as an experimental tool, as one considers its advantages over other techniques, what can it afford that other techniques cannot? For example, in pain, what can you gain by using hypnosis that you cannot get with drugs designed for pain relief?

HILGARD: Understand, I am not setting hypnosis in competition with drugs, but there are certain situations in which it is to be advised. There are certain medical and surgical situations in which you want the responses of the patient in his normal state, not subdued with drugs, and there are heart problems, conditions where the side effects of drugs would be worse than hypnosis.

EVANS: Can you state with some certainty that the side effects of hypnosis are less than those of drugs? Is this one area that there is some agreement on?

HILGARD: I think that is a rather safe statement. You know you always have some qualifications in terms of a particular person, but it is quite a safe thing. In certain burn cases, for example, where circulation must be preserved in a skin flap, and a hand, say, must be kept on the ankle for several weeks—to reduce the discomfort and pain by using morphine for that length of time is to run the danger of addiction. But such a person can be kept under hypnosis without any addiction, without any discomfort, and with no side effects from the hypnosis when the time is over. Childbirth is another example, where the woman under hypnosis is able to assist in the birth process and be aware of what is happening without discomfort. Women who have had babies both ways tend to prefer the hypnosis.

EVANS: In the area of drugs and drug research, of course, one recalls the considerable criticism that has been leveled at the work with LSD and the so-called mind-expanding drugs. This consciousness-expanding property has also been connected historically with hypnosis. Do you see any parallel here?

HILGARD: There is the problem of susceptibility. You have to have a rather susceptible subject for hypnosis, and we are working on the problem of how well you can train an unsusceptible subject to be susceptible. There has also been some work suggesting that many of the effects of LSD are the results of suggestion, that is, if a person is with a group that is involved in a religious experience, he may, under LSD, have a religious experience, or he may believe he can design buildings if he is with an architectural group. But the experimentation of this type has been shut down.

EVANS: The induction of a hypnotic trance does not require a person with a PhD or a medical degree. Suppose that some of our young people who have been involved with drugs like LSD become involved in hypnosis as a form of consciousness-expansion. What would be the probability of injury to the subject compared, say, to the drugs we now know have indeterminate, long-range effects?

HILGARD: I don't like to put it in a versus case because they are different, but I would express caution with the use of hypnosis here. It is not as dangerous as LSD, and I think I can say that confidently. But it is not something to be played with. I suppose it is no more dangerous than caffeine. Anybody can get himself a cup of coffee, but if he starts experimenting with caffeine to see how much he can stand, that wouldn't be a very wise thing to do. It is something that should be kept to a professional setting. Most people working with it would like to see hypnosis taken off the stage, too. I don't think it should really be used for entertainment.

EVANS: I have heard it suggested that we might develop a body of skilled persons—paraprofessionals—who are highly trained in inducing hypnotic trances, who would be available to physicians and dentists and others, and this might extend its use into the professional fields. Would you care to comment on this?

HILGARD: I think this arises out of a misunderstanding of how hard it is to induce hypnosis. If anybody really understands it, he can have a tape or a phonograph record that would do it just as well as an assistant. We have done a number of studies on this and we have not been able to demonstrate any particular difference in the hypnotist.

EVANS: Looking toward the future use of hypnosis as a tool in research, you have mentioned your own interest in pain and the question of control, but what are some of the other applications to contemporary research areas?

HILGARD: I believe that a much wider use of it will be made in the study of memory, in dream research, in all kinds of control of levels of arousal—things like that. The interest is not in hypnosis, but in something else. You know, a stethoscope doctor isn't just a stethoscope doctor. He is a doctor first, and he is a stethoscope user second, and a hypnotist psychologist shouldn't be just a hypnotist. He should be a psychologist first, and a hypnotist second.

EVANS: That's a very interesting way of putting it.

HILGARD: Both the British Medical Association and the American Medical Association are urging that hypnosis be taught in medical schools now, so we're making some gains. It's slow, but it's moving.

EVANS: In conclusion, Dr. Hilgard, you have written an introductory textbook, and kept in pretty close contact with introductory students in psychology. You mentioned that at Stanford, senior members of the faculty teach introductory psychology. Perhaps you could make some suggestions as to how we can make this a learning experience that goes beyond the content of the course, for many of these students will carry this concept of psychology into society with them as their only exposure to it.

HILGARD: Well, you know we've had this long argument in the profession as to whether it should be psychology-centered or student-centered. The psychology-centered people say, "Let's show them what psychology really is, and what our problems are, and what our methods are, and what our tools are." Some rather successful courses are taught that way, and it has a tendency to bring into the profession people who won't be bored by it, because they like this kind of thing. The opposite is to say that student questions are legitimate, even if we are not quite ready to answer them. Let me say that I personally prefer the second method; that is, to say "You are going to see how psychology approaches certain problems, but they ought to be relevant to your own lives and you might very well look around in your own experience for examples of the things we talk about."

REFERENCES

Bandura, A., Ross, D., and Ross, S. 1961. Transmission of aggression through imitation of aggressive models. *J. Abnorm. Soc. Psychol.* 63: 572–82.

Berreman, J. V., and Hilgard, E. 1936. The effects of personal heterosuggestion and two forms of autosuggestion upon postural movement. *J. Soc. Psychol.* 7: 289–300.

Evans, R. 1968. *B. F. Skinner: the man and his ideas.* New York: Dutton.

Guthrie, E. 1935, rev. ed. 1952. *The psychology of learning.* New York: Harper.

Hilgard, E., and Marquis, D. 1940. *Conditioning and learning.* New York: Appleton.

———, and Bower, G. 1975. *Theories of learning.* New York: Appleton.

———. 1975. Hypnotic phenomena: the struggle for scientific acceptance. *Amer. Scientist* 59: 567–77.

Hull, C. 1943. *Principles of behavior: an introduction to behavior theory.* New York: Appleton.

Lewin, K. 1935. *Dynamic theory of personality.* New York: McGraw-Hill.

Pavlov, I. 1927. *Conditioned reflexes.* New York: Oxford.

Skinner, B. 1938. *The behavior of organisms: an experimental analysis.* New York: Appleton.

Thorndike, E. 1932. *The fundamentals of learning.* New York: Teachers College.

Tolman, E. 1932, rev. ed. 1967. *Purposive behavior in animals and men.* New York: Appleton.

Wertheimer, M. 1945. *Productive thinking.* New York: Harper.

B. F. Skinner

(1904–   )

B. F. Skinner completed his Ph.D. degree in psychology at Harvard University in 1931, after which he spent five years in basic research, including three years as a Junior Fellow in the Harvard Society of Fellows. He then embarked on a highly productive research and teaching career that included posts at the University of Minnesota and Indiana University, after which he returned to Harvard where he is currently Edgar Pierce Professor of Psychology. Considered one of the most influential contemporary psychologists, Professor Skinner has made many significant contributions, including the concept of programmed instruction and the powerful and precise techniques he terms operant conditioning. His novel Walden II *brought his ideas to the attention of society at large. He has been awarded the Distinguished Scientific Award by the American Psychological Association and the President's Medal of Science.*

Behavior: A Very Precise Definition/Pavlovian Reflexology and the Notion of the Operant/"Empty Organism" or "Irrelevant Organism"//A Positive Shift/ Positive Reinforcement and the Problem of Control/Examples from History, Education, Religion, and Politics/Punishment/Negative Reinforcement/ Aversive Control//The Russians Need an Incentive System/On-the-Job Applications of Scheduled Positive Reinforcement and Fixed Ratio Schedules/ Psychotics Are Psychotic Because of Their Behavior/Institutional and Therapeutic Applications//A Question of Method and Not Individual Worth/ Humanistic and Behavioristic Approaches/Teaching Machines/Educational Applications//A Genuine Science of Behavior/Psychological Training/ Basic and Applied Research//

As we begin our discussion, Dr. Skinner defines behavior precisely and traces the emergence of the notion of the operant, which led to his widely discussed technique of operant conditioning. He reacts to the stimulus-response (S-R) and stimulus-organism-response (S-O-R) paradigms and clarifies his position on the "empty organism." He responds to the criticism that behaviorists view

---

This discussion is an excerpt from the book *B. F. Skinner: The Man and His Ideas* by Richard I. Evans. Copyright © 1968 by Richard I. Evans. Reprinted by permission of the publishers, E. P. Dutton & Co., Inc.

man as merely a machine, comparing the goals of both humanistic and behavioristic approaches. We discuss negative and positive reinforcement, the historical-cultural trend away from aversive control toward positive control, and Dr. Skinner offers some examples from religion, education, and political science to support this trend. He describes some of the more subtle forms of control, as well as the direct ones, used by governments, educators, employers, and others in daily activities, and suggests some alternate solutions to the problems involved. He also describes the therapeutic and institutional applications of his techniques with psychotic patients and severe retardates. We discuss the development of the teaching machine, and he differentiates between this method and computer programming systems. We conclude our discussion with his ideas on psychological training and applied versus basic research, as he comments, "I'm very much impressed by work with exceptional children, psychotics, retardates, and so on, in which the scientist brings to bear on the problem special techniques acquired under more rigorous conditions. There's enough reinforcement for a man working in that area to last him a lifetime. I've done both."

EVANS: Dr. Skinner, most present-day theories of motivation lean heavily on the physiological notion of homeostasis or balance. In these theories, motivation involves all of the conditions which arouse, direct, and sustain the organism. How do you feel about this approach to dealing with motivation from the *behavioral* standpoint?

SKINNER: There seem to be two issues here. One concerns the dimensions of behavior itself. I would define behavior as the movement of an organism in space with respect to itself or any other useful frame of reference. This is a pretty specific way to define behavior, and most people fall back on a more general description, using terms such as "adjustment," "adaptation," "homeostatic development," and so on. On the other hand, to identify the variables which lead an organism to adjust, you must be more specific about the behavior and its causes. It isn't enough to say, "Oh, there's a totality of conditions within the organism which bring about behavior." If you want to identify manipulable causes, you must isolate them and then test yourself by manipulating them and observing what happens. If you have a situation in which you can observe the frequency with which an animal or a man engages in a given activity, then you can search for all the variables of which that frequency is a function.

EVANS: A major field of interest in contemporary psychology is learning. Central in any consideration of learning is the concept of conditioning as conceived by Pavlov (1927). How did Pavlov's work on the conditioned reflex affect your thinking as you began to develop your approach to learning?

SKINNER: Well, I certainly took off from the notion of the reflex and the conditioned reflex in the early years of my work as a psychologist.

But I soon realized that something was wrong, and before the publication of *The Behavior of Organisms* (Skinner 1938), although I still used the word "reflex" more freely than I do now, the basic notion of an operant emerged. An operant is quite different from a reflex, and different from the Pavlovian conditioned reflex. You define an operant in terms of its effects, and study it by means of its effects on your apparatus. Operant behavior, as I see it, is simply a study of what used to be dealt with by the concept of purpose. The purpose of an act is the consequences it is going to have. Actually, in the case of operant conditioning, we study the consequences an act has had in the past. Changes in the probability of response are brought about when an act is followed by a particular kind of consequence. It can be positive or negative reinforcement as the case may be, but the datum that you watch and follow is the probability that a response of a given type will indeed occur. An operant, then, is a class of responses, and a response is a single instance of that class.

EVANS: Dr. Skinner, historically we have seen psychology deal with the stimulus-response, or S-R paradigm, as well as the stimulus-organism-response, or S-O-R paradigm. We find that these two paradigms are still developing concurrently. It appears to be difficult for the student of psychology to decide what is implied by being an S-R psychologist. To be scientific must we speak of an "empty organism"?

SKINNER: I think there are two issues here. Let me emphasize first that I do not consider myself an S-R psychologist. As it stands, I'm not sure that response is a very useful concept. Behavior is very fluid; it isn't made up of lots of little responses packed together. The stimulating environment is important among the variables of which behavior is a function, but it is by no means the only one. It is a mistake to suppose that there are internal stimuli and to try to formulate everything as S-R psychology. I don't think hunger, for example, should be considered a stimulus. There is stimulation associated with states of deprivation, but deprivation does not act by producing stimuli which then affect behavior. The topography of a response is only one property. If you take rate of responding as the datum, then details of any one response become less important. Once you are observing the rate, you look around for anything which has influence on it. Some of the influences will reasonably be described as stimuli, and some will not.

I think, however, that the problem goes deeper than that. If the O represents the organism and S-R represents input and output, then the question arises, How important is the O? I guess I'm even more opposed to postulating the influence of O than I am to the strict S-R formulation. As I see it, psychology is concerned with establishing relations between the behavior of an organism and the forces acting upon it. Now, the organism must be there. . . . I don't really believe in the "empty organism." That wasn't my phrase. I hope that this particular something will be investigated just as rapidly as possible. At the same time, I don't want to borrow support from physiology when my formulation breaks down. If I can't give a clean-cut statement of a relationship between behavior and antecedent variables, it is no help to me to speculate about something inside the organism which will fill the gap. As far as I'm concerned, the organism is irrelevant either as the site of physiological processes or as the locus of mentalistic activities. We begin with an organism as a genetic product. It very quickly acquires a history, and we, as students of behavior, must deal with it as an organism with a history.

EVANS: Humanists often accuse behaviorists of having no concern for human values or human good because behaviorists view man as being merely a machine. How do you react to this criticism of behaviorism?

SKINNER: If by "machine," you simply mean any system which behaves in an orderly way, then man and all the other animals are machines. But this has nothing to do with the interests of the humanists, or of the interests of any man of compassion who deals with his fellow man. Though I call myself a behaviorist, I don't particularly like the term. However, we see that the humanist and the behaviorist have different conceptions of man and the nature of man. But if it is the goal which matters, rather than the conception, then I feel that the weight of evidence is all on our side. For example, in education, we can specify materials and methods which bring about the changes in the student we want to bring about and in a very effective way, much more effectively than the person who thinks of the student simply as an individual whose wishes must be respected, who must make decisions, and so on. He may make decisions, but the forces which lead him to do so must be taken into account.

EVANS: Dr. Skinner, some psychologists seem to be shifting from a purely environmentally and socially determined conception of man to a conception that reflects more concern with individual responsibility. I wonder where you stand in relation to this issue?

SKINNER: I'm not arguing for the organism's self-responsibility. But the distinction you make is really a shift from aversive control to positive reinforcement, and it's a very important issue. The early Christians and Jews, in the Kumran community and the monasteries, were submitting themselves to external authority in order to control themselves. You put yourself under a punishing authority and are then responsible for your actions in the sense that if you do not behave properly, you will be justly punished. In the Hasidic movement and with Freud, it is not that inner sources of control have been substituted for the external, authoritative, orthodox sources, but that there has been a shift from negative reinforcement to positive reinforcement. The notion of personal responsibility just isn't relevant. The control is still there. This is a point on which I argue with Carl Rogers, who claims that somehow or other you are going to find within the client himself the controlling forces that will solve his problem. His methods work with clients who have emerged from a tradition, such as the Judeo-Christian, which gives them reasons for behaving well, but if a client suddenly announces, "Ah yes! I see it now. I should murder my boss!," you don't just let him walk out of the office. You don't tell him that he has really found the solution to his problem. Every solution comes from some source of control.

EVANS: Your emphasis on positive reinforcement, then, might be said to be reflecting an already existing historical-cultural trend away from aversive control toward positive control.

SKINNER: Yes. I'm really a little embarrassed to say this, because I don't believe in arguing from history. However, I do think it is interesting to watch what is going on, even though I don't like to make predictions on historical evidences. Civilization has moved from aversive control toward a positive approach. There are only a few places in the world today where slavery is still practiced, where labor is coerced by the whip. We have substituted the payment of wages for physical punishment, and are even concerned with finding other reinforcers. You hear claims occasionally that we've got to start whipping our school boys and girls again, but this simply reminds us that until very recently, education was openly aversive. In England, the cane is still used, but there is a movement away from punishment, and an effort to find positive reasons for studying. The same is true in religion. There is less and less emphasis on hell-fire and the threat of damnation; people are to be good for positive reasons, for the love of God or their fellowmen. There is a parallel trend in politics and government. In a famous case in the thirties the Agricultural Act provided that farmers be paid for not planting acreage, instead of making it illegal to plant. I'm not a historical determinist to the point at which I would predict that this trend is going to continue, but I hope it does. A punitive society is not supported by the people under it, whereas a society which is full of good things is likely to be strong.

EVANS: I know, Dr. Skinner, that your experimental work led you to make distinctions among the conceptions of *punishment, negative reinforcement,* and *aversive control.* Could you discuss these distinctions?

SKINNER: You can distinguish between punishment, which is making an aversive event contingent upon a response, and negative reinforcement, in which the elimination or removal of an aversive stimulus, conditioned or unconditioned, is reinforcing. Aversive control is a way of generating behavior. When you say you punish a child to make him work, you are misusing the word "punish." You are arranging conditions which he can escape from by working. When you punish a child to keep him from misbehaving, however, you are trying to suppress behavior. In my earlier experiments punishment did not suppress behavior as it had been supposed to do. Punishment may only be reducing a current tendency to respond. As soon as punishment is withdrawn, the behavior bounces back. This isn't always the case, because extremely severe punishment may knock behavior out for good, at least so far as we are able to determine. I object to aversive control in general because of its by-products. If you make a student study to escape punishment, then he will soon escape in other ways; he'll play hookey, be a truant, or become a dropout. Or he may counterattack. Vandalism against school property is easily explained just by looking at the techniques schools use to control their students. Another common reaction is a kind of inactivity —an apathy or stubborn do-nothingness. Positive reinforcement does not generate comparable by-products, and that's why it's better.

EVANS: Any discussion of systems of control in society, of course, raises questions of what systems of control actually operate in communist societies. For example, how about the Soviet Union?

SKINNER: I'm not too impressed by what I've seen in the Soviet Union, and theoretically I think they are wrong. I don't think they even subscribe to their own theory. Marx's principle, "to each according to his need," is, of course, scriptural; it is not St. Karl, it's St. Augustine. But the principle misses the boat because the important thing is what a man does at the moment he receives what he needs. That's where reinforcement comes in. Khrushchev reportedly told the then Senator Humphrey that the "crazy Chinese" still believed you should give to each according to his need. Yet Khrushchev promised the Russian people that by 1980 food, housing, clothing would be free. If he actually meant free, that these things are to be given away and not made contingent on productive labor, then there will be no reason for people to work. I once argued this with a Russian economist whom I met at a reception in England. I said, "If this happens, why will a man work?" He took a very smug stance, and said, "Ah, they will work for the common good." But as Karl Marx himself knew, there is a great gap between working at a given moment and participating in the common good at a later date. The Russians need some sort of incentive system.

EVANS: All of the properties of this incentive system would not necessarily be positively reinforcing, would they? There would likely also be some aversive elements in the system, as I understand your meaning here, wouldn't there?

SKINNER: Oh, yes. Many people, and textbooks as well, cite the weekly wage as an example of a scheduled positive reinforcement, but actually that's quite wrong. If you reinforce a man only at five o'clock on Friday afternoon, he will work only, say, from five minutes before five to five o'clock. The reason he works on Mondays is that if he doesn't he'll be fired; he will be unable to collect his money on Friday afternoon. There's another schedule I've studied in some detail, the fixed-ratio schedule of reinforcement. It's seen in operation in the piece-rate system, where the worker is paid in terms of the amount of work he does. This does not require supervision, and on this type of schedule, an organism will indeed start work long before reinforcement because he must start if he is to reach the point of being reinforced. Actually, that schedule is so powerful that most labor unions oppose it; it can burn a man up, exhaust him. Incentive systems are a mixture of the two schedules. There is enough of the periodic pay to provide a satisfactory base so that the ratio-type schedule doesn't completely take over. A proper mixture of salary and commission yields productive work which is also free of supervision, yet without the excessive effects of a ratio schedule in a piece-work system.

EVANS: Isn't the positive shaping of response and environmental manipulation being systematically applied in psychotherapy? Of course, some have challenged this method by saying that it ignores the "private world" of the patient and reduces his interaction with the therapist and his environment to such a mechanical, superficial level that the deep, underlying "psychodynamics" of his problem are ignored. How do you feel about this sort of criticism?

SKINNER: I don't think you really lose out on anything. A psychotic patient is psychotic because of his behavior. You don't institutionalize a person because of his feelings. You may say that the behavior is a result of his feelings, but the feelings must be the result of something too. When you look farther, you find environmental factors. I see nothing demeaning, nothing undignified or ignoble, about building a world in which a psychotic person can lead a decent life. Many psychotics are certainly sick or damaged organisms, and they can never successfully return to an ordinary environment. But under the control of simplified environments, their lives can then be happier and possibly more productive.

EVANS: How could these efforts be made most effective?

SKINNER: There are two possibilities: One is to eliminate the poor contingencies which now prevail in those institutions where, for example, it is the troublemaker who is reinforced by getting the attention of the hospital attendants. The alternative is to be much more explicit about it and build a world which is admittedly contrived. It will not be a natural environment; but these are not natural cases. You can contrive a situation in which such people will live reasonably effective lives from day to day with a minimum of care.

EVANS: Similar methods are being applied to the mentally retarded. Do you feel the same way about this area of application?

SKINNER: Yes. Several of my colleagues and I have experimented with institutionalized retardates whose IQ's ranged around 50 (whatever that may mean). They respond well to a simplified environment, and I am sure that institutions which care for them could be reorganized along the same lines.

EVANS: The principles which you outlined so carefully in your *Science of Human Behavior* (1953) could become quite effective if, say, a hostile government were to gain control and proceed to shape the development of children, putting such techniques totally into use. Could this not lead to a rather dangerous situation for the world?

SKINNER: There's no doubt about it, but what are you going to do? To impose a moratorium on science would be worst of all. It does not solve the problem to say we must not increase our knowledge or publish what we already know because it might fall into the hands of despots. The best defense I can see is to make all behavioral processes as familiar as possible. Let everyone know what is possible, what can be used against them.

EVANS: Dr. Skinner, to turn now to the field of education, I know this to be an area which is of profound interest to you. You were the significant developer of programmed learning. In describing this method of teaching, do you not use the term "teaching machines"?

SKINNER: Yes, I'm afraid I'm responsible for it. The original teaching machines were the equipment in operant laboratories which arranged contingencies of reinforcement. That's all teaching is, arranging contingencies which bring about changes in behavior. Machines bring them about more rapidly than the natural contingencies in daily life. The contingencies arranged without instrumental aid are often quite defective.

EVANS: So many people feel that merely programming material in a progressive sequence achieves the reinforcement that you describe. What other elements are there that affect the efficiency of learning?

SKINNER: In the first place, there is the progressive shaping of a complex response. I sometimes give a classroom demonstration with a hungry pigeon and a food dispenser. You can't wait for the pigeon to pace a figure eight before you reinforce it; you'd wait forever. You choose any response which will contribute to that figure eight. That is one kind of programming. Another kind of programming brings the response under the control of a particular stimulus. The pigeon paces a figure eight only when the light is on, say, and not when it is off. Another kind of programming brings behavior under the control of intermittent reinforcement. If you reinforce every response, then every second response, then every fifth, then every tenth, twenty-fifth, fiftieth, and hundredth, you can get a pigeon to go on indefinitely, responding one hundred times for each small measure of food. In most studies of learning, organisms are plopped down into terminal contingencies of reinforcement and allowed to struggle through. They may reach the terminal behavior, or they may not. It is called trial and error, but that term doesn't really describe a behavioral process at all.

EVANS: What specific reinforcers might be used in a hypothetical example of teaching arithmetic?

SKINNER: The teacher doesn't have too many reinforcers at her disposal. That's one of the tragedies of education. There are a number of contrived reinforcers, such as prizes or tokens, pats on the back, approval, attention, and that sort of thing. But the important thing is that the child sees that he is progressing toward some ultimately desirable state, even if only the state of getting through school. Any little indication of progress, such as being right so that you can move on to the next step, is enough. I don't define a reinforcer in any biological sense. Some reinforcers have an obvious relevance to biological conditions, some don't. The human organism is reinforced simply by being effective.

EVANS: Some of those who have resisted the use of teaching machines have maintained that shaping behavior in this manner is detrimental to the development of individuality, and contrary to the spirit of democracy. Do you see the possibility of controlling behavior in a manner consistent with your principles without doing violence to individuality?

SKINNER: The humanist who uses persuasion, argument, inducement, emulation, or enthusiasm to get a student to learn is controlling the student just as definitely as the person who designs a program or a teaching machine. The whole thing is a question of method. That's the crux of my argument with Carl Rogers; I'd like people to be approximately as Rogers wants them to be. I'm convinced that I can specify methods which will be more effective than Rogers'. I just don't think his conception of inner determiners is valid. We agree on our goals; we each want people to be free of the control exercised by others—free of the education they have had, so that they profit by it but are not bound by it, and so on. This is all part of the educational design which I'm trying to implement, not only with teaching machines but with the application of an experimental analysis to classroom management. It boils down to a question of method, not of the ultimate worth of the individual. I want to preserve the dignity and worth of a man, too.

EVANS: This leads us into a somewhat related area which has become important to contemporary writers who have criticized our educational system and general cultural climate from a different perspective. Do you feel it's a meaningful statement to say that man is overconforming?

SKINNER: I think man could be much less conforming than he is. But that would raise problems on its own; a world in which people were freely and wildly original could be a very difficult world to live in, too. A certain amount of conformity is needed for just the ordinary articulation of a group. You want people who are making the most of themselves, and this usually means people who are least under the control of manners, customs, and other people. I seldom think in terms of conformity; I don't think it's a useful concept.

EVANS: Dr. Skinner, one issue of increasing importance on the contemporary scene is the challenge to psychology to solve human problems. For example, the war on poverty or the problems of civil rights, mental retardation and mental illness present challenges to our profession by government at a level greater than ever before in history.

Still the most scientifically prestigious manner for a psychologist to operate would appear to be to work in his isolated laboratories engaging in basic animal research. How do you feel about this question?

SKINNER: He can be both, or be either one separately. This should be left up to the individual. Human behavior and animal behavior are extremely complex subjects. You can no longer deal with them with a few general principles. We need a lot of dedicated people who love nothing more than going into the laboratory and spending a lifetime in research. On the other hand, I always point out to my students the implications of this kind of work, because I feel they should know what they are really doing, and see what it all amounts to. I'm very much impressed by work with exceptional children, psychotics, retardates, and so on, in which the scientist brings to bear on the problem special techniques acquired under more rigorous conditions. There's enough reinforcement for a man working in that area to last him a lifetime. I've done both.

EVANS: There are some within the applied field of psychology who may be dealing with highly specific areas with little generalizing of results possible, such as building systems and doing research for various agencies such as the Department of Defense. How do you feel about this trend?

SKINNER: I'm not sure such research involves them as psychologists. I'm not at all impressed by the model builders, the information theory analysts, the systems analysts, and so on. Many of them seem to be looking for an alternative to an empirical science, and I don't believe there is any such thing. I don't look for much help from these people; the learning theorists who set up mathematical models don't keep up with the data, or they generate data using large groups of subjects. They aren't contributing anything we can use, and in fact, what they are doing usually seems rather ludicrous. It scares me to think that the Pentagon hires these people to decide whether or not to push the button.

EVANS: This is interesting, since there are some who would say that the use of elaborate programming involved in choice-making decisions is similar to the auto-instructional methods you've described in your own work. I gather, then, that you do not feel there is any similarity between the two kinds of programming activities?

SKINNER: No, I don't. Programming a computer and programming instruction are very different things. I'm interested in analyzing behavior. There are others—many in the field of decision-making—who confine themselves to analyzing the contingencies of reinforcement to which behavior is submitted. An analysis of the contingency is not a substitute for a study of the way in which the organism responds to contingencies.

EVANS: In the area of training psychology students, what do you feel is important? We continue to teach students to use a hypothetico-deductive orientation, and there seems to be a great deal of importance placed on it.

SKINNER: I prefer to bring my students into contact with subject matter as quickly as possible, and show them how to spot useful lines of investigation and how to discard useless. No student of mine to my knowledge has ever "designed an experiment." Once formulated, such methods must be stretched to fit research to which they aren't adapted and in the end nothing of interest comes out of it.

EVANS: How broad should the student's training in psychology be?

SKINNER: I see no reason why every individual must climb the tree of knowledge all the way from the roots. If I were to design a course for students who did not have to answer someone else's final examinations, who were genuinely interested in understanding human behavior, and who wanted to be effective in dealing with it, I should not bother with ordinary learning theory, for example. I would eliminate most of sensory psychology and I would give them no cognitive psychology whatsoever. I would include very little of mental measurement or testing. My students would never see a memory drum. They would study a bit of perception, but in a different guise. I don't mean that I want a really narrow curriculum. I want students to know some history and some literature. And other sciences. I would much rather see a graduate student in psychology taking a course in physical chemistry than in statistics. And I would include other sciences, even poetry, music, and art. Why not? You could include some of these in place of learning theory.

EVANS: Dr. Skinner, of all the many intriguing and provocative contributions you have made to the field of psychology, many of which we have touched on in our discussion, which do you feel to be the most significant?

SKINNER: Let me preface my answer by saying that I have had a lot of luck in my scientific career. As I look back on it, it seems to me that two important things were the use of rate of responding as a basic datum and the so-called cumulative record which makes changes in rate conspicuous. Once you have rate of responding as a dependent variable you can begin to look for variables which influence that rate. I began in the field of motivation—deprivation and satiation—but I quickly moved into conditioning, contingencies of reinforcement, stimulus control, and so on. As time has passed, of course, records have become smoother and smoother, as we have gained control over more and more variables. This is the heart of the experimental analysis of behavior.

EVANS: As you look to the future, Dr. Skinner, do you feel that in this era of the proliferation of nuclear bomb capability, there is any way to solve the increasingly complex problems we see challenging the hopes for peace in the world—or for that matter, avoiding the destruction of man?

SKINNER: Of course, this isn't the first time we've developed lethal devices and I feel quite sure that man will survive this one too. He probably will do it by developing a genuine science of his own behavior.

We're pretty well along toward an effective science, but implementation is the next step. I'm very much disturbed by the kinds of opposition one encounters when trying to apply a science of behavior to human betterment. People who genuinely want to help me are taking positions which may prevent the application of behavioral science for a long time to come.

REFERENCES

Evans, R. I. 1968. *B. F. Skinner: The man and his ideas*. New York: Dutton.

Pavlov, I. P. 1927. *Conditioned reflexes*. New York: Oxford.

Skinner, B. F. 1938. *The behavior of organisms*. New York: Appleton.

———. 1948. *Walden two*. New York: Macmillan.

———. 1950. Are learning theories necessary? *Psychol. Rev.* 57: 193–216.

———. 1953. *Science of human behavior*. New York: Macmillan.

———. 1954. Critique of Psychoanalytic Concepts and Theories. *Sci. Monthly* 797: 300–05.

———. 1956. A case history in scientific method. *Amer. Psychol.* 11: 221–33.

———. 1957. *Verbal behavior*. New York: Appleton.

———. 1959. *Cumulative record*. New York: Appleton.

———, Solomon, H. C., and Lindsley, O. R. 1954. A new method for the experimental analysis of the behavior of psychotic patients. *J. Nerv. Ment. Dis.* 120: 403–06.

———. 1968. *The technology of teaching*. New York: Appleton.

———. 1971. *Beyond freedom and dignity*. New York: Knopf.

Donald Norman

(1935–   )

Donald Norman completed his undergraduate work at Massachusetts Institute of Technology for a degree in electrical engineering. He received his M.S. in electrical engineering and in 1962 was awarded a Ph.D. in mathematical psychology from the University of Pennsylvania. He spent two years as a National Science Foundation postdoctoral fellow at the Harvard Center for Cognitive Studies, and served as a lecturer and research fellow at Harvard University until 1966. Dr. Norman is now chairman of the department of psychology at the University of California at San Diego, where his current research includes computer implemented studies in sensory perception and simulation of human semantic memory and cognition. His significant contributions to the field of human information processing, particularly in the areas of short and long term memory, have been widely heralded.

I View the Field Differently/ What Are the Parts of the Mind?/We're Talking About One Mind/Perception/Cognition/Thinking/Experiential Phenomena/ Behavioristic Techniques/Cognitive Psychology Is Right in the Middle// How We Remember/Derivation/Frameworks/Introspection/Functional Rules/How to Get Out of the Box/The Interpretation of Reinforcers/Piaget and the Right Questions//Cybernetics/Feedback Systems/Computer Modeling/Artificial Intelligence/I Want to Know What the Components Are//IQ/Intelligence/Prior Understanding/Psychology Doesn't Know What Intelligence Is/Intelligent Behaviors/Problem Solving/Creativity/Short- and Long-term Memory/A Continuum of Memory States//The Power of Constraints/Trying to Make a Model//

Outlining what he believes were the early flaws in the field of cognition, Dr. Norman states the kinds of questions he feels ought to be asked. He addresses the problem of the differences between perception, thinking, and cognition and the relationship of cognitive psychology to the controversy between behavorism and phenomenology. We discuss the use of introspection as a tool in the study of memory and the criticism this technique has faced. I ask him about his views on some of the previously well-established principles concerning memory, such as the law of exercise and the law of effect. In answering, he tells us what he feels is fundamental to the ability to remember. We discuss the concept of "information" and whether reinforcement is necessary to learning. There has been much recent activity in the areas of cybernetics and computer modeling and Dr. Norman considers the potential contributions of such research. I ask him about the controversy over the question of genetic determination of intelligence, and he comments on the problem of defining "intelligence." Asked what he considers to be his major contribution to psychology, he discusses the evolution of his work on memory, then describes his current research. He reacts to criticisms of his work, and ends with a brief description of a technique he now uses and calls "the power of constraints." Dr. Norman's philosophy is straightforward: "What I've tried very hard to do is ask the right questions. My main philosophy of life is to be curious."

EVANS: Dr. Norman, I think those of us who have been looking at the field of psychology with any perspective at all are aware of the fact that there has been a kind of revitalization of the field of cognition. I think that your work stands out as being a particularly significant component of this. It would be interesting to have you share with us some of your perspective. Why was there a need to go in a different direction from the way the field developed from the 1930s through, perhaps, the early 1960s. Of course, you may not accept this premise.

NORMAN: Yes, I view the field differently. When I entered psychology in the late 1950s and early 1960s, I was very surprised to discover that nobody seemed to have asked how psychological mechanisms work, what the psychological mechanisms were, how the mind worked. I entered psychology from the field of electrical engineering and to me it was just a very natural thing to ask, What are the parts of the mind? What are the structures? Yet, when I read the psychological literature, I found extreme emphasis on studying the inputs to the organism as a whole and the responses of the organism, with no attempt to unravel the different pieces that were inside. I was rather unaware of the literature of psychology that had gone before me, but steeped in the contemporary viewpoint of behaviorism, which in fact thought it was not appropriate to ask what went on inside the organism. My first area of study was psychophysics, and from there I moved to the study of short-term and long-term memory. It seemed obvious to me that we must have several different kinds of memory systems. That's when I discovered Donald Broadbent (1963, 1971), who, it turned out, had asked these kinds of questions in Great Britain. I discovered William James (1950) whose writing was very sympathetic to my thoughts, and I found it to be very contemporary. I think what happened in the 1950s was that a new field called mathematical psychology had developed in this country, and perhaps the people who were doing applied work in Great Britain, especially on attention and other aspects of performance, were starting to look at what the components might be. The attention people said that we know a person's attention is limited; where is the limitation? As soon as you ask the question, "Where?" you're asking a question about the mechanism. When you ask, "What's the difference between short- and long-term memory?" you're asking a question about the mechanism. And I think these kinds of questions have revitalized the field of cognition.

EVANS: I think students are very perplexed by the way many of our introductory psychology textbook writers deal with three constructs: perception, thinking, cognition. Is there some way you look at these three constructs that might help the students separate them? Is there some way that these *can* be separated?

NORMAN: My belief is that we're talking about one mind. It's a mistake to try to separate perception from cognition, from thinking.

EVANS: About the time you were entering this field, there were efforts to reintroduce phenomenology; the work of MacLeod (1964), for example, figured very prominently. Suddenly we shifted from disciplined analyses of reacting to stimulus to focus more on the naive response, the perceptual response of the person to phenomenological experience. The early work in social perception over and over again demonstrated that perception is a function of our needs, values, and past experience. How did you look at that work?

NORMAN: Well, my approach has always been the naive response approach. But my main view has been that you simply can't ignore a person's introspections. I have certain ideas about the way in which I function, and I think it's criminal to ignore this. Now it's perhaps equally criminal to take it extremely seriously, because an organism can have only a fragmentary glimpse into its own operation. But there is a mind in there, and we've got to use all the evidence we can to get at it.

EVANS: That introduces a polarity that has been around for a couple of thousand years in philosophy. On the one hand, you have present remnants of logical positivism; in psychology you have strict behaviorism: you have Skinner (Evans 1968), who argues that the important thing is the response of the organism and that the real issue might be arranging the contingencies of the environment to increase the probability that certain responses occur, which you can then measure, etc. The behaviorists might argue that a lot of these other constructs like thinking and memory, even in the neurophysiological dimension, are very interesting, but rather irrelevant to the business of the scientist in the analysis of behavior. On the other hand are the phenomenologists, the existentialists, who argue that we should study experience, and that ultimately we cannot really understand or even deal with a person effectively without understanding experience. In other words, we seem to have one group looking for understanding and the other being satisfied with controlling and predicting behavior. How do you see the present thinking in cognitive psychology relating to this particular battle?

NORMAN: I find cognitive psychology right in the middle. The goal is to understand the mind. The techniques, however, are scientific techniques, mostly those developed during the era of behaviorism. Our theories are often very abstract, but end up predicting behavior that we can actually observe and measure. The phenomena I look at are more like the experiential phenomena; the techniques I use to get at this are more like the behavioristic techniques.

EVANS: Could you give us a specific example to demonstrate how these two approaches interact in your work?

NORMAN: Do you know Charles Dickens, the novelist?

EVANS: Yes.

NORMAN: What's his telephone number?

EVANS: I don't know, of course!

NORMAN: You don't know it. But how did you know that you didn't know it? You obviously didn't search through your memory to declare that you don't know it, but rather you know right away that it's a silly question. I'm trying to use questions of this nature to get at techniques one might use in examining memory. You know about the death of Charles de Gaulle and about the landing of the first men on the moon. Which happened first? Most people remember both events but have very little idea about the interrelation in time between them. I try to find out how people get at these memories. There are a number of phenomena I don't know how to explore, but often I consider these the most important phenomena.

EVANS: Let's take the example of de Gaulle and the man landing on the moon. What kind of mechanism would you now use to explore that further?

NORMAN: Marigold Linton (1975), who is now at the University of Utah, has been studying questions of exactly this sort. She's found that it's very important to get a data base, to try to find out if people really can or cannot answer these questions, and if people do remember relative times, how they get at it. She finds that it's done by deriving. You remember who was President, let us say, when the first man landed on the moon, and that gives you a rough time period, or you might remember some personal incident. There is a lot of derivation like this.

EVANS: Now, you're using successive introspection as a tool. Introspection has been attacked as being inadequate because there is no way of verifying it.

NORMAN: But we're asking about events that we know about, that we can check reliably upon. I can, perhaps, give you a laboratory example. One thing I've become very interested in is how people learn, and when I say learn, I don't mean learn a set of nonsense words; I mean learn complex subject matter, such as learning to play the piano or learning a language. What I believe happens is that you fit new knowledge onto a framework of old knowledge. Well, that sounds nice, but it's very vague. How do you get at something like this, something that takes so very long? One thing we're doing is studying how people learn particular topics. A particular topic we're studying now is the history of the American Civil War. We train people, say, in the battles along the Mississippi River. This is a nice situation because we can make fictional battles. We can make the battles consistent with the geography going along a simple time course, or we can make them inconsistent with one aspect of the situation, but consistent with another. We can actually put these together in ways that will test our theoretical ideas. Later, perhaps a week later, we can test the person on his knowledge of the war, which is a mixture now of real and false facts, real and false situations. Now, we can look at introspective evidence, comparing it against a solid base of what we know we have told a person. We get an understanding of the kind of functional rules a person is using to derive his introspective knowledge.

EVANS: Of course, in a lot of the early work on memory, nonsense syllables were used, for example, to eliminate past associations, so that memory could be studied in its raw, most basic form. You seem to be doing exactly the opposite; the context out of which you're operating is the richest context. Now, that's not an accident, is it?

NORMAN: No. That's what life is about, I feel, to establish meaning and understanding of what goes on in the world. The attempt by Ebbinghaus (1964), and behaviorists ever since, to use nonsense syllables was nonsense.

EVANS: Do you think that perhaps this artificial context study of memory, which characterized virtually all of the work of the 1920s, 1930s, and 1940s, has led to some hypotheses about memory that are, or will be proven, fallacious, rather than being the well-established principles that many of our introductory textbooks seem to think they are?

NORMAN: I don't think they'll be fallacious. I think they'll be irrelevant.

EVANS: Let's consider a few of these principles. Take the law of exercise: for learning to occur, we must repeat things. Things are over-learned, in which case there will be much less forgetting. If they are under-learned, a lot of forgetting will occur in the first few minutes after learning. You know, it's a typical curve that's used over and over again and is accepted uniformly.

NORMAN: Let me tell you about the law of effect instead of the law of exercise. It, I feel, is nonsense.

EVANS: The law of effect is: If a given response leads to punishment, it will tend to be extinguished; if it leads to reward, it will tend to be continued and so on.

NORMAN: Well, I don't like the idea of the reward. I like the idea of information. I think the law of exercise is an incorrect law because what is really happening is the new knowledge is embedded within the framework of our old knowledge. I have a paper that I've been trying to write for the past several years entitled, "Why Is Life Easy to Remember?" I didn't laboriously try to memorize my way to this hotel, or my path up to your room, or to the restaurant, or the size and shape of the menu and what I ordered, but right now I remember all that, and I dare say I'll remember it for a long time. The curve of forgetting of this information will be very slow and gradual. Yet had I spent the same amount of time trying to learn, oh I don't know, a Russian–English vocabulary, I would have almost no retention right now. As I go through life and observe things, they fit well within the framework I have. Not so with a Russian–English vocabulary.

EVANS: Related to this is the trial-and-error learning paradigm. Let's consider the Thorndike "puzzle box" situation, the precursor of the "Skinner box." You have an organism trying to get out of a situation. As it makes response, it may, by accident, kick the lever and open the door. If you put it back in there, as you plot it over time, there will be fewer and fewer incorrect responses. Finally, he will consistently make the correct response. By contrast, in the classic Köhler (1925) study, you have a chimpanzee in a cage with a banana hanging on a string from the ceiling. The chimpanzee jumps on a fairly high box, tries to reach the banana, and can't do it. It tries a little lower box. Then suddenly it sees the relationship between the two boxes and the banana; it puts one on top of the other, jumps to the top and pulls the banana down. There is no laborious trial-and-error process. Here are two contrasting analyses. Now, how do you resolve them?

NORMAN: My philosophy is that the organism—all organisms—is engaged in active hypothesis formation. We're trying to figure out what on earth to do to get out of the box. When the box opens, we believe that we caused it to open; so we try to remember what we did. This is an information approach, which results in the kind of response that behaviorists have indicated: namely, that we think it was the last thing we were doing, so in the same situation, that's what we would do again.

EVANS: You use the word "information." This work has also been described as "information processing." Could you give us a definite example?

NORMAN: An example comes to mind of an experiment reported by Azrin (1968). He was a behavior modifier, and for those who wanted to stop smoking, he devised a lovely cigarette case. Every time a person started to take a cigarette out, he would get a shock. That's punishment, negative reinforcement. Azrin soon learned, though, that all he had to do was use a buzzer. The information that the person was doing something wrong was a sufficient reminder. He didn't have to really punish the person. I feel that most negative and positive reinforcers really have their effect because they are interpreted in either positive or negative ways.

EVANS: When Skinner started working on teaching machines, he had a problem. The teaching machine was kind of a step-by-step process in which the child would be exposed to a simple task until mastering it, then allowed to go on to the next task. Of course, there would be all sorts of variations of those models of programmed instruction. But at a certain point, one questions: Why does a child keep learning? In discussing this with Dr. Skinner he sort of alluded to the reinforcement of being right. Isn't that really what you're saying, that as a matter of fact, information or knowledge can be a reinforcer?

NORMAN: Oh, poor Skinner. He believes that in order to keep behavior going, there has to be a reinforcer, at least every so often. And when you have somebody going to school for twelve or twenty years, my goodness, where are the reinforcers? Well, I don't feel that everything must have its reinforcer, but I am also quite willing to say that I don't understand what keeps complex behavior going.

EVANS: In a wild derivation of Piaget (Evans 1973), we might argue that there is a powerful reinforcing value to knowledge itself. As a matter of fact, the ethologists are very interested in what they call the curiosity drive. Does that make any sense?

NORMAN: I think it does, but I'm not at the point where I want to postulate a mysterious knowledge drive, a curiosity drive. To me, that's just naming a phenomenon; it does nothing in terms of explaining it.

EVANS: In a sense, however, Piaget has seen a succession of developments in a kind of seeking-knowledge pattern in the child, and has even tried to establish models. He argues, of course, that they are programmed in the genome, but will not be activated unless there is some environmental impact on the organism.

NORMAN: I see Piaget as *the* great twentieth-century psychologist. He has asked questions that other psychologists have not dared ask. Yes, the function of a person is to understand what goes on around him, and that may be what you're getting at. That may be my answer to your question.

EVANS: It seems that understanding does not have to take the form of language as we know it.

NORMAN: Oh, no, absolutely not. As far as I can tell from the latest studies, perhaps from the moment of birth, the child is actively exploring.

EVANS: You are clearly among the group of psychologists who are identified as having a very sophisticated mathematical perspective. What kind of input has this kind of thing had toward the increased understanding of the nature of human knowledge?

NORMAN: Well, the early mathematical psychologists, of whom I was perhaps second generation, were in a field that I feel was empty of content. They were very behavioristic; they began by looking at the responses of an organism to stimuli converging on them. They did not ask questions about mechanisms, and I feel for that reason the field died. Today, many of the old mathematical psychologists are the top researchers in the field of cognitive psychology.

EVANS: Not unrelated to this is Norbert Weiner's (1965) cybernetics and the whole idea of computer models as an analog of man's thinking process, cognitive process. There have been those who want to make big jumps with it. We have even extended to systems theory, systems analysis. In fact, we've adopted a lot of engineering language without quite the precision with which the engineer uses it. How do you see the computer models and cybernetics, and where do you see it pointing today?

NORMAN: You're talking about two different fields. Cybernetics, or feedback systems, is one and computer modeling with artificial intelligence is another. They're quite different. Again, the cybernetically based people didn't look inside the organism; they looked at it as a whole and tried to use feedback analysis to describe what was going on. I never felt there was any insight whatsoever gained from their work about psychological mechanisms. In a sense they were premature. I myself have been called a cyberneticist, and I've never quite known how to deal with that. In the field of artificial intelligence, however, there are a number of people attempting to build intelligent computer systems. These people are deliberately trying to model human brains and human psychological processes, and in that sense I think that they have a lot to contribute to psychology and psychology has a lot to contribute to them.

EVANS: I wonder if you could be a little bit more precise. What exactly do you mean by a computer model of the brain? We're not talking about the entire brain.

NORMAN: No, we're talking about the way it operates—functionalism—not about all of the components. Components are of no relevance to one another. Suppose I use Bob Abelson's (Abelson et al. 1968) sentence, "I went into three drug stores yesterday." What might another person ask in response to it? The kind of response a normal person would give is, "How come the first two didn't have what you wanted?" This question indicates you know why people go to stores, and that one doesn't normally go to three. You've got to have a tremendous amount of knowledge about the meanings of the words, the way the sentence is put together, and the way the world is constructed, world knowledge. That's what I want my computer model to do.

EVANS: Suppose you had constructed the model; where would you go with it?

NORMAN: I don't care about the model once it works. If I ever see a computer model that mimics human behavior at that level, then having seen it is enough. I want to know what the components are because I know there is some kind of intelligent mechanism inside. When we have the ability to compare human intelligence and another intelligence that we understand, we should learn something about both.

EVANS: You know, recently, in the work of Jensen (1969), Herrnstein (1973), Shockley (1972), and others, there has been a whole new controversy around the nature of human intelligence. You're talking about artificial intelligence, a very fascinating concept. Do you mean the same thing by intelligence that Lewis Terman (1937) meant and that Jensen now means?

NORMAN: I know very little about the concept of intelligence. What little I do know says there is no single dimension of intelligence, that there are going to be a lot of different areas where a person is more or less capable. I discovered in my work in teaching that the matter of one's prior knowledge makes an unbelievable difference in ability to deal with the field. And I'm afraid that much of what is passed off as a difference in intelligence may really be a large difference in prior understanding.

EVANS: Lewis Terman was suggesting that 65 percent of variance in intelligence, as measured by this test they were using, could be accounted for in genetic terms. More recently, Jensen is saying this was about 80 percent of the variance, and he tries to demonstrate it by massive intercorrelational analysis. He goes so far as to separate intelligence into two types: Type I, a more basic, concrete type of intelligence, and Type II, a much more abstract intelligence. Does that make any sense to you, to develop such a construct and measure it by a test, and from this purport to show racial differences, ethnic differences, differences between urban and rural populations, and so on?

NORMAN: I believe that psychology does not know anything about what intelligence is. Maybe cognitive psychology someday will know something about the nature of intelligence, but until we do, I think it is patently ridiculous to use a test, of which we know nothing, that gives us very precise numbers, about which we know nothing, and try to use these to make statements about society as a whole.

EVANS: When you were speaking of building an artificial intelligence, you did use the word "intelligence" in describing it. It would be interesting to hear in this very relative sense what you mean by intelligence. Obviously it's quite different from the sort of thing that's measured by current intelligence tests.

NORMAN: I'm just talking about an understanding of intelligent behavior, which means the understanding of perception—even so simple a task as recognizing that those are pictures on the walls. That's an unsolved problem today. I think it's unsolved because even perception requires cognitive skills, thinking, problem solving. I also want to understand language behavior at a very deep level, one that requires world knowledge that interacts within the sentences. I want to understand problem solving, and eventually I want to understand creative behavior. I refuse to label any of those as the core of intelligence, but I think that everyone agrees that these are intelligent behaviors.

EVANS: What, of your work, do you feel is most significant?

NORMAN: Let me put it this way. What I consider significant about my work is the philosophy of the work, not any particular study, because every study that I do and every particular theory that I propose is wrong. It isn't known to be wrong when I propose it, but it will be shown to be wrong, if not by someone else, then by me. What I've tried very hard to do is to ask the right questions. I learned this from Georg von Békésy, who is perhaps my idol as a scientist. I've tried to ask questions about thought and intelligent behavior. I've developed large numbers of questions that I ask myself and ask others. I've tried to guide the research to look at general problems and not be confined to very narrow psychological areas but to restrict it to narrow psychological tests. I feel it is very important to my work to get the philosophy of this approach into the science.

EVANS: You have propounded some theories and done some studies; granted that they may eventually become less important, which would you, yourself, cite as being particularly interesting?

NORMAN: Well, perhaps the one that is best known is the study on the distinction between short- and long-term memory. I'm certainly not the first person to pronounce this distinction, but the work that I did with Nancy Waugh has been widely cited (Waugh and Norman 1965). At the time we wrote that there was a distinction between two memory systems. We called them primary memory and secondary memory; we took the terms from William James. We discussed the mechanisms one used in the transfer of material from one memory system to another, and one kind of mechanism was just exactly one you suggested earlier, the law of exercise, repetition. Today many workers have questioned the difference between short- and long-term memory, although accepting that there is some type of difference. It is said that what seems to be important is not the law of exercise, but what is called depth of processing—how deeply one processes the information, and to this I would add, and how readily the information is assimilated into the prior framework of knowledge one has. So what there appears to be is a whole continuum of memory states, not just the simple short-term and long-term memory, which we should have recognized years ago.

EVANS: Are there particular articles that you might cite that represent the study and elaborate on it?

NORMAN: Well, the first would be the paper by Nancy Waugh and Donald Norman in *Psychological Review* (Waugh and Norman 1965), and the latest paper would be Donald Norman and Daniel Bobrow (Norman and Bobrow 1975).

EVANS: This seems to demonstrate the evolution of an idea, as you spoke of it earlier. You asked the question; you had some work that looked fairly definitive; you even had an explanation in terms of the law of exercise.

NORMAN: Yes. It accounted for it beautifully. The theory of short-term memory went on and the field then became very popular. Thousands of papers appeared in the literature, all supportive. We looked at the encoding factors in short-term memory and found it to be phonetically based. Pretty soon the problem became uninteresting; it had been solved, and I went on to other problems. I got involved in what long-term memory was, what meaning was, what it meant to understand something, how you use the information in long-term memory and problem solving—what thinking was about. In the process of studying thinking and the learning of complex materials (the Civil War again), I began to realize that short-term memory played an integral role, that there was a different kind of short-term memory from that I had talked about before. This long path, which took five years, made me realize the earlier work on short-term memory was incorrect.

EVANS: Where did that leave all the investigators who supported and replicated your early ideas?

NORMAN: Oh, I think the replications, the experiments themselves, are valid and correct, and those data are important data. But someone who slavishly takes another person's ideas and believes them without any critical thought perhaps deserves to be left in the lurch. I think the heaviest critic of my work has always been myself.

EVANS: Unlike some of the memory and cognitive researchers, the information processing group, you have always been interested in the larger picture, the applications. I notice that throughout your career, even when working on rather basic problems, you've also been involved in broader things, such as instructional systems, computer-assisted instruction, this sort of thing. Do you try to take concepts you've gained from your basic research and apply them to these larger systems?

NORMAN: Well, my main philosophy of life is to be curious. Whenever I do anything, I examine what's around it and ask myself why or how? I just like to see how things work; maybe it's my engineering background. Before I came to psychology, I was designing and building computers, and I'd never felt there should be any strict line between theory and application.

EVANS: Are there any of these computer-assisted instructional programs you've developed that might be described?

NORMAN: Well, you've got to be careful because I don't call it computer-assisted instruction. What I'm doing is trying to understand what goes on in the learning situation. I'm very much attracted by a tutorial learning situation where there's a dialogue, much like this, which I feel just can't go on in the normal instructional situation where you've got large numbers of students. I'm trying to see if perhaps we can automate a machine to have a dialogue not unlike what we're having. But that is a long way in the future.

EVANS: Have you made any progress that you can report at this time?

NORMAN: Well, we've made a fair amount of progress toward understanding what goes on in learning. I'm also very much interested in applying what I know to instruction in the real classroom, in my daily activities as a teacher. I've been experimenting with a self-paced instruction plan.

EVANS: You have certainly challenged the established notions in the area of memory, learning, and thinking, and as a result, I'm sure that those who've been wedded to the old positions have been rather critical. Have any of these criticisms seemed to you unfair?

NORMAN: Well, I don't consider that I've overthrown any old notion in psychology. I've considered my work to be evolutionary, not revolutionary. I think that what I've done has evolved in a fairly consistent way from the background of knowledge in the field. And the longer I've been in the field, the more I've read older works, the more I discover that is consistent with what people have been saying all along. Often these thoughts have been out of the spirit of the times, and so they've been lost. The major criticism of my work, which has come from a number of my friends (I don't know what other people might think) and from myself, says (a) Is the work that I'm now doing really psychology, and (b) How do I get experimental tests of the work done? Well, I try to study mental processes in the human, and I certainly believe that's a fundamental issue of psychology—one that's been surprisingly ignored over the past forty years in the United States, largely because it was so very difficult to get evidence. I don't know how to get evidence for some of the new ideas I have. And that's, in fact, probably the weakest point in my research. There is one technique that I use that people don't understand thoroughly yet, and that's the power of constraints, the power of converging evidence. I look at the cross-disciplines in psychology, at all that is known about human interaction and human thought, and then I try to make a model, try to understand the mechanisms that might give rise to all that is known. Now, even though everything that is known is very weak and vague and hard to pin down, the different aspects have strong, important constraints upon each other when you try to put them together. You usually have very few theories, often just one, that can account for all of these things at the same time, and I find that to be an extremely powerful tool.

REFERENCES

Abelson, R., et al., eds. 1968. *Theories of cognitive consistency: a sourcebook.* Chicago: Rand McNally.

Azrin, N., and Powell, J. 1968. Behavioral engineering: the reduction of smoking behavior by a conditioning apparatus and procedure. *J. Appl. Behav. Anal.* 1: 193–200.

Broadbent, D. 1963. Flow of information within the organism. *J. Verb. Learn. Verb. Behav.* 4: 34–39.

————. 1971. Cognitive psychology: an introduction. *Brit. Med. Bull.* 27: 191–94.

Ebbinghaus, H. 1964. *Memory: a contribution to experimental psychology.* New York: Dover.

Evans, R. 1968. *B. F. Skinner: The man and his ideas.* New York: Dutton.

————. 1973. *Jean Piaget: The man and his ideas.* New York: Dutton.

Herrnstein, R. 1973. *I.Q. in the meritocracy.* Boston: Little, Brown.

James, W. 1950. *Principles of psychology.* New York: Dover.

Jensen, A. 1969. How much can we boost IQ and scholastic achievement? *Harvard Educational Review* 39: (1) 1–123.

Köhler, W. 1925. *The mentality of apes.* New York: Harcourt.

Linton, M. 1975. Memory for real-world events. In *In cognition,* eds. D. Norman and D. Rumelhart. San Francisco: Freeman.

MacLeod, R. 1964. Phenomenology: a challenge to experimental psychology. In

Behaviorism and phenomenology: contrasting bases for modern psychology, ed. T. W. Wann, pp. 47–78. Chicago: University of Chicago Press.

Norman, D. 1969. *Memory and attention: an introduction to human information processing.* New York: Wiley.

————. 1971. Human information processing. *Viewpoints* 47: 48–65.

————. 1972. The role of memory in the understanding of language. In *Language by ear and by eye: the relationship between speech and reading,* eds. J. Kavanagh and I. Mattingly. Cambridge, Mass.: MIT Press.

————. 1973. The computer in your briefcase. *Behav. Res. Meth. Instr.* 5: 83–87.

————, and Bobrow, D. 1975. On data-limited and resource-limited processes. *Cog. Psychol.* 7: 44–64.

————, and Rumelhart, D., eds. 1975. L. N. R. Research Group Explorations. *In cognition.* San Francisco: Freeman.

Shockley, W. 1972. Dysgenics, geneticity, raceology: a challenge to the intellectual responsibility of educators. *Phi Delta Kappan* Jan. 1972, 297–307.

Terman, L. 1937. *Measuring intelligence.* Boston: Houghton Mifflin.

Waugh, N., and Norman, D. 1965. Primary memory. *Psychol. Rev.* 72: 89–104.

Weiner, N. 1965. *Cybernetics of the nervous system.* Amsterdam: Elsevier.

J. B. Rhine

(1895–)

J. B. Rhine completed his work for the Ph.D. in plant physiology at the University of Chicago in 1925. His strong conviction that science should have no limits, coupled with his interest in certain unexplained phenomena, led him to resign his post in the botany department of the University of West Virginia and to return to Harvard University to study these ideas further. Professor Rhine moved to Duke University in 1927 where he was instrumental in establishing the Institute for Parapsychology, pursuing a line of research that has sought to bring rigorous scientific controls to the investigation of such exotic areas as clairvoyance, psychokinesis, precognition, and telepathy. As the director of the institute and as editor of the Journal of Parapsychology, *he has made significant contributions to understanding this new field.*

Science Shouldn't Have Any Limits/Sixth Sense or Extrasensory Perception/
Psi/Perception Without the Senses (ESP)/Extramotor Phenomena:
Psychokinesis (PK)/Clairvoyance/Precognition/Telepathy/Retrocognition//
A Gambler, a Preacher, and Mind Over Matter/The Beginning of the PK
Research/Card Guessing and Mathematical Probability/The Space-Time
Continuum//Belief Is Something of an Emotional State/What the Evidence
Indicates/Methodology/Conclusively Established Evidence/Firm Data/
Everyday-life Applications/Another Matter/Misconceptions and
Criticisms//ESP in Animals/High Psi/World Research/Jung, Freud,
and ESP/The Future—A Precognition?//

As we begin our discussion, Dr. Rhine tells how he became interested in the field of parapsychology and how he moved into it from a university career in another area. He defines the terms currently in use, distinguishing between clairvoyance, precognition, and telepathy (ESP) on the extrasensory side, and psychokinesis (PK) on the extramotor side. He describes the beginning of the research, and the strict methodology behind the card-guessing and dice-throwing demonstrations of ESP and PK. He states that the term "belief" is too emotionally loaded, and restricts his comments to the indications of the evidence. He feels that applications of the research are not yet practical, and answers some of the criticisms that are commonly leveled at this area of study.

Dr. Rhine speculates on the possibility of ESP ability in animals, and discusses the characteristics of the "high-psi" subject. He describes the research
being carried on in other parts of the world, and the interest of both Jung and
Freud in this area. Dr. Rhine outlines the training offered his graduate students, and then talks about the future: "This must have tremendous importance. But you see that, too, against the background of the history of science.
Man holds himself back, wisely, in not pushing application beyond its reasonable possibilities."

EVANS: Well, Dr. Rhine, I notice in your background that you
actually have a Ph.D. degree in plant physiology from the University of
Chicago. Now with this, how did you happen to get into the field of
extrasensory phenomena?

RHINE: It wasn't directly connected with plant physiology, of
course. I went as far as I could in that—actually taught some, but in the
meantime, there had been these claims of unusual happenings that science was not dealing with. Now, we (my wife and I) grew up with the
idea that science shouldn't have any limits as to what it considers. We
thought these happenings were possibly very important, so it bothered
us to see that nobody was giving them proper attention in our country.
We began looking into it, and there was nothing in plant physiology that
seemed as important to man if there was anything in this.

EVANS: Well, to be more specific, just exactly what transpired in
the contacts that you and Mrs. Rhine had that first led you into this area
of research?

RHINE: There were claims at the time, let's say around the early
twenties, of spirit communication with the dead. Now it seemed just as
ridiculous to us as it did to anybody else, but, again, we wondered if
there could be anything in it. There were some very respectable people
looking into it. William James was looking into it. We heard about
William McDougall, a psychologist, who was just coming to Harvard
in 1920. It seemed to us that we ought to try it just as an avocational
interest. There came a point, however, at which it seemed as though we
ought to take a step. I resigned my position at West Virginia University
in the Botany Department and went to Harvard, spent a year there, and
came to Duke in 1927.

EVANS: I think it might be valuable to hear from you, at least
briefly, definitions of some of the major terms that have been used in this
field for all these years. Now, do you still find "extrasensory perception"
to be a generally acceptable term to describe the entire field?

RHINE: Well, we could improve it now, but it's hard to change
when everybody knows that term, and especially its abbreviation, ESP.
"Extrasensory perception" was an improvement on an expression that
was in use when we came in—"supersensory perception." We also
rejected "extrasensory cognition." We thought it had belonged in a

loosely considered concept of perception. Actually it was the response of the organism or person to the environment without the intermediation of sensory functions. At first we said "known sensory functions," but as our understanding grew, we could see that there was no sensory basis. That is, there was no reception of a stimulus. There was not even any inter-mediating function. So we then abandoned the idea of sensory functions —the "sixth sense," and so forth—and defined it as "perception without the senses." But there was, at the same time, the corresponding "extra-motor" side. The organism or person reacted upon the environment with-out muscular intermediation, and we needed a term. Fortunately, we found that Charcot had already coined the word "psychokinesis." We found it in the dictionary. It was defined as the direct action of mind upon matter.

EVANS: First time a psychologist found a word in the dictionary instead of making up a new one.

RHINE: Yes, well, it's a handicap to introduce new terms; so we abbreviated that to "PK." But by the time we had come to this stage, we had realized that these various phenomena were essentially unified in operation and function. We began to suspect that there was one common operation. About that time a leading English psychologist, Robert Thouless, of Cambridge, decided we ought to call these two systems by one name. We'd been saying "parapsychological activity" or "parapsy-chological ability." He said why not just call it "psi ability." "Psi ability" for us means ESP and PK combined as one basic function, reversible—on the one hand, extrasensory, and on the other, extramotor. Of course we divide extrasensory perception into its types, subtypes, according to what is perceived. "Clairvoyance" is the simplest concept: awareness of an object. Awareness of a future condition or future event has been termed "precognition." There's a third one. Clairvoyance, precognition, and the more familiar "telepathy": perception from another person's state of mind or thought. Those are the three types of extrasensory perception. On the motor side, or extramotor side, are the types of PK. They're not characterized by names as yet, but they're easily described.

EVANS: We might think in terms of having some perception of the past, along extrasensory. . . .

RHINE: Retrocognition? You can't investigate it. Precognition we can investigate because we can check it later.

EVANS: All of these attempts to restore images of the past, events of the past, and so on—the problem here is that you cannot empirically verify such reports?

RHINE: That's right. There's no reliability test that you can apply. You can verify predictions of the future event, just as you can verify attempts to perceive or identify what another person is thinking of at a given time. You do it indirectly; of course all of our work has to be done indirectly. Extrasensory perception and psychokinesis are both uncon-scious phenomena.

EVANS: Perhaps we might do something here to help put all these in perspective. Now, here's one common report: The individual is away on a trip; he comes back and his mother says she woke in the middle of the night feeling extremely concerned and anxious because she thought he had an accident. And he says, "Yes, Mother, at that time I was driving along and I just barely averted a fatal accident." How would you label this?

RHINE: That's a little difficult to classify because, you see, we try to separate a telepathy experience from a clairvoyant one. To illustrate an experience that would have to be clairvoyant—couldn't be telepathic and wouldn't be precognitive: a woman, out at dinner, who had left her husband home, ill, and asleep in bed, got up in the midst of dinner and insisted that she be driven home. She found the house afire, and her husband was still asleep. It was an awareness of an objective situation. Now, if he had been awake and frightened by the fire and unable to get out, you wouldn't know if it had been his state of mind that she shared, somehow, at a distance; it'd be very likely that's the case. Sometimes, it's almost certain to be a state of mind, like the case of the boy whose hair turned white when he landed on Anzio beach—ah, that awful experience. His fiancee, who was a student here at Duke, dreamed of him with white hair, wrote and asked him what it meant. He said, "This must have been God's way of telling you what I couldn't write you; the night we landed on Anzio beach, my hair did turn white." This was likely telepathy.

EVANS: Experimentally, how would you make this distinction because it's very clear from these anecdotal types of reports that it may be rather difficult to put these into categories?

RHINE: Let's begin with a test of clairvoyance, because that's what we chose as our starting point for testing the question of extrasensory perception. We chose it because we need only one person at the time; telepathy calls for two. We arrange a simple objective situation in which the object to be identified is completely hidden from sensory contact or from any kind of rational inference. Way back in the seventies and eighties, the early explorers in this had begun with playing cards, probably because the casino games seem to imply that if you're lucky, you have some ability that goes beyond your sensory-motor functions. Also, the mathematics of probability first developed around those games; it was already available. At any rate, all we needed to do when we began at Duke, skipping over some other intermediate steps, was to take the card-guessing technique and the methods of probability, simply improve them a little, and with the help of colleagues from the department and from other departments, we had methodology for clairvoyance. Now, telepathy had to wait. It was ten years, twelve years, before we got a really firm telepathy test. No matter how carefully we planned it, there was always some way in which you could imagine that clairvoyance could work to get around the pure, mind-to-mind transfer.

EVANS: So, you began with the research in clairvoyance; then you went to the research in telepathy.

RHINE: We skipped over telepathy. What we did go to was precognition. To you, perhaps, and to most people, it will seem like a great step to go into the testing of the capacity to go into the future. But actually, we had already made two or three steps that made it easy to go over. We had tested a subject right close to the deck of cards—a yard away, behind a screen; we had tested him two rooms away; we'd tested him across the campus. And we found no decline with distance, according to the inverse-square law; we found no decline at all. We thought this suggested that this is not a function geared to the space-time continuum, and then we remembered that the cases that had been reported of precognitive experiences were among the most numerous that we had, and they're the most verifiable. So, we decided when we had a subject who performed well in a clairvoyance test to ask him to predict the order of the cards as it would be when we shuffled them for four minutes or forty times, or something. We compared it to asking him to call down through the deck without disturbing the cards. The two experiments, running side by side, gave about the same results with this one, outstanding subject. And the conditions were awfully good. You don't have any difficulty with sensory cues when you're going to shuffle the cards afterward. With that success, we started on the long trail—approximately two decades—to refine the method. That's precognition, now. But in the meantime we had already started on this PK work. Ah, that's quite an interesting little story in itself, we always thought.

EVANS: Would you like to elaborate a little bit?

RHINE: We were visited by a young gambler who had heard about our experiments. He said, "You know, Doc, I could tell you something else. You know about mind over matter?" I said, "Well, yes, I've heard about it; I'm very interested." He pulled a pair of dice out of his pocket, and we soon were keeping records of the numbers of high dice that he could get in so many throws. Sure enough, he was able to beat chance. Of course I suspected his dice and tricks of throwing, but he was very earnest about it. He was quite convinced that he had the ability to influence the dice. I soon called in my best subject on ESP. The man who had done the highest scoring at a hundred yards distance was a divinity school student, whom I suspected hadn't had much experience with dice. He was able to beat this other boy quite markedly, throwing high dice and low dice and sevens and so forth. We began a program, then, of testing the ability of the individual to influence the roll of dice for a specified target combination under conditions of control. We proceeded to eliminate, first, the types of throwing. We had them throw not with open hand, but with cups and containers, and then we set up little systems to allow the dice to fall by gravity alone, and with rotating cages. We kept on through the years improving the conditions and improving the statistics of the handling of the results.

EVANS: Well now, to go back to these various categories, do you believe there is clairvoyance on the basis of your research?

RHINE: I never use the word "believe." The reason is that if one reaches a point of belief, it's something of an emotional state. We say we have such and such evidence. Each one may then believe what he wants to about it—make up his own mind. In fact, it's a matter of judgment—not a final judgment; we expect to go on to other conditions. In fact, each step confirms the last one. That's the way we think we build a firmer structure, by mounting round by round, or mounting stratum by stratum of evidence. The data become better, or the experimental results become better as we introduce new types of methods. We come down to the work of the Institute now, with Dr. Schmidt's new machines, which permit the subject just to sit down, as he would at a piano or at a typewriter, and make guesses at something that is hidden in the machine. The machine is completely locked, sealed, and results are recorded on a tape over in some other room.

EVANS: What about the anecdotal data which, for example, the British Psychical Society is gathering? Are you, at this point in your research in clairvoyance, more likely to be wanting to use your electronic apparatus?

RHINE: Well, that would be a great mistake. In fact, the more we are able to go ahead, through improvement and diversification of methods, and broaden our coverage, the more we need to broaden also our perspective as to what there is to investigate. In parapsychology, we have numbers of workers that are devotedly interested in this case material, and they help us to bring this material into close relation with experimental findings. We can see how far we've come to match it, experimentally. Would you like to see the gaps we've left on that?

EVANS: Yes.

RHINE: Take the field as a whole and just imagine a chart of a circle here, and suppose that one half of it deals with ESP, and the other half of it deals with PK. Suppose in the first sector we're dealing with clairvoyant ESP; that's been confirmed. Precognition is the next one, then telepathy. Now, over on the other side, we have three types of PK. We began down here with PK of moving objects. It's easier, we think, to think of influencing a moving object—a rolling die or a streaming electron—than it is to think of moving a rock or something static. Divide the field for the world of matter into the categories of moving matter, static inanimate matter, and this other bracket of living matter. Experiments are going on in the field, particularly successfully in France, on electrons. That's all in the moving area. But we were always interested in the possibility that this PK could affect living matter. There are so many claims about it, claims of people who think they're able to heal some kind of organic disease by molding the state of the mind of the subject or, perhaps, directly affecting the diseased tissue. And we don't, in attempting to investigate, employ any belief in this claim. That's not necessary. And we don't even, later, on say, "Now we believe in it," but, rather, "Now we have some evidence that looks as if there is a basis." We say something is suggested, something is indicated, something is conclusively established. We don't come very easily to this last—conclusively established. That would mean simply that we now don't have any uneasiness about our ability to reproduce this, if we were given adequate conditions and time and so forth. We have a good many things that are in that category. At this point, for instance, we can say that clairvoyance, precognition, and PK of moving targets are in the very firm category. But the other things, like telepathy, they're strongly indicated, and PK of living material, now experimentally in the laboratory, is in a similar category. But, come to this last one, static targets; we don't have any really firm evidence of that at all.

EVANS: What do you feel are the major misconceptions of your work? You certainly are aware of these from your travels and the correspondence you have and the way you're quoted in the various media. Let's start out by what you consider the major misconceptions that colleagues in psychology may have.

RHINE: It's surprising that there aren't more misconceptions when there is relatively as little communication as there is. Our stuff is off in our own journal; we're only a few people; we can't communicate a lot. So there isn't a great deal of misconception. But such as there is, is largely a repetition of some of the early criticisms that were offered. There's distrust, among many people who don't know thoroughly what we're doing, of our statistics, when all the while (I'll have to make a strong statement, but I do it under pressure—the pressure of your question) we have been setting a mighty good example for the behavioral sciences as to how to handle new, exploratory material carefully. Actually, we've had people come here, people of eminence, like Professor Huntington of Harvard, who spent three days going over our methods, went back and wrote a report. The *American Scholar* for spring of 1938 has his article in which he concludes in our favor on the statistics of ESP. I could go on listing other things: books, articles, so forth. That was the first thing we had to deal with. Now there was a similar wave of criticism about our conditions. We must be letting sensory leakage in—they would find something wrong with some of the cards we used, overlooking the fact that those cards might have been in another building, or in an opaque envelope, or behind a screen, but making it look as if we were just a bunch of careless, slovenly people. When all the while, we were doing such tight experiments that Bob Rosenthal. . . .

EVANS: You're referring to Robert Rosenthal, of Harvard, who's most recently been writing on the whole matter of self-fulfilling prophecy, or experimenter bias, of course.

RHINE: Yes. He told me, when we had our conversation over these matters many years ago, that he didn't see anything substantially wrong with the way we did our experiments.

EVANS: What about some of the misconceptions that you think the layman may have?

RHINE: The general lay groups, especially if they're affiliated with other groups, such as the spiritualists or some occult group, tend to criticize us for placing so much reliance on very objective methods, of doing things in such a cut-and-dried way. We're scorned sometimes for our statistical experiments. They think we're losing something precious when we have a subject guess a card. They want them to try to show evidence of reincarnation or to experience an astral projection—what would be, for much of the general public, a more interesting type of phenomenon.

EVANS: Do you think that you can train individuals to heighten their various extrasensory capabilities? This would be the important ultimate question, wouldn't it?

RHINE: It is one thing to be able to reproduce the results sufficiently well to be able to go on studying them effectively. We are making great progress in that. Being able to produce results, demonstrate results sufficiently well for application to the important practices in life and society, that is another matter, which we are beginning now to take seriously. We're making some progress on it, but it would be unwise to lead people to think that we are going to do that in a short time.

EVANS: With your research on ESP and PK in lower organisms—mice and cockroaches, for example—you certainly are beginning to raise some questions about some of the early beliefs that ESP resided in the higher neurological function of the human organism. You're really saying that higher neurological functions may not really be involved in ESP at all. Is that correct?

RHINE: Yes. It's something on which we've had to change our own minds. People first thought of these abilities as having a supernatural origin. In fact, the religions have used these capacities, or assumed these capacities, as the essential type of communication for the world of spirit realities. It is what is often called a "spiritual" power. So, we began with that background and came around, slowly, to recognizing that there's no real division between the species on these matters. We have certainly now a pretty well established case for ESP in animals. We are not ready to conclude anything with any finality about the PK capacity of animals of other species. But the evidence is accumulating.

EVANS: Well, Dr. Rhine, perhaps one of the most frequent questions is about the personality characteristics of those individuals who seem to show an unusually high degree of psi. Have your studies over the years pointed to any differences in personality and other characteristics of those of high and low psi capability?

RHINE: We began, very early in our work, to see whether we could get the key to this thing through personality characteristics. We found that it was not possible to pin down the psychic personality type. We came to conclude, tentatively at least, that everybody had the ability.

We found, however, that the conditions of personality, or state of personality, or state of mind that made a subject score high in a test were something within the range of general psychology. Various types of personality measures proved useful to us. We found that we could get an important difference in ESP scoring between extroverts and introverts, and between compressives and expansives, and we found that it made a great deal of difference what the subject's attitude toward ESP was— his skepticism. These all were, however, general characteristics of individuals and need not have anything to do with the ability. The only thing we've found that a person has to have to show this psi ability (it's true for everybody) is motivation. He can't do it if he doesn't want to, if he isn't interested, if he's negative about it. This motivation, then, with certain attitudes, personality, does make high scorers or their converse. It may make very low scorers, who will score below mean chance expectation; this tells us something, perhaps the most important thing that psychology has yet come up with, namely, that we have a way, probably general, of thwarting the normal functioning of the unconscious operation of personality.

EVANS: Now, I wonder if you might like to tell us about some of the other centers for research in this field besides your own; just briefly describe what they're doing, both in the United States and abroad.

RHINE: Well, there's one right here, in Durham, which I helped to set up many years ago. One of our supporters wanted to pursue more actively the question of postmortem survival—communication through mediums; so, we persuaded him to set up the Psychical Research Foundation. In Charlottesville, Virginia, in the university medical school, there is a division of the department of psychiatry in which there are at least three men giving pretty largely full time to parapsychology. And they're doing important work. In Philadelphia there is a small center at St. Joseph's College. In New York there are several centers: the old American Society for Psychical Research, which was going on before we began, has established an institute or a laboratory for work right on the grounds, which is an important new step. At City College, in the psychology department, a psychologist has been carrying on this work for twenty years, and doing important work. Over at Maimonides Hospital, in the department of psychiatry, they have what they call a dream laboratory, and they're doing some work on ESP in dreams, which attracts attention, deservedly. There's the Newark College of Engineering, where work is being done with college approval, by one of the professors there. Those are leading places.

EVANS: Yes. Now what about in other countries?

RHINE: The most active country abroad right at the present time is probably Japan. India is quite a good place for the subject. There is some important research going on in Paris. The Eastern European countries have a great deal of interest in this subject. Their people naturally tend more readily to the recognition of what they used to call the supernatural (which we call the superphysical) aspects of parapsychological phenomena. It looks as though they are pinned down a little more tightly by the state philosophy of materialism. But they find ways of changing terminology using a covering theory, implying it's a sort of "higher" materialism that they're looking for, another energetics of personality that's beyond the physical basis that we know.

EVANS: Are you including the Soviet Union in this statement?

RHINE: Yes. I'm definitely thinking of the Soviet Union. Now, the best work behind the Iron Curtain, in the past, came from Czechoslovakia. At present, we want to watch Russia—do not underestimate the abilities of Russian scientists. When they go in for something, they go in so thoroughly, so extremely well, that if they get started, they may easily pass ahead of anything else in the world. But at present there's no indication that they have that much freedom to go ahead with this subject.

EVANS: Regarding the matter of publication in this field, it seems that the things that seem to get the most attention are obviously not necessarily those in your own journal, the *Journal of Parapsychology*. There are all sorts of events occurring—poltergeist phenomena, for example, that get a lot of publicity. Rarely do we hear a lot of people talking about the more careful research that's being published in your journal.

RHINE: You did at one time. In fact, we published our first report in 1934 very modestly, in a Boston society for psychical research. But Walter McKendrick, *The New York Times* science editor, got hold of a copy. He saw immediately the potential of this, and he wrote about it in his forceful way. Immediately then, the public, the other editors and publishers, were after it. And you can't stop that kind of thing. What happened was this, when we did begin to cooperate and allow ourselves to be interviewed and allowed ourselves to get into a radio program . . .

EVANS: Was that the old Zenith program?

RHINES Yes, 1937, 1938 . . . it was overdone. That's always the way with anything where the commercial hand comes in; if you make a little money, you want to make a little more, and so it's overdone. There's nothing to stop you as long as it's good for business.

EVANS: And of course, in those days they were attempting to actually conduct experiments.

RHINE: Yes, and it was a mockery of experimentation. I resigned; Gardner Murphy resigned—we were two of those on the committee. We pulled back and became very conservative again. And the editors just went to somebody else. They got stuff from the wrong people and they wrote sensational things that we didn't like. To some extent we just figured, well, it'll all straighten out in time; let's get on with the main research. But gradually we lost control of the air, you might say, or the public relations. And that's a good bit the way it is now.

EVANS: Yes. In other words, rarely do you or your group have a chance for critical input, the way this is being used in the mass media today. That is, I know that in England from time to time there are programs on the BBC related to these phenomena, and occasionally there will be something on a network special that will be related to parapsychology.

RHINE: Yes, they do a better job in England and in Canada. They're more thorough and handle it more cooperatively with those concerned. Over here, what happens so often is that we are mixed up with a bunch of charlatans on the same show, and the audience can't tell one from the other. They put up a package that's got a lot of dash and flash and entertainment, and so I've quit going on television until I've got adequate written assurances, that is, from people in this country.

EVANS: To move to another area of discussion, there are a number of figures in the history of psychology who have been interested in extrasensory perception, and their interest has led to a lot of speculation. For example, I know in the dialogue that I was able to complete with Dr. Jung (Evans 1976b), he did refer to his interest in extrasensory perception particularly; he called his concept "synchronicity," and he also referred to you.

RHINE: I first made contact with him through Professor McDougall, who was a good friend of his. I wrote and asked him for a report of some of the phenomenal things that he had mentioned to Professor McDougall, and he responded very cordially. When he came to this country to give his series of lectures at Yale, we had a delightful, long conversation of several hours in New York. He was older and already established; he took the attitude of having known about all this that we were investigating from observations of cases, not from experimental studies. He felt pretty much convinced of it all, but he was very appreciative, at the same time, of the fact that it was being studied by laboratory methods and confirmed. So we got on well. Later, in correspondence, he presented his "synchronicity" view and explained how he arrived at it on the basis of work we were doing. I think that we were both disappointed that I couldn't see the great merit of the concept, but I respected his interest and his own thinking about it.

EVANS: Now Freud was very interested in the telepathic nature of dreams. In fact, I discussed this with Ernest Jones, Freud's biographer, and he said that Freud was always very keenly interested in this whole area of parapsychology. Did you have any contact with Freud at all?

RHINE: I sent him a copy of my first book. Dr. Smiley Blanton was there at the time and said he thought well of it. He was interested in that. That's the only communication. There are many of these depth psychologists interested in this. But so far as the practice of psychiatry as a discipline is concerned, I don't know of anything that it has contributed that would justify our going off into it. They are laymen in this thing, just the same as if they'd been bishops or lawyers. The only thing we can say is they're open-minded, broad-minded. Broad-mindedness is stimulating; we appreciate it. But the synchronicity theory or Freud's attempt to interpret telepathy in terms of his system—that's just as good and no better than the theories that you get from these various other systems, cults, and so forth. It doesn't mean anything. Frankly recognizing that is part of the game of science.

EVANS: Dr. Rhine, in our mentally ill population, it's interesting that delusional systems so often have involved with them some of the components of, at least what appears to be, a belief in extrasensory powers. How do those of you working in this field look at this?

RHINE: We never found any of these delusional cases to be, so far as parapsychology is concerned, any less delusional than they were from the sensory-motor point of view. If people were easy to work with, we would get about the same results as with normal people.

EVANS: Would you tell us a little about your institute here? Do you have a number of young investigators working in your laboratories?

RHINE: We try to have somewhere from three to six or seven young people in training. It's the only way in which we can get people trained in this field, since there's no Ph.D. program, as yet, in this country.

EVANS: How do you go about selecting the trainees? Do you have certain standards that you use to select those that you would want to work with your center?

RHINE: We don't have any system of screening. As people apply, we take those who have shown the most preparation—reading, or a little experimenting.

EVANS: You don't have stipends available?

RHINE: Generally, we support them.

EVANS: Now, what is the source of your funding for this sort of research?

RHINE: The present situation is that we are mainly dependent upon certain accumulated capital which, over the years, has come through interested friends. A few foundations have helped us.

EVANS: How large a staff do you have?

RHINE: On the whole, we have about a dozen people, about half of them more or less permanent, not always full time; and about half a dozen, at most, in training. Some of those only come for three months, some for six, some for twelve. We've had a program for training people from different countries and that is the way in which some of the workers in other places got started. And in this country a good many of the people who are working in the field now got started in our training program.

EVANS: Sir Julian Huxley once told me that he sees a very severe problem for mankind. He thinks that our technology has moved far beyond our knowledge of human relations. He really feels that we have developed the means by which we can destroy ourselves, but we have not really been so fortunate in learning about how we can get along. Is it possible that your study of psi, if it moves to the point where psi can be controlled, could have some effect on man's very survival? Does it have promise for having an important effect on the very nature of man, would you say?

RHINE: Yes, I think so. I think that it is obvious, if one once takes the whole thing seriously; this must have tremendous importance. But you see that, too, against the background of the history of science. Man holds himself back, wisely, in not pushing application beyond its reasonable possibilities.

In my laboratory, back in the mid-thirties, the best performer we had discovered called twenty-five cards accurately in a row. We were under great tension. Now I was satisfied that there was nothing but ESP that could have enabled him to do that. Circumstances were very good. I had the cards completely screened; after each card was a reshuffle or realignment of the cards. Now take that phenomenon, which took probably five minutes or so. I take it seriously, but I couldn't do it again; in fact, the man said, "He'll never get me to do that again." It was a terrific ordeal. We can wait. But I know now that there is something voluntarily controllable. The way this man worked, with my help, was something that's within human range. And the ability is so general, we think now. What will happen when we get to that stage of control, even if it is only under some limited conditions? You bring yourself almost to that point that man symbolized in his religion when he endowed his divinities with an omniscience and an omnipotence. This ability isn't limited by distance. It isn't limited to the present. Now, what else is there to the concept of omniscience? You see how religion came to be. Over on the PK side, allow things to happen like some of the things we're doing, and you've got the omnipotence. If men can do those things, there's no power of the imagination now that can deal with it. So I just think it's better not to spend our time stirring ourselves up because the thinking we do may look pretty silly someday. But it's not silly now to think of it as the greatest challenge of man's intellectual history.

REFERENCES

Evans, R. I. 1976b. *Jung on elementary psychology.* New York: Dutton.
Rhine, J. B. 1942. Evidence of precognition in the covariation of salience ratios. *J. Parapsychol.* 6: 111–43.
———. 1954. *New world of the mind.* London: Faber and Faber.
———, and Brier, R. 1968. *Parapsychology today.* New York: Citadel Press.

Joe Kamiya

(1925–   )

After completing his Ph.D. at the University of California at Berkeley in 1954, Joe Kamiya held positions at the University of California and the University of Chicago prior to becoming professor of medical psychology in residence at the Langley-Porter Neuropsychiatric Institute of the University of California. A recipient of a National Institute of Mental Health Research Science Development Award, Professor Kamiya is well known for his pioneering work in the area of biological control by feedback, biofeedback, and innovative approaches to sleep and dream research. He now directs the activities of the psychophysiology of consciousness laboratory in exploring the physiological processes of psychological health and growth, including the concepts of heightened awareness and wisdom.

Dr. Kamiya and I talk about the age-old mind-body problem, tracing some of the earlier work in this area, and he explains the methodological integration that led him to his breakthrough research in the field of self-control of autonomic responses: biofeedback. He describes the various rhythms present in EEG recordings of the brain's electrical activity, and the particular state, "alpha," that has been the basis for much of his research. He outlines an alpha experiment, the theory behind it, its implications, and the replication of it by other researchers. We discuss the possible interrelations between biofeedback, meditative states, hypnosis, and other altered states of consciousness. Dr. Kamiya comments on the matter of training autonomic responses as a medical technique, and his more general interest in the underlying processes and the new trend toward sleep and dream research. In conclusion, Dr. Kamiya reacts to commercial applications of his work and speculates on the future, "Until the scientist can develop himself as a human being and can understand the nature of man in its most fundamental aspects, he is going to be unable to raise very far-reaching scientific questions."

EVANS: Dr. Kamiya, in psychology and medicine, and probably, I guess, from the very beginnings of philosophy as well, there's been a question about the so-called mind-body problem. There are a lot of ancient philosophical arguments that the mind and body are separate or the mind and body are one; and of course, the implications of this in the area of, say, psychosomatic medicine have been ultimately that there is nothing the body does that is not influenced by the psychological makeup of the organism, and there is nothing that happens psychologically that isn't affected by the body, and so on and so forth. As a matter of fact, these complexities are what got Freud (1953) involved in his early work. He began to study hysteria when he could find no real physiological or neurological basis for his patients' symptoms in cases where they had, say, a paralyzed right arm or whatever. Finally, he found that through hypnosis he could get these patients to become symptom-free for a while, but as soon as hypnosis disappeared, they had these symptoms once again. Freud could only conclude that a psychosomatic interaction was occurring, and of course, this triggered off the entire Freudian revolution. This has been revitalized in recent years by far more experimental work, and I think it might be interesting to hear from you how the whole psychosomatic issue has become crystallized or coalesced in what we now sometimes call the biofeedback movement.

KAMIYA: Well, I think that it is an interesting part of integration of methodology that hinges both on physiological measurement techniques and self-reports of the individual's experiences. And since the general, fundamental process is that of training the individual in the achievement of self-control of a physiological process, such as heart rate or brain waves, by means of a signal that is fed back to the subject or patient, and since that voluntary process involves the individual coming to grips with his own internal states, it seems to be a natural for psychosomatic considerations.

EVANS: It seems that the first real excitement was generated in this area when they began to demonstrate "self-control" of autonomic functions in the area of electroencephalogram, or EEG, readings. It is rather fundamental here to have you describe electroencephalography, as you see it, and some of the brain waves that are emitted.

KAMIYA: Why sure, we can do that very easily. All humans—from infancy through old age, at all hours of the day, awake or asleep—show electrical activity of the brain. There is a particular rhythm seen in all adults and young (at least from adolescence on) that is called the alpha rhythm that is especially prominent at the back of the head, overlying the occipital cortex. This rhythm is characterized by a particular frequency, which is about eight to twelve cycles per second, and it has the further characteristic of waxing and waning all the time. It is made especially strong when people close their eyes and enter a rather relaxed state of mind. So long as they keep themselves awake and are in a darkened room with their eyes closed, many people will show this. Not all have alpha rhythms, but most people do show them. The point I'm making now is that they do wax and wane over a period of time. And the question that started us in the whole query was really the question of whether individuals could be trained to discern any kind of consciousness associated with those waxings and wanings.

EVANS: Now in addition to the alpha rhythms, the brain emits waves that have been described as beta, theta, and delta rhythms. How do these differ from alpha?

KAMIYA: All right. The chief characteristic used to distinguish the different types of brain waves is really the point in the frequency spectrum at which the brain wave occupies the total activity. For example, delta rhythms, which are the slowest of all, occur at rates of from less than a fraction of a cycle per second, to two or three or four cycles per second. Theta rhythms occupy the spectrum from about four to seven per second; alpha from about eight to twelve, and these are differentiated into fast alpha and slow alpha. There is something known as the sleep spindle, sometimes called the sigma rhythm, that is about thirteen to fourteen cycles per second; it is noticeable only during sleep under normal conditions. The beta rhythm is much faster; it goes from fifteen to twenty-five. There are other kinds of rhythms, kappa, mu, etc., but they really are just names for different parts of the total frequency spectrum. At any one moment in time, if one were to do a complex electronic analysis of the frequency composition of the brain wave, let's say over a period of about five or ten seconds, he would likely find representation at each of these frequencies, and it's only a question of which one is most predominant. When we say that alpha rhythms are noticeable, we mean that the activity in the region of eight to twelve cycles per second is especially prominent—so prominent that it can be seen in the graphic record.

EVANS: The alpha rhythm that you selected for research, then, can be charted for easy examination; even the layman can recognize the difference in the various rhythms you described.

KAMIYA: Oh yes. It takes no time at all to train the average layman to recognize each of the different characteristics that I have described. Getting exact measurements is something else again, but simply to identify the dominant frequency is really quite easy.

EVANS: So, if you were to take a printout from an electroencephalogram (EEG), which is the device that's used to measure brain waves, an unskilled observer could look at this alpha rhythm and know whether the subject was in a sort of relaxed state or in a somewhat more normal, perhaps slightly more agitated state and so on. Is that correct?

KAMIYA: Anyone can spot these fluctuations, but to be able to say at one moment that this person is more relaxed than at another moment is something else again. The whole business of identifying the subjective properties of these fluctuations is still very much debated. I hold a particular point of view, but perfectly respectable investigators working along with me dispute some of my interpretations. We have to do basic empirical work to nail down the subjective qualities, such as, for example, relaxedness, calmness, happiness, sereneness, or whatever. One thing nobody disputes is that when a person closes his eyes he will have more alpha rhythms.

EVANS: What does closing the eyes really mean though? The act of closing the eyes seems to be a simple motor act.

KAMIYA: Yes, the alpha rhythm, especially from the back of the head, is reflective of the activity of the visual cortex—perhaps one should say the *inactivity* of the visual cortex. The rhythm is especially prominent when the brain is not processing visual input; so when the person closes his eyes, the rhythm increases in amplitude. Martin Orne and others who have been doing research in this area have argued that that's all there is to alpha, that if you just close your eyes in a completely darkened room, that's when alpha will be maximum. No other operation, including feedback training, will necessarily cause it to get bigger. My own view about the matter is somewhat different. It is that the alpha rhythm reflects more than the absence of visual-occulomotor inactivity or visual information processing. I believe that it is heightened by a particular kind of attentional deployment that seems to be focused essentially internally where the individual is quite alert, but relaxed. It is also my belief that the individual can, in fact, learn to cause increases in the size of those rhythms with practice and with a technique called "feedback training."

EVANS: All right, at this point let's take kind of a big leap. It seems that during the era of the sixties and seventies there's been a tremendous interest among our students, and perhaps in society in general, in various types of consciousness-expanding mechanisms. We went through the drug scene, and now a lot of the focus is on various meditative techniques, and the meditative state has been linked with alpha rhythms. It is believed in many of the Eastern cultures where they have been practicing meditative techniques for centuries that this very fine state is emotionally relaxing, that it is therapeutic, etc. What is your general reaction to that? Surely you've been plagued with questions about this.

KAMIYA: Well, I haven't been plagued by it. I think it is among the most important questions of all that can be raised. Every time it is raised, it's worth going into with special care. I hope we will have time to get into some of the fundamental challenges that psychology seems to be missing, and one of those seems to be the psychology of internal states and altered states of consciousness. Anyhow, there's no doubt right now that when meditators, such as those of the Zen and Yoga traditions, meditate (usually this involves a sitting posture with eyes half-closed or closed altogether, a particular form of breathing, and a certain muscular set), there is an increase in alpha activity following fairly soon after the onset of meditation, and it persists for a period of time after meditation. This has been proved by several different investigators in Japan and India, and now here in the United States.

EVANS: Can you mention a few typical papers a student might want to read, if you happen to recall them?

KAMIYA: Yes, there is a new book out by Tomio Hirai (1974) called *Psychophysiology of Zen*, which I am going to review for the magazine, *Psychology Today*, if I get around to getting myself together on it. There is Charles Tart's (1969) *Altered States of Consciousness*, which has been published in several different versions. The studies done by Hirai and Kasamatsu (an EEG study on the Zen meditation) and Anand, Chhina, and Singh (some aspects of electroencephalographic studies in Yogis) I believe are included in that one. And they all pretty much agree on the abundance of alpha during meditation.

EVANS: This is directly in opposition to those who feel that the alpha state is simply a function of eye-closing.

KAMIYA: I would say that certainly it would be a challenge to those who believe that all there is to alpha activity is visual activity. Now it may be that they can readily show that in fact it is related to minor fluctuations in degree of visual processing, but my own hunch is that there is much more involved than that. Our own experience with EEG alpha in the last sixteen years is that it's considerably more than that.

EVANS: So you were really one of the pioneers in looking at this. Now could you describe a typical experiment in which you have demonstrated the control of alpha, which is very much related to the whole issue of what, in fact, the basis for alpha is.

KAMIYA: For example: We bring an individual to our laboratory, record his EEG in a totally darkened room with his eyes closed. We've monitored his eye movements as well as his occipital alpha rhythm. We have a way of measuring the alpha activity that takes into account the fluctuations in the size of alpha in a continuous way rather than asserting, as many systems do, that the rhythms are larger or smaller than some arbitrary criterion, and then expressing a percent-time presence of the rhythm. We feel that way of measuring is inadequate. What is required is the integration of the actual amplitude over unit time, and that's what we achieve. We get that over several sessions of baseline, and then we undertake feedback training.

EVANS: Could you describe feedback training? I think that one of the things that has complicated this whole situation has been the borderline commercial utilization of feedback training, which promises, perhaps, a good deal more than a scientist like yourself might suggest.

KAMIYA: Well, it's really quite simple. The subject is first presented with a tone, which is controlled by his brain rhythm in such a way that as the brain's alpha activity grows larger, the tone gets louder, and as his alpha rhythm gets smaller, the tone gets softer. For about five seconds every two minutes, the tone cuts out altogether. The subject has been informed that at that moment he can open his eyes and see a three-digit score displayed in the panel in front of him that reflects the exact amount of EEG alpha that he had for that two-minute period. This quantitative score, I found, is quite important in keeping the subject motivated and performing well. It prevents him from getting lost as to whether he's had more or less alpha in the last two minutes than in previous periods. A tone fluctuating all the time is quite hard to get a level of adaptation for, and people can learn quite well if you give them a score and keep them working at their task.

EVANS: This gives them kind of a reference point in a sense, doesn't it?

KAMIYA: That's right. So we have two kinds of feedback. There is the tone and then the intermittent two-minute score, and the subject is told to try to find ways that he can cause the tone to get louder and the score to get larger over a period of several sessions. He's told, first of all, that he shouldn't expect to get results in the first session, necessarily, and we keep working with him to cause increases in the signal. After training we compare his performance with a control subject, who is given a tone and scores from a typical experimental subject. This is what is called "yoke-controlled design"; he gets the same kind of tone as the experimental subjects and he also expends effort trying to cause an increase in tone and scores. In our studies the experimental subjects do learn, on the average, to increase their alpha amplitudes above baseline, whereas the control subjects do not. One of the important questions that has been raised is whether subjects can really cause elevations of alpha activity beyond their highest levels in baseline data in relatively short periods of time.

EVANS: Behavior theory, of course, argues that in order for a certain behavior to be evoked most effectively, you have to be very specific. In other words, you want to be sure that the subject knows exactly what he or she has to do. How specific are you in the instructions you give that subject in order to train him to alter the alpha rhythm?

KAMIYA: Well, it certainly has to become a meaningful task for him. If it is no challenge, or if he's really bored, or if he really doesn't want to—doesn't give a damn about your experiment—he will not get motivated to do it. The task is never defined in terms of what they must do internally. I never tell the subject what they must do unless I feel that it would be of some interest to explore whether such instructions affect the outcome. You see, when we started our experiments, and to a great extent to this day, it is of some importance for us to get the subject's own unbiased judgment of what is involved in handling that tone.

EVANS: In other words, you're trying to get what we call experiential or phenomenological data then.

KAMIYA: That's right. That's been our basic approach. We have also said to the subject, "Well, there are certain kinds of things that we find helpful." I believe now that I can coach people into learning to increase alpha a little bit because I've heard many hundreds of subjects describe how to do it.

EVANS: You're learning something from phenomenological data.

KAMIYA: That's right. But in the end, I must say that the words that people use are not always very communicative or useful to new subjects. It seems as though this is indeed a task that each person has to learn for himself. For instance, I can tell everybody that in the first few moments of their efforts, they will actually have less alpha than if they were not trying to increase it. This is invariably true. Everything that the person does at the outset is wrong. I can tell people and they know that, and they can try not trying, but they'll still get reductions in alpha level. So not everything that I tell them has the quality of direct utility. They have to learn it themselves; perhaps it's like bicycle riding. I can give you the theory of bicycle riding so it might help you to some extent, but I suspect that most of it will be learned just simply by your getting on, trying it, and falling a few times in the process.

EVANS: Have you recorded any overt behavior during this process?

KAMIYA: I don't think I can spot any at all; maybe some expert in facial or body expressions could spot a few of those, but I doubt that, actually, because really what is involved are such subtle things as learning how to let go of conscious control. That sounds paradoxical, but many, many subjects tell us that they do best when they forget about trying deliberately to control that tone, and instead just sort of let the spontaneous fluctuations go and then follow them—just let them happen.

EVANS: Isn't that what some of the evaluations of successful induction of hypnosis seem to indicate?

KAMIYA: Yes, I think so, and this is why I was not totally surprised when Perry London (1969) and others began to talk about a relationship between hypnosis and the EEG-alpha activity; although of late they have been saying that their data do not support their earlier observations.

EVANS: This relationship would be a logical inference, wouldn't it?

KAMIYA: Yes, I think so. I believe that there is much in common between learning to do hypnosis, control of imagery and so on under hypnosis or even outside it, and learning to control an internal conscious state.

EVANS: In fact, one of the things people like Hilgard and others have pointed out repeatedly is that becoming a successful hypnotic subject is a question of learning. Is that the same sense?

KAMIYA: Yes, I believe so. I think it takes a certain kind of practice for those who do not have the basic skills to start with. I believe it is something that everybody or nearly everybody can learn. What we are now touching on is a fairly fundamental thing from a methodological point of view, which may actually begin to point to the reasons for disparities in alpha learning in different laboratories.

EVANS: When you talk about disparities, you mean that some labs like yourselves can demonstrate this repeatedly, and others can never demonstrate it?

KAMIYA: Yes. For example, I've never seen a report out of Martin Orne's laboratory that indicated that alpha amplitude increases could be learned. I think he's always found that it can't be learned. This poses a very interesting question. There are a number of specific techniques for specifying alpha that differ from his techniques; however, I believe that the way the subject is set to the task and psychologically maintained to stay with it can make an enormous difference, and may account for the different results.

EVANS: The experimenter bias operating, for example?

KAMIYA: Oh, I'm sure that experimenter bias operates very much in this experiment in the sense that motivation and expectations are set differently by different experimenters.

EVANS: In addition to brain waves, there were other areas studied for control of autonomic responses (assuming that you call alpha rhythm an autonomic response). Blood pressure is always classed physiologically as an autonomic response. Did you always feel that you could move away from alpha rhythms into other areas of autonomic functioning and demonstrate control? Or had you, almost from the start, felt that this was related to the state of consciousness?

KAMIYA: What do I think about all other attempts to change autonomic control? I've done them myself from a fairly early phase, without as much emphasis in my total research, but we have done things like train people to control their blood pressure. I believe that the whole matter of training other autonomic processes is very important here in our trying to understand the whole process of voluntary control of internal states. I think it is highly arbitrary, and has always been, to set up autonomic versus nonautonomic, skeletal-motor versus autonomic processes. I don't think you can find a really defensible division in the brain, functionally or anatomically, that will reflect it. Obviously, in emotion or any direct experience, there's an enormous range of bodily processes involved, of which the brain is but one part. There is the cardiovascular response, the respiratory response, the galvanic skin response, and many other kinds of things that are really quite important. It happens, as a matter of historical emphasis though, that there seem to be two general trends that people are seeking to pursue in biofeedback work. One is in gaining control of autonomic states for the specific purpose of its utility in psychosomatic medicine. You can cure people of various kinds of stress-related disorders, as you know, hypertension, headaches, and so on. The pathway that I've been following is actually, in some way, less applied. I'm really more interested in the question of the degree to which this tool known as biofeedback can be used in exploring consciousness, the varieties of it, its control, and so on. And so, whether it's brain waves, or finger-pulse volume, or respiration, I'm interested in the extent to which that process of self-control is related to consciousness. I'm interested in trying to develop a map of the entire subjective space that's related to the physiological parameters.

EVANS: You have looked into another obvious phenomenon of this study, the dream. I wonder if you could trace, very briefly, some of the more controlled dream research, and then talk a little bit about your work in dreams in relation to your broader interest in consciousness.

KAMIYA: As I think is well known now, it is now possible to index with a fair degree of probability the time and occurrence of dreaming by means of the electroencephalograph and the record of eye movements during sleep. The correlation is quite high in most people, though it is important to stress, not perfect, and that has made possible a great enlargement of studies of dreaming. But interestingly, not so much work has occurred in the way of developing the subjective aspects of dreaming processes. And essentially, I don't think we've made very substantial progress about the dreaming process since the time of Freud.

Johann Stoyva and I wrote a paper in 1968 in *Psychological Review*, indicating that what we seem to have in the case of physiological indicators of something so subjective as dreaming is a significant departure from the earlier ways of indexing dreaming. Throughout history, we've always indexed dreaming by verbal report. But now, quite independently of the verbal report, we can have physiological indicators indexing the fact that dreams are occurring. What we wrote in that article, and still believe, is that we have two independent, though fallible, indicators of the same hypothetical process called dreaming. (We call it hypothetical because no one has ever seen anyone else's dreams.) And it is now getting to be quite exciting to see the areas where the two indicators converge and where they don't converge. I believe that we will soon find out more, for example, about the dreaming process in relation to such events as sleeptalking and sleepwalking, which seem to occur outside of the REM periods of sleep. We will know many more things about dreaming in general. I feel strongly that psychology simply has to account for certain subjective facts such as dreaming; otherwise, it just simply isn't complete.

EVANS: Not unrelated to this, of course, is the very, very fascinating work of William Dement (1957, 1958), who has looked at sleep and dreams. Now, the logical antithesis to the study of consciousness would be the study of one of the most widely known, relatively nonconscious states, which is, of course, sleep itself. Have you looked at sleep itself in this total context?

KAMIYA: Well, that's what we're currently getting into. Let me say, first of all, that it was William Dement who showed me how to attach the electrodes and record the dream process at the laboratories of the University of Chicago back in 1957. Our own work now currently hinges on the process of sleep onset. We're interested in knowing whether people can be trained to put themselves to sleep voluntarily by means of a signal that indexes their stages of wakefulness, and since the EEG is exquisitely sensitive to levels of arousal, we think there may be some hope in training people to follow their EEGs, so to speak, into the process of sleep itself. Certainly we all do things of an operant sort to get ourselves to sleep. We lie down and close our eyes, we relax our musculature, and we encourage certain mental activities in the head that help us get to sleep. I suspect, though this is still highly speculative, that the sleep process is not just merely a matter of muscular relaxation, which is indexed by electromyographic activity, but that sleep will also include some kind of significant departure from the ordinary cognitive processes to some other form, like hypnagogic imagery (free-floating dreaminglike states) and so on.

EVANS: It would be interesting to get you to react to the plethora of commercial preoccupation with biofeedback. Some rather marginal operators are now advertising, "Biofeedback—you, too, can become an expert," etc.

KAMIYA: Wherever there are technological developments that have the ring of something new, there's almost certain, in our culture at least, to be some kind of unjustified exploitation of them. I regret the development of this exploitation, but I think it's also a reflection of where our culture is. Exploitation does develop long before there's any substantial empirical base. And those of us who are in the professional societies will do the usual kinds of things to try to keep the public on its toes, so they don't just get raked off by all kinds of phony claims. However, I do not think that there is yet any grave danger. There seems to be a wisdom of the general economy; the fad sort of thing does have a way of dying out in a few years. To the extent that any commercial biofeedback operations are schlock and not genuinely useful, I think that the marketplace will take care of them.

EVANS: All right, a more serious question then, which we referred to earlier, is about the matter of the need for an open mind toward innovative looks at meditative states. How do you feel about that? Do you think psychology is missing a bet not to take these things really seriously?

KAMIYA: Oh, you bet I do! I think that psychology has been far too uptight about what constitutes its subject matter. It has decided by and large to say that gross behavior is its subject matter, because this is what we can look at with our current instruments and our current methodology. One area that I feel is quite important, and I believe that psychology can contribute to it, is the process of personal growth. I think that concept is a valid and interesting one. It is true that people are somehow psychologically more mature or less mature, more wise than others, and more enlightened than others. I think, too, that every one of us is concerned with the question of whether what we are doing is really helping us, really "getting us there." We're constantly facing it; we lie on our backs in bed before we go to sleep pondering it. Now this is an area that is typically not considered scientific; we have succeeded in fooling ourselves that because we cannot give certain kinds of definitions in working on them, they are not scientific issues. But certainly, a man lying on his back, wondering about whether he's really getting on, or how life is being fulfilled for him, is engaged in a biological process, viz., thinking. We cannot afford to say that because that's too hard to handle, we shall leave it out of our discipline. Why shouldn't we include ourselves as subjects for research? Meditation is one form of self-observation—why not use technology to help it?

EVANS: Being involved as one of the pioneers in the field, in the biofeedback movement, has been a mixed blessing, hasn't it?

KAMIYA: I think there are a lot of people who have taken the point of view that I've been rather sloppy in my work, and I suspect they're right. There are lots of times that I haven't done the neat little experiments and written up all the details and then gone on to the next one. I have not been the scientific good citizen in that respect. But that's rather a minor matter. I think the fundamental question that has to be answered is: What is it that we really ultimately want to make of our field? What is it that really matters? I think it sort of follows as the night the day, when you really get down to it, that until the scientist can develop himself as a human being, and can understand the nature of man in its most fundamental aspects, he is going to be unable to raise very far-reaching scientific questions.

REFERENCES

Dement, W., and Kleitman, N. 1957. Cyclic variations in EEG during sleep and their relation to eye movements, body mobility and dreaming. *Electroencephalography and Clinical Neurophysiology* 9: 673–90.

———, and Wolpert, E. 1958. The relation of eye movements, body mobility and external stimuli to dream content. *J. Exper. Psychol.* 55: 543–53.

Freud, S. 1953. *The standard edition of the complete psychological works of Sigmund Freud*, ed. James Strachey. London: Hogarth Press.

Hirai, T. 1974. *Psychophysiology of Zen*. Portland, Ore.: International Scholarly Book Service.

Kamiya, J. 1961. Behavioral, subjective and physiological aspects of drowsiness and sleep. In *Functions of varied experience*, eds. D. W. Fiske and S. R. Maddi, pp. 145–74. Homewood, Ill.: Dorsey.

———, and Stoyva, J. 1968. Electrophysiological studies of dreaming as the prototype of a new strategy in the study of consciousness. *Psychol. Rev.* 75: 192–205.

———. 1968. Conscious control of brain waves. *Psychol. Today* 1: 57–60.

———. 1969. Operant control of the EEG alpha rhythm and some of its reported effects on consciousness. In *Altered states of consciousness*, ed. C. Tart, pp. 507–15. New York: Wiley.

————, and Timmons, B. 1970. The psychology and physiology of meditation and related phenomena: a bibliography. *J. Transpersonal Psychol.* 1: 41–60.

————, and Nowlis, D. 1970. The control of electroencephalographic alpha rhythms through auditory feedback and the associated mental activity. *Psychophysiology* 6: 476–83.

————. 1971. Preface to biofeedback and self-control. In *Biofeedback and self-control*, Chicago: Aldine.

————. 1971. Conditioned discrimination of the EEG alpha rhythm in humans. In *Biofeedback and self-control.* Chicago: Aldine.

————. 1972. Abdominal-thoracic respiratory movements and levels of consciousness. *Psychonomic Science* 27: 173–75.

————. 1974. Posterior alpha-wave characteristics of eidetic children. *Psychophysiol.* 11: 603–06.

————. 1974. Autoregulation of the EEG alpha: a program for the study of consciousness. In *Operant control of brain activity*, Brain Information Service. Brain Research Institute, University of California at Los Angeles. Vol. 2 in *Perspectives in the brain sciences*, ed. Michael Chase.

————, and Hardt, J. 1976. The measurement of EEG alpha: percent time vs. amplitude integration. *Biofeedback*, in press.

London, P. 1969. *Behavior control.* New York: Harper.

Lynch, J., Paskeivitz, D., and Orne, M. 1975. Inter-session stability of human alpha rhythm densities. *Electroencephalography and Clinical Neurophysiology* 36m: 538–40.

Tart, C. 1969. *Altered states of consciousness.* New York: Wiley.

Section Three
Physiological Psychology
Motivation
Emotion

In this section of the book, we include a group of individuals whose work represents a highly creative approach to various areas of physiological psychology, motivation, and emotion. Motivation and emotion have often been investigated in terms of psychological analysis, in which case the focus is on the cognitive, subjective, or external response to the motive or emotional state; the stimulus that gives rise to that emotional or motivational state is measured. Increasingly, however, a physiological analysis has been brought to bear on this area. Where the concern in the past was for the specific physiological determinants of motivational or emotional states, now the interaction between the physiological and psychological components is of wide interest. Significant new directions of research have been developed in the area of physiological psychology, aside from the previously explored relationships between physiological psychology and motivation and emotion.

David Krech describes the development of physiological psychology and his gradual move toward this area from the traditional behaviorism of his early training. He discovered that his rats didn't act according to straightforward behavioristic principles. His attempts to understand their behavior led to his brilliant research relating brain function to behavior, brain chemistry, and related work.

David McClelland's work represents a more psychologically oriented study of motivation. His interest in achievement motivation and power motivation is reflected not only in the projective measures of these motives that he employs, but in his application of research findings to such diversified social problems as increasing productivity in underdeveloped nations and alcoholism.

Early in his career, Stanley Schachter explored the psychological aspects of motivation, as seen in his intriguing work on affiliation. As he moved into such areas of motivation as hunger, however, he became increasingly concerned with physiological aspects and the biochemical changes involved, and this phase is illustrated in the research on smoking and stress that he discusses in this section.

Neal Miller began his career strongly influenced by his psychoanalytic training, so his earlier work reflects a more psychological approach to

behavior. Impressed by his clinical observations of the effects of conflicting motivations, he searched for underlying mechanisms involved,
which led to work in brain stimulation and control of autonomic responses utilizing biofeedback techniques. His research emphasizes the
interrelationship between physiology, biochemistry, and pharmacology.

James McConnell gained prominence for his work on the specific
memory-storage properties of RNA, with the implication that memory
not only goes through the information-processing sequence emphasized
by cognitive psychologists, but that the storage of information may, in
fact, be a transferable biochemical event. He has now moved into the
utilization of operant conditioning to modify social behavior in prisons.

11

David Krech

(1909–   )

Starting a highly speculative line of research during his early years of study at New York University, where he completed his master's degree in 1931, David Krech earned a Ph.D. from the University of California at Berkeley. He then spent several postdoctoral years at the University of Chicago where he explored the physiological bases of behavior, particularly the brain-behavior problem. Moving for a brief period into social psychology, he made significant contributions to social psychological theory, and to learning theory, before returning in 1947 to the University of California where he established a brilliant line of research on the biochemical aspects of brain and behavior functions. Now retired, he is a professor emeritus of the University of California.

Dr. Krech and I discuss a career that has spanned half a century, and he tells how he chose psychology—science without tears, no memorizing!—and then goes on to describe his movement away from the strict behaviorism of the times. He recounts an experiment done in the early thirties that led him to suspect that his rat subjects were also hypothesizing! His rats taught him his favorite law: "Nothing in science, no matter how complex, if analyzed correctly, does not become more complex." Under the influence of Lashley, he became interested in the physiological aspects of behavior, working under the assumption that physiology could be expanded to encompass psychology. We discuss some of the intriguing research he has done in the area of brain chemistry, biochemical factors affecting brain development, and memory. After describing the search for "memory drugs," he speculates on the future directions of physiological psychology, emphasizing nutrient and hormonal research. In conclusion Dr. Krech and I discuss the biofeedback movement, and he summarizes for us, "If you're open to experience—and to the complete psychologist, nothing human should be foreign—you can open up new areas of research."

EVANS: Dr. Krech, your background seems to show an evolution in thinking that I think might be interesting to students in psychology. As a student, you were influenced by the very early radical behaviorism of John Watson (1924). Later, you moved away from this and began to consider the importance of experience to the organism. Could you tell us a little about the evolution of your career?

KRECH: As a young man in the mid-twenties, I was very much interested in becoming a scientist. One reason was that I had read popular books in which the scientist was always the hero—books like *Arrowsmith* and *The Microbe Hunters*. In college at New York University I discovered that, as it was taught, science subjects involved a tremendous amount of what seemed to me uninteresting, repetitive memorizing, with no emphasis on function. In biology there was an emphasis on anatomy; in chemistry and physics, we were taught to memorize what had already been discovered.

As a prerequisite to another interest of mine, which was law, I decided to take a psychology class. My instructor was a rabid behaviorist. Here I was, a naïve sophomore, being told that such vague things as "human behavior," the "human world," "desires," could be put under a microscope and studied as rigorously and scientifically as the drosophila or the salt molecule. And this without a tremendous amount of memorizing because behaviorism at that time (and I suspect the same is true right now) was a very simplified and maybe even simple-minded business. So psychology, I thought, was going to be science without tears—no memorizing! There was also a fundamentally correct and appealing notion there: that we need not depend upon the philosopher or the theologian for insight into human behavior; we could study humanity honestly and objectively. Well, I just fell for that—hook, line, and sinker.

EVANS: Don't you see a parallel today with Skinnerian theory? It has some of the same seductive qualities for the young student.

KRECH: Very, very much, but Skinnerian theory is seductive, I would think, for students who are in psychology not because of their interest in humanity, but because they want to be "scientists," and because here is one realm of science which is so challenging. I'm afraid that was my original motivation, also.

EVANS: The change in your career came when you left N.Y.U. to finish your doctorate here at Berkeley, where you came under the influence of Edward Chase Tolman (1967). In brain study, you were introduced to the very interesting and then revolutionary work of Karl Lashley (1929), which introduced alternatives, which suggested examination of human experience and/or the brain. Is that not correct?

KRECH: That's correct except that I had begun to prepare myself unwittingly, as it were, unconsciously, for Tolman even before I met him. I took my master's degree at N.Y.U. under Ted Schneirla, the famous "ant psychologist," who was a hard-shelled, 100 percent, true-blue behaviorist and remained that way until his death. Under his direction, I was doing animal research, but the rats refused to behave according to straightforward behavioristic principle. That's when I did my "hypotheses in rats" experiments.

EVANS: Your paper, " 'Hypotheses' in Rats," is regarded by many as a classic of sorts. Describe it briefly; I think it is still extremely intriguing.

KRECH: Well, it was finally published in *The Psychological Review* (1932). Fundamentally, what it said was that we have underestimated the complexity of the "mind" of a rat. A properly trained rat can learn to solve a simple discrimination problem about as quickly, say, as a four-year-old child can. Such a problem would be for the rat to learn to choose a lighted door to go to over a darkened door, without regard to which door is on the right or left. The behaviorist would have us believe that to learn that the rat attacks the thing in a purely random fashion, and every time he goes to the lighted door he gets a piece of food and every time he goes to the dark door, he can't get through, or he gets a bump on the nose. As the number of light responses accumulate, there will be a greater and greater tendency for him always to go to the light. He doesn't know what he is doing or why. It just works this way mechanically. Well, my rats didn't behave that way at all. My rats, from the very beginning, behaved as though they were following some plan or hypothesis. To begin with, when the typical rat is first presented with the problem, he may start by always choosing the right-hand door. He'll do that systematically, regularly, way beyond chance. Then, I would say, he finds that that only pays off about half the time. What will he do? He might then shift to the left every time. Some rats will even make a fairly complex hypothesis and alternate right, left, right, left. Finally, the rat would begin to go always to the light. From the very beginning the animal behaves systematically.

EVANS: There's another rather interesting study that you were connected with relating to rigidity in rats' behavior. Does this stem from the early " 'Hypotheses' in Rats" study, that brain damaged animals persisted stubbornly in solving the problem in the same way over and over again?

KRECH: Yes. I never got away from the lesson those rats taught me. They taught me two fundamental things: never to underestimate the complexity of the mind, even the rat mind, and that what looks simple, if analyzed carefully, becomes complex. This last is a paraphrase, by the way, of what has become my favorite law. I call it Anderson's law because I first saw it in a science fiction book by Paul Anderson. His statement went something like this: Nothing in science, no matter how complex, if analyzed correctly, does not become *more* complex. Be very suspicious of the simple analysis, no matter how simple the behavior.

EVANS: Isn't this almost exactly the opposite of what we would see today in Skinnerian thought?

KRECH: Oh, completely, and you might be interested to know that Lashley also started life as a rigid behaviorist. He worked with Watson and after many years of work with rats ended up convinced that everything he had learned at Watson's laboratory about learning theory was wrong.

EVANS: I wonder if you might briefly describe the important things Karl Lashley did that influenced you and that have made him such a singularly important individual in neuropsychology.

KRECH: Well, I think *the* important thing that Lashley did was to wed the objective study of behavior with a sophisticated neurological approach. You see, before Lashley's time, there were people who worried about how the brain is involved in behavior. Many of them were very good anatomists; many of them were good neurologists; but they knew nothing about behavior and didn't bother with studying it. Their position was, "Any fool can observe people behave. What we have to know how to do is how to look at the brain." Lashley maintained that you had to be just as disciplined, just as precise in your behavioral measurements as in your neurological and anatomical measurements. So what Lashley did was to combine the two skills; he taught the psychologist neurology and anatomy. We can really say that physiological psychology in that sense began with Lashley, who, by the way, learned it from Shepard Ivory Hanz, the psychologist.

EVANS: Since you have been identified as a physiological psychologist it might be interesting to hear a brief description of what that is.

KRECH: I'll try. I think that the objective of the physiological psychologist is to investigate the relation between the biochemical events, such as the neurological and endocrinological (hormonal) events, that take place in the body and the behavior of the individual. You can formulate a number of simple questions in my area of physiological psychology. How is the brain involved in memory? What part of the brain, if any single part, is primarily involved in creative thinking? What is the physiological substrate for the emotion of love, for hunger or thirst, for aspiration after power—all these things. To be a physiological psychologist, not just a physiologist or not just a psychologist, one has to follow the great lesson of Lashley and be very skillful in both fields. And another thing, my position is that if a physiological phenomenon contradicts an observed psychological phenomenon, give preference to the psychological phenomenon, because we can be more certain of what we observe behaviorally than what we observe physiologically. A nice illustration of that, I think, is Lashley's demonstration that according to the physiological, neurological theory of behavior of his time, it was impossible for nervous impulses to be transmitted fast enough for a pianist to play some of the very rapid cadenzas that every pianist played. We have a choice here. We can shoot the piano player and then there will be no behavioral observation to disagree with the physiologist, or we can shoot the physiologist. It's clear that we should shoot the physiologist; he's obviously wrong. The problem of the physiological psychologist is not to reduce psychology so that physiology can explain it; it is to expand physiology so that it can encompass psychology. Now sometimes, this means we can expand physiology only through speculation. Science thrives on speculation, but it has to be the disciplined speculation of the good psychologist who is also a good physiologist.

EVANS: Today the field of physiological psychology is branching out in several directions. We have memory-transfer work, biofeedback work, all sorts of work on neuromechanisms, and the productive and very important work in chemistry of the brain, which is the area of your considerable contributions. Would you describe your work for us and tell us which of these other areas you consider to be particularly significant?

KRECH: Well, because of my work in the field, I suppose, my prejudice is that the area which at the moment is the most interesting, the most exciting, and may even be the most significant in both the scientific and social sense, is the area of brain chemistry and memory. We know a great deal now about the behavioral side of memory in both animals and people, and we know about diseases of memory—senility in older people, injury to the brain through accident or disease, mental retardation. And in the last fifteen or twenty years, we have begun working on the brain chemistry of memory. Developments there are proceeding so rapidly that we now have a respectable body of information about it with research on everything from earthworms to man. So what we need now is the synthesis of chemical and behavioral information. This is what I see as the great promised land for the next couple of decades of research in physiological psychology. Its social implications are obvious. I think that very soon with chemical therapy we will be able to alleviate some of the failings of the mind which many people assume to be the inevitable misfortune of old age. It's very important, not because some of us are becoming older and older, but also because the general population is becoming older and older, in that more elders survive now.

EVANS: I wonder if you would describe how you got into this particular field and describe a few of the experiments that you thought were particularly significant.

KRECH: Well, after I finished my work with Tolman on the hypothesis material, I went to work with Karl Lashley at Chicago where I became interested in the whole business of the brain and behavior. Lashley's approach to the problem was ablation. That is, to discover what part of the brain was concerned with what kind of behavior, you trained an animal, opened up his skull, and destroyed this or that part of his brain. Then after he recovered, you checked him out to see what he remembered and what he had forgotten. In this way you eventually gained some information about what part of the brain did what. Well, I worked in that area for a number of years, even tried to find out what part of the rat brain was involved in hypothesis behavior. I think I found some results of interest, at least for rat watchers.

EVANS: This is where you did your interesting study about persistent rigidity in the brain-damaged rat?

KRECH: Yes. Many years later, back at Berkeley, when I returned to the study of the brain, I decided not to use the ablation approach. As someone said, using ablation to discover how the brain works is similar to hitting a typewriter with a sledge hammer and then examining it to see whether it can still type Shakespearean sonnets. If it can't, you know damage has been done. The ablation method was a crude, sledge-hammer approach. What I wanted to do was to study the normal brain and what goes on in the brain in behavior. Brain chemistry, for the first time, was really coming into its own, but the accumulating information was almost entirely in the hands of biochemists, organic chemists, and perhaps a few neurophysiologists. Very few psychologists knew anything about it, including myself. Fortunately, Melvin Calvin, a biochemist, became interested in what I was talking about, and he suggested that perhaps his laboratory might collaborate with me. He recommended Edward Bennett. All the brain chemistry in our work comes from Bennett. Then Mark Rosenzweig, who was also a physiological psychologist, joined us, and the three of us began trying to find chemical processes in the brain that somehow were related to the behavior of animals. We examined bright rats, dull rats, rats preferring this kind of hypothesis, or rats preferring that kind. Then we sacrificed them (that's a nice way of saying we decapitated them), and did chemical analyses of their brains to see whether these animals, whose carefully observed and recorded behavior differed one from another, also had different brain chemistry. Now, you can't do that just blindly, looking for any old chemical response, because there are too darn many chemicals to look at. You say, "Well, we know that such and such an enzyme may be important for transsynaptic firing, or such, so let's check out that enzyme." Frequently, of course, you look at the chemical not because it's highly important, but because it's easy to measure. In science, you get your grasp on a problem however you can, and that's what we did. We began to look for relations between behavior and an enzyme called acetylcholinesterase, which is very important in the process of transsynaptic conduction of impulses. That paid off, not in the way we expected, but it did pay off. By analyzing the brain chemistry of the beast we were able to tell you what kind of an animal it had been behaviorally (in terms of its hypothesis preference, etc.) before we had sacrificed it, and as far as I know, this was the first time that anyone had been able to get any relationship between these two things. By that time, we had been joined by Marian Diamond, a neuroanatomist, and I think from that point on, her work probably was more important than the biochemistry work.

Everybody has assumed for many, many years that whenever we learn something, there must occur a permanent change in our brain. This residual brain record could be anatomical, it could be chemical. We didn't know, but we had some opinions. So we decided to train a group of animals and then compare their brains with the brains of an untrained group to see what we could see. If we were to find consistent differences, we might get our first clue about the residual messages left in the brain as the result of experience. Since we expected the differences to be subtle, we tried to do a very strong experiment. We adopted a litter-mate control design using only males; we divided our rats at birth, putting one randomly picked brother into the experimental group, and the other brother into the control group. We did this to be certain that they had come from a similar genetic background, etc. Now, the experimental group, almost from the day it was weaned, lived in an enriched environment. They lived in a group of about fifteen; they had rat toys; they were given all the food and water they wanted; they were taken out and petted; they were given little problems to solve for sugar, etc. We even encouraged the graduate students to walk around the laboratory playing transistor radios. We stimulated them (the rats, that is!) in every way we could. Their brother rats, meanwhile, although they were fed the same food and water, lived in a very impoverished environment. They were put one in a cage in a dark, soundproof room with no social stimulation. After eighty or ninety days, both groups were decapitated the same day. Their brains were given to the chemist and the neuroanatomist, coded so that neither knew which rat came from the enriched environment and which from the impoverished group. Diamond and Bennett did their damnedest with these rat brains looking for any possible chemical or anatomical differences, and lo and behold, they found lots of them. The rats from the enriched environment had heavier brains; their cortexes were thicker; the blood supply to their brains was better; the cells were larger. Let me stress again that the brother rats came from the same genetic background, had the same healthy care, the same food, etc. So it wasn't genetics and it wasn't physical care. We also found a difference in the chemistry of the experimental and control brains, which we had expected. So here we had definite evidence that the result of an enriched early environment was literally a better brain. I really got a charge out of those experiments! While this was merely a beginning, we thought it might be an indication of where to look for the engram of memory; we thought we were on the trail of the physiological, anatomical, chemical basis of memory.

EVANS: Dr. McConnell at the University of Michigan and George Ungar at Baylor Medical School, who have worked in the brain-chemistry area, have now been trying to look at the nature of acetyl-cholinesterase. Is it some kind of an amino acid molecule? What are we dealing with here? I was wondering how you feel about the developments moving from the very early work of McConnell, which seemed to be very, very dramatic, to where we're beginning to think we may be looking at the RNA; that we're looking at something very, very understandable. Not only can you find evidence in the brain of the enriched environment, but that the memory can perhaps be transferred, etc.

KRECH: Well, in the first place, I don't know that memory can be transferred. Memory transfer here refers to the transfer of a memory from one animal or organism to another by transferring bits of the brain or brain substance from one animal to another. Well, Bennett and I tried to do some work in that field; we've even published a couple of things, and we got very discouraging results.

EVANS: When did you publish this and where, Dr. Krech?

KRECH: It was published in a fairly recent book called *Chemical Transfer of Learned Information*, edited by Ejnar Fjerdingstad. It is one in a series called "Frontiers of Biology," published by the North Holland Publishing Company of Amsterdam. Well, we got negative results really, fundamentally very discouraging results.

EVANS: Did you try to replicate McConnell's work with the planaria?

KRECH: No. We thought we had a new approach which would guarantee us results if there were anything at all to the notion of chemical transfer with learned information. But Bennett has tried for many years to replicate Ungar's results. He has worked with Ungar. Ungar has sent him samples of his material and so on, and Bennett has been unsuccessful in replicating it. So my position at the moment is a cautious, negative one. What do I think of the more molecular analysis, that perhaps we're dealing here with some kind of an RNA molecule? I think that may be a very good lead, but that does not come from the McConnell or Ungar school. That, of course, comes from the Swedish school of research, and I suspect that the time will come when we will be able to specify in some detail the molecular components of the chemicals primarily involved in memory. But of course, it isn't just the chemicals. It's always a chemical thing in an organized, prepared, anatomical vessel, as it were. It's got to be in the brain. Those chemicals in the test tubes don't remember a damn thing.

EVANS: Although the memory transfer work is very dramatic, there must be other directions to take from your demonstration that something did happen biochemically as the result of learning or enrichment.

KRECH: Yes, for instance, one of my students, James McGaugh, has done some brilliant work in another direction: a search for drugs or chemicals that would improve the learning capacity of an individual. A number of drugs have been isolated now which literally can improve the learning and memory ability of the brain. Now again, this has been done only with animals, but McGaugh is hoping to test some of these things on mental retardates, on children. We use drugs to improve the functioning of other physiological organs—the heart, the liver, and so on. Well, why not the brain? Not only does such a discovery pay off in a medical or social sense, but also in a scientific sense, because once you discover a drug that has such a capacity, that gives you a clue as to *why* it does, and that, of course, is the business of science.

EVANS: If you were not retired now and were in your laboratory working in the area of brain chemistry and behavior, in which you were one of the pioneers, where would you go?

KRECH: I'll tell you, there are two areas that I would go into. One area is the interaction of the nutrient status of the organism and the development of the brain insofar as it affects behavior. For example, we know the human brain is pretty much fully developed by the time the infant is born. Some development takes place after that, but the story has pretty much been set. The uterus is the environment in which it develops. Having nothing to do with the genetics of the mother, some of these environments are good and some are bad. If, for instance, the mother should become very ill right after conception, obviously the developing embryo is going to be nourished and grow in a sick environment. The heart and lungs are going to be affected, and the brain is going to be affected. How does it affect the brain? We really don't know. But, significantly, one of the things that's easy to change and to observe is the mother's nutrition. It necessarily affects the brain because the brain makes tremendous demands on the nutrients in the mother's blood supply. If the mother doesn't have the proper nutrients, the probability is very high that you will have a child born with an underdeveloped brain, and it may never be able to catch up. Well, we know nothing about that really. We know that children of parents who have been chronically hungry (meaning there's no excess fat in the mother for the embryo in the uterus to draw upon) tend to score low on IQ tests, but what does this mean? And why? And how? This is one area I'd certainly go into.

The other area I would go into is the interaction of hormones with brain performance. The brain, of course, like every organ, is bathed continuously by the fluids of the body, primarily by the blood. The brain, as a matter of fact, is so completely dependent on the fresh blood supply, that just a few seconds of obstruction of the blood to part of the brain can kill it. Well, now. The blood carries not only the nutrients the brain absolutely needs but also whatever happens to be in the blood. Suppose you have two people with entirely different hormonal structures. I may be a very excited and excitable person, full of adrenaline and all kinds of juices in my blood. Those juices are bathing my brain. You may be a very solid, stodgy, unexcitable person with a low level of adrenaline and so on, and your blood is bathing your brain. Now let's assume we start out with exactly the same brains, but they are living in different environments, and when we both start working on a mental problem, your brain—the action, the physiology, the biochemistry of your brain is involved in that behavior—must be influenced differently by your blood supply than my brain. Put in a more general frame, what is the interaction, the relation between personality or excitability or what have you and intellect? And how about the brains of men and women? Assuming they're the same, identical, we know very well that the hormonal conditions are different, at least before the menopause period. The woman's sex hormones are different from the man's. It's very difficult for me to believe that the biochemical events in a woman's brain are not different in kind from those in a man's brain. These differences may make no great difference to be sure, but how sure are we?

In any event, here is another problem: the interrelation between personality, motivation, emotion, and the brain.

EVANS: I noticed that you did not include an area like memory transfer, which has become very visible journalistically, or the area of biofeedback, which deals with the receiving of feedback on biological processes and exertion of self-control over them. You were right here at Berkeley when one of the early workers, Joe Kamiya, got involved in this. Now, of course, Barbara Brown has come up with a definitive book. We've had Neal Miller who did an early study which he himself says he has been unable to replicate. Of course, that disturbs him a great deal, because from the credibility of his general approach much has sprung up. I was wondering how you feel about this movement.

KRECH: Well, I do take a dim view, but a cautious dim view, of the transfer stuff because I was involved in it myself and I think I know something about it. But the biofeedback material, I have no first-hand information about it. I think that it is important and we may learn a considerable amount from it about how the brain works. Of course, we're only referring to the more or less orthodox stuff that comes out of laboratories, not the kind of stuff that makes the Sunday supplements. The only reason I didn't refer to that field is that I have never worked in it and don't really know what the possibilities are. But I might make one point. This I know—the impetus for that work did not come from the laboratory. This is one of its strengths, by the way; it came from the observations of the mystics, the meditation people, etc. who insisted that these things happened. And if Kamiya had been a hard-shelled behaviorist, paying no attention to anything outside the laboratory, or outside the pigeon brain, he would never have observed this thing, and would never have brought it into the laboratory. If you're open to experience—and to the complete psychologist nothing human should be foreign—you can open up whole new areas of research.

REFERENCES

Krech, D. [Krechevsky, I.] 1932. "Hypotheses" in rats. *Psychol. Rev.* 39: 516–32.
———. 1933. Hereditary nature of "hypotheses." *J. Comp. Psychol.* 16: 96–116.
———. 1935. Brain mechanisms and "hypotheses." *J. Comp. Psychol.* 19: 425–62.
———. 1938. A study of the continuity of the problem-solving process. *Psychol. Rev.* 45: 107–33.

———. 1946. Attitudes and learning. *Psychol. Rev.* 53: 290–93.

———, and Crutchfield, R. S. 1948. *Theory and problems of social psychology.* New York: McGraw-Hill.

———. 1950. Dynamic systems, psychological fields, and hypothetical constructs. *Psychol. Rev.* 57: 283–90.

———, et al. 1954. Enzyme concentrations in brain and adjustive behavior patterns. *Science* 120: 994–96.

———, Rosenzweig, M. R., and Bennett, E. L. 1960. Effects of environmental complexity and training on brain chemistry. *J. Comp. Physiol. Psychol.* 53: 509–19.

———. 1969. Does behavior really need a brain? In *William James: unfinished business,* ed. R. B. MacLeod. Washington, D.C.: American Psychological Association.

Lashley, K. S. 1929. *Brain mechanisms and intelligence: a quantitative study of injuries to the brain.* Chicago: University of Chicago Press.

———. 1951. The problem of serial order in behavior. *Cerebral Mechanisms in Behavior.* New York: Wiley.

Tolman, E. C. 1967. *Purposive behavior in animals and men.* New York: Appleton.

Watson, J. 1924. *Psychology from the standpoint of a behaviorist.* 2d ed. Philadelphia: Lippincott.

David McClelland

(1917–   )

David McClelland took his undergraduate degree from Wesleyan University and his master's from the University of Missouri. In 1941 he received his doctorate from Yale. After posts at Wesleyan and Bryn Mawr, he moved to Harvard University where he is now professor in the department of psychology and social relations. His research in the area of motivation, in particular the need for achievement and the power motive, has been highly innovative. It has led to significant theoretical contributions and highly creative measurement tests. In addition his research findings have been applied to a wide variety of social problems in such areas as management and organization, alcoholism, and increased productivity in the world's underdeveloped nations.

Biological and Social Determinism/The Discrepancy Hypothesis/A Theory of Expectancies/Learning Affects Adaptation Levels/Some Universal Incentives/Achievement/Challenge/Power/The Desire for Impact//The Achievement Motivation/The Need for Achievement/Defining the Field/ Measurements/N-Ach/V-Ach/Achievement and Values/The Origins of Achievement/It's Never Too Late to Learn Achievement/ Some Very Important Applications//Power Motivation/Historical Perspective/ Authoritarianism/Looking at the Motive/TAT/Folk Tales/Cross-Cultural Studies//The Achievement Motivation and Underdeveloped Countries/You Do It Because They Want You To//Research Ethics/Academic Freedom/ The LSD Controversy/Reactions to Criticism/It Troubles Me Very Much/ Introducing Measurement to a Soft Area/The Cause and Cure of Heart Disease!/A Look at the Future//

Dr. McClelland and I discuss his early work on social motivation, and he recalls the development of the theory of expectancies, the discrepancy hypothesis, and his work on adaptation by the organism. He describes the techniques used to measure achievement, and his systematic study of the need for achievement in humans—achievement motivation. He explains what he means by both need for achievement and value achievement, and what he believes to be the origin of these needs. He reacts to questions concerning the heritability of IQ, and offers an interesting alternative: ". . . one of the worst things that is inherited is the opportunity structure. It's got nothing to do with your genes; it's got to do with society." He then tells how achievement-motivation training has been effective in working with problems of schoolchildren from deprived environments, underdeveloped nations of the world, and in business opportunities for minority groups. We discuss his current research on power motivation, and he connects it up with the serious problem of alcoholism. Dr. McClelland tells how the TAT is used to measure fantasy in delineating both the achievement and the power motivation, and the interesting and novel way he applied this concept to cross-cultural studies. We discuss research ethics and academic freedom, and he then reacts to criticisms of his work. In conclusion, he outlines some of his current research, including the relationship of power motivation to stress and alcoholism.

EVANS: Dr. McClelland, looking back at the evolution of your thinking, one notes that even in your earlier work, such as your 1951 textbook on personality (McClelland 1951) you were trying to demonstrate how social motivation develops, anticipating a social-learning mode that is becoming extremely important in psychology today. The traditional homeostatic model, of course, defines motivation as all the conditions that arouse, direct, or sustain the organism, and argues that certain unlearned, primary drives are part of the inherited nature of the organism, while drives of a higher order, social drives, are learned. This thinking has been challenged by ethologists such as Lorenz (Evans 1975b) who believe that what we call social motivation, the need for social approval, may really be programmed in the genome and that we are overestimating the importance of learning. In fact, they say such motives as social approval may be as innate as the need for food, the hunger drive. How would you react to this?

McCLELLAND: You will remember from that book, that I had developed a somewhat different theory that combined biological with social determinism, what I called the discrepancy hypothesis. The basic idea involved a certain relationship between a stimulus and the adaptation level of the organism for that stimulus, which either gives pleasure or pain. That provides for both learning and biology, because learning affects adaptation level. I used the example of adapting your mouth to a saline solution. If you adapt at a certain level, you can then take a new level that would seem pleasant to you in relation to the adaptation level, but would be very unpleasant without that adaptation. I applied this idea, generally, to expectancies. My basic theory of motivation was, and I guess still is, a theory of expectancies. If you expect something will happen—100 percent—and it does happen, you don't get any particular reaction on the affective side. It just confirms, and if anything, you get boredom. It may even be a bit negative if you have the same expectancy confirmed over and over again. So far as motivation like the achievement motivation is concerned, it still looks clear to me that it's a discrepancy between what you expect and what happens. If the discrepancy is small, it interests you, it catches your attention and challenges you, and you're more attracted to that particular situation. If it's too different from what you expect, you avoid it. So approach and avoidance motivation are basically tied to this biological thing.

EVANS: Actually, that's not too far removed from what the ethologists would agree with.

McCLELLAND: I developed this theory right out of ethology at the time. I haven't done much with it for the past twenty years because I found it very hard to measure, very hard to get at. It makes good theoretical sense, but in practice it's very hard to determine on what level people are adapting. I don't think it's untrue; I think it's one of those theories that gets left behind because it hasn't been tested. The person who has worked with it the most is Jerry Kagan (1970) at Harvard. He has worked a lot with infants, on what causes an infant to smile—the pleasure response—if it sees a face that is a little different from the face it is used to seeing; if the face is very different, the infant may not smile and may even avoid it. Now in the social motives, it's clear to me that there are certain incentives that are quite universal, however they are derived. In the case of achievement motivation, for example, the incentive of challenge—something just a little beyond what you can probably do—is universal for members of the human species. In the case of power, it's more apt to be the desire for impact.

EVANS: One of your many innovative contributions to psychology that students will identify immediately is your work on achievement motivation. Going back to the area of measuring achievement, we think of Murray's (1938) classification of needs, such as need for avoidance, need for affiliation, and of course, need for achievement. Did your work begin from the kind of thing Murray was talking about, or had you become interested quite independently?

McCLELLAND: What I borrowed from Murray was, essentially, fantasy as a technique for measuring motivation, but I brought to it an experimental approach. I did it systematically. What is the effect of hunger on motivation? What is the effect of achievement arousal—what I used to call ego involvement?

EVANS: I know it's impossible to be absolutely precise in constructs like this, but what did you mean by "need for achievement"? What were you describing?

McCLELLAND: There are three different ways to answer that question. First, we had an arousal technique: we aroused what we felt was the achievement motive in people and detected its effects on fantasies. That's a little like injecting somebody with something and taking a blood sample to see what happens. Then second, we had a coding definition; that means we coded fantasies to find instances of achievement—imagery, we called it. That is probably the closest to a good definition; the concern for doing something well, or better than it has been done before. The third way was the actions shown by people high in this need, whose fantasies were high in need for achievement. We know these people act in ways that maximize their feedback on how well they're doing. They like situations that are moderately risky because they have a chance of succeeding, and they like to be personally responsible for what's going on, so if they do succeed, they can take the credit. They want feedback on how well they're doing, so they do something concrete. All of this suggests that the motive is the desire to do something better, *measurably* better.

EVANS: Another interesting thing I recall is from a series of lectures you gave quite a few years ago. This was your description of two directions in which achievement motivation could move. In one direction is the individual who attempts to achieve in terms of social reinforcement, for the immediate reward, so that people will applaud him. But you also talked about another direction, not "n-ach," the need for achievement, but "v-ach," value achievement, a type of achiever who exercises his need for achievement in such a way that he doesn't care about external reinforcement, about people saying he's great. It's more a personal sense of satisfaction, the kind of thing that Maslow and Rogers (Evans 1975a) imply when they talk about a higher level of individuation. Is this kind of artisan's self-satisfaction the kind of achievement you were thinking about?

McCLELLAND: I think it's analogous. This is the person with a high need for achievement as we measure it in fantasy, who could be happy on a desert island constructing a swing in a palm tree. If it worked, he'd get complete satisfaction out of building some little gadget, even though nobody else knew he'd done it. The person with high v-ach, and we measure this essentially from self-ratings, rates himself high in achievement motivation. We find such people to be influenced by what experts consider to be good, what other people think is right. They are more apt to be influenced by that.

EVANS: There seem to be two problems that confront the scientist in this area. One is the question of measurement which we've discussed and the second is the source. Where does it come from? One line of thought relates it to early childhood rearing practices. If the child receives a great deal of independence training, right from the start, there seems to be a great achievement-need developing, while too much of a dependency relationship results in somewhat less need for achievement. Is this what you were speculating?

McCLELLAND: I was very much influenced by the culture and personality field that argued that basic things like motives were laid down early in life, that they were laid down preverbally so they weren't terribly conscious, and that they continued to influence you disproportionately for the rest of your life. We found evidence that mothers who encouraged their sons and set high standards for them, who gave them lots of encouragement in achievement areas, tended to have sons with a higher need for achievement. At the time, it seemed that the encouragement had to come at just the right time, so that the child's reach would just exceed his grasp. And I found that fathers who were authoritarian tended to discourage their sons from developing achievement motivation. I'm less sure now that it's some particular thing that happened at a particular time of life. We've been giving achievement-motivation courses for adults, and we can teach them achievement motivation when they're twenty-five, forty-five, or sixty-five. It's never too late to learn achievement.

EVANS: You're saying, then, that first you were thinking in the tradition of Freud's early five years of life, or what Adler described as a kind of life style that's embedded and almost irreversible. Then you began to find that it's not irreversible, that persons can be retrained to become more achievement-oriented.

McCLELLAND: I was also influenced in all this by the civil rights movement in the sixties, because all this early childhood training looked like it was fatal to the blacks, seemed to condemn them forever. It was believed that their characters couldn't be changed. We found, in fact, that they could be changed. I began to think of it like learning to play tennis. It may be easier to learn certain things about tennis when you're young, but you can certainly learn them when you're older. In fact, you may learn it better because you can hold the racquet better.

EVANS: The point you made about black children brings to mind the stir and furor that has evolved around the work of such people as Herrnstein, Jensen, and Shockley. Take Jensen (1969) for example, who began to look at Head Start and such programs designed to take children from so-called deprived environments—the kind of environments that may deprive them of the enrichment that may lead to higher need for achievement. These programs try to provide this enrichment and intercept these deficits so that the child can function better. Jensen is a very thoroughly statistically minded psychologist, out of the tradition of Thorndike and Spearman, and he began to think this deficit couldn't be accounted for entirely in terms of environment; that perhaps as much as 80 per cent of intellectual functioning might really be genetically based. If there is some limit fixed by heredity, and one that is racially linked, what effect would this have on training children in achievement motivation?

McCLELLAND: Jensen is just wrong about saying that compensatory education doesn't work. Lots of compensatory education doesn't work, but achievement-motivation training *does* work. There's a very careful study by Richard DeCharms (1975) in St. Louis, done with a variant of achievement-motivation training that he called "origin training." He trained the principals and teachers in black districts of St. Louis, and there were very marked changes over a two-year period in the test scores of the kids, after motivation training. Psychologists don't believe in motivation training; they believe in skill training. I would argue that the motivation problem is central, that we do know how to work on it and that we have worked on it successfully. DeCharms showed that it really worked there.

EVANS: Then you believe this training can overcome the deficits some of these children face, even if the problem is inherited?

McCLELLAND: Undoubtedly, there are some things that are inherited—skin color, eye color, things like that—and one of the worst things that is inherited is the opportunity structure. If you're black, you inherit less opportunity, all along the line. It's got nothing to do with your genes; it's got to do with society. If you develop some goals, some reasonable goals for a young person to make, and then you are systematically prevented from achieving those goals, not from your own lack of ability, but simply because you're black, that discourages your achievement motivation. That's another kind of inheritance. I went back and looked at the famous studies of Terman (Terman and Oden 1947) that everyone quotes about IQ, and which are usually cited as an example of the heritability of intelligence. If you'll look at his data, you'll discover that the kids with high IQs came from better families; their families were richer and could help them more—to go to college, for example, and pay their way through college. These kids were happier; money helps people be happier, and they inherited money along with whatever genes they inherited. You can't conclude from Terman's studies whether it was better opportunities that led them to be more successful, or better achievement motives, or higher IQs.

EVANS: You are saying that achievement motivation is an overriding factor; that even the person with a high IQ is still going to function in a context of achievement motivation?

McCLELLAND: I would say some motivation. There are all kinds of other motives, but you're absolutely right. He's not going to use his intelligence at all unless he's motivated to do something.

EVANS: Moving away from achievement motivation, I'd like to talk about another motive that I know you're presently interested in. In fact, I believe you have a book soon to be published on power motivation (McClelland 1975). Historically, the older philosophers seemed to see the world operating in terms of power. Nietzsche talked about man in terms of a power-oriented organism, and Jung (Evans 1976) disagreed strongly with Freud in the juxtaposition of power versus sex. Jung clearly felt that power was a very important motive and they must have had some interesting discussions because their own relationship was really a power relationship. What seems to be strange is that here we have a very important motive, central to the behavior of man, and yet it has not been studied in a systematic way. Why do you feel there is such a resistance to studying power as a motive?

McCLELLAND: We have been studying it very intensely for the past five years, although a lot of the work hasn't been published yet. As to why it wasn't studied earlier, I think the answer is very clear. American social scientists, and I would say Americans in general, are afraid of power. They don't like it, they're against it, they don't think it should be exercised, they dislike people who have it, and of course, there are some very good historical reasons for this. Almost everyone knows stories about fleeing from tyranny, about Nazi tyranny, about the exercise of power. Power was a terrible thing. It was associated with authoritarianism, race prejudice, everything bad. *The Authoritarian Personality* (Adorno, et al 1950) kind of killed the field.

EVANS: You think *The Authoritarian Personality* killed the field?

McCLELLAND: It made power a swear word. Authoritarianism is definitely a bad thing. You shouldn't have power motivation. Obviously power motivation can take that form, but I'm saying that power motivation is much broader than that. A mother is exercising power when she protects and nurtures her young, and we consider that good. It's still the power instinct, the power drive.

We started systematically measuring it about ten years ago and a very good book has come out by David Winter (1973) called *The Power Motive*. Then my own work on alcohol, described in *The Drinking Man* (McClelland, et al 1972), turned out to be related to power motivation. We discovered that drinking increased power fantasies, and we tied that in to power motivation.

EVANS: How did you study these motives? The historical pattern is to name a motive, then define it. . . .

McCLELLAND: Wait, let's be clear. We do not define in advance. We define only well enough to arouse it, and in the case of power motivation, we used three different ways. We used student candidates who were awaiting election returns, and had them write TATs while they waited. We figured their power motives would be aroused. We compared their scores with the scores of other students under neutral conditions—a very careful comparison, almost phrase by phrase—and out of that, we got a base line. Next, we put somebody in the role of experimenter —that's a powerful role—and then we had subjects watch a hypnotist, a power-related experience, and we had them write fantasies under these conditions. We found the results were similar in all the conditions.

EVANS: You mentioned the TAT—the Thematic Apperception Test —and it might be interesting to have you describe a typical power response, or a typical achievement fantasy, to show the distinction.

McCLELLAND: Well, let's say we show a picture of a guy in shirt sleeves working at what appears to be a drawing board. A typical story might go: "This is George. He's working late on some project. He's new on the job and eager to do well. He's working on a new system that's going to save the company money, and he works late and succeeds and goes home happy and gets promoted." It's a simple story, but full of achievement imagery because he clearly wants to do better, wants to find a new way, and he's happy because he succeeds. Even if he had failed, it would have scored for achievement because the concern is still with doing well. Another story might go, "This is George. He's working late and he wants to come up with something that will win him the prize in some kind of architecture competition because he knows the person who wins that prize will be proclaimed the greatest architect in the world. His wife will respect him more if he wins because she had some doubts about his being an architect. If he wins that prize, he will get worldwide recognition and fame, and his wife will love him. And he does." That's clearly not concerned with doing a better job or with performance; he's wholly concerned with recognition.

EVANS: You have done some very interesting cross-cultural studies with achievement motivation. How do you approach the measurement of something like the motivation achievement or the achievement of power from one culture to another?

McCLELLAND: We code the fantasies the same way, and there are certain actions that are similar the world round, like moderate risk taking. The thing that varies from culture to culture is the area in which people take risks. That varies enormously from culture to culture and even in our own culture, between the sexes. There are great differences because of culture patterning, of what men do, typically, and what women do. Women may take moderate risks and act like achievers in, say, the social area, and men may take more risks in the mechanical area.

EVANS: You say *moderate* risks. The amount of risk is a form of innovation, isn't it?

McCLELLAND: It leads to shortcuts.

EVANS: What type of material did you use in the cross-cultural studies? Obviously the TAT cards would not work in every case.

McCLELLAND: Whole cultures produce something very much like fantasies, namely folk tales, so we started coding these folk tales. We coded them for achievement motivation and found it enabled us to predict certain things, such as the number of entrepreneurs, and so on. Although social psychologists had completely discarded the study of "group mind," we found we could get measures of motives on countries through coding children's stories—stories in children's textbooks—and from them tell if the country had developed rapidly, whether it would go to war, and so on.

EVANS: One thing that has characterized your career is your idea of starting out with a theory, developing a measure and then putting this together in a "training package." You have even gone into underdeveloped countries to attempt to train them in such things as achievement motivation, haven't you? How did you happen to get involved in this?

McCLELLAND: When I finished my book, *The Achieving Society* (McClelland 1967), I had traced the role of achievement motivation in the development of entrepreneurs and the relationship of that to economic growth, and I had done historical studies showing that countries that were high in achievement motivation developed more rapidly. I

conceived the idea that maybe we could develop achievement motivation, and I had a little ambition—a very power-oriented ambition—to
create an achieving society, to influence history, so to speak. It was a
long, hard struggle because people found it difficult to take me seriously. There is a strong prejudice that psychologists have that it's really
hard to change something like motivation in adults. Well, we've done it
at least a dozen times, all over the world, and we've done a number
of careful follow-up studies, and the results are very predictable. We
always get about two-thirds results. That is, about two-thirds of the
people are turned on by this training. Our trained people do about
twice as well as untrained people who are otherwise comparable. We're
doing it on a large scale for minority business enterprises in this country—blacks, the Chicano communities—and we're having real success.
There's no question about these people doing better—their profits are
up 90 percent, on the average, in six months. We did our first work in
India, and that is written up in a book called *Motivating Economic
Achievement* (McClelland and Winter 1969). It's the first of the evaluation studies. We started there twelve years ago, training small businessmen in one city, matched with a control city where there was no training.
We don't know whether it was because of what we did—we like to think
it was—but the city where the businessmen were trained is doing much
better today than the control city.

EVANS: There's a criticism that I'm sure you've heard, about your
moving into these underdeveloped countries and trying to make them
become more achievement-oriented. There are those who say, "Why
can't we leave quiet, cooperative, nonproductive countries alone?"

McCLELLAND: The answer is simple. You do it because they want
you to. Our first talks take approximately the following form: "You've
got dysentery. You've got all kinds of aches and pains. Do you like that?
Do you want to be rid of it?" And the answer is usually, "Yes." You
say, "You've got to quit drinking the water from the pond. It has organisms in it that cause the trouble." Now, is that wishing your western
way of life on him? I think not. I think that's giving him information
he didn't otherwise have. It's still up to him whether he wants to do
anything about it.

EVANS: Now here's a question I'm sure you've heard before. The
power of the experimenter has been involved in several recent examples of research—Stanley Milgram's (1974) obedience to authority work,
and Philip Zimbardo's (1973) simulated prison experiment are two
that have caused a great deal of stir—and the question of experimenter
ethics is being given a lot of attention. Your own experience at Harvard,
when Leary and Alpert were involved in their research with LSD, represented one of the early ethical challenges to psychology's use of subjects. Do you feel that your actions at the time were justified in light
of more recent concerns about ethics?

McCLELLAND: That's a complicated issue. The concern for ethics is extremely important. Some experimenters find it easier, and I honestly suspect some of them find it more fun, to shock people than to do something nice for them. Margaret Mead once said to me, "You can't lie to subjects." And I said, "What do you mean, you can't lie to subjects?" She said, "They know something is wrong." There's a lot in that, and I've never forgotten it. The LSD controversy didn't involve deceit; the subjects in that study were all too willing to take LSD. It involved the question of how far you can stretch the mantle of academic freedom over innovative research. And it was a case of somebody doing something that was very unpopular and somewhat dangerous, more than misuse of subjects. The kickback on personality research in the long run was more serious. Other psychologists are always suspicious of personality people because personality people, by definition, work with the more difficult, delicate areas of human behavior—sexuality, homosexuality, criminality—all of the things that make people nervous. They make psychologists nervous too. Unfortunately, that's our job as psychologists, to understand those phenomena and just keep working on them. It might interest you to know that I've kept records from that time, and of all the graduate students involved at that time in LSD research, none takes LSD today, to my knowledge. Leary is the only one who, as far as I know, continued to recommend its use and to take it himself.

EVANS: What are some of the criticisms of your work that have troubled you? Perhaps "troubled" is too strong.

McCLELLAND: No, it's not. It troubles me very much. I've never understood why it's so difficult for psychologists to take work based on fantasy seriously. After all, the instructions for writing a story are not very different from the instructions for a memory task, running nonsense syllables on a memory drum. I've followed all the rules, statistical tests, experimental controls, everything that a good psychologist ought to do, but I feel that my data have never had the same acceptance as they would if I had stuck to something more traditional. That seems unfair to me.

EVANS: It would be interesting to hear you assess your own work. What do you consider to be your own most important contribution?

McCLELLAND: I'd like to think it's measurement in the area of motivation. Everybody has talked about motivation, but until I got around to measuring it, we weren't really able to make the kinds of breakthroughs I think we have now. I think, overall, that's the major contribution I've made. I introduced measurement into a very soft area that otherwise is dealt with by "common sense," "good clinical judgment," "conventional wisdom," and so on.

EVANS: In assessing your contributions, it seems to me that you have moved into a very devastating problem with alcoholism and have come up with a whole new direction of research. Could you describe some of that work?

McCLELLAND: We discovered that people who drink too much are people who want a "power rush." Drinking produces an adrenaline response, and this gets into fantasy in the form of power imagery, particularly for people who don't have power, or who have had power and have had it taken away from them. Let's say an army officer is passed over for promotion, and his former subordinates are now kicking him around. He turns to the bottle, not to "drown his sorrow," but just to feel stronger for a little while. We've done a very carefully controlled study with severe alcoholics in which they learned why they were drinking and how to discover alternative outlets for their power drives. A control group received the standard AA group therapy, outpatient treatment at the veterans' hospital where we conducted the study. At the one-year follow-up, about 25 percent of those who got the standard treatment were still on the wagon. Of those who got the additional power-motivation training, 50 percent were doing better. It works because we had more specific knowledge of what was wrong in the first place, so we could treat it better.

EVANS: You focused on the power dimension very precisely. We've found in our own research in persuasive communication that specificity is a far more important variable in communication than the character of the message. You're applying this specificity to a very complex problem.

McCLELLAND: One thing that psychologists really know is that feedback works. The human organism is so constructed that it can adjust very quickly, but if your feedback is fuzzy, it's very hard to have learning. In the area of alcoholism, people were telling alcoholics that all sorts of things were wrong with them, but these things weren't pinpointed.

EVANS: What are you working on at the present time?

McCLELLAND: I have just finished writing a paper on the stress syndrome and power motivation. People high in power motivation have a higher resting level of adrenaline production; they act as if they're under stress even when they're not. You keep pouring adrenaline into your circulatory system and eventually you damage the cardiovascular system. You get this circulating adrenaline that's not burned up by large muscles, and some people become addicted to what I call the "power rush." What we need to do is a longitudinal study on high power motivation in adolescence and how it correlates with essential hypertension in the thirties and heart attacks in the forties. A very fascinating study by Herbert Benson (Wallace and Benson 1972) at the Harvard Medical School has shown that meditation techniques specifically decrease the secrection of adrenaline and the whole stress syndrome associated with it. So I have now given you the cause and cure of heart disease! It will need to be checked out, of course.

EVANS: But it's a very interesting set of hypotheses. It is most interesting the way you take a particular motive, like power, make a subtle conversion into a specific and damaging disorder, and then use your training methods and evaluation procedures to yield long-term longitudinal data. If you get the long-term changes, you're going to have a lot of people knocking at your door. They probably already are.

REFERENCES

Adorno, T., et al. 1950. *The authoritarian personality.* New York: Harper.

DeCharms, R. 1975. *Enhancing motivation: a change project in the classroom.* New York: Irvington.

Evans, R. 1975a. *Carl Rogers: The man and his ideas.* New York: Dutton.

———. 1975b. *Konrad Lorenz: The man and his ideas.* New York: Harcourt.

———. 1976b. *Jung on elementary psychology.* New York: Dutton.

Jensen, A. 1969. How much can we boost I.Q. and scholastic achievement? *Harvard Educational Review,* 39: (1) 1–123.

Kagan, J. 1970. Attention and psychological change in the young child. *Science* 170: 826–32.

McClelland, D. 1951. *Personality.* New York: Free Press.

———, et al. 1953. *The achievement motive.* New York: Appleton.

———. 1967. *The achieving society.* New York: Free Press.

———, and Winter, D. 1969. *Motivating economic achievement.* New York: Free Press.

———, et al. 1972. *The drinking man.* New York: Free Press.

———. 1975. *Power: the inner experience.* New York: Irvington.

Milgram, S. 1974. *Obedience to authority.* New York: Harper.

Murray, H., et al. 1938. *Explorations in personality.* New York: Oxford.

Terman, L., and Oden, M. 1947. *The gifted child grows up.* Stanford, Calif.: Stanford University Press.

Wallace, R., and Benson, H. 1972. The physiology of meditation. *Sci. Amer.* 226: 84–90.

Winter, D. 1973. *The power motive.* New York: Free Press.

Zimbardo, P., Haney, G., and Banks, C. 1973. Interpersonal dynamics in a simulated prison. *Int. J. Criminology and Penology* 2: (1) 69–97.

Stanley Schachter

(1922–   )

Stanley Schachter studied at Yale University, Massachusetts Institute of Technology, and in 1950 completed work for a Ph.D. at the University of Michigan. He was a Fulbright professor at the University of Amsterdam and spent several years at the University of Minnesota before accepting a position at Columbia University in 1961. There he has served as professor and chairman of the social psychology department and as Robert Johnston Nivens Professor of Social Psychology. Professor Schachter has done landmark research in the fields of group dynamics and communications and in 1969 received the American Psychological Association's Distinguished Scientific Contribution Award. His current research involves the more physiological aspects of motivation related to such areas as hunger, stress, and smoking.

Why People Want to Be Together/The Need for Affiliation//How Can I Describe What I'm Feeling?/Social/Cognitive/Physiological Interrelationships//How Do You Extinguish a World of Food Cues?/ External Cue Determination of Behavior of Obese Humans//The pH Factor/Smoking and Stress//Crime and Chlorpromazine/Some Intriguing Extrapolations of the Adrenaline-Emotion Studies//Go Where the Problems Lead You//

Dr. Schachter and I discuss the influences that led him to his well-known work on affiliation. He outlines the experiments that clearly defined the area of need affiliation and generated several broad new lines of research. We draw some comparisons between his research on obesity and parallel studies on smoking behavior. Dr. Schachter describes his current research on the physiological components of nicotine addiction in such a way that even the beginning student can follow the design of the experiments, the development of the hypothesis, and the intriguing results. He then comments on the theoretical implications of the adrenaline-produced anxiety studies with some possible generalizations to the criminal psychopath. Reacting to a question about his work in several areas, Dr. Schachter comments, "There's no such thing as a tough area. An area's tough only if you don't have an idea." In conclusion, Dr. Schachter discusses the work he has found most personally satisfying in an outstanding career.

EVANS: Dr. Schachter, although your more recent work has moved in other directions, your early work in the field of social psychology is still widely discussed in introductory and social psychology textbooks. One area of particular interest is your work on affiliation. What led you into this line of research? How did you first become interested in the need for affiliation?

SCHACHTER: I had been working with Leon Festinger and Kurt Lewin on the whole business of social influence, social comparison, how people evaluate their opinions, the social determinants of opinions, and so on. It simply struck me that though we had paid a great deal of attention to the consequences of being with other people, we had paid almost no attention to why people bothered associating at all. Social psychology started from the premise that people do affiliate; they do associate, they do want to be with each other, and it goes on from there to examine what happens when they are together. I became very curious as to why, in a nonobvious way, people want to be together at all.

EVANS: You say in a nonobvious way. Could you expand on what seems to be a key to your whole program of research, as I see it?

SCHACHTER: There are certain needs that obviously you can satisfy only with other people—sex is a clear one, and bridge and tennis, and so on. You have to do these things with other people. However, people spend immense amounts of time together beyond such simple need-satisfactions, and it's really not obvious why. Historically, the thing that got me into affiliation was a talk by Don Hebb (1949) about his sensory deprivation work. If you remember these studies, they involved putting people into social isolation and sensory isolation, sometimes for days on end. Hebb reported tremendously dramatic effects. Many of his subjects had hallucinations, most of them seemed to suffer a great deal. I wondered how much of this was due to sensory deprivation, as Hebb claimed, and how much to the fact that they were simply alone. So I read a number of autobiographical reports of people who had spent a great deal of time alone—people who had sailed around the world alone, monks, prisoners, hermits—and it did appear that the state of being alone, in and of itself, was immensely painful.

EVANS: Can you recall some of the early studies that you did in that area?

SCHACHTER: I tried a couple of case studies in which paid volunteers lived in a room alone, seeing no one for days at a time. There was some evidence of suffering; but from these cases alone, it was difficult to figure out just why this should be the case. And so I started a series of experiments on the relationship of anxiety to the affiliative need—a pure guess, at first, that if you're upset and frightened, you want to be with other people. It turned out that if the subjects were badly frightened, they wanted very much to be with other people, and if they were calm, not nearly so much so. Comparatively, the intensity of their need to be with others was far less when the subjects were calm than when they were anxious.

EVANS: Is it possible to take a need, like the need for affiliation, and separate it from social needs that seem to overlap in so many ways? For example, the need for social approval might overlap with this, or be a problem of the sort David McClelland (1953) had with the need for achievement. We're not always sure that we're getting that specific thing. Did you have any problems in looking at this, in measuring it?

SCHACHTER: I never assumed there was anything such as a generalized need for affiliation. I simply didn't think in terms such as Mc-Clelland's notions of needs, or those of his forefather, Henry Murray (1938).

EVANS: This is a very important point because in Murray's original list of needs, he set up a pattern that stated, if you did a factor analysis, that you'd find all these specific needs, which, without measurements, is pretty hard to do. You weren't thinking, then, in terms of this framework.

SCHACHTER: No. It seemed to me that if you talk about something like a need for affiliation, you assume there must be some people who are high in this need and some who are low. You would expect people who are high to want more to be with other people than those who are low. From casual observation, however, there seem to be times when people want very much to be with other people and times when they want very much to be alone. So my view was: What are the situations that lead people to want to be with others? What are the situations that lead them to want to be alone? I never thought of it in trait terms, which I think essentially is what McClelland and Murray have done.

EVANS: This is the distinction I was trying to evoke, the idea that a trait concept of a need is really quite different from yours. Do you feel that your need for affiliation has sometimes been presented incorrectly in introductory textbooks?

SCHACHTER: No, not particularly. To pursue the contrast between my approach to affiliation and the trait view, it did seem to me that implicit in the notion of a traitlike need affiliation is the expectation that no matter what the circumstances, people who are high in that need will want to be with others more than people who are low in that need. In some of our experiments we deliberately manipulated conditions to show that there are situations where such people want to be with others, and there are situations where they want *not* to be with others. With such a pattern of results, it is simply more useful to think in terms of what people get out of being with one another rather than in terms of a traitlike need affiliation.

EVANS: I'm glad you underlined that. Looking at some of the specific studies, what are the one or two experiments that you find particularly intriguing, as you look back on that work?

SCHACHTER: The very first experiment, of course, the one in which we simply manipulated fear, making some subjects anxious and some calm, and then gave them a choice of being together or being alone. That they wanted to be with others when they were frightened opened up the whole problem. It was a real phenomenon, a real fact, we had a *finding*. What the hell did it mean? That question led to the whole series of experiments described in my book.

EVANS: *The Psychology of Affiliation* (Schachter 1959). Those experiments must have led you to look at this whole area much more closely.

SCHACHTER: The only other experiment in this series that was intriguing for me was the experiment that opened up the next line of research and suggested that one of the reasons people choose to affiliate, to be with other people, is to better evaluate how they feel. Experimentally we had created a novel, rather startling, and frightening situation for our subjects, and there was no real way for them to decide, "How do I react?" "What's the most appropriate response that I can give?" "How can I describe what I'm feeling?" I suggest in that book, and there is some support for it, that one of the reasons they choose to be with other people in that context is so they can literally understand what they're feeling by comparing themselves with other people. They want to be with others so they can evaluate their own reactions to the situation. Those studies led into the whole line of work that I've been doing ever since. In general, since the affiliation studies, I've been concerned with the interrelationships of social, cognitive, and physiological determinants of feeling states.

EVANS: It would be interesting to hear your comments on a more recent line of research that does get into affiliation. You may recall the line of bystander-apathy research that Latané and Darley (1970) have done. One of the concepts that has come from this research is the "diffusion of responsibility" idea—if you're with a lot of other people, you're less likely to help them than if you're alone. It just occurred to me that you might have something to say about that. Is there something related here in terms of anxiety affiliation behavior?

SCHACHTER: I'm sorry, but I've never thought about the connections explicitly. I suppose, since Latané was my student, that the two bodies of work are loosely connected, but I confess that's a glib, off-the-top-of-my-head, answer.

EVANS: Some research that is of interest in our society right now and that I have found valuable in interpreting various phenomena, is your work on how cues are related to the hunger drive, particularly for the person who tends to be obese, and the special nature of sensitivity to cues. I was speaking recently to a group of people who are interested in the area of oral hygiene, and they were concerned with why people cannot be taught to brush their teeth properly. I referred to your work, pointing out that when you're trying to modify an eating habit, you're plagued constantly with cues that stand out, saying eat,

eat, eat, every time you pass a grocery store or listen to a commercial. But there are no cues shouting at a person about his tooth-brushing behavior. The possibility for altering that behavior might be much greater than altering the behavior that leads to obesity, and such disease-prevention behavior also may be parallel to the area of smoking. I am presently embarking on a massive study supported by the National Heart and Lung Institute, designed to train school children to cope with pressures to smoke cigarettes, and your work opens some very interesting lines of thought about precisely how much the person is bombarded by cues. Are these interpretations too wild?

SCHACHTER: No, very sane, very sensible. I'm fascinated to hear you make that analogy to smoking because I've been working on that for the last three years.

EVANS: The big problem is taking the work of a person like yourself, a very rigorous scientist looking at these things carefully, and then extrapolating to the larger problems. We were considering your work and making generalizations that might be put into antismoking spots on television, for example.

SCHACHTER: I now believe that these findings on external cues and eating don't generalize to smoking; but to get into the eating and obesity business, the gist of what we found on obesity is pessimistic indeed if you're in the therapy business, and helps explain why recidivism is so astonishingly high with the obese. Almost any treatment is effective in the beginning, and why shouldn't it be? All you have to do is cut down eating a little bit and you must lose weight—God says so. But the recidivism rate is an astonishing 90 percent. It seems to be the case that the obese eat in terms of environmental cues rather than in terms of satisfying any particular physiological need, and the world is full of food cues. If a cue triggers eating, then if a person is exposed to food cues, he'll eat. And with the world built as it is, it's almost impossible to avoid food cues. The behavior modifiers, as you might guess, love these findings because they imply that for the obese the stimulus world is what triggers the eating behavior, and for B. F. Skinner (Evans 1968) all that would have to follow is to extinguish the connection between the food stimulus and the eating response. Problem is, how do you extinguish a world of food cues?

EVANS: This obesity work has caught the imagination of almost everyone who's obese, of course. Thinking about the problem of these findings, you seem to see this person surrounded by almost an overload of food cues. In addition to that, there is the question of why some people will and will not eat, reacting to these cues. Some of us respond more than others. Have you conceptualized something that would account for distinctions like this? Do we learn to respond to cues as a function of something going on internally or for other reasons?

SCHACHTER: The genesis of it hasn't really been my concern, but there are two ways to look at it. Hilda Bruch (1971) thinks that you are taught to respond to the world too often by being rewarded with food.

She's an analyst, and she's done extensive work with the juvenile obese. She says that all her obese patients have a mama who is the comedian's version of the Jewish mama—if the baby cries, give him a cookie; if he's cold, give him a cookie; if he comes in upset because he's had a fight with another kid, give him something to eat. The consequence, she suggests, of raising kids in this manner is a dissociation between the internal physiological state and the actual act of eating. Such people eat in response to *any* disturbing situation, rather than in response to a state of true physiological hunger.

EVANS: Has this notion been supported by any of your own work, or have you approached this problem in other ways?

SCHACHTER: I suppose Bruch's ideas are plausible enough, particularly if you're inclined to learning theory, but in my work I haven't been following up her developmental ideas. In the last work I did on obesity, I had grown intrigued by some of the remarkable resemblances between the behavior of obese human beings and the behavior of animals that have been made obese by a lesion made in that part of the hypothalamus called the ventromedial area. I don't know what the hell to make of these parallels. Is there something about the structure of the obese person, some strange muck-up in his hypothalamus that means he is particularly responsive to cues? The only evidence is the tempting kind of analogy that exists between this particular animal preparation and the obese human being, and the analogy has paid off in a fair amount of experimental work. So you have two views—the analyst's view that mama made them that way, and the physiologist's view that there are some human beings who are going to be fat because that's how God built them.

EVANS: Is there anything specific in your work that a student might read that develops more fully the ideas you've briefly presented here?

SCHACHTER: The best place for the work on the external cue determination of the behavior of the obese human is a book I wrote called *Emotion, Obesity and Crime* (1971a). The work on the parallels between the lesioned animal and the obese human is presented in a paper that I did for the *American Psychologist* (1971b) called "Some Extraordinary Facts About Obese Humans and Rats."

EVANS: Moving from obesity to smoking, you said that you believe that this is not an analogous situation. It would be interesting to have you discuss more fully some of your ideas about smoking behavior and why it doesn't exactly parallel the work you did on obesity.

SCHACHTER: The parallel doesn't hold up because one is tempted to assume casually that the heavy smoker is like the obese eater. If anything, though, the reverse is the case. One of my former students, Peter Herman, compared the effects of smoking cues, as well as of nicotine deprivation, on the smoking behavior of heavy and light smokers. It turned out that smoking cues, such as the sight of someone else lighting up, have far stronger effects on light than on heavy smokers. Heavy smokers seem to smoke largely in terms of the amount of nicotine in them. I got absorbed with some of the physiological implications of Herman's findings on heavy smokers, and that's what I'm working on now. The first thing I did was to run a study using heavy and light smokers. I gave them each a carton or two of cigarettes—one week they'd get a very low-nicotine cigarette and the next week a very high one—and then I simply asked them every day how many cigarettes they had left. We found that the heavy smokers smoked a great deal more when they were on the low-nicotine cigarettes. This is a finding that has amusing implications for the frequent suggestion that if heavy smokers are unable to give up the habit, they should at least switch to low-nicotine cigarettes. From these findings, you'd suspect that if they did so, they'd end up smoking more cigarettes, they'd get about the same amount of nicotine, and since they're smoking more, get far more of the combustion products.

EVANS: Let's look more specifically at why these cues break down. One would have to hypothesize that addiction, habituation, enters in some way. Addiction or habituation can obviously be reinforced by something like nicotine, or for that matter, sugar, anything that is perceived by the person in some unusually satisfying way. Are people addicted to cigarettes in the same sense they're addicted to hard narcotics?

SCHACHTER: It depends on what you mean by addiction. If you mean that the absence of the presumed addicting agent leads to withdrawal symptoms—that people suffer if they don't have it—and if you mean that people track the amount of the addicting agent—that is, if they have only a small amount of it in their system, they will go through hell and high water to get more—then that is the essence of the experiment I just described. The people who smoked low-nicotine cigarettes— and they didn't know that's what they were getting—smoked more cigarettes. There is something that knows how much nicotine is in the system, and when the system is deprived of the amount to which it is accustomed, there are signals that say, "Smoke, light another cigarette." I do tend to see smoking as an addiction, nicotine as an addiction, and that's why it's not in any way an easy thing to treat.

EVANS: Perhaps you could describe some of the physiological effects of smoking, of nicotine, on the body, as you see it.

SCHACHTER: Rather than do that, let me tell you what happens to nicotine when you smoke. We know that when one lights a cigarette and inhales, the nicotine is picked up by the network of blood vessels in the lungs, goes first to the brain, and then it's distributed around the body. The liver metabolizes nicotine, and the kidneys flush out the metabolites, as well as some raw, unmetabolized nicotine. That's the way the body copes with it. Nicotine is an alkaloid, and it turns out that the rate at which you get rid of nicotine depends to some degree on the pH, or the acidity, of the urine. If you have very acid urine, you simply pee out far larger quantities of unmetabolized nicotine than you do if you have an alkaline urine. Given this fact, in one of our experiments we attempted to manipulate the acidity of the urine by having the subjects take either bicarbonate of soda, which is a very effective alkalizer, or vitamin C, a safe acidifier, or a placebo. Then we kept a systematic record, over a period of weeks, of how much the subjects smoked. We did find that they smoked about 20 percent more when they were on vitamin C. We were also able to show that this is true of other acidifying agents as well, so these results aren't due to some magical property of vitamin C but do appear to be associated with acidification. Given these facts about the metabolic rate of nicotine, let's turn back to psychology and ask why and when do smokers think they smoke? If you ask them, most smokers will tell you that they smoke more when they're tense or anxious. And it's true; in an experiment designed to test this we found that smokers smoke about 50 percent more when they're anxious than when they're calm. Now the question is why? Most psychologists tend to interpret this fact in terms of the reinforcing or anxiety-producing properties of smoking. For the analysts, for example, it's all oral dependence. Presumably it all starts at mama's teat, and anxiety reactivates the suckling impulse and so you smoke. For the learning people, smoking under stress is somehow reinforcing and anxiety-reducing. Well, maybe, but let's look at another possibility and ask, What is the effect of such presumed psychological determinants of smoking as stress on the machinery that we know controls nicotine metabolism?

EVANS: That's a very interesting approach. What experiments were you able to set up to look at this problem from both a psychological and a physiological point of view?

SCHACHTER: The first thing we did was a series of studies that examined the effect of anxiety on urinary pH. In experiment after experiment we got the same result. The urine is more acid when people are frightened than when they're calm. So now we have two facts— stress increases smoking and also increases urinary acidity; which is still a long way, of course, from proving that urinary acidity causes the increased smoking observed in stress, but at least such a hypothesis now becomes a possibility. In order to get at the causal chain we designed an experiment in which we deliberately pitted psychology against urinary acidity. We manipulated stress so that half our subjects were frightened and the other half calm. At the same time we manipulated urinary acidity by having half of the subjects take a placebo and the other half bicarbonate of soda. Bicarbonate is an alkalizing agent which stabilizes pH or the degree of acidity so that for a time nothing short of drinking a glass of vinegar will increase acidity. The results were fascinating. In the placebo conditions, frightened subjects had a more acid urine than calm subjects and they also smoked considerably more. In the bicarbonate conditions, the stress manipulation had no effect on acidity and no effect on smoking. With bicarbonate in them, frightened subjects smoke no more than calm subjects. Given this pattern of results, it's a little difficult to take purely psychological explanations of smoking very seriously.

EVANS: You're research is very persuasive. I think this should be an interesting field for a student who's looking at the problems in psychophysiology. It's a very tough area, though.

SCHACHTER: There's no such thing as a tough area. An area's tough only if you don't have an idea.

EVANS: In your book, *Emotion, Obesity and Crime* (Schachter 1971a), why did you relate emotion to obesity and crime?

SCHACHTER: It's an offshoot of some of the emotion-adrenaline experiments that we had done, which in turn came out of the affiliation studies. One of the reasons people want to be with others is so they can evaluate their own reactions and feelings in a disturbing situation. That's obviously saying there's a cognitive component in an emotion. So we embarked on a line of research in which we tried again to manipulate independently the physiological and the psychological. We used injections of adrenaline which forces the body to respond in the way it normally does when you're emotional, and then we put the subject either in a situation that was frightening, or in one that should make him euphoric. Subjects with adrenaline tend to react more emotionally than those with placebo, whether the situation is one designed to make them angry or to make them euphoric. In control conditions, if you make the situation such that they know exactly how they feel and why—that their heart is beating faster because you have given them an injection of adrenaline—then they don't react emotionally at all. The gist of the study was that these two factors—physiological and cognitive—interact in determining any emotional state at all.

EVANS: You then applied these findings to several areas of study, as I recall—cheating, pain perception, and others. Is this how the "crime" part came in?

SCHACHTER: The crime part came in when we asked what effect adrenaline—something that tends to block the endogenous activity of the sympathetic nervous system—would have on an anxiety-producing situation like cheating. By manipulating the degree of anxiety and fear by the arousal of the sympathetic nervous system, you should be able to manipulate the likelihood that a crime will or will not be committed. We blocked off the action of the autonomic nervous system, presuming that autonomic arousal is the physiologic component of fear. We found that about twice the proportions of subjects cheated when they had taken the tranquilizing and sympatholytic agent chlorpromazine as when they'd taken the placebo. This is an interesting alternative explanation for the frequent observation students make that they do much better on exams when they take a tranquilizer.

EVANS: Again, the big problem is extrapolation of this to larger problems. How could this be done?

SCHACHTER: We did it directly. We went into prisons and tried to identify criminal psychopaths, the type that, clinically, have been labeled chronically bad boys. Cleckley (1955) in his book, *The Mask of Sanity* describes them as people who are emotionally flat. They don't have any great joys or any particular fears. Cleckley hypothesizes, and David Lykken (1957) produced some data that demonstrate that this kind of person is anxiety-free. Perhaps the reason they are chronic criminals is that anxiety is one of the chief inhibitors of being a crook. We replicated some of Lykken's work on the inability of the psychopath to learn to avoid pain. When they are injected with adrenaline, however, the physiological correlates of anxiety are forced on them, and they appear to learn pain-avoidance. The data are tentative but potentially wildly intriguing.

EVANS: In conclusion, Dr. Schachter, which of the many contributions that you've made do you consider to be the most important?

SCHACHTER: The one that has the most theoretical significance is the adrenaline-emotion study I just described. But of all the work I've done, the project that I've found the most fun is this series of studies of smoking. I confess, I adore the idea of reducing apparently complicated psychological phenomena to the pH of the urine.

EVANS: Are there any particular criticisms of your work that have troubled you, in the sense that you think they are basically unfair?

SCHACHTER: I tend to get criticism from people who seem to feel that a social psychologist shouldn't get involved in physiological problems. Some of the criticism is fair; some of it is silly. Probably the silliest was an attack on the fact that I measured heart rate by putting my fingers on a subject's wrist rather than plastering him with electrodes and wiring him into a cardiotachometer.

EVANS: Are you fairly optimistic about this present line of research?

SCHACHTER: I'm immensely excited about this tie-up between smoking and the chemistry of the body as it copes with nicotine. I do like the idea of being able to reduce presumably complex phenomena to small ones.

EVANS: Do you feel that these conclusions will be borne out, replicated?

SCHACHTER: We've done so many experiments on the subject by now, that it's hard to believe that we could be seriously wrong. That's a little extreme, but we keep finding these things, and they tie together.

EVANS: What I'm really trying to get at is this, that as someone moves into a line of research that is very unique and creative and in the early stages looks very positive and then five years later, someone does another piece of research and knocks it out. I want our students to share with you, as you move through these stages, what goes on in your mind.

Do you maintain an optimistic mood, or do you say it might turn up to be wrong?

SCHACHTER: Oh, on any of these I could be wrong. I sometimes think that there isn't any finding in all of psychology, my own findings, God knows, included, which *someone* won't fail to replicate. Replication is a problem that bugs me. Someday let's have a conversation about that.

EVANS: It's remarkable to me that you, as a sort of neophyte, could move into this field and in a relatively short span, come up with what seems to be breakthrough constructs. The idea that this could happen is, in itself, exciting. This may illustrate the need for something other than very limited specialized training.

SCHACHTER: It's hard to talk about some of these things without sounding pompous. But if I were forced to give advice, I'd say, get problem-oriented, follow your nose and go where problems lead you. Then if something opens up that's interesting and that requires techniques and knowledge with which you're unfamiliar, learn them.

REFERENCES

Bruch, H. 1971. Eating disorders in adolescence. In *The psychopathology of adolescence,* eds. J. Zubin and A. M. Freedman. New York: Grune and Stratton.

Cleckley, H. 1955. *The mask of sanity.* 3rd ed. St. Louis: Mosby.

Evans, R. I. 1968. *B. F. Skinner: the man and his ideas.* New York: Dutton.

Hebb, D. 1949. *The organization of behavior.* New York: Wiley.

Latané, B., and Darley, J. M. 1970. *The unresponsive bystander: why doesn't he help?* New York: Appleton.

Lykken, D. 1957. A study of anxiety in the sociopathic personality. *J. Abnorm. Soc. Psychol.* 55: 6–10.

McClelland, D., et al. 1953. *The achievement motive.* New York: Appleton.

Murray, H., et al. 1938. *Explorations in personality.* New York: Oxford.

Schachter, S. 1959. *The psychology of affiliation.* Stanford, Calif.: Stanford University Press.

———. 1971a. *Emotion, obesity and crime.* New York: Academic Press.

———. 1971b. Some extraordinary facts about obese humans and rats. *Amer. Psychol.* 26: 129–44.

14

Neal Miller

(1909–   )

*Neal Miller took his undergraduate training
at the University of Washington, completed
his master's degree at Stanford University, and
received his Ph.D. from Yale University in
1935. Trained as a psychoanalyst, he combined
clinical observation and a broad line of research that led to such important contributions
as the frustration-aggression hypothesis and
social learning theory. Searching for the un-
derlying causes of conflicting motivation, he moved into the area of brain
stimulation and then to an interesting and highly controversial series of studies
involving the control of autonomic responses utilizing biofeedback techniques. After
a distinguished career at Yale and the Institute of Human Relations, he moved to
Rockefeller University in 1966 where he continues his interests in physiology, biochemistry, and pharmacology. Professor Miller served as president of the American
Psychological Association in 1969.*

A Broader Picture of Psychology/The Psychoanalytic Background//The
Human Animal Is Very Social/Social Learning and Imitation//The
Flexibility of Innate Programming//The Frustration-Aggression
Hypothesis/A Contemporary View//Looking for the Connection/Brain
Stimulation and Motivation//A Change in the Whole Attitude/Modifying
Autonomic Responses//A Series of Bridges/Some Implications for
the Future//

Dr. Miller and I begin the discussion with his evaluation of the psychoanalytic
background of his training, and then move into his work in social learning.
Dr. Miller talks about the specific nature of imitation and copying and the
question of learning versus genetic programming. He then describes the
evolvement of the frustration-aggression hypothesis and its influence and implications for both psychology and society. After discussing his research in
behavior modification, Dr. Miller tells how the study of motivation led him to
brain-stimulation research and then the possibility of modifying and controlling autonomic responses. We discuss the implications of the biofeedback
movement, and Dr. Miller suggests that new areas, such as behavioral medicine, may develop as applied fields of the future. In conclusion, Dr. Miller
looks back over a career that has encompassed a broad area—learning theory,

psychoanalysis, motivation, physiological and biochemical components of behavior—and sees himself as a builder of bridges between disciplines: "It
hasn't been any one spectacular bridge, but rather, a series of bridges."

EVANS: Dr. Miller, as one looks over your illustrious career as a
scientist, one is struck by the variety of interests you've had, and also
by the number of things you did early in your career that have, very
recently, become central to many areas of psychology. You were involved
in psychoanalysis; in fact, you've been analyzed yourself. You worked
at Yale with Clark Hull (1943). You worked with the drive reduction
model, and with the significant frustration-aggression hypothesis. Then
you moved into the area of the brain and brain stimulation, and finally,
the work that has received tremendous attention recently is your work
on conditioning of the viscera. Looking back, to what degree did your
early experience in psychoanalysis affect your thinking? In other words,
would you recommend to the scientist that he get psychoanalyzed?

MILLER: Well, I think it was a valuable experience. You learn quite
a bit about your own motivations and about human motivations in
general; it gives one a broader picture of psychology to be exposed to
psychoanalysis. Indeed, I think that it may be much more valuable from
that point of view than it is as a therapeutic technique. It's a pity, in
my opinion, that normal people are not studied in the detail that abnormal people are, but of course, they don't have the same motivation to
cooperate. I think that the clinic in general, not only psychoanalytic, but
neurological, is to human behavior what field observation is to animal
behavior. It shows one the human animal struggling with some of the
difficulties that occur in its natural life, and hence, gives one a perspective.

EVANS: One of your classic contributions is in the general area of
social learning and imitation (Miller and Dollard 1941). Of course, today
we have a tremendous thrust in the area of social learning. There is the
work of Albert Bandura (1963), and many, many others. Suddenly it
has become central, not only to social psychology, but clearly to clinical
psychology as well. What were some of the basic principles that you
were attempting to communicate in your earlier work on social learning
and imitation?

MILLER: As a result of being at the Institute of Human Relations
at Yale, where I was thrown into contact with sociologists and anthro-
pologists, I was impressed with the strong importance of social influences
on our lives. Of course, the human animal is a very social animal, and
the group is the most important aspect of his environment. I was impressed with the influence of the group on behavior, and one of the ways
that this is demonstrated is by imitation. A person imitates the behavior
of the other members of his group, or uses them as models. John Dollard

and I did this series of experiments to show that the tendency to imitate could, itself, be learned and be influenced by learning. In those days, my view was that imitation was primarily the product of learning. Nowadays, I think I would change that view. There is probably some strong innate basis for imitation in people and other primates, but this certainly can be greatly modified by learning. As some of our early experiments showed, if a given model's behavior is imitated and that imitation leads to success and reward, then that model acquires prestige and his behavior is more likely to be imitated. If imitating a particular model leads to failure and lack of success, the model loses his prestige and is less likely to be imitated.

EVANS: You were looking at a pattern that, at that time, people were particularly interested in because of its implications for child development, for example. We were trying to understand something about the whole developmental sequence. In your work you also used the term "copy." How did you distinguish between copying and imitation?

MILLER: We divided imitation into two aspects. The division certainly isn't an absolute one. One is "matched dependent behavior," where a person uses another person's behavior as a cue and is guided by it, but is not essentially responding to the similarity or difference in his own behavior and the other person's. In "copying," the person is responding to the difference between his own behavior and the other person's behavior, and is making corrections to minimize this difference.

EVANS: Would this occur at a later stage of development in the individual? Are you suggesting a conscious choice here?

MILLER: Well yes. We still don't understand too well what "consciousness" is, but using it as a layman uses it, yes.

EVANS: Would we find copying in lower animals or in infants?

MILLER: I strongly suspect that one would, but I would not want to make an assertion without studying the problem. I think the essential thing about the copying analysis is that it was a very early example of what now would be called a cybernetic type of analysis. When the individual is responding to a difference and trying to minimize it, it's what I call a relative response to a relative cue. That is, he is responding not to an absolute but to a relative difference. In his own behavior, it can be a difference between his goal and his achievement. That gives him much more flexibility. I think that a lot of our behavior is this kind of behavior. We aim for something; we miss it slightly, and we correct on the basis of that discrepancy.

EVANS: In the work of Albert Bandura (1969), he uses the term "modeling" rather than "imitation," and of course, he's looked at the way the model operates and how the behaviors that are generated by the model are maintained. Do you see your earlier constructs centering on imitation differing from the more recent concept of modeling?

MILLER: I have been so busy in other areas that I haven't read the literature on modeling very thoroughly, but in what I have read, I'm struck by the similarities rather than the differences.

EVANS: You indicated that earlier you believed most of this behavior was learned, but as you looked more deeply into things, you began to recognize the innate basis for some of these patterns. That innate aspect, of course, is not stressed in the more recent work. How can you account for this battle raging today between those who argue that some behaviors might be programmed in the genome, and others who argue that behavior is almost completely learned?

MILLER: To the extent that the situation you describe actually exists, I think it's due to a misunderstanding. There is no incompatibility between learning and innate. The old view was that man's behavior is so flexible because he is, more or less, a tabula rasa and everything is learned, that man has far fewer instincts, should we say, or fewer species-specific behaviors than lower animals. My current view is that it's more plausible to contend exactly the opposite: that man's behavior is so flexible and so influenced by learning and by culture precisely because he has such a great variety of species-specific, or innately programmed, behaviors. I'll give you a very simple illustration. The kangaroo, because of its innate organization, can only hop; I may be doing the kangaroo a slight injustice here, but let's suppose that he can only hop. In this case, learning cannot do anything to modify the kangaroo's gait. Now let's take an animal like the cat, which, at the spinal level, has not only hopping reflexes, but organized stepping reflexes, trotting reflexes, and galloping reflexes. Such an animal, by having a greater number of innately programmed types of locomotion, can have its locomotion changed much more by learning. Thus, instead of having a conflict between innate mechanisms and learned behavior, the former can provide the essential basis for the latter.

I think that the same thing I have postulated here on the motor side applies also on the perceptual side. If you have a great variety of innately programmed feature detectors, or feature extractors, at different levels, of the kind that have been partly studied by Hubel and Wiesel (1959) and others, I think your possibilities of learning to respond to a variety of subtle aspects of the environment are greatly extended. I believe people have a very rich endowment of feature extractors on the sensory-perceptual side, a very rich endowment of innately programmed, different types of motor behavior, and also of innate patterns of social behavior —something that we've scarcely begun to study or to understand at all.

EVANS: Apparently, then, you wouldn't take exception to a point Konrad Lorenz (Evans 1975) recently made to me. We were discussing traditional motivational theory that argued there were certain basic drives with certain characteristics, such as hunger, thirst, and so on, and there were certain secondary social drives that were primarily learned, or at least were derived from the primary drives. It's ridiculous, he was more or less implying, to say that this is completely learned; you can find this kind of behavior in animals. It could be just as nearly genetically programmed as the need to satisfy the hunger drive. You wouldn't disagree with this at all, then?

MILLER: No, I wouldn't disagree with it. I think people have very rich endowments of motivations that we don't understand well enough to describe. But I believe that innate motivations can be modified or channeled by learning (Miller 1959). Take even as basic a drive as hunger. You have to habituate an animal to a specific kind of food before you can use it effectively as a reward in an experiment. If it's a completely strange food, he won't eat it. So you can see that even such a basic drive as the hunger drive is affected greatly by learning. There are, of course, innate limitations; you probably couldn't get anybody to like to eat asbestos, or fiber glass, or something of that kind.

EVANS: Your frustration-aggression hypothesis (Miller 1941) is still discussed in introductory psychology and social psychology. I recall that in the early formulations on animal behavior, you were attempting to manipulate the environment, frustrating the animals in order to study them under various kinds of frustrations. What did you find in that early work on frustration that led you to the formulation of the frustration-aggression hypothesis?

MILLER: The frustration-aggression hypothesis didn't grow entirely out of animal work, by any means. It just seemed to be a hypothesis that explained a lot of data on animals, a lot of data from the clinic, and that caused a lot of sociological and anthropological observations to fit together. It does seem that one of the important consequences of frustration is aggression. Now, I think there are other consequences of frustration in addition to aggression and other things in addition to frustration that are responsible for aggression. Furthermore, the forms of aggression, and even the tendency to express aggression, can be modified considerably by learning.

EVANS: I know that later you modified your earlier formulation in which you might have stressed to an unduly high degree the aggressive reaction to frustration. You began to reformulate that slightly as you moved along, did you not?

MILLER: Yes. One reaction to frustration can be depression, shall we say—experimental extinction, discouragement. Another reaction can be substitute activity of various kinds. Another reaction can be problem-solving. Without some kind of frustration, you don't have a problem, so you don't do any creative thinking.

EVANS: Of course, since your early formulations on aggression, this whole subject has taken on unusual interest in American psychology and, for that matter, in our culture in general. It seems that now we are caught up in some very interesting dilemmas, somewhat like the one we were discussing earlier. Again, the contemporary social-learning individuals, such as Berkowitz (1969), focus on the learned nature of aggression. The ethologists, such as Lorenz and Tinbergen, focus on the fact that aggression is, to a great degree, genetically programmed. In fact, Lorenz (Evans 1975) insists that aggression will occur quite spontaneously.

MILLER: This business of whether aggression will occur spontaneously is a little different from whether it's innately programmed. A computer can be completely programmed, but the program doesn't go into operation until somebody presses the button, so the question is a little different. Is there some specific quantum of aggression which builds up in a person, and which, if it isn't released in one way, has to be released in another? I don't think we have enough evidence to be sure, but certainly what evidence there is suggests that this is not true. If indeed there is any truth in it, the different ways that the aggression can be expressed are so wide and diverse that many of them can scarcely be regarded as harmful. I think it's quite possible there may be an innate basis for aggression, but certainly the degree to which it is elicited will depend on the degree to which the circumstances press the button, so to speak, and the ways in which it will be expressed are certainly subject to learning.

EVANS: This question has very great importance for our society.

MILLER: I couldn't agree more. I think the survival of the human species depends on our mastering this problem. As yet, we haven't had much success in control of nuclear armaments; we have the capability of killing the population of the world several times over. As the number of countries that have nuclear weapons increases, the odds that something will go wrong are being multiplied considerably. Although the innate and social psychological factors in aggression are important, I think to understand this picture, we need a far wider perspective. We need to bring in economics and political science, and we'd better start working much harder on these problems!

EVANS: You anticipated still another area that has become very central to contemporary psychology. Today, we call this behavior modification. It's an offshoot of behavior therapy, which is is a spinoff, more directly, from the work of B. F. Skinner (Evans 1968). Now in those early days, you were already formulating a behavior modification approach to psychotherapy. What was involved in your model of psychotherapy, as you recall it?

MILLER: The basic assumption was that functionally abnormal behavior, in other words, abnormal behavior that's instrumental in meeting some need or achieving some goal, must be learned. Similarly, psychotherapy, the degree to which one can modify such behavior by non-pharmacological means, must be a process of relearning or emotional reeducation. That was not a unique idea; other people had had it. I think John Dollard and I worked it out in more detail by applying it to combat neurosis (Dollard and Miller 1950), where the circumstances of learning are very clear and the learning is recent, and to other examples of neurotic behavior. I believe the importance of this work was that it provided the intellectual and scientific rationale for psychologists being involved in psychotherapy at a time when there was strong pressure in this country to regard psychotherapy as a strictly medical problem. Dollard and I took psychoanalysis as a point of departure for analyzing psychotherapy as learning, and some of the more radical behavior therapists have not liked this point of departure—have thought that this was the wrong tack. But it is my general impression that as both psychoanalysts and behavior therapists have to cope with the reality of the clinical situation, these two superficially opposite camps are being brought nearer together, and that they are converging toward the point of view that Dollard and I expressed in *Personality and Psychotherapy* (Dollard and Miller 1950). For example, when the behavior therapists say that it is important to discover and treat the real phobia rather than what the patient at first describes, they are approaching our point of view; and when the psychoanalysts place more emphasis on the fact that the patient gets well in real life, they also are approaching our point of view (Porter 1968). I think, however, that the really fundamental thing is for all of us to realize that our therapeutic techniques are actually rather poor. We need continual freedom to innovate, both theoretically and technically, and we need as rigorous an evaluation of these innovations as we can possibly achieve.

EVANS: As your career evolved, you began demonstrating increasing interest in the brain, attempting to understand better something about brain function. As I recall, one of the most important areas that you moved into and rapidly achieved eminence in was the area of brain stimulation. Could you talk a little bit about what you were looking for and what you were finding?

MILLER: In psychotherapy, clinical observation revealed the importance of conflict; many of these miserable people had severely conflicting drives. You can argue about the importance of drives for learning and performance in many situations, but in a conflict situation, it is clear that the outcome is dependent to a very considerable degree on the relative strengths of the competing drives. For example, in an experiment on approach-avoidance conflict, the rat's behavior depends on the strength of the hunger motivating the approach to food and the strength of the electric shock motivating avoidance (Miller 1944). In an attempt to bring a number of observations together, Mowrer, Hull, and I were all involved in developing the drive-reduction hypothesis of reinforcement. The attempt to secure more critical evidence on the drive-reduction hypothesis of reinforcement and to learn more about the mechanism of drives led me in the direction of physiological psychology (Miller 1957). At this time, the physiologists were making advances in their techniques of measuring motivations. I saw an opportunity to bring these two advances together. This work started with simpler interventions, such as making a fistula in the stomach of an animal so you could put food directly in. You could thereby bypass the consumptive response which, according to one hypothesis, was the basis for reinforcement. Incidentally, we did find that food introduced directly into the stomach served as a reward to produce learning by the hungry animal, but that an equal amount of distension of the stomach by a balloon served as a punishment. So this combination of behavioral and physiological techniques led to some interesting extensions of our understanding. Indeed, this approach could, in my opinion, lead to still further research on just how much an animal can discriminate about food in the stomach. Can he discriminate between fats, carbohydrates, and proteins? What are the sensory capacities of the stomach with respect to recognizing food?

EVANS: This, of course, preceded the brain work, and presented an interesting model for it, in fact.

MILLER: That model was to use a variety of behavioral techniques to measure the effects on motivation of normal behavioral interventions and of abnormal physiological ones. I got involved in the brain when I learned from Bob Livingston about the lesions in the ventromedial nucleus of the hypothalamus that caused rats and other animals to over-eat so that they became fat. Could this be a region of the brain involved in the regulation of hunger? If so, would stimulating this region electrically cause animals to stop eating and would recording from it be a more direct measure of hunger? Different behavioral techniques were used to measure the motivational effects of these lesions. But we found that these lesions, which caused animals to eat more, did not cause them to work harder for food or to be willing to tolerate more adulteration of the food with the bitter taste of quinine. In fact, these lesions had the opposite results—a paradox that has been the basis for considerable research since then, research that has replicated our findings and is increasing our understanding of these phenomena.

Twenty years earlier, Hess in Switzerland had devised techniques for implanting chronic electrodes in the brains of cats to stimulate them. Among other responses he had elicited eating behavior. But it was not until considerably later that some of his publications (e.g., Hess 1954) came to my attention. This work increased my hopes for combining behavioral techniques with those of direct stimulation and recording from the brain. If we could use such a recording as a measure of hunger, would this drive be momentarily shut off while the animal was eating a small pellet of food and then afterwards return to normal?

It took more than a year just to solve the technical problems of putting electrodes into a rat's head, getting them to stay, making connections to them, and all the little details that now we can teach a student in a couple of days. But we were working at a high level of excitement (Miller 1973). Since then, of course, other work has confirmed the motivational effects of electrical stimulation of the brain; it has shown that such stimulation can arouse a considerable variety of motivations, or perhaps some more generalized drive states, and that the responses to this electrical stimulation can be considerably modified by learning (Valenstein, Cox, and Kakolewski 1968, 1970). I think such modification is an area that needs further study. To what extent can the motivational effects of electrical stimulation of the brain be modified, and what are the laws governing such modification?

EVANS: Maybe ten years ago you began thinking about the whole autonomic system. In psychology, physiology, and the biological sciences, it was generally believed that the autonomic system was automatic. You began to wonder to what degree autonomous functions could be controlled by the organism. Would you tell us a little about how you moved into this?

MILLER: Well, that's a long story. Some of my very earliest work as a graduate student, strongly influenced by Professor Clark Hull, was devoted to documenting the similarities between the trial-and-error learning originally discovered by Thorndike (1898) and the classical conditioning, which was discovered by Pavlov (1927). It had been thought that these were two considerably different types of learning. Watson (1916) had tried to bring them together by saying that all behavior consisted of units of conditioned reflexes that were put together like building blocks. Hull's (1932) approach was considerably different; he thought the conditioned reflex was a peculiarly favorable situation for discovering laws of learning. What our group at Yale did, under the leadership of Professor Hull, was to show that the detailed laws of conditioning worked out by Pavlov were applicable, point by point, to the trial-and-error learning situation; namely, that immediate rewards and punishments are more effective than delayed ones, that a rewarded response will be strengthened but if not reinforced, experimentally extinguishes. After a period, however, you get spontaneous recovery from experimental extinction. We found that a gradient of stimulus generalization, which was demonstrated by Pavlov in classical conditioning, applied equally well to trial-and-error learning (also called operant conditioning) and that discrimination was built up by the joint action of stimulus generalization, reinforcement, and extinction. Of course, Spence (1936) was heavily involved in this work. Since the laws were so similar, in *Social Learning and Imitation* (Miller and Dollard 1941), Dollard and I asserted that classical conditioning and instrumental learning were different examples of the same learning process. This meant that if autonomically mediated responses can be modified by classical conditioning, it should be possible to modify them also by instrumental learning.

EVANS: But your interest in the problem did not stop there.

MILLER: I worried about this problem for a long time because, if you could have instrumental learning of these autonomically mediated visceral responses, this learning would allow psychosomatic symptoms to be reinforced in the same way that the hysterical ones seemed to be.

But I was busy doing other things, and I also probably was deterred to a certain extent by the strong, generally held belief that this was impossible. Then Bykov's (1957) book was translated into English, and this book showed the large number of visceral responses that were subject to classical conditioning. It greatly increased the practical importance of the problem because that meant there were far more of the visceral processes that could be modified by learning, either as psychosomatic symptoms or therapeutically. In addition, by now I had accumulated considerable physiological equipment. The combination of having the technical capacity plus the added importance of the problem pushed me over the threshold of action. We did a lot of fumbling around at first, but Carmona and I finally succeeded in using water to reward changes in the salivation of thirsty dogs (Miller and Carmona 1967). After this, Trowill (1967) taught rats paralyzed by curare and reinforced by brain stimulation to either increase or decrease their heart rates. Then the results seemed to come very fast, with six different students working on quite a number of different responses, all getting good results from their rats paralyzed by curare. As you may have heard, more recently we have had difficulty with this kind of experiment; the results seemed to have been getting poorer with time. I still have no idea what was occurring during the time the results were getting poorer. Now Dworkin and I have vastly improved our techniques for maintaining animals paralyzed by curare; so hopefully, we are in a position to learn more about this problem.

EVANS: Parallel to this is the so-called biofeedback movement, in which it is maintained that if you can display to a subject the measurement of some autonomic response, such as blood pressure, heart rate, or brain waves, he can affect the incidence by concentration or will. This has become an almost astounding demonstration of the interrelation between psychological and somatic problems. Of course, your work has been perceived by some as legitimizing the biofeedback work. What do you think you did that more or less triggered this off?

MILLER: Earlier, there was a strong inclination to believe in the impossibility of modifying any visceral responses by learning. I think that this was due to our cultural background, to the spirit of the times. But since then, there has been a complete change in our whole attitude. I don't understand the reasons—perhaps it is the interest in Oriental religions and in meditation that has prepared young people to swing over to the opposite extreme.

I wasn't the only person who was working on visceral learning. There were others working with people at the same time, at first having a very hard time getting their results accepted. I think that the experiments in my laboratory on the animals paralyzed by curare were especially carefully designed; the results seemed to be very clear-cut and I think that the conviction they carried gave things a big boost. There were also the rapid technical developments. Over a period of a half-dozen years, with the solid-state equipment, the miniaturization, the integrated circuits, and all of the computer developments, it has been vastly easier to get superior equipment to do this kind of work. That has made a big contribution. But what I really want to emphasize is that although there is no doubt in my mind that people can learn to control some of these autonomically mediated responses in one way or another, there are still two very thorny and difficult issues to be resolved.

EVANS: What are these issues?

MILLER: One is the degree to which the control of these visceral responses is direct, the degree to which skeletal responses may mediate the control, or the degree to which both skeletal and visceral responses may be part of a centrally integrated pattern. Workers in my lab have found that if a person is rewarded for changing his heart rate, the first thing he will do is to change his respiration, which will change his heart rate. In working with patients with severe polio or muscular dystrophy, which paralyze the skeletal muscles but don't affect the autonomic system nearly as much, we have found, for example, that if the person commands his paralyzed muscles to squeeze a ball, although he is unable to move even a little bit, he can raise his blood pressure and heart rate. This result demonstrates the central integration of the skeletal and vasomotor responses. In this case, however, when these patients have learned voluntary control over their blood pressure, these learned changes did not affect their heart rate. The specificity of the learned change in blood pressure distinguished it from the change occurring as part of the central pattern involving commands to the paralyzed muscles. To the extent that we are unable to make any distinctions like the foregoing one and are forced to conclude that specific skeletal and visceral responses are inseparable parts of a fixed centrally integrated pattern, the original traditional idea that visceral responses can be modified by classical conditioning and that skeletal responses can be modified by instrumental learning becomes meaningless. This issue is not yet definitely decided. There may be some correlations that we haven't yet discovered between subtle specific skeletal responses and specific visceral responses. On the other hand, it may be possible to separate some normally integrated patterns of skeletal and visceral responses just as it is possible to separate the parts of the pattern of walking and swinging one's arms. This remains a tricky problem which requires very careful investigation.

EVANS: You mentioned a second difficult issue.

MILLER: Yes, therapeutically, the foregoing problem is not so important. For example, it is well known that when some people have attacks of paroxysmal tachycardia (that's when their heart suddenly begins to beat wildly), they can arrest such attacks by taking a sudden deep breath. Now, therapeutically, it doesn't make any difference whether or not they use this skeletal response provided that it is effective. But with therapy there is a different thorny problem. This problem is whether the patient is showing a genuine effect that is specific to the type of training he is given, or whether he is showing a nonspecific placebo effect—the kind that can be produced by a sugar pill. If the person believes he's going to be helped, he may not only feel better, but also be better. It's interesting to note that in double-blind tests to determine whether or not a drug is effective in modifying blood pressure, quite a number of the patients who get only the placebo sugar pills will show progressive improvement over a period of months. In one such study the forty-eight placebo patients showed a reduction of twenty-five millimeters mercury in systolic and twelve millimeters mercury in diastolic pressure. This shows the importance of purely psychological factors. Studies of the effects of suggestion on visceral responses show that they are not as automatic and independent as they have been thought to be, but are subject to subtle psychological influences. Such results open up an important and new area of study: just how does the placebo effect work?

EVANS: Dr. Miller, what do you see for the future of psychology?

MILLER: That's a big question, like asking: What is the climate of the Americas? In the general area that we have been discussing, I see the possibility of what one might call "behavioral medicine" developing, on the one hand as an area for basic research, and on the other hand as an area of therapeutic applications. I see a number of developments, with the work on visceral learning and biofeedback being one small part of the picture. Another important part would include the research being done showing that the immune system is subject to modification by psychological factors, particularly by stress, and that the hypothalamus, which is involved in emotion, plays a significant role in affecting the immune system. I see the work that psychopharmacology is doing with the amines—determining the effects of behavioral variables on the monoamines and the emotional and the behavioral effects of changes in these amines. I see additional investigations of psychological effects, such as fear, on the cardiovascular, pulmonary, and gastrointestinal systems. I see investigations of the effect of learning on homeostasis. I see increasing use of behavioral techniques to help patients to reduce maladaptive illness behavior and to achieve better health-promoting activities; for example, rehabilitation patients to exercise and achieve better voluntary control and children threatened by scoliosis to achieve better posture. I see these and other developments advancing the new area of behavioral medicine.

EVANS: Now I think it would be only fair to have you comment on some of the criticisms of your work, particularly the question of replication of your experiments on conditioning the visceral responses, heartbeat and blood pressure.

MILLER: Well, certainly the brute fact that we cannot now repeat the earlier experiments is posing difficult problems. I've been working very hard on that for the last three or four years (Miller and Dworkin 1974). It's extremely frustrating. The problem isn't resolved yet; so one has to view the earlier work with reserve. It may be that the nature of the rearing of the rats, the constituents of the extract of curare, or something else has changed. Or it may be that there were some hidden errors in the earlier experiments. Working on this problem, Dr. Dworkin and I have vastly improved the techniques of respirating and maintaining the curarized rat. I'm sure that something of value will come out of these improvements—perhaps a better preparation for studying the instrumental learning of visceral responses, but if not that, an alert but immobilized animal suitable for the use of microelectrode techniques in the study of neural circuits involved in classical conditioning.

EVANS: In conclusion, I'd like to ask which of your contributions you yourself consider to be the most important.

MILLER: I would say that such importance as I have had comes from having done a series of things, and especially from building a number of bridges between different disciplines. In the early work, it was bringing together anthropology, sociology, and learning theory, and also bringing together some notions from clinical studies of psychoanalysis and from experimental studies of learning. Briefly, Dollard and I pointed out how the social sciences supply essential information on the conditions of human learning, while psychology provides information on the principles of learning. In order to understand human behavior, one must know both the conditions and the principles. Then the clinic provides a vital view of the human animal struggling to learn to adapt to the social conditions of his culture, class, and cliques. More recently, I have tried to bring together some concepts and techniques from physiology, biochemistry, pharmacology, and behavior. My work hasn't been on any one spectacular bridge, but rather on a series of bridges between different disciplines.

EVANS: What are you working on right now?

MILLER: Well, just at the moment, I am working with Dr. Dworkin and Dr. Eissenberg on the problem of trying to replicate the earlier results on visceral learning by curarized rats. I am also trying to help my associates to push on further the learning of visceral responses by human subjects. Mr. Brucker and I seem to be finding that patients who are paralyzed by a lesion of the spinal cord have an unusual ability to learn increases in blood pressure. Conceivably, this lesion helps visceral learning by relaxing certain homeostatic controls. Are there other ways of producing antihomeostatic effects? Dr. Dworkin, Dr. Eissenberg, and I are testing a behavioral approach to the treatment of children with scoliosis, which is an S-shaped curvature of the spine. For the cumbersome and socially traumatic Milwaukee brace, we are trying to substitute a lightweight, inconspicuous, electromechanical device that informs the child whenever her posture is incorrect and helps in maintaining the correct posture. Dr. Vertes and I are recording in the freely moving rat from certain large neurons in the pontine region of the reticular formation that respond specifically to a conditioned stimulus for electric shock. You will remember that one of the original ideas that led me into work on the brain was the hope that I could record there from neurons whose activity would yield a direct measure of drive. But the effects of direct electrical and chemical stimulation of the brain were so interesting that I never did get to the recording. Now Dr. Vertes and I hope that recording during approach-avoidance conflict will yield significant information on the detailed dynamics of such behavior. It is conceivable that the recorded activity of these neurons will provide a moment-to-moment index of either fear or of a state of arousal related to fear.

REFERENCES

Bandura, A. 1963. *Social learning and personality development.* New York: Holt.
———. 1969. *Principles of behavior modification.* New York: Holt.
Berkowitz, L., ed. 1969. *Roots of aggression: a re-examination of the frustration-aggression hypothesis.* New York: Atherton.
Bykov, K. 1957. *The cerebral cortex and the internal organs,* ed. and trans. W. Gantt. New York: Chemical Publications.
Dollard, J., and Miller, N. 1950. *Personality and psychotherapy.* New York: McGraw-Hill.
Evans, R. 1968. *B. F. Skinner: the man and his ideas.* New York: Dutton.
———. 1975. *Konrad Lorenz: the man and his ideas.* New York: Harcourt.
Hess, W. 1954. *Das Awischenhirn: Syndrome, Lokalisationen, Funktionen.* 2d ed. Basel: Schwabe.
Hubel, D., and Wiesel, T. 1959. Receptive fields of single neurones in the cat's striate cortex. *J. Physiol.* 148: 574–91.
Hull, C. 1932. The goal gradient hypothesis and maze learning. *Psychol. Rev.* 39: 25–43.
———. 1943. *Principles of behavior: an introduction to behavior theory.* New York: Appleton.
Miller, N., and Dollard, J. 1941. *Social learning and imitation.* New Haven: Yale University Press.
———. 1941. The frustration-aggression hypothesis. *Psychol. Rev.* 177: 449–51.
———. 1944. Experimental studies of conflict. In *Personality and the behavior disorders,* ed. J. V. McHunt, pp. 431–65. New York: Ronald.
———. 1957. Experiments on motivation: studies combining psychological, physiological, and pharmacological techniques. *Science* 126: 1271–78.
———. 1959. Liberalization of basic S-R concepts: extensions to conflict behavior, motivation and social learning. In *Psychology: a study of a science,* ed. S. Koch, study 1, vol. 2, pp. 196–292. New York: McGraw-Hill.
———, and Carmona, A. 1967. Modification of a visceral response, salivation in thirsty dogs, by instrumental training with water reward. *J. Comp. Physiol. Psychol.* 63: 1–6.
———. 1971. *Neal E. Miller: selected papers.* Chicago: Aldine.
———. 1973. Commentary on Delgado, Roberts and Miller's "Learning motivated by electrical stimulation of the brain." In *Brain stimulation and motivation: research and commentary,* ed. E. S. Valenstein, pp. 53–68. Glenview, Ill.: Scott, Foresman.
———, and Dworkin, B. 1974. Visceral learning: recent difficulties with curarized

rats and significant problems for human research. In *Cardiovascular psychophysiology*, eds. P. A. Obrist, et al., pp. 312–331. Chicago: Aldine.

Pavlov, I. 1927. *Conditioned reflexes*. Trans. G. V. Anrep. Oxford: Oxford University Press. Reprinted 1960. New York: Dover.

Porter, R., ed. 1968. *The role of learning in psychotherapy*. London: Churchill.

Spence, K. 1936. The nature of discrimination learning in animals. *Psycho. Rev.* 43: 427–49.

Thorndike, E. 1898. Animal intelligence: an experimental study of the associated processes in animals. *Psychol. Rev. Monogr. Suppl.* 2: vol. 8.

Trowill, J. 1967. Instrumental conditioning of the heart rate in the curarized rat. *J. Comp. Physiol. Psychol.* 63: 7–11.

Valenstein, E., Cox, V., and Kakolewski, J. 1968. Modification of motivated behavior elicited by electrical stimulation of the hypothalamus. *Science* 159: 1119–21.

———, Cox, V., and Kakolewski, J. 1970. Reexamination of the role of the hypothalamus in motivation. *Psychol. Rev.* 77: 16–31.

Watson, J. 1916. The place of the conditioned reflex in psychology. *Psychol. Rev.* 23: 89–116.

James McConnell

(1925–   )

James McConnell completed his undergraduate work at Louisiana State University and received his master's degree and in 1956 the Ph.D. from the University of Texas. While there he first began the line of research that was to evolve into the exciting and highly controversial memory transfer hypothesis: that the storage of information may be a transferable biochemical event. In addition to this work, Professor McConnell has instituted and directed studies on the application of operant conditioning techniques in a novel way to such problems as criminal behavior and mental illness. Joining the faculty at the University of Michigan in 1956, Dr. McConnell is currently professor and resident psychologist.

Memory Transfer/When You Shock a Worm, It Scrunches/Classical Conditioning in the Flatworm/All Five Pieces Remembered/The RNA Hypothesis/It Shouldn't Matter How You Get the Chemical to the Brain/ The "Cannibal" Studies/You've Got to Give a Rat the Weekend Off/ Replicating Memory Transfer in Rats/Some Implications for the Future// Behavioral Technology/Operant Conditioning in Attitude Change and Social Behavior/The Prison Experiments/Learning Better Control/Behavioral "First Aid"/The Reinforcers/Creature Comforts/The Joy of Learning/Social Interaction/The Further You Get from Aversive Control, the Better/Training Patients to Get Well/Conditioning Good Health/Changing Society//

Dr. McConnell and I discuss the origins, development, and implications of his work in the area of memory transfer. Tracing the learning mechanism in the brain, he trained planarians, or flatworms, using classical conditioning methods, and then attempted to transfer the learning from an "educated" flatworm to a naive one, through a variety of methods, including the well-known cannibalism studies. He reacts to the critics of this work, emphasizing both his own findings and those of others who have successfully replicated this research. He also describes memory-transfer and learning-transfer experiments in rats, and then tells why he decided to move into another area, away from the biochemical thrust and into the work he calls behavioral technology. "I guess I have always been an applied psychologist. I enjoy doing things with worms, but I prefer doing things with people." By modifying and applying operant conditioning techniques in an attempt to change attitudes and social behavior in a wide range of social groups, including patients in both mental and general hospitals, and prisoners, he says, "We help them learn better strategies for taking control of their own lives. We train patients to get well, condition them for good health."

EVANS: Dr. McConnell, some years ago, in the area of physiological psychology, you did research that had to do with the matter of memory transfer. How did you happen to get into that line of research?

McCONNELL: In 1953, when I was a graduate student at the University of Texas, Robert Thompson, who was another graduate student, came to me and tried to talk me into working with him on training flatworms—planarians. I wondered what the hell he wanted to do that for; you can't be respectable in psychology unless you train rats. But he had just been reading Donald Hebb's (1949) great book, *The Organization of Behavior*. God, what an influence that book has had on us. Hebb was interested in what was going on inside the brain when an organism learns. He had a notion, also found in William James (1950) and other sources, that perhaps there had to be a rearrangement in the basic connections of the nerve cells of the brain whenever anyone learned anything. When you put information into a computer, you have to make some kind of physical change in the computer, either at the switching level or the program level. You could really reach out and touch the memory, if you knew where to look, either on the memory drum, or within the switching arrangement. Hebb and others began saying, "Well, there must be the same sort of change in the human computer we call the brain. What is it?" We call it an *engram*, but we still don't know what it is. Hebb had thought that perhaps at the point of learning you connected up nerve cells in different pathways; he called them cell assemblies. It was a brilliant idea. He was thinking in terms of functional connections rather than structural changes among the nerve cells, but I don't know that you can ever have a functional switching arrangement in the brain, unless it is also structural.

EVANS: How did the worms fit into this?

McCONNELL: Well, Thompson said, "Let's try to train a flatworm, because if Hebb is right, the synapse, which is the junction point between two nerve cells, must be involved in memory." The flatworm, as it happens, is the simplest animal to have true synapses in a true brain; therefore, Thompson said, "If a flatworm can learn, then that proves that synapses are involved." Well, years later, we learned that animals that don't even have synapses, or nerve cells, or brains can learn, but they are obviously animals that haven't read Hebb's theory, so the hell with them. We were the first to train planarians using classical, or Pavlovian, conditioning, which was Thompson's idea. (The professor in charge of the lab at Texas didn't like our research, so we had to do it in my kitchen.) We built a little water-filled trough that these flatworms could wiggle through; it had electrodes at either end so we could shock the animal. The shock was the unconditioned stimulus that caused an unconditioned response—a scrunch. When you shock a worm, it scrunches, as I like to say, because that communicates what really happens better than our technical jargon. We had a light above the trough. We turned on the light; this was a signal the shock was coming, and presumably, if the flatworm could learn, it would eventually begin scrunching when we turned on the light, before the shock arrived. So, we sat down in the kitchen for about three months, training flatworms, and they did seem to learn.

EVANS: Did you have a comparative group?

McCONNELL: We had the usual numbers of controls that one might wish: groups that had shock only, or light only, and they showed a decrease in their response rate. The only group that showed an increase were the experimental animals that got light and shock paired. Thompson and I thought we had proved that flatworms could learn. I don't know that we had done quite that, but we published it in 1955 (Thompson and McConnell 1955), and no one really gave a damn about it, to tell the truth. It was just another study. But at any rate, I went to Michigan and sort of continued the work. First, I trained students who did all the work and had all the good thoughts, and I sat back and watched them and encouraged them, which is my way of doing research. But assuming that a worm can learn, where do you go from there? If you cut a flatworm in half, it doesn't die; it simply regrows the missing parts, so you end up with two worms. If you cut the flatworm in ten pieces, each of these pieces will regrow to the size of the original animal and become a sexually mature adult. We thought if we cut up a trained flatworm, the front end, which has the brain, would remember, if anything were remembered. The tail, which has to grow a new brain, obviously would not remember.

EVANS: Yes, that would seem logical.

McCONNELL: We decided to try it (McConnell, Jacobson, and Kimble 1959). We had a number of control groups, and we asked ourselves stupid questions that we don't usually ask, like: How much would you expect a flatworm to forget in a month? It was really pretty nicely designed research, I think. What we found about the cut-up worms was that the trained heads that grew new tails remembered just as much as before they were cut, so apparently losing your tail doesn't affect your memory, if you're a flatworm. To our surprise, the tails from the original worms remembered even better than the heads. Now you ask yourself, how could that be? But it's not a really startling finding. During the time that the tail is growing a new head, it is protected from any environmental inputs; it does not have eyes; it sits in a bowl and does not move for about ten days. With some of the tails, it seemed as if the response that had been learned in the original animals now was almost an innate reaction, and not a learned reaction. Many of the tails showed perfect performance right from the very start. That's difficult to explain in terms of simply shuffling around connections among nerve cells. We began to ask ourselves: What goes on in the brain when an organism learns, because obviously learning is not stored just in the head. We took a worm, trained it, and cut it in five pieces. All five pieces remembered. We took a worm, trained it, cut the head off, let the tail grow a new head, cut the old tail off, let the new head grow a new tail. The animal still remembered. No part of it was the original animal. The only thing I could figure out was that there was some chemical change in the animal when it learned.

EVANS: Was this the first time such a thing had been suggested?

McCONNELL: I went to the literature and found, as usual, that there were ten people who had said the same thing long before I did. There was a great tradition, not a very well believed tradition, but it was there. We simply stole the ideas from other people and began thinking that maybe when a flatworm learned something, the engram basically was a chemical change, a molecular change, probably in the RNA, perhaps in protein. These words sometimes confuse us; I don't know why they do. The structure of the brain has to be coded in the genetic code, because we all have almost identical brains. Our basic reflexes are instinctual responses, innate responses that have to be carried in the molecule, what we call DNA. If DNA codes for species memory, and that's really what an instinct is, then perhaps RNA, which is manufactured by DNA, could code for individual memories. The blueprint that hooks your brain up in the beginning must be flexible. Perhaps it is the RNA that adds the flexibility, that reshuffles the connections among the nerve cells, so that you have a combination of Hebb plus biochemistry.

EVANS: Did you, at one point, actually take one of the worms that had learned the response, cut it up in little pieces and have another worm ingest it?

McCONNELL: Right. This is the cannibalism study (McConnell 1962). When we began thinking that chemicals had to be involved, and maybe it was RNA, the next question was: How do you prove it, because no one's going to believe that nonsense. My thought was that if two flatworms learned exactly the same trick, the same conditioned response, the chemicals in their brain would be the same, and it shouldn't matter how you get the chemical to the brain. Flatworms are fun, because if you tire of the way your animal looks, you can rearrange its body in a lot of ways. As a matter of fact, if you want to, you can cut the head off one beast and graft it on to the body of another, and you have a worm with a head at both ends; then they argue about which way they're going to go. We grafted a trained head onto an untrained body to see if we could transfer the mechanism for learning that way. It turns out you can do it about one time in fifty if you're very clever about it. It's theoretically possible, but not very practical. Next, we decided we'd grind up worms and inject the juice from the trained worm into an untrained animal. We had huge needles and small worms, and we left such big holes that everything we injected oozed right out. Then, as a result of a letter from a friend, it occurred to me that these worms are cannibals, and we could let them do the transfer for us. We trained worms and then fed them to untrained worms of the same species. We had another group that got fed untrained worms, and a third group that got just liver. Then we compared the learning speeds, and we found to our delight that the cannibals that had eaten uneducated victims did not show any increase in their learning; the animals that had eaten educated, or trained, victims showed considerable speed.

EVANS: You're obviously not implying that the cannibals were immediately able to exhibit this response? You're saying that they learned more quickly?

MCCONNELL: We were using the method of "savings" to measure learning, but there are other methods. For example, we could feed a worm the trained worms, and simply test it in an unreinforced situation to see if there were any change without encouragement. We would expect some "transfer" there, too.

EVANS: The "savings" concept would be demonstrated in, say, someone who had learned typing at the age of seven or eight; then, without having typed in the interval, at the age of twenty-two began learning again. He would learn more quickly—have a savings score— than a person learning for the first time.

MCCONNELL: It's a very sensitive method, and that's why, I think, we used it. Well, with the transfer thing, when we first got the results, and we did show a significant savings, we knew we had something, and we also knew no one would believe it. One of the questions with this kind of research is, Do you have an unconscious bias; are you getting the kind of results that you want? We call this experimenter bias. We had to run an experiment in which the people who were training the cannibals didn't know what they'd eaten so they couldn't bias the results. We tried filming what went on, so anyone could look at it and judge whether or not the response was there. I think with the replications we've had, it's pretty clear that the results are there.

EVANS: Of course, other replications involve other laboratories, people who start out, perhaps, with the premise that you're all wrong. Was there such research? Were there attempts to replicate your methodology?

MCCONNELL: Science is such an odd human behavior. It depends as much on gossip as on anything else. The gossip in this field is that it is difficult to repeat or replicate these studies, and the real truth is that this work has been replicated more than almost any other I know of in the whole field of psychology. It is not all that difficult to do if you follow directions. After we got the original transfer by cannibalism study done, we did one more study. We asked ourselves again, O.K., if there is transfer via the gut, what is the chemical involved? So we did a study in which we trained worms—we had to train several hundred for each group—ground them up, and extracted this chemical called RNA and a lot of other things and injected this "soup" from trained worms into untrained worms, using a very tiny needle, and got a transfer this way. So we were pretty sure that it was RNA, or a related chemical, that was involved. No one had ever extracted RNA from a living tissue to inject into other tissue, and there are a lot of things you have got to do biochemically. We didn't know much about it; it was not as well controlled as later. It is now done with machinery at dozens of labs around the world.

EVANS: Do you recall some of the particular problems?

McCONNELL: Well, one funny thing I remember. The medical students who were doing the extraction for us wanted me to come and watch. I saw the trained worms, five hundred of them—I don't know if you know how long it takes to train five hundred worms, but it's a long time—they ground them up, put them in the worm-blender, and extracted the RNA. They had it in a little glass test tube; they dropped it on the floor and the glass shattered. There was about three months of work gone. So they took a little glass pipette and sucked the RNA up off the floor, and said, "We'll clean it up, don't worry." You don't do that now, of course. But after we showed that you could transfer learning chemically, people began using animals other than worms, and this is when we began to get into difficulties in replication. There were, in 1964, laboratories in four countries—Denmark, Canada, the United States, and Czechoslovakia—that began training rats, grinding up the brains, taking the chemicals out, and injecting them into untrained rats. All four labs got successful results with a series of experiments. We began working with rats in 1965. By 1966, there were thirty successful experiments in print. But in 1966, a group of scientists in seven laboratories tried and failed. They reported their results very carefully in *Science*.

EVANS: Who were the authors of that particular article?

McCONNELL: The major author was William Byrne (Byrne, et al 1966). They said that perhaps they had not done the same thing that we and the people in the other labs had done, and that this was, perhaps, to be expected. No one read that part. Between the time Byrne wrote the article and it was published, he had gotten successful results, and so did several other people. Of course, they reported that later, but you can't change an article once it is in print.

EVANS: Here you're trained as a physiological psychologist, learning psychologist, whatever term you want to use, and you're venturing into a very complex area—molecular biology, in particular biochemistry, and as you say, RNA is still in many respects a very mysterious substance. Do you think that to some degree this might have been a factor in the readiness of some to reject your work?

McCONNELL: Sure. We don't like it when people come into our area and tell us how we should work with humans or with worms. The molecular biologist, the neurophysiologist, didn't like this smart-ass psychologist coming in and upsetting some of their notions, and I don't blame them. We were very stupid about our public relations. We didn't try to write in terms they could understand.

EVANS: What was the essence of your study on the rats?

McCONNELL: Suppose you want to train a rat to press a lever to get milk. Typically, you want the chamber where the milk is to be as close to the lever as possible. The rat smells the milk, approaches it, bumps into the lever, hears a click as the milk mechanism operates, allowing the rat to get to the milk. So first the animal learns that click sounds get milk, then the rat learns to press the lever to get the click, and then get the milk. You can slow down the learning a great deal if you put the milk chamber on the opposite side of the box from the lever. It's a very difficult connection for the animal to make, between pressing the lever on one side and running over and getting the milk on the other side, because the milk disappears about ten seconds after the click. We decided we would try to transfer this response. When the milk is on the opposite side from the lever, the first thing you do to train the rat is simply stand by the milk, and any time the rat is close to the milk delivery mechanism, you press a button that makes a click and gives the rat the milk. So when the rat hears a click, it goes to one side and gets the milk. After it has learned that, anytime it happens to hit the lever, which is on the other side, it hears a click and runs over and gets the milk. So what we did was to train animals to go to the milk when they heard the click, then we ground up the brains, extracted the RNA, and injected it in tiny quantities directly into the brains of another group of rats. We put these rats in the box, but we never gave them the milk-click training. We wanted to see if they could spontaneously learn to press the lever on one side to get milk on the other. We had two groups, six animals in each group. We found that the animals injected with RNA from trained brains all learned in a matter of two or three days with no further training. None of the animals that got untrained RNA learned.

EVANS: There have been some directions this line of work has followed, and one, of course, is to vary kinds of learning in this transfer phenomenon. Another is trying to pin down, at the biochemical level, precisely what is operating here in the RNA. We know that at Baylor Medical School in Houston, Georges Ungar (1970), who is really a neurophysiologist, is working in the lab. As you see it, what is he doing and what has he found?

McCONNELL: Well, we've replicated most of his findings, so I'm reasonably sure that they're right. But let me tell you a story about

Georges, because it shows the trouble with replication, which we've been talking about. Georges was one of the first four to work with rats and did some most intriguing research. He wanted to find out what the chemical was, and he's come closer than any of the rest of us. His training is such that he might be expected to. Georges trained rats to avoid the dark. They usually prefer the dark, but if you shock the rat when it is in the dark chamber of a box, it's smart enough to learn to stay the hell out; after a few days of training, it will avoid the dark continuously, something it normally wouldn't do. Georges took chemicals from the brains of animals that had been trained to avoid the dark, injected these chemicals into untrained rats. Within about twelve hours after the chemicals have been put in, suddenly the rat no longer goes into the dark, but avoids it. If you force the animal toward the dark, it begins to squeak, to bite, to urinate, to defecate; it shows emotionality. It's a really interesting set of responses from the animal; it looks like you're transferring some kind of innate fear. We tried to repeat this experiment that Georges had run. The first time we did it we succeeded. We tried for eight months to repeat that first study, and it didn't work. And every time we tried, I'd call Georges up on the phone, and say, "Now, Georges, what the hell did you really do?" He would say, "Oh, I forgot to tell you this." But none of these variations was really successful, and so we quit that and went on to something else and discovered an effect that explained what Georges was doing that we weren't. We found that in training donors, if you give them rest periods of several days off in the middle of training, you get better transfer than if you don't. You get better learning, too. Psych labs tend to run rats every day, and you don't report it because everybody does it. When Georges trained his rats, he trained them for five days and took off for the weekend. He did not report that. So we went back and repeated Georges' work taking weekends off, and it worked. Well, a lot of replications fail for simple, stupid reasons that you don't know about. Georges went on to do a chemical analysis of the brains of four thousand trained rats. He found one chemical, which he called *scotophobin* (from the Greek meaning fear of dark). He found a small protein that has fifteen amino acid residues hooked into a chain, like beads on a necklace, and he identified pretty well what those beads were, what chemicals were involved. He then could specify what the memory molecule was for fear of the dark. The next thing he did was to synthesize this material, take nonliving chemicals and hook them together, and the synthetic material worked as well. He sent us some synthetic scotophobin, and we replicated his findings.

EVANS: As fantastic as it may sound, are we coming to a point now where we could somehow see a projection into controlling human behavior?

McCONNELL: I think so. I think that probably within a few hundred years we will know enough about memory and learning so that we will be able to speed up learning on certain subjects—anything we want—very, very rapidly. Look, we already know that if you give a person caffeine during the time he is trying to learn, he learns faster. We've already found certain general learning facilitators and inhibitors. We're going to be more specific in the future. We will have synthetic memories we will be able to inject, and I see nothing wrong with this; it's like being vaccinated against smallpox. That's a learning mechanism; your body learns to reject the smallpox before it encounters it. Now there are limits to this. As far as I know, you can't really shape attitudes; what you are shaping is responses. But I think we are going to have some controls; that is, I would want the person to be allowed to decide what kind of injections he or she is going to get.

EVANS: More recently, you have begun to take some of these operant conditioning procedures and move into real life settings. Of course, widely disseminated recently was your prison project.

McCONNELL: There are three levels that I think psychologists try to analyze things at: mind, body, and social behavior. I was interested in all three, from the start. I started teaching in the area of social, and really, clinical work. I tried to get some research funds to do what we now call behavior modification with hospital patients. The worm work was not controversial so they gave me the money for worms, but they wouldn't give me any money for research on behavior modification with people. By 1970, I had learned enough about worms and rats to know that only a biochemist was going to make the next leaps forward. They didn't need me anymore. But suddenly, we began to realize we had built a technology of personal change that we hadn't had before. I guess I have always been an applied psychologist. I enjoy doing things with worms, but I prefer doing things with people.

EVANS: Were you influenced by B. F. Skinner (Evans 1968) at this time? Had you been reading his work?

McCONNELL: Skinner is the other really major influence in my life besides Hebb. I was asked by the Department of Defense to do a monograph in 1958. Its title was "Persuasion and Behavioral Change." I surveyed the entire field of experimental psychology to see what could be dredged up that might be of interest to the Department of Defense on how to change people, how to control them, how to shift their attitudes. And I discovered that there were a great many things that psychologists had been doing that could be applied.

EVANS: Where was that particular paper published?

McCONNELL: I eventually published it, of all things, in *The Art of Persuasion in Litigation Handbook* (McConnell 1966). That's a legal publication put out by the American Trial Lawyers Association. Trial lawyers were very interested in this, of course, because they've got to persuade the jury. Anyway, I read everything Skinner had written, and I admired the man greatly. I think he has some limitations, which are that he hasn't dared to go beyond the narrow scope of behaviorism, as we might call it, looking just at the physical responses of the organism. What I have tried to do in the last few years is to show that these techniques that Skinner developed so beautifully for training animals or for training people can be used to change thoughts and to change social attitudes and to change social behavior as well. Skinner, I think, was one of the first people to work with mental patients, using what we now call behavioral technology, or behavior modification. He tried programming them to act in a sane way. You have to be very hard-minded, look at the stimuli, look at the responses, and connect the two up. That's what Skinner did so well. The next thing that Skinner discovered was that if you reward people instead of punishing them, they learn faster. He gave us that. Skinner suggested, and we have now begun to prove, that many of the mental problems people have are a matter of training. They have been trained to do the wrong things. And this whole idea of rewarding people for doing the right things, instead of trying to give them some kind of cognitive insight alone, or punishing them when they did the wrong things, is one of the most powerful discoveries that anyone has made.

EVANS: How did you apply these ideas to the prison system, which is a social organization a little different from most?

McCONNELL: When I began teaching behavior modification in 1970, my students said they didn't want to sit in class and hear me discuss theory; they wanted to try it out themselves. So we started a laboratory class. We sent undergraduates into prisons and hospitals, into the Ann Arbor school system, into businesses, and a whole lot of places, and told them to try to get people to change their behaviors. Sometimes we called it psychotherapy; sometimes we called it education. God knows what it should be called. It's behavioral technology. Some of the students went into the federal prison near Ann Arbor, and began working with volunteer prisoners (McConnell 1970). The prison system assumes that you have awareness of your actions, which nobody does really, and that when you commit a crime, you do it deliberately, because you are evilly motivated, and the only way to change you is to punish you until you are purified of your evil intent. Then they'll let you out. The major reason that most people commit crimes, I think, is that they don't know a better way of getting what they want. You're not going to change our prison population or cut the crime rate until you learn to train these people in the skills they don't have, and that's what my students started doing. It was incredible. They found that if they gave nothing but rewards to prisoners—not punishment, because they get enough of that, God knows—the guys could learn rapidly, not only things like reading, writing, and arithmetic, but to control their impulses. They began to learn better strategies for getting along with the guards and for taking control of their own lives.

EVANS: In my discussion with Skinner (Evans 1968), we were dealing with this question of taking these operant principles and applying them to hospitals and to psychotherapy and so on, and we were discussing his concerns about these methods. And he said something like, "Well, the thing that bothers me is that some people believe if you know a few principles of stress and strain, you can build a bridge." And of course, as you described this, with your success, I'm sure that some people might get the impression that it's a little easier than it really is. You're really shaping a complex response.

McCONNELL: We applied first aid; that's all we did. Obviously, there are some cases that need the help of a skilled practitioner over a long period of time. But many can be helped simply by aiming them in the right direction, giving them a couple of strategies and they can take care of it themselves. When the students apply this first aid, believe it or not, they have about a 90 percent success rate. We have that documented. We have all the case histories, something like 800 cases. Another thing is that the students are the most creative resource that you have. I have now seen several senior therapists come in and watch my students, first with horror at the thought that an undergraduate is performing therapy with only two courses under his or her belt, and then with awe and amazement.

EVANS: There seems to be in the last, perhaps, three years, a shift in the area of behavior technology away from the limited, token, economy notion of reinforcement, the "M&M" candy notion. Is that true?

McCONNELL: Yes. Skinner focused on just the body; he wouldn't agree with that, but in my analysis that's what he did. M&M's are a creature-comfort reinforcement, and almost all of Skinner's work is aimed in that direction. (Programmed learning is maybe an exception, and maybe it isn't.) I think we have to realize that there are three classes of reinforcers. One is creature comforts. One includes intellectual pleasures: beautiful music, a lovely sunset, a painting, a chess problem. These are very rewarding to many people. This is what an educational psychologist would mean by the joy of learning, and I don't think that it is a secondary reinforcer; I think it's primary. And then we also have social relations, social interactions. They are just as primary in their own way as food and water. You and I have different reward schedules. You want some things more than I. We have many creature-comfort types— typically, small children, highly deprived prisoners, people in mental hospitals. . . .

EVANS: In concentration camps. . . .

McCONNELL: In concentration camps. They are deprived of more creature comforts and usually those are more powerful reinforcers, but not always. So you have to find out what the person wants. Good therapy, I think, uses all three types of rewards.

EVANS: What are some of the criticisms of your work that have bothered you the most?

McCONNELL: Two lines of criticism: the one we've already covered, that the worm work can't be replicated. It has been, again and again.

I'm just tired of hearing people say it can't be. But the real criticism that bothers me, I suppose, at the level of the behavioral technology, is that what we're doing is really a matter of brainwashing, that what it involves is punishing people, whipping them into shape, using psychosurgery and bad things. If there's anything I have learned, it's that these things don't work very well. The further you get away from aversive control, the better off you are. Punishment works only as far as I know, in one situation: where you have to set limits for the safety of the organism or society.

EVANS: What are you working on right now?

McCONNELL: Lots of things. I want to find better ways of writing textbooks so that students are turned on to learning instead of turned off, and the way to do that is to get the students to participate, so that learning is a contract. I have my own institute, my own clinic in Ann Arbor, with a colleague of mine, Chan Smith. He and I are training people in business and industry. The major theory in motivation in business is the "hot poker" theory. You tell a worker to do something and you stick a hot poker up his rear end if he doesn't. And that doesn't work very well. We've got to change our society so that we begin to reward people when they do something right instead of punishing them when they do something wrong. We're working in prisons; we're working in mental hospitals; one great area that we're having fun with now is in regular hospitals, training patients to get well, conditioning good health.

EVANS: In conclusion, Jim, in terms of what we've been discussing here, what would you particularly recommend among your many publications?

McCONNELL: The book that I've just published, called *Understanding Human Behavior* (McConnell 1974) lays this out probably better than anything else that I've written. And the early worm work is covered in a number of different places. There's a book by Georges Ungar (1970) that is perhaps as good as any.

REFERENCES

Byrne, W., et al. 1966. Memory Transfer. *Science* 153: 658–59.

Evans, R. 1968. *B. F. Skinner: the man and his ideas.* New York: Dutton.

Hebb, D. 1949. *The organization of behavior.* New York: Wiley.

James, W. 1950. *Principles of psychology.* New York: Dover.

McConnell, J., Jacobson, A., and Kimble, D. 1959. The effects of regeneration upon retention of a conditioned response in the planarian. *J. Comp. Physiol. Psychol.* 52: 1–5.

———. 1962. Memory transfer through cannibalism in planaria. *J. Neuropsychiat.* 3: 45.

———. 1966. Persuasion and behavioral change. In *The art of persuasion in litigation handbook.* West Palm Beach, Fla.: American Trial Lawyers Association.

———. 1970. Criminals can be brainwashed—now. *Psychol. Today* 14: 3, 11, 14–16.

————. 1974. *Understanding human behavior: an introduction to psychology.* New York: Holt.

Thompson, R., and McConnell, J. 1955. Classical conditioning in the planarian (*Dugesia dorotocephala*). *J. Comp. Physiol. Psychol.* 48: 65–8.

Ungar, G. 1970. *Molecular mechanisms in memory and learning.* New York: Plenum.

Section Four
Personality:
Behavioral
Social
Existential

The field of personality psychology has become increasingly vague since at various times almost all ideas concerning human psychology could be subsumed under this title. This section of the book includes a group of contributors whose work might be described as focusing particularly on behavioral, social, or existential perspectives as they relate to personality.

Perhaps one of the most integrated attempts to deal with personality is found in the work of Gordon Allport. His interests included the measurement of personality, the behaviors reflective of specific personality organization, and as evidenced by his classic work in prejudice and communication, the social determinants of personality as well. His study of values was not only examined at an objective level but began to be synthesized in his increasingly active examination of ultimate subjective or existential dimensions of personality.

Carl Rogers and Ronald Laing are two contributors who have focused on the subjective-existential-phenomenological components of personality.

Carl Rogers recognized that the psychotherapeutic process might actually increase the dependence of the patient on the therapist rather than contribute to his personal growth and independence; he evolved a therapeutic approach that he called nondirected or client-centered. Additionally, he attempted to look at personal growth in the larger milieu of society, such as our educational system. Presenting an avowedly humanistic philosophy, he, like Gordon Allport, had no doubt that the psychologist should not fear commitment to a value system.

Ronald D. Laing focuses quite brilliantly on the phenomenology of schizophrenia, and through this persistent focus, has begun to challenge basic concepts of the notion of mental illness. He has become increasingly skeptical of the prescribed analysis and treatment approaches of his psychiatric colleagues. His philosophic sophistication and persistent skepticism has led to much [undeserved] misinterpretation of his work.

In the more purely behavioral realm of personality analysis, certainly Albert Bandura and Hans Eysenck are at the forefront.

Albert Bandura, beginning his career as a clinical psychologist, like

Neal Miller in the previous section, began to recognize the need to examine the clinical behavior-modification process in more precise terms. The learning theory of Hull and Spence, and more recently, Skinnerian theory and the concepts of modeling and imitation have resulted in a broader, more socially oriented approach to behavior modification. His work in the study of aggression reflects in a particularly clear manner, a blending of concepts he calls social learning theory.

The work of Hans Eysenck, who also began his examination of clinical psychology through a Hull-Spence learning model, began to systemize this approach into what he finally called "behavior therapy." However, the diversity of Eysenck's work goes far beyond his interest in behavior therapy, as in the tradition of the British measurement psychologists; he has utilized factor-analysis approaches to personality measurement and has always attempted to rigorously relate such measurement to specific behavior.

Gordon Allport

(1897–1967)

The contributions of Gordon Allport to psychology represent perhaps the most integrated approach to personality theory of any contemporary psychologist. Educated at Harvard University, Professor Allport took his A.B. in 1919, spent a year teaching in Turkey, and then returned to Harvard to complete his Ph.D. in 1922. This was followed by two post-doctoral years in Europe. Except for a two year period at Dartmouth College, his entire career was spent at Harvard where he was the first Richard Cabot Professor of Social Ethics and was instrumental in the formation of the department of social relations. Involved in all areas of personality, Professor Allport's most significant contributions included the measurement, organization, and social determinants of personality, his classic work in prejudice and communication, and his approach to a systematic study of values. He was president of the American Psychological Association in 1939 and received the Gold Medal of the American Psychological Foundation and the Distinguished Scientific Contribution Award of the American Psychological Association.

S-O-R/The Nature of the O/Stimulus-Response versus Individual-Centered Psychology//A Frame of Reference/Traits//A Sense of Self/The Functional Autonomy of Motives//Who Am I?/A Sign of Growing Maturity/ Existentialism//An Element of Ignorance/The Nature of Prejudice// Extrinsic or Intrinsic Values/The Religious Dimension of Personality//How Are You Going to Know?/Personality Testing//

We begin the discussion as Dr. Allport reacts to the stimulus-response (S-R) versus the stimulus-organism-response (S-O-R) model, relating his answers to such areas as determinism and personal responsibility. "Man has a great deal more freedom than he ever uses," Dr. Allport explains, "because he operates out of habits, prejudices and stereotypes." He reevaluates his concept of traits in personality theory, distinguishing between nomothetic and morphogenic, as well as central, cardinal, and secondary traits. Our discussion of motivation

---

This discussion is an excerpt from the book *Gordon Allport: The Man and His Ideas* by Richard I. Evans. Copyright © 1971 by Richard I. Evans. Reprinted by permission of the publishers, E. P. Dutton & Co., Inc. Awarded the 1971 American Psychological Foundation Media Award in the Book Category.

leads to the concept of functional autonomy, and **Dr. Allport** clarifies self, ego, and proprium. We explore existentialism and the nature of man and the thinking that led to the study of prejudice. After defining prejudice and discrimination, **Dr. Allport** makes some suggestions about dealing with both areas, and the direction he feels is most productive of change. We discuss the religious dimension of personality, and he connects it with the extrinsic and intrinsic values of the individual. In conclusion, **Dr. Allport** explains why he thinks personality testing is a valuable tool for the psychologist and the way in which he believes it should be done.

EVANS: Dr. Allport, your writing and thinking has transversed an important shift in theoretical orientation in psychology, where the stimulus-response (SR) paradigm which de-emphasizes the organism has been increasingly challenged by the stimulus-organism-response (SOR) paradigm which attributes more importance to the organism and its characteristics. Do you feel that it would be possible for the young scholar to accept the validity of these two diverging streams of thought and still make some sense out of psychology?

ALLPORT: I think that he should first of all realize that the simple SR model is extremely attractive because it is based on a very healthy desire to know exactly what is going on, and both stimuli and responses can be measured quite accurately. On the other hand, it seems to me that with some nine trillion brain cells, what's going on inside the organism simply cannot be adequately depicted in terms of SR. I would argue for a small "s" and a small "r," but a very large "O," because it seems to me that all the interesting things in personality lie in the inferences we must make about what's going on in these intervening variables in terms of motivation, interests, attitudes, values, and so on. On the other hand, I may add one warning about the nature of "O." You could also consider the "O" as a being trying to establish an equilibrium of contradictory forces impinging on itself, and that "O" represents this homeostatic mechanism at work. If you consider the O as having tension-reducing propensities, or as establishing homeostasis or equilibrium, that is one view of O. Actually, however, I take a more proactive view of the nature of O. As I see it, it not only tries to establish equilibrium under some circumstances, but also attempts to maintain disequilibrium. It even goes out to seek disequilibrium in order to maintain tension. So your conception of the nature of the O forms the basis for your notion of what personality really is.

EVANS: Does this not also embrace the notion of personal responsibility or self-determinism? We might ask how much emphasis should the organism be given in the self-deterministic model of human behavior.

ALLPORT: You have leapt into the most difficult question of all—the problem that the philosophers call human freedom. Speaking as a psychologist and a scientist, I have to say that I think man has a great deal more freedom than he ever uses, simply because he operates out of habits, prejudices, and stereotypes, often going off, as it were, half-cocked. If he reflected and kept uppermost the selective set to ask himself, "Is this my style of life or isn't it?" he would have a lot more self-determinism than is reflected in the traditional materialistic, mechanistic view of man as a reactive being. Of course, our behavior is to some extent determined by society, heredity, and our organic nature, and we must acknowledge that; but beyond that it revolves around whether we consider O a proactive or just a reactive organism. I am inclined to think that the answer lies in the direction of proaction, thereby admitting into psychology the importance of such concepts as goals, purposes, intentions, plans, values, and the like. I would not, however, argue for the absolute untrammeled freedom espoused by some of the existentialists. The answer lies somewhere in the middle course.

EVANS: Dr. Allport, you have, of course, been identified with the personality trait and the way in which it can be used in assessing personality. It would be very interesting to know a little more about how you happened to develop this focus and how you feel about the label "trait psychologist" which some psychologists have given you.

ALLPORT: When I was a student just beginning to be interested in differential psychology, this field was most clearly represented by William Stern, who held that it is just merely a matter of measuring degrees of intelligence. Stern invented the I.Q. concept, which was a rating of degrees of intelligence or degrees of dominance, anxiety, and what not. That's been going on ever since. When I studied with Stern later in Hamburg, we developed the ascendence-submission dimension as an early personality test of the same sort. I liked to get at the dimensional aspects of values, and used the six values of Spranger (1928) as a base. I called these variables traits; there was nothing original about that. But to put a label of "trait psychology" on my work since then is to misrepresent it. I've been troubled by misinterpretation of the distinction between common traits and individual traits. At first I thought I could make clear the distinction between common traits, which are the abstracted trait categories we use for measuring personality, and the individual traits, which represent the way a given individual is actually organized. I found, however, that people merely doubled the use of the word "trait" and heard me to be suggesting traits again. Recently I've tried to change the terminology so that common traits would still be a valid field for research, but personal dispositions would focus on the morphogenic study of the individual in order to find out how he is organized. We have morphogenic and molecular biology, and I think the parallel represents the distinction I'm trying to make in psychology. It seems to me that to adequately distinguish these frames of reference, one could use nomothetic to mean general laws, principles, and dimensions, as opposed to morphogenic to mean the unique individual organism.

EVANS: You've made the point here that we should not become confused between common traits and the unique characteristics of the individual. You have, however, also written about central traits, cardinal traits, and secondary traits, and I wonder if you might distinguish among these for us.

ALLPORT: I didn't intend for these to become fixed classificatory schemes at all. It is simply a means to call attention to the fact that if you know one thing about a person's trait system, you could predict his attitude toward a great many other things. Most people have some important foci of development, but we can usually distinguish six or eight, and these would be more central traits. There would likely be secondary ones which are not as well integrated as the others, as well as reflecting situational and opportunistic expression. The trait categories I postulated are meant to be a sort of continuum between the very central, central, and more peripheral or accidental developments in the personality.

EVANS: The distinctive feature of organizing character on the basis of your system would be that you emphasize the uniqueness of the individual rather than his conformity to a set pattern of characteristics. You emphasize the uniqueness of the individual also in your concept of motivation. Many theorists still emphasize a biocentric theory of motivation which ascribes maintenance of the organism to physiological drives such as hunger, thirst, and so on, but allows for the development of various drives derived over time from these fundamental physiological drives. These would include the various social motives. It is about this point where your rather controversial concept of the functional autonomy of motives comes in. In your writings you have tried to explain that there are many drives, motives, or needs influencing our day-to-day behavior which are not clearly derived from the primary drives; that they are for the individual functionally autonomous, and become self-sustaining. To illustrate this point, you had a generation of students rather seasick as they read your description of the sailor who went out to sea and remained there long after his early *original* needs for going out to sea were outgrown. His continuing urge to go out to sea you suggest is an illustration of functional autonomy. Would you care to elaborate on this notion?

ALLPORT: To me it was simply a way of stating what was perfectly obvious to me, that motives change and grow in the course of one's life. I still can't understand why a person would challenge that basic proposition unless he were a die-hard believer in reactivity instead of proactivity, of homeostasis instead of transcendence, of balance or equilibrium instead of growth. To me it is more or less self-evident. I realized that it wasn't self-evident to others when I had to defend it and try to answer the very difficult question of how functional autonomy comes about. Most theories stress the importance of events which occur early in life through conditioning, and the analytical theory requires that the life be traced backward in time. But people are busily living their lives forward; they are oriented toward the future, and therefore, the psychologist cannot be correct if he's oriented entirely to the past, simply because his subject is not so oriented. One must have some proactive view of human motivation to explain plans and intentions, and self-image and long-range goals, which are not like those of childhood, and are not just conditioned reactions. They are proactions and plans, and it seems to me to be basic to a valid theory of personality that they be accounted for.

EVANS: Just to illustrate how functional autonomy works, could you give us an example of autonomous motivation in operation?

ALLPORT: Let's take, for example, the phenomenon of the son following in the father's profession, such as politics. I don't question that they might have had a father identification when they were six years old; most boys do. If daddy made a speech, the son would play that he made a speech; if daddy went to work, he would go out to work, and so on. But is that what sends senators to the Senate to work hard for what they believe in? Does their committee work represent an attempt to be daddy at age fifty? It seems perfectly ridiculous to me to believe that a normal person can be so motivated. But, giving Freud due credit, I can conceive of a neurotic who is still trying to step into daddy's shoes, or still trying to win mother's approval by making like daddy. But we would be able to distinguish this kind of neurotic motivation by its compulsive, inappropriate, and not age-related character.

When people ask how functional autonomy comes about, I have to say there are two different levels. There is first a perseverated mechanism in the nervous system which is evident in repeated observations, that what has started tends to continue. This kind of mechanism is well known even in lower animals, where you can establish a rhythm by training and then take away the training or the food or the reward, and the rhythm continues for a very long time. At the human level, we see that children are enormously repetitive. This kind of perseverated functional autonomy is a mechanism which feeds itself. But this does not fully satisfy me as a basis for behavior. I labeled another kind of functional autonomy "propriate functional autonomy," which refers to oneself. Perseverated functional autonomy is still within the sphere of reactivity; something stimulates, feeds back, and stimulates again—the person is reacting to himself, his own circuits, and not to outside stimuli. But we are, after all, also proactive, and given to a kind of functional autonomy that responds to interests, goals, purposes, and relates warmly to one's sense of self. This is what I call propriate functional autonomy. If you ask me how it comes about, I would have to say merely that it is the nature of the human organism.

EVANS: Your discussion of functional autonomy suggests that you would agree with the late Professor Kurt Lewin's (1936) emphasis on a contemporaneous, ahistorical view of personality and motivation. Is this correct?

ALLPORT: Yes. I think Lewin and I both stress contemporaneity of motives. What drives the individual must drive him now, and if the past is at all relevant it has to be incorporated into the present. We do have memories and skills that we call on under specific motivational conditions, and so the past can be active in the present. I think that Lewin and I would agree that in normal behavior, the regions of the personality under tension at a given moment are the motives, and they are affected very much by the field or the situation that one is in.

EVANS: The same growth factor that you postulate as necessary for functional autonomy would be needed to describe the concepts of self and ego, and in fact, focusing on ego autonomy is one important contemporary approach to understanding personality. Your concept of propriate, which relates to self and ego, while it implies this growth factor, doesn't appear to be exactly the same as ego or exactly the same as self. It seems to have a unique quality. I wonder if you would elaborate on this.

ALLPORT: To explain why I have coined the term "proprium," and especially the adjectival form, "propriate," I would say that in the literature I found at least eight different uses or definitions of ego and self. Both terms are practically interchangeable by different authors, so I don't think we can make a systematic distinction, even though all the meanings were acceptable. To avoid the question-begging approach involved in the usage of the words self or ego, I felt that we might take a word that is fresh so that every time it was used it wouldn't have to be defined, nor would it be cluttered with the baggage of former connotations of self or ego. But in my books, I do use self, especially in relation to the development of the self or sense of self evolving from childhood, and I feel it is an important construct.

EVANS: The developmental approach to the concept of self is not as broad in perspective as the notion of proprium as you have proposed it. What often happens when some one proposes a term that has growth connotations in psychology is that some individuals accuse him of being transcendental or even metaphysical, and while I'm certain you had no intention of proposing a metaphysical concept, I wonder how you would defend the concept of proprium against this kind of criticism.

ALLPORT: Anyone who says it's transcendental or mystical just hasn't read what I've written. I stated very carefully that the idea of an agent, a separate agent, whether metaphysical or mystical, is not what I intended. I've often said that proprium is an entirely operational construct which is necessary and can't be avoided in a systematic personality theory. I would define proprium in terms which might be considered phenomenological by saying it's that part of the personality which seems to be warm and central to the person, involving matters that are of importance in this life over and above the mere matters of fact in it. If you begin from the phenomenological core it can be demonstrated that this sense of proprium, when it is present, makes an operationally demonstrable difference in behavior.

EVANS: As soon as we discuss terms such as proprium, self, or ego we begin to relate to the existentialist or phenomenological points of view introduced into psychology by individuals such as Robert McCleod and Rollo May. The notions of phenomenology or existentialism cause us to ask to what degree must a psychologist be concerned with "under the skin" facets of the individual. Might we, for instance, go too far in introducing such nonoperational frames of reference into the science of psychology?

ALLPORT: To say that we go too far is a matter of subjective judgment. I think we can go a good deal farther than we have before we've exhausted the value that comes from reports of experience when they're done thoroughly. We've neglected subjective reports in psychology so long that I'm not immediately worried about being too phenomenological.

EVANS: When we examine a developmental model such as Freud's which postulated that the child at first is irrationally nondiscriminating and emerges slowly to a point where its own rationality begins to govern its behavior, we encounter the same problem of determinism. Even though the child has evolved what Adler called a style of life, he still seems to have introjected a great deal from his period of development when he was essentially dominated by irrational behavior. Can we accept such notions of the effects of early influences on present behavior? Certainly, virtually all contemporary developmental models, with the possible exception of Piaget's (Evans, 1973) (which views the child as being in a sense rational from the beginning), stress the importance of these chaotic early influences.

ALLPORT: We must look for truth somewhere in the middle. We sometimes, I think, much overdo the emphasis on early life. A factor important to the socialization process which has not yet been mentioned is the self-image of the individual. One's conception of what one is, one's proper style of life, must fit into the present style of being, and is an important factor in making or breaking habits and in forming attitudes, and so on. Individuals are in a constant process of becoming. Many factors enter into the process, including some mechanical learning out of habits from the past, but all these factors must be accounted for when we attempt to determine how personality becomes what it is. We may learn to keep to the right in traffic or how to run a machine or some skill which might be explained by traditional theory, but the concept of becoming includes also the self-image, maturation, identification, and all forms of cognitive learning. They must all be accounted for in an adequate theory of personality.

EVANS: You would be inclined to agree, then, with Jung's (Evans

1976*a*) discussion of the individuation process. He felt that individuation is an important process even into middle age, and his ideas are consistent with the emergence of the existential movement in that the individual begins to raise questions of "who am I," "what am I here for," and so on. Do you feel that it is a healthy thing for the individual to become more and more preoccupied with thoughts of his own existence?

ALLPORT: When you raise questions about aging, you almost invite me to speak introspectively, but I realize that you are getting at the increased length of life which allows a man more time for such questions. I would say that there are probably as many ways of aging as there are individuals because I argue for uniqueness at every stage of being. The Hindu psychologists tell us that it is very characteristic of older people to seek a fourth stage of life which is called meaning or liberation, but represents a disengagement from the activities of the first stages that are more pleasure—and success—seeking and doing one's duty. The fourth stage is the one you referred to which brings up the questions, "who am I," "what's it all about," "what next," and so on. It's a natural concern as one grows older, but not peculiar to old age alone. Perhaps it's characteristic of our times that the question will have a more subjective, personal tone to it. The Aristotelians asked the question, "what is man," and that led to all the sciences of man, but we today are asking it more personally, as "who am I." This shift of emphasis is part of the so-called existential trend of our times, and I don't think it's either good or bad, though it's probably good because we have a right to know the answer to both the questions, "what is man" and "who am I."

My one criticism of the existential movement is that it tends to be rather egghead and philosophical and ascribes to all human beings the same existential vacuum. The eggheads and the elite would give to all men their own anxiety, nausea, and alienation. I just don't think it's true that every man goes through this anxiety and anguish and alienation in his effort to find meaning. However, as the educational level increases, more people read more books, and ponder more the questions they encounter, and I suppose it's natural to have more and more of this type of concern.

EVANS: It's interesting that you suggest that this whole existential question could be the product of an intellectual culture. Though the question of existence is dealt with differently by different religions, another problem with existentialism is that it is very loosely defined. Each writer defines it differently and it may be that its only definition comes from within the individual and can't really be intellectualized at all.

ALLPORT: The movement is a broad one, of course, and solutions have been offered from both the atheistic and the theistic points of view. Some stress alienation and some stress the need for commitment and responsibility; some search for meaning, and others for different things. It's rather lately come to America, but the American version has a little less of the pessimistic or fatalistic flavor than the European existentialism. America has produced her own existentialists, but they are generally more hopeful that in confronting the mysteries of life, even when starting with anguish and despair, one can work out a commitment and a solution adequate to himself.

EVANS: Do you feel that man will arrive at a stage in development where he will become increasingly less concerned with this existential question?

ALLPORT: The history of ideas has always been a reflection of historical conditions: plagues, wars, etc. The danger of the atomic bomb and the terrible tragedies which it implies has thrown this century into a kind of reflective mood. I am inclined to think it's a sign of growing maturity to ask the question "who am I"; to ask whence and whither, without being overcome by the need to adjust to the realities of technological advances. It puts more strain on the personality to do the adapting and the socializing and to continue to meet the economic problems of life while at the same time going on as a human being to think about one's own nature and destiny.

EVANS: Dr. Allport, you've contributed a great deal over the years to the understanding of prejudice. Perhaps we might begin by asking you to define prejudice.

ALLPORT: Oddly enough, the best definition for prejudice is a slang one: "Prejudice is being down on something you're not up on." We can be down on something that we are up on, too. We can be against criminals, assassins, Hitler's gang, and so forth; and for good reasons— because they violate our values—we are up on them. But in prejudice there is always an element of ignorance—unwarranted hostility—or else it's not prejudice. Prejudice must be defined as having two variables— one is hostility, and one is ignorance or erroneous judgment. Let me add, of course, that there can be prejudice in favor of others.

When I wrote *The Nature of Prejudice* (1954), the problem of causation was so large that it took several years for me to figure out the table of contents for the book. There is no single, simple thing that causes people to be prejudiced. I've divided the causes into rough levels for the purpose of analysis: historical, sociocultural, character and personality factors, perceptual factors, and the qualities of the victim himself. For example, if you don't know anything about the history of slavery in this country, you wouldn't know much about the nature of current prejudice. And on the sociocultural level, factors including a way of life that gets established must be included with some of the distal factors which are actually translated into behavior. Psychologically, elements which entered into the character, structure of personality, attitude, and training of the individual must be considered, while perceptual elements such as the way individualism in the minority group is perceived are important. Finally, you must take into account the qualities of the victim himself because sometimes his behavior is perceived more or less corruptly and it puts an element of factuality into the judgment which may or may not support his prejudice. It's a very complicated question which would have to include perhaps eighteen to twenty distinguishable causal factors.

EVANS: And you see that these factors originate both from within the individual, his psychological makeup, and from the environment or culture in which the individual operates, resulting in a wide variety of interactive effects.

ALLPORT: Yes, but I would emphasize that the historical and sociocultural factors have to be translated into the nervous system of the individual. They don't act automatically. The term that is missing here to describe the interaction is conformity. We have never answered why people pick up the historical and sociocultural traditions and translate them into attitudes and behavior.

EVANS: Another question integrally related to prejudice is the concept of discrimination, toward the elimination of which we are spending a great deal of energy in our country. Would you, with your orientation toward the individual, be satisfied that merely changing the environment through legal means would be an effective means to cut down prejudice and/or discrimination?

ALLPORT: I would concede here a little to my sociological colleagues. If it's a matter of attitudes and prejudices, will we not have to effect changes in the education and exhortation of children to make long-range changes in prejudice? It does not seem to follow from what I have previously said because when an external situation is changed by fiat or through law, you may have eliminated discrimination but you have not necessarily also eliminated prejudice. After discrimination has been eliminated and people come into equal-status contact with one another, then their attitudes may be affected away from prejudice. I would not, of course, rule out intercultural education, or exhortation, or working with individuals, but I really feel it's more efficient to begin with a large-scale change in the social structure.

EVANS: Could we consider now the question of religion and the part it plays in the personality structure. There are some who feel that psychologists are not sympathetic to religion, but you have given the subject a great deal of thought and exposition.

ALLPORT: The study of religious values is an outgrowth of my interest in personality theory, which is the basic concern out of which all my professional work has come. In 1937, I postulated a general theoretical approach in my book, *Personality: A Psychological Interpretation* (1937), but since then a lot of special problems have arisen that must be dealt with: what is the nature of attitudes in personality structure; what can you do with personal documents; what is the formation of prejudice that makes it so central to personality structure; what about some of the major values, etc. The work I did on the Study of Values Test is an aspect of the interest in more complex levels of personality. Religion, obviously, belongs in the same category as one of the complex sentiments that many, if not most, people develop. It represents a problem of personality—perhaps a specialized part of personality—and I think it's ridiculous for a psychologist to neglect it or overlook its importance in the structure of personality. In order to bring religion into line with a comprehensive study of personality, I presented six lectures on the subject which were later published in the book *The Individual and His Religion* (1950).

EVANS: Would you summarize some of the main ideas you presented in those lectures to give us an insight into how you feel about the religious dimension of personality?

ALLPORT: I think it is helpful to take the developmental approach in this study. A child is totally incapable of understanding the abstraction of theology, and so he takes on the family religion simply as a matter of course, just as he takes to brushing his teeth or speaking the English language or taking on political sentiments. This is particularly true during the period of his close family identification between ages eight and eleven or so. Ordinarily the normal child begins after a while to question the family pattern simply because the statements are obviously abstract, and some of them sound rather outrageous to his literal-minded ears. Usually he goes through a period of questioning, but it's not that he's questioning religion as such. He's questioning what he thought his parents taught; he's questioning the dogmas as he understood them, not as the parents understood them. He's questioning his own childish approach, and that is the essential element for any personality if it is eventually to grow up. There are some, of course, in whom the childish formations and beliefs don't change; they go through life with essentially a juvenile, undeveloped religion. But about sixty percent, I should say, of the college students report having a very acute adolescent rebellion. What happens to them after that is subject to a wide variety of differential influences, and the personality develops in an individual style.

EVANS: The adolescent rebellion you refer to here is rebellion against what they believe to be some of the basic dogmas of religion?

ALLPORT: Yes, I'm glad you made that point clear. The adolescent think it's the parents' fault, so it takes its place among other emotional upheavals or rebellions he undergoes in his attempt to get away from parental domination. Then later he attempts to resolve this turmoil by a variety of means, such as adopting the same attitude his parents had when he has children of his own. This phenomenon often occurs around the age of thirty or so. The twenties are perhaps the least religious age of man.

EVANS: Several early studies investigating the effects of religion in the individual personality found a high correlation between religiosity and prejudice, which would seem to indicate that religion was narrowing the individual. Still our later study (Evans, 1952) has suggested that there might be two aspects of religion which operate differentially on the individual; the one reflected in more humanitarian concerns while the other is reflected in a more selfish aspect of religion. Do you feel that this notion, opening the possibility of a differential impact of religion, is consistent with your experience?

ALLPORT: We are presently engaged in a research project which deals with this very question. All research indicates that churchgoers on the average are much more prejudiced than nonchurchgoers, and that's a fact. It would seem to be a curious finding in view of the fact that most of the people who have devoted themselves to brotherhood are religiously motivated, and some good examples of this are Albert Schweitzer, Mahatma Gandhi, and Martin Luther King. There must be some kind of contradiction going on here, and so reviewing the research makes it obvious that we must distinguish between two kinds of religious orientation, the extrinsic value and the intrinsic value. When we tested for these dimensions using a scale for extrinsicness and one for intrinsicness, lo and behold, we found that the extrinsic attitude is correlated with prejudice, and the intrinsic is correlated with very low prejudice. I have to define extrinsic here as something that the person uses for his own purposes: to make friends, influence people, sell insurance, good times, prestige in the community, comfort, or wish fulfillment. He uses his religion in the same way that he uses his social groups and memberships. It's an exclusionistic point of view that can lead to prejudice because it is part of the fact that religion is solely for his benefit, and other people are not for his benefit. It's a very self-centered orientation and you would have to say a majority of people take their religion that way because the majority of churchgoers show this bigotry. On the other hand, there is a sizable minority whose attitude toward religion is quite the opposite; it plays an entirely different function for them because they serve it, it doesn't serve them. They have decided that the creeds and doctrines, including the doctrine of human brotherhood, are necessary for their value system, and they adopt for themselves the entire religious system, then live by it.

EVANS: Another area of current and continuing interest in psychology is the area of personality testing and measurement in that it seems to imply a nomothetic approach where the tester looks for common traits, as you call them. In order adequately to understand the individual, one must use phenotypical (descriptive) information, and yet at the same time know that it doesn't do adequate justice to the individual. Is there a means by which we can handle this dilemma?

ALLPORT: Yes, I've worked on that problem, and I think that I have the proper direction to look for an answer. We've simply neglected the study of personal dispositions which I think can be done purely quantitatively. For example, when Cantril asks people to define the best possible way of life for themselves and the worst possible way, then he puts those on a ladder of ten rungs. Then he asks the people where they stand now, where five years ago, and where they expect to stand two years from now. This gives him a morphogenic anchorage point, and indicates their best possible way of life. It's more than just a common trait. Another example is the case of personal documents which represents strictly morphogenic material. I have some very fascinating material called *Letters from Jenny* (1965) which one of my former students, Professor Al Baldwin, used in a course to count the relationship of ideas in Jenny's mind.

The approaches used by people like Dr. Magda Arnold with the Thematic Apperception Test try to get at personal characteristics through a fairy-story sequence which serves as a diagnostic indicator, but is not scored routinely according to an established pattern of responses. These are problems which have not yet been adequately resolved.

EVANS: Some people have suggested that this projective testing emphasizes the unconscious unduly, making it difficult to validate them properly. Do you feel there is a legitimate place for them in psychological research?

ALLPORT: Yes, I certainly do feel they have a place. What I've said about them is that they should never be used without also using direct methods. If a person, for example, is consciously and unconsciously anxious, it means something very different from when he's only unconsciously anxious. How are you going to know that you're tapping the unconscious unless you know also what is conscious? I think I would be dogmatic and say that we should never use projective tests unless we also use direct methods of interview or pencil-and-paper tests in order to make comparisons between them.

EVANS: Would you feel this way also about the use of dream interpretations?

ALLPORT: Yes, I think so.

EVANS: Incidentally, we couldn't engage in a discussion of personality measurement without pursuing further the significant personality measure which you yourself have developed along with Professors Vernon and Lindzey, the Study of Values. It's another example of the use of ostensibly nomothetic measurement designed to get at individuality, is it not?

ALLPORT: That particular instrument is a curious hybrid. Actually, that instrument stands halfway between dimensional and morphogenic methods in a curious respect. There are, at the outset, six common traits: the theoretical, aesthetic, social, political, religious, and economic. These were defined by Spranger (1928) originally, and our test invites you to indicate the relative strength of these six values in your own personality. Consequently, your score cannot be compared with anyone else's because the test reflects relative strengths of those values within your own personality. We begin with an instrument which measures six common traits, but end with a profile that is strictly personal and individual.

EVANS: In a different vein, Dr. Allport, would you share with us your feelings concerning the contributions you have made to psychology that you feel to be the most important?

ALLPORT: It seems odd, perhaps, but I have never thought about this matter at all. All my work has focused on personality theory, particularly on the structure and the motivation of the personality. Everything has been focused around the central question of the nature of the human being. I have attempted to get reasoned empirical answers that shed some light on the issue, and they have come from different directions.

REFERENCES

Allport, G. W. 1937. *Personality: a psychological interpretation.* New York: Holt.

————. 1942. *The use of personal documents in psychological science.* New York: Social Science Research Council Bulletin 49.

————. 1943. The ego in contemporary psychology. *Psychol. Rev.* 50: 451–78.

————. 1950. *The individual and his religion.* New York: Macmillan.

————. 1954. *The nature of prejudice.* Cambridge: Addison-Wesley.

————. 1955. *Becoming: basic considerations for a psychology of personality.* New Haven, Conn.: Yale University Press.

————. 1961. *Pattern and growth in personality.* New York: Holt.

————. 1965. *Letters from Jenny.* New York: Harcourt.

Allport, G. W., and Vernon, P. E. 1933. *Studies in expressive movement.* New York: Macmillan.

Evans, R. I. 1952. Personal values as factors in anti-Semitism. *J. Abnorm. Soc. Psychol.* 47: 749–56.

————. 1976a. *Jung on elementary psychology.* New York: Dutton.

————. 1973. *Jean Piaget: the man and his ideas.* New York: Dutton.

Lewin, K. A. 1936. *Principles of topological psychology.* Trans. F. Heider and G. M. Heider. New York: McGraw-Hill.

Spranger, E. 1928. *Types of men.* New York: Stechert.

Carl Rogers

(1902–)

Carl Rogers' belief that the psychotherapeutic process should contribute to personal growth and independence led to his formation of client-centered or nondirective therapy, an approach that has generated a number of highly creative developments in psychotherapy, psychology, and education. Dr. Rogers took his B.A. from the University of Wisconsin and received the Ph.D. from Columbia University's Teachers College in 1931. He held positions at Ohio State University, the University of Chicago, and the University of Wisconsin prior to his present post as fellow of the Center for the Study of the Person. Here he continues his research, writing, and exploration of new approaches to therapy. Dr. Rogers was President of the American Psychological Association in 1955, and received that organization's Distinguished Scientific Contribution Award in 1956.

Motivation: A Basic Tendency Toward Growth/Perception: All We Know Is What We Perceive/This Desire to Grasp Something Meaningful/Redefining the Unconscious: A Continuum//Self: Acceptance and Awareness/ Actualization/Real Versus Ideal Self/Congruence versus Incongruence// Client-Centered Therapy/A Deep Sense of Communication/The Therapist/ Congruence/Acceptance/Empathy/Group Therapy//The Mysteries of the Human Condition/Science Versus Scientism//Self-Determination/The Awareness to Make Choices/The Encounter Group/Today's Applications and a Warning About the Future//

Dr. Rogers and I discuss such basic principles as motivation, perception, and learning. He describes the development of his theories in these areas, the ways in which they differ from more traditional models, and the effectiveness of these theories in generating practical applications and new ideas. He discusses the growth of his concept of self, elaborating on the real and ideal self and the notions of congruence and incongruence. We then talk about client-centered therapy and the impact of his work in this area on psychotherapy.

He emphasizes the need for a deep sense of communication between therapist and client and the importance of the therapist's own self-understanding and self-acceptance. He compares the effectiveness of individual and group therapy and the special uses of each. Looking at the field of behavioral science today, he offers both a criticism and a challenge: "There are really only a few psychologists who have contributed ideas that help to set people free, making them psychologically free and self-responsible, encouraging them in decision making and problem solving." We discuss the notions of self-determination and the relative effects, cultural, biological, and environmental influences, and Dr. Rogers suggests ways to develop the awareness necessary to make choices. We conclude the discussion with a look at encounter groups, encounter-group training, and future implications of this type of therapy.

EVANS: Dr. Rogers, I'd like to relate some of your views to three of the important dimensions that are almost always dealt with in psychology—motivation, perception, and learning. Beginning with motivation, in psychology we have tended to define this as all conditions which arouse, direct and sustain the organism. This generally is interpreted as a homeostatic model, taken from biology—that the organism seeks to reduce tensions and maintain a state of equilibrium. I gather that your theory is not developed out of this particular approach to motivation. Is that correct?

ROGERS: Yes, I do not agree with that point of view because I think the organism is definitely not trying to achieve *stasis*.

EVANS: In other words, in not accepting this homeostatic model, you feel that man is almost striving for tensions rather than seeking to reduce his tensions?

ROGERS: Always. I think there is plenty of evidence now that this is true. In man, we call it curiosity. In lower animals, it's a tendency to seek more complicated stimuli rather than simple ones.

EVANS: Let's look at needs as they have been studied in psychology. There have been attempts to look at very specific needs, attempts to develop an understanding of how they come about and develop. For example, McClelland (1953) deals with need for achievement. Do you think there is a value to psychology in taking a specific need and tracing back to early childhood patterns that contribute to its development?

ROGERS: No, I think it was of value to McClelland and I think there is truth, some truth, in all such approaches. However, rather than try to comment on such approaches to motivation, I'd rather say something about my own view of motivation. The much more basic thing is that every organism has a tendency to maintain itself, to enhance itself if possible, eventually to reproduce itself. To me, that basic tendency toward growth, toward maintaining and enhancing the organism, is the central aspect of all motivation. Now, you can say, yes, and some of that seems to be describable as a need for achievement and so it cer-

tainly is channeled into a sexual drive, and so forth. I'd prefer to emphasize what to me is much more basic than any of those single concepts.

EVANS: Of course, the homeostatic model to which you have been
taking some exception was basic to Freudian theory. Since so many
writers have cited your work as an "alternative to Freud," it would be
interesting to get your reactions to some of Freud's views. Let's start
with his construct of the unconscious. Particularly in his early work,
Freud (1953) seemed to see man as primarily irrational rather than
rational in the sense that most of man's behavior is unconsciously determined. In fact, he introduces the concept of over-determinism, which
suggests that man does nothing by accident—that everything he does
has unconscious determinants. How do you regard this construct of the
unconscious?

ROGERS: I think that I see the same sort of phenomena that Freud
saw, for which he developed this concept. I think that psychologists in
general, and perhaps psychology students especially, tend to make things
out of these concepts when they are really attempts by someone to
understand an observable set of phenomena. I'd prefer to think of a
range of phenomena: first, those in sharp focus in awareness right now—
the height of consciousness; secondly, a range of material which could be
called into consciousness, that you really know and can call into consciousness but you don't have in "figure" right now—it is in the "ground"
or background; then, finally, some phenomena which are more and more
dimly connected with awareness, to material that is really prevented
from coming into even vague awareness because its coming into awareness would damage the person's concept of himself.

EVANS: So in a way, you're redefining Freud's views of the unconscious in a more rational sense.

ROGERS: Yes. You see, I feel that whether or not I totally agree or
disagree with Freud's concept of the unconscious is, in itself, not very
helpful. I'd rather point out that the way I conceptualize the same kind
of phenomena is along this spectrum I just mentioned: a continuum
from material that is sharply in focus to the individual at the immediate
moment to material that would be too threatening to even permit into
the awareness at all.

EVANS: Do you feel that early childhood experiences can continue
to determine the individual's behavior over and over again? Do you think
they are that powerful in their impact?

ROGERS: Yes, I think that early experience is a powerful force. Attitudes and values that are interjected from the parent do have a continuing influence and consequently would repeatedly influence behavior.
You see, all along through here, I'm objecting to putting hard-and-fast
labels on these processes. I don't like the pigeonholes that Freudian and
other theories have promulgated. I think people handicap their thinking
when they think in terms of so many labels. I'd rather they observe the
phenomena themselves.

EVANS: I mentioned earlier another central area in psychology, perception. You are certainly aware of the rather interesting developments in the area of perception in the last few years. From an interest in the more precise studies of perception which merely emphasized the study of sensory processes by relating the individual's response to a very specific stimulus, we have moved to examining the individual's overall experience in its more naive, natural state. This phenomenological approach is more interesting to many psychologists today than very precise reactions to specific stimuli. Is this movement to phenomenology in line with your own interests?

ROGERS: Yes, very definitely. I think that I am really characteristic of the trend you mentioned. I recognize the narrow field of perception as a neurological event very worthy of study, but it is of relatively little interest to me. I am more interested in the gestalt of what the person perceives in his environment and in himself. One thing that seems very true to me is that there is no such thing as a perception without a meaning. That is, the human organism immediately attaches a meaning to whatever is perceived. I may, out of the corner of my eye, see a plane in the distance. But if I turn my head that way, I discover it's a little gnat flying close by. In other words, in each case I attach a meaning to that perception immediately, even though it may be an erroneous meaning, as in the first case. For me, the perception is reality as far as the individual is concerned. I don't even know whether there is an objective reality. Probably there is, but none of us every really know that. All we know is what we perceive, and we try to test that in various ways. If it seems to be perceived in the same way from several different aspects, we regard it as real.

EVANS: We've briefly discussed motivation and perception, two central constructs in psychology. Another fundamental construct is learning. It's clear from looking at your work that you have not ignored learning and have been very interested in it. As in perception, there is a spectrum in learning theories. At one end, we have what might be called cognitive learning which emphasizes the individual's experiences and cognitions and their development and organization. The other extreme attempts to stress the behavior of the organism rather than its experience and cognitions. You would be more interested in the individual's experience as we study learning and would not be content to focus primarily on behavior. Is that correct?

ROGERS: Yes, I certainly would be closer to that view. I've never been particularly interested in the atomistic theories of learning. However, I think that the kind of view that I have of learning is not entirely cognitive, either. I think it is holistic, that the individual learns as a whole, which includes the nature of the stimulus and the response as well as the individual's cognition and affect. As I mentioned earlier, this desire to enrich the stimuli with which one is faced is a very deep desire. Out of it grows our whole desire for play. I have known prominent scientists who are strongly motivated by that notion of play. They like to play with new ideas, new theories, new possibilities, new hunches. I think this desire for learning, this desire to grasp something that is meaningful to the self, to the person at the moment, is something that needs to be nurtured rather than molded. That's why I grow a little fearful of some of the possible results of the use of Skinner's theory, and his notion of "operant conditioning," which focuses primarily on modifying the behavior of the organism. Rather than being planned, as Skinner would have it, I believe that learning should be highly spontaneous and should occur as the person feels that which is to be learned is related to his own needs and his own desire to enhance himself.

EVANS: So, aren't you saying somewhat the same thing about learning that you said about perception? The precise study and analysis of this process is not the really important factor because the learning process is more complex than more precise analysis can reveal.

ROGERS: Well, you're giving one definition to precision. I think that we can make precise studies of complex phenomena, too. I would be interested in seeing more precise studies of the way in which the human being reaches out to grasp material which has meaning to him. But I think that to be precise in the atomistic fashion is a matter of less interest.

EVANS: In looking more specifically at some of the principal ideas with which you deal in your own writings and research over the years, it seems that you were among the earliest group of individuals in psychology to stress the self. Of course, self may be defined in many ways. What does the concept of self mean to you?

ROGERS: I think I might lead up to that by saying why I became interested in that particular construct. I certainly didn't start psychological work being interested in anything as vague as the self. To me, that seemed like old-fashioned introspectionism. I was really forced to examine self and forced to define it for myself, because my clients in therapy kept using that term in all kinds of significant ways. They'd say, "I think I've got a pretty solid self underneath this kind of phony exterior," or, "I'd be terribly afraid of getting to know my real self." They showed in all kinds of ways that for them, self was a significant construct. I felt I should take a more direct look at it. To me, the self includes all of the individual's perceptions of his organism, of his experience, and of the way in which those perceptions are related to other perceptions and objects in this environment and to the whole exterior world.

EVANS: In the history of psychology, many individuals such as Carl Jung (Evans 1976a), as he discussed the individuation process, viewed the self in terms of a process of growth toward an actualization. Kurt Goldstein (1939) formulated this notion in his concept of self-actualization. Your view of the self also takes into account this notion of growth, does it not?

ROGERS: Yes, ideally, the organism is always endeavoring to actualize itself. Of course, this is what I was referring to earlier when we discussed motivation. When the self is aware of what is going on in the organism, then it keeps changing, growing and developing in the same way that the organism does. In most of us, the static aspects of the self are what really constitute maladjustment. Maladjustment would result if I persisted in holding a set view of myself which doesn't correspond with what's actually going on in my organism. An extreme example relates to a boy I knew a long time ago. He had been raised in a very strictly religious home. He had no sex feelings or sex desires that were a part of his self-picture. I saw him because he was arrested for lifting the skirts of little girls. In other words, his organism was experiencing all kinds of sexual curiosity and desire, but as far as his self-picture was concerned, that was not a part of it at all. When he was arrested, he said that it couldn't have been him and that he couldn't have done it. In the strictly technical sense, his self-picture couldn't do it, and didn't do it. In that sense, he was right, as his organism was experiencing all these drives and acting on them. Now to change that to a picture of adjustment, he would need to be aware of it and accept his sexual drive as well as the other aspects of himself. Then his picture of himself would match what was going on within his organism, and I would say that he would then be much closer to psychological adjustment. Self-actualization implies that the person is acceptantly aware of what's going on within and is consequently changing practically every moment and is moving on in complexity.

EVANS: Are you really suggesting that a balance among the "selves" that may exist in the person is somehow achieved?

ROGERS: Yes, but it should be mentioned that some students of mine stressed too much, perhaps, the notion of different selves, although I don't quarrel with that idea particularly. This idea hasn't had as much meaning for me as the notion of a more complex unified picture of self which keeps expanding to include new experiences, even though some experiences may be shut out as being too threatening. It seems that each of us endeavors to preserve the concept or picture that he has of himself and that a sharp change in that picture is quite threatening. That really is what therapy is all about—to help drop the barrier so that a person can realize, "Yes, I do have these parts of myself and parts of my experience that I have hitherto thought were totally unacceptable."

EVANS: In this same respect, how would you relate your terms *ideal self* versus *real self* to our discussion?

ROGERS: Those terms grew up in an attempt to measure the self-perception. I might say that one reason I was so reluctant to use the concept of the self was that if I got into something that vague, it could never be measured. We could never do research on the self. That's why William Stephenson's (1953) development of the Q-sort came along at just the right moment, as far as I was concerned. Here was a way of getting an objective picture of this highly subjective phenomenon—the self. Then we realized that a person does not value every aspect of himself, so we asked the subjects in our research to sort the Q cards for a picture of the self they would like to be, which gave a picture of the ideal self as compared with the self as currently perceived. That proved to be quite a valuable way of bringing objectivity into the study of this ephemeral phenomenon. When you get the valued self as against the perceived self, all kinds of interesting comparisons can be made.

EVANS: Based on your description of the self, there are obviously certain important resolutions that the human organism must undergo. To delve a bit more deeply into this, you have introduced an interesting polarity—congruence versus incongruence—to describe this process of integration of self and experience. What do you actually mean by congruency versus incongruency?

ROGERS: Incongruence results when the individual's experience is quite discrepant from the way he has organized himself. A common example is the person who is convinced that he's intellectually inferior. He may actually do creative and good things that show he has a fine intellect, but he can't believe those. The discrepancy between the picture he has of himself and what he is actually experiencing is called incongruence. What we are working toward in counseling or therapy is a greater congruence of self and experience so that the individual is able to be aware of what he's experiencing, which means that he is not too defensively organized. He's able to be aware of even things which might change his concept of himself and can organize those into the Gestalt of the experience in regard to self. The term may also be used in relationship to congruence in the therapist, which is very important in the relationship. It is very important for the therapist to be himself in the therapeutic relationship. He, too, may be an incongruent person in other ways, but it's important that in the therapeutic relationship he should be what he is experiencing. Otherwise, he comes across to the client as a little bit phony or somewhat of a facade, and therapy is not nearly so likely to take place. So one description I've given of what it means to be congruent in a given moment is to be aware of what's going on in your experiencing at that moment, to be acceptant toward that experience, to be able to voice it if it's appropriate, and to express it in some behavioral way.

EVANS: You've introduced the notion of psychotherapy in the answer to this last question, Dr. Rogers, and this leads us to one of the most obvious areas of discussion that one would ever have with you. Your work has had such visible impact, it would be difficult to find anyone who has ever had anything to do with any type of profession relating to interpersonal relationships who is not aware of it. In your book, Counseling and Psychotherapy, (Rogers 1942) you were talking about non-directive counseling, and as time passed, you began using terms like "client-centered" psychotherapy. Can you trace in more detail the evolution of this important contribution?

ROGERS: I guessed you might be raising some questions along that line, and I was thinking about it in terms of the books that I've written. It really goes back further than you mentioned, because my book, *Clinical Treatment of the Problem Child*, which was really written in 1936 and 1937 and published in 1939, shows where I stood at that point. I was working with children then and my whole aim was to manipulate the conditions under which the child lived so as to improve his adjustment. We made a diagnosis of the child's situation. We developed a treatment plan. We brought in all the different agencies, the school, the courts, whatever was needed to make sure that the plan was carried through. So that shows my approach at that time, at least to the child, was on the whole a planful but basically manipulative approach. But you'll find traces in that book of a beginning notion of something a little more than that, which attempted to get in touch with the individual client with whom one is dealing. Then by 1942 when *Counseling and Psychotherapy* came out, quite a little of that was still directed negatively: "Don't diagnose, don't advise, don't interpret." The central theme was the notion that the potential for better health resided in the client, and it certainly was quite a technique-oriented book. The counselor's responses were to be of the sort which would enable the client's potential to develop. Then *Client-Centered Therapy* was written in 1949 and 1950 and published in 1951. There the hypothesis was becoming a little more sophisticated—that the counselor's basic premise was that the individual has sufficient capacity to deal with all those aspects of his life which come into awareness. There was a great deal of stress on both the philosophical and attitudinal characteristics of the therapist, and a definite move away from techniques with perhaps a bit of groping toward a close personal relationship. It was at that time that I began to formulate the three conditions of the therapy which I'll mention a little more fully later on. Then in 1961, when I published *On Becoming a Person*, which contained papers from 1953 to 1960, I had come to recognize quite fully that the therapist must be present as a person in the relationship if therapy is to take place. It is a much more I-Thou kind of relationship that develops between the therapist and the client filled with the same philosophy of not imposing.

EVANS: Martin Buber (1965) used these I-Thou terms earlier. Can you define the terms as they have become most meaningful to you?

ROGERS: I think that some of Buber's phrases would do the best job. When there is a real trendless immediacy in the relationship, when you're aware of nothing but this person and he's aware of nothing but you, and there is a deep sense of communication and unity between the two of you, that's the thing I refer to as I-Thou relationship.

EVANS: Which is in contrast to what?

ROGERS: In contrast to an I-It relationship where I'm seeing the client as a complex object, a machine whose functions may be in disrepair in certain ways. The whole diagnostic look at an individual is in sharp contrast to the I-Thou kind of relationship.

EVANS: Emerging from this I-Thou relationship, of course, was your idea of how important compassionate non-direction by the therapist was, instead of direction. In fact, you've been accused of being so non-directive that you wouldn't respond to a client's literal cry for help. Would you say today that you have perhaps qualified somewhat this notion of being non-directive?

ROGERS: No. I think perhaps I enriched it, but not really qualified it. I still feel that the person who should guide the client's life is the client. My whole philosophy and whole approach is to try to strengthen him in that way of being, that he's in charge of his own life and nothing that I say is intended to take that capacity or that opportunity away from him. It is changed in this respect, that I would try to be aware of my own feelings and express them as my feelings without imposing them on him. I would express even negative feelings. I might tell a client, "I'm really bored with what you're saying." It doesn't guide him. It does provide him with some rather jolting data which he must handle in some way or other.

EVANS: Would you discuss the technique you feel is necessary to psychotherapy?

ROGERS: We've gradually built up a fairly solid theory, and backed it up with some pretty satisfactory research which shows that if these conditions are not the ultimate or best statement of what fosters personal growth, they are at least an approximation of it. The existence of these three conditions is very important to the relationship. First, and most important, is therapist congruence or genuineness—his ability to be a real person with the client. Second is the therapist's ability to accept the client as a separate person without judging him or evaluating him. It is rather an unconditional acceptance, that I'm able to accept you as you are. The third condition is a real emphatic understanding. That's where the term *reflection* was used. If it is simply reflection, that's no good. That's just a technique. It must be a desire to understand empathically, to really stand in the client's shoes and to see the world from his vantage point. If some of that can be communicated to the client, that I do really see how you feel and understand the way you feel, that can be a most releasing kind of experience. The effect that can have is really fascinating. It is this aspect that enables the process of therapy to go on.

EVANS: There has been a tremendous revolution in our whole conception of psychotherapy, and obviously your work has contributed to this. Increasingly we have moved away from individual face-to-face therapy into the area of group therapy. Group therapy is still growing by leaps and bounds. Aside from group therapy as such, variations of group encounter techniques such as sensitivity training, an out-growth of the group dynamics orientation, have taken on new importance. Even more broadly, the whole personal growth movement has moved into what we call the encounter group. Dramatic variations, such as nudity among participants, touching, massaging, spiritual and various transcendental dimensions are becoming a part of group encounters. In other words, in terms of trying to develop this interpersonal encounter you've been talking about, it seems that suddenly the message is: "Yes. Use every technique of communication, tactual, visual or what have you." How do you see yourself in regard to this whole movement?

ROGERS: Let me focus on my encounter-group aspect of it because, as you know, I've completed a book on that (Rogers 1970) and it's a field in which I'm very interested and very much involved. I think that in many ways it can, and in some respects has, gone completely wild, and I regret that. In its more solid aspects, it's one of the most significant social inventions of this century because it is a way of eliminating alienation and loneliness, of getting people into better communication with one another, of helping them develop fresh insights into themselves, and helping them get feedback from others so that they perceive how they are received by others. It serves a great many useful purposes. In my own work with encounter groups, I have very much the same theory and philosophy that I've been talking about. As a group facilitator, I would try to hold much the same attitudes that I was describing as effective in individual psychotherapy. And one reason for my great interest in encounter groups is that I have seen very positive results from them in a relatively short space of time.

EVANS: What are some of the fears that you have about this movement? It seems to have gone beyond the bounds of the rational orientation that you've just described. Do you think there's some danger here that these extremist offshoots could actually set this whole movement back seriously?

ROGERS: Yes, I think that's a definite possibility. I don't really object, basically, to people trying various approaches—Zen, mysticism, even nude groups if they want to. The social effect that will have, though, is going to be very bad because I think the general public may get turned off and feel that all groups are bad.

EVANS: I recall a conversation that I had with Sir Julian Huxley in London a few years ago which suggested something that's both challenging and disturbing to the behavioral sciences. He used a thermometer analogy. He pointed out how our world is increasingly jeopardized by problems such as pollution and the possibility of nuclear war for which solutions will depend largely on knowledge of human relations. Our knowledge of the technology which created these problems registers high up on the thermometer. Our knowledge of human relations necessary to solve these problems barely registers above zero on that thermometer. Do you share his pessimism? Is the gap between potentially destructive technical knowledge and knowledge of human relations too wide to resolve?

ROGERS: I have a great deal of confidence in man's potential for resolving his own problems. This grows out of my experience in therapy and in groups. But that confidence is based on the condition that the person is really aware of the facts. What really troubles me about today's society is too little awareness of all the facts. I feel that a great many people—politicians, government officials, industry, extreme right wing, extreme left wing—are all in the business of concealing facts. I don't know if man will have the facts available to him to make sensible and sound decisions in this very crucial period. Someone asked me not long ago if I was an optimist or a pessimist in regard to mankind. I responded that I had enormous confidence in the individual, and in the small group, but for the reasons I've given, my attitude toward the future of our culture is that we're on a knife-edge balance. I don't know whether we will make it or not. If there should be, say, a right-wing take-over—which I regard as probably much more likely than a left-wing take-over—psychologists would have a great deal to contribute to anyone who took over the dictatorship. Psychologists have prided themselves in predicting and controlling behavior; they could instruct a dictator in manipulating public opinion and molding behavior. When you try to figure out the contributions of psychology or the behavioral sciences to a viable democracy, that is a much more difficult thing. There are really only a few psychologists who have contributed ideas that help to set people free, making them psychologically free and self-responsible, encouraging them in decision-making and problem-solving.

EVANS: You would say that one of the problems is the very lack of commitment of the psychologist. You're almost saying that he's hiding behind science.

ROGERS: That's right. I feel it's so true that it hurts. He is clearly rejecting the possibility of trying to build a science as other sciences have been built, through careful naturalistic observations first, then more and more refined approaches to the problem. One leap will make it into the minutely refined methodology of an advanced science, and in his heart of hearts, I think he knows he doesn't belong there. Psychology is not that far advanced, so he's an insecure scientist who does have more of a scientism than does a true science. He isn't particularly commited to any social view of man or man's problems. He's fearful of doing anything that would really look into the mysteries of the human condition. He wants to just stick to the things he's sure he can measure and measure exactly.

EVANS: There is renewed interest in the free will versus determinism issue generated by B. F. Skinner's book, *Beyond Freedom and Dignity* (1971). Individuals argue that Skinner posits an ultimate social-environmental determinism, which says that man is almost completely shaped by his environment. Freud and the biologists who influenced him, and many biologists today, continue to believe that man is a product of his genetic capability, that in spite of all other influences the biological make-up of man ultimately controls him. Of course, in psychology, we are inclined to conclude that all these factors converge in the individual. How do you resolve this determinism issue?

ROGERS: I suppose I would say that I am not an extremist along those lines, but it's true that I focus on the self-deterministic rather than social-environmental or genetic-deterministic values in my training of students. I'll try to explain what I mean. There is no doubt that our genetic inheritance sets certain limits on what an individual is going to be and become. Those limits are more capable of being stretched than we had supposed, but there are limits. There's no question in my mind that we are very much shaped by what happens to us in our childhood, in our family life, and in our contact with society. You only have to think of what ghetto living does to an individual to realize what a curse he's been shaped by to a considerable extent. But then, there is also the fact that in the present moment, it is the person himself who is able to understand those factors that have contributed to who he is, and to choose his own future. I think as the person becomes aware of these various factors in his background, he can make realistic and sensible choices as to how he's going to both live with, and transcend the circumstances of the past.

EVANS: Looking back at your work, even as you're still so active, what do you perceive as your most important contribution?

ROGERS: One thing that comes to mind at once that often has amazed me is that I seem to have enunciated principles in regard to interpersonal relationships that have been useful to an incredibly wide spectrum of different groups. That must mean something. It means something to me to know that business executives read my stuff, educators at all levels, psychiatrists, psychologists, social workers, priests and ministers. The range of impact that my work has had is fantastic. I stand in awe of that myself, and the only thing I can attribute it to is that they seem to feel that I have voiced some principles, if you will, of interpersonal relationships, of the way to promote growth and development in people in any situation, which they've found useful in a very wide variety of professional groups. I suppose one other contribution that I've made is a very simple one in one way, but I think it's had quite a wide influence, and it is the fact that I have been willing to pay attention to the raw data of interpersonal relationships: recorded interviews, all that kind of thing. It has given courage to some others to stop dealing only in abstractions, and to really get down to the basic raw data, and then to begin to theorize and build from that. I guess something I take some pride in is that I always wanted to get close to the raw data. I've not been a person who lives happily in a completely abstract world. I suppose related to this fact are my efforts to make objective studies of very subjective phenomena. When I first came into the field of psychology, the thought that anyone could study a thing like empathy or congruence, or anything of that sort, would have seemed utterly ridiculous.

EVANS: We are getting to the point where we are writing primers for the individual on how to shape and modify behavior, or come to grips with his true, humanistic inner being. Do you think that we know enough now in either of these approaches to hand a primer to a layman, show him a film or two, and provide insights that imply, "O.K., now you, too, can do this"?

ROGERS: No, I don't think so. I'll just speak about what you call my end of it. I think that one reason I say no to your question is that the whole encounter-group movement is an experiential type of learning, and will never be fully captured within the covers of any book, primer or otherwise.

EVANS: What about those who direct, supervise and consult in the process of developing such groups? Do you think that we should maintain standards of minimum training or experience for them? Do you think that we could almost allow anyone to begin practicing this "art" now?

ROGERS: No, I think that they do need training, but I think the training that they need is not typical or conventional training. It is more experiential. As for setting up minimum standards and so on, that's a very knotty question. I lean further and further away from that. I think all our attempts to set up minimal standards—I had a part in setting up the Board of Examiners in Professional Psychology and I'm not very proud of that—tends to freeze a given state of the art and science in a way that is not particularly helpful. It becomes a dead hand of the past where its whole intent is simply to protect the public. Even in the encounter-group movement, I know of no way of avoiding the risks that are involved in many people going into the field. I can only hope that the public will begin to discriminate between those who seem to provide helpful experiences and those who do not.

REFERENCES

Buber, Martin. 1965. *The knowledge of man*. ed. M. Friedman. New York: Harper.

Evans, R. I. 1976a. *Jung on elementary psychology*. New York: Dutton.

———. 1975. *Carl Rogers: the man and his ideas*. New York: Dutton.

Freud, Sigmund. 1953. *The standard edition of the complete psychological works of Sigmund Freud*, ed. J. Stracher. London: Hogarth Press.

Goldstein, Kurt. 1939. *The organism*. New York: American Book.

McClelland, David C. 1953. *The achievement motive*. New York: Appleton.

Rogers, Carl R. 1939. *Clinical treatment of the problem child*. Boston: Houghton Mifflin.

———. 1942. *Counseling and psychotherapy: Newer concepts in practice*. Boston: Houghton Mifflin.

———. 1951. *Client-centered therapy: its current practice, implications and theory.* Boston: Houghton Mifflin.

———, and Skinner, B. F. 1956. Some issues concerning the control of human behavior. *Science* 124: 1057–65.

———. 1961. *On becoming a person.* Boston: Houghton Mifflin.

———. 1969. *Freedom to learn.* Columbus, Ohio: Merrill.

———. 1970. *Carl Rogers on encounter groups.* New York: Harper.

Skinner, B. F. 1971. *Beyond freedom and dignity.* New York: Knopf.

Stephenson, William. 1953. *The study of behavior: Q-technique and its methodology.* Chicago: University of Chicago Press.

R. D. Laing

(1927–   )

Ronald David Laing read medicine at Glasgow University, graduating in 1951, after which he spent two years as a psychiatrist in the British Army before returning to Glasgow to complete his advanced training in psychiatry in 1956, working both in city mental wards and the university's teaching hospital. He moved to Tavistock Clinic in London in 1957 and completed the first draft of the book, The Divided Self, *that was to bring his work to the attention of a wide cross section of readers around the world. His work has continued to focus brilliantly on the phenomenology of schizophrenia, an area where he has challenged many basic concepts, bringing both a philosophic sophistication and a persistent skepticism to bear on contemporary approaches to therapy.*

As we begin our discussion, Dr. Laing reacts to psychoanalysis and other basic concepts and expresses a deep concern for the validity and effectiveness of certain current trends. He suggests that Freud may have underestimated the earliness of childhood experiences and discusses Jung's construct of archetypes. We discuss the problems inherent in diagnosing and classifying disorders with behavioral manifestations and contemporary research into both causes and

---

This discussion is an excerpt from the book *R. D. Laing: The Man and His Ideas* by Richard I. Evans. Copyright © 1975 by Richard I. Evans. Reprinted by permission of the publishers, E. P. Dutton & Co., Inc.

therapeutic techniques. In discussing schizophrenia, Dr. Laing comments on the problems of both therapist and patient, and compares contemporary treatment to Inquisition methods. We explore the factors that lead to the "double-bind" family situation and he presents a brief case study to illustrate this point. As we talk of the professional role today, he makes an analogy to a prostitute relationship, and speculates on whether the capacity to communicate is cultured out of mental health training. We discuss bystander apathy, and Dr. Laing generalizes to broader issues, both contemporary and historical, including the apathy of the Jewish people in the face of extermination by the Nazis during World War II. He then tells me about his investigations of Eastern meditation during an extended trip to India, and compares some of his findings with western psychoanalytic practices. He explains the thinking behind the Kingsley Hall-type experimental houses, and in conclusion, challenges his critics to make a more accurate reading of his work.

EVANS: Dr. Laing, although you've abandoned psychoanalysis in a formal sense, you were trained in psychoanalytical theory, and involved in the psychoanalytic movement in your early years of practice. Looking at the field today, what do you still believe to be valid?

LAING: It's very difficult to say what psychoanalysis means today, since there are so many people who call themselves psychoanalysts, and practice so many different things under that name. I don't think there's one psychoanalyst who'd be prepared to recognize everyone else who calls himself that. It's a very zany, peculiar field that we're talking about if we go beyond its public presentation.

EVANS: You are often perceived as having departed radically from psychoanalysis in your own thinking as well as in your therapeutic procedures. With respect to some of Freud's (1953) ideas, how do you feel about his theory of psychosexual development, the importance of overdeterminism, the unconscious, the Freudian defense mechanisms? Do these ideas continue to be of value to you in your work?

LAING: In some way or another, very early experiences from conception influence all people significantly, I believe, but not all people in an obvious way, necessarily. Perhaps Freud didn't fully realize the earliness of those effects. Without diminishing anything that Freud said about later development, it seems plausible to me that the intrauterine experience, from conception, before implantation, all the way through implantation and after-birth experiences are mapped into our system in some way or another, and stored to express themselves later, especially surfacing after physical growth ends, and postpubertal adult life begins. Our responses are a product of G (genetic system) and E (environment). In our lives, professionally, personally, family-wise, and in different stages of life, we are often so hard-pressed that there's almost nothing we can do except fight for survival. We live, often, in states of polyvalence. Generally speaking, in my life, my reaction to situations, my experiences, the emotional heights and depths and transformations I go through, seem to me to display a form and a syntax which I learned like language. I think there's a logic of the heart, a syntax common to every culture. We can't take any of the things that happen in our emotional lives out of the context of that structural field. This realm of discourse Freud explored. We must emphasize the social weave, the interrelatedness of psychic life, the interplay of our feelings, our ideas, our perceptions and experiences of the world within the warp and woof of our life together.

EVANS: Would you say, then, that psychoanalysis has not done an adequate job of accounting for cultural effects on the individual, or the effects of the present? A theory of universal historical determinants is not sufficient to account for the entire behavior of the individual. Is this correct?

LAING: It's difficult to get down to what universal constants of behavior exist in any one species. Conduct is not only a specific set of movements, but a set of actions, with apparent ends in view toward which the actions are aimed. If we both move to lift a pen off this table, we could move on the left hand tack or the right hand tack. If we imagine ourselves studying behavior from a position suspended in space, we look about the size of ants on the face of the planet. As Loren Eisley says, it looks from that position as though the human species at present is a sort of congerie of spores, building capsules into spore-heap cities, crowding until they explode three feet out of the dung to another stuffed heap. Our perspective depends on whether we put ourselves on this planet or into space. I can entirely agree with the last chapter of Levi-Strauss' *The Savage Mind* (1966), where he says that we cannot naïvely adopt any particular form of total world view or *Gestaltian* meaning our mind happens to find plausible. We can, however, place all these views—all of which display dramatic characteristics, reduced by Levi-Strauss to diachronic transformations of binary elements— within the general framework of world view.

EVANS: Your comments on Loren Eisley bring to mind one of Carl Jung's (Evans 1976a) most controversial constructs: the idea of archetypes and the whole notion of the so-called race or collective unconscious. As you know, Jung argues that in this collective unconscious reside the archetypes, quasi-Lamarckian, tradition-inherited symbols such as the mother, the father, evil, etc. How do you feel about this line of thought?

LAING: I think it's one of the most fundamental notions the human mind has come up with. The nature of possible and actual basic structural, schematic forms that *in*form the human mind, and find representation in images, have been considered long before Jung. Expressed through basic schemata, experience presents itself to us, patterning particular sets of redundancies we tend to take for granted, and tend nowadays to construe as being either environmentally and/or genet-

ically programmed. The data is incontrovertible. Everyone who studies the human mind comes up against the data to which such theories
point.

EVANS: But this idea of the collective unconscious, the race unconscious of Jung (Evans 1964), is considered controversial though it
has really been presented from Plato on by many writers. Are you saying that it's validated from your own observations?

LAING: Not quite. I said that the *seen* confronts the *seer*. Jung
presents more than observation. One of his observations is that many
people's minds are closed to the observations upon which his theories
are based. There follows many abstract generalizations, influences, and
assumptions—a certain amount of which isn't entirely clarified—that
attempt to give the most acceptable, rational account of certain phenomena that we have before us in our own and other people's minds.
Jung was prepared to look at these physical manifestations of mental
phenomena, at psychic realities of what the human mind makes and
creates. That such productions of the human mind often appear to us
grotesque and bizarre is itself a scientific datum. Jung's theory attempts
to put it together and say there are underlying structures traversing the
board, universal processes at work, mental as well as physical genetic.
This field is up for grabs. It needs someone who can really develop it
further.

EVANS: Dr. Laing, perhaps the most widely noted observation made
in your various writings has been your reaction to the whole matter of
classifying mental disorders. Kraepelin (1883) came up with a book of
mental disorders divided into categories—neurosis, psychosis, the various
subtypes—and the American Psychiatric Association periodically brings
them up to date. They have become almost a bible to the traditional
psychiatrist as he attempts to deal with his patients, to decide whether
or not the patient will be hospitalized, for example, or how he can be
treated. What exactly is your criticism of the classification of mental
disorders? After all, we generally use diagnostic categories in the field
of medicine.

LAING: I'm not saying that we should not use diagnostic categories
as a matter of principle. But when persons are checked over completely
and found, in the present state of our knowledge, to have nothing the
matter with them physically, they are said to have something the matter
with them mentally. This is a device, an extended metaphor or analogy,
that has become institutionalized and politicized. We have installations
that are supposed to treat disorders of the mind, dogmatically regarded
as due to disorders of the body at the molecular level, or the deeply
programmed genetic level. It is part of what Ivan Illich (1975) has
recently called the medicalization of everything, as a feature of our
proliferating medico-industrial complex. Here it is the medicalization of
mind. There are equally strong objections to the medicalization of the
body. When we talk about having something or nothing the matter

physically, we are often also in a zone of speculation, infinite cultural variation and non-medical value judgments.

EVANS: To help clarify this, let me be more specific. Admittedly, the term *functional* is very ambiguous, so let's go to the term *organic*, in the sense of organic psychosis. This seems to be an area where the classifiers of mental disorders feel on firmest ground. Let's take a case such as alcoholic psychosis. Surely some of the neurologists believe that you can find real pathology or brain damage that causes this psychosis. Don't you agree?

LAING: That won't be easy to do. What's cause and effect? It has to be post-mortem, doesn't it?

EVANS: Yes, and even that is not conclusive. So-called organic psychosis is not always that apparent.

LAING: Definitely not.

EVANS: I realize you're not suggesting that neurologists could never correctly see any type of organic pathology in some types of psychosis, but perhaps it would be a fairer inference, perhaps more important than whether or not there is some pathology, that there might be a heavy psychological loading in some of these disorders. In fact, maybe the psychological loading could be much more important than the pathology itself, even if it is found. Is that correct?

LAING: If I am disturbed, I may be disturbed spiritually, intellectually, emotionally and physically. Many neurologists, once they find something as they say organic, think that's it. The content of that heavy loading is of no interest. Even the notion that a social system does have "organic" effects is remote to many doctors.

EVANS: There are those who argue that there is no such thing as a functional disorder, in the sense that functional means no final neurological basis, that ultimately we will find something biochemical going on. Heath (Heath et al., 1967, 1960, 1958, 1957) and his group at Tulane University in New Orleans have been working in this area for many years. There are also those who feel that we're dealing with a genetic phenomenon. The early work of Kallman (1958, 1953) for example, argues that schizophrenia is of genetic origin. Would you also have reservations about accepting a genetic or biochemical basis for the so-called functional disorders?

LAING: I would have great reservations. In the first place, I do not always regard those people, to whom the diagnosis of functional disorder is applied, as necessarily having anything the matter with them. Suppose a person is placed in an environment set up to disorder them. Animals used in ordinary laboratory experimentation have been deliberately driven crazy by environmental experimentalists, just to show how easy it is. We know, at least we ought to know, that there is nothing more sensitive to social, psychological, communicational, and environmental influence than the chemistry of the body. The body chemistry is a contingency of unremitting resonance with its social situation. A catastrophic situation reverberates through the adrenals, the pituitary, the lymphatics; the whole endocrine system is brought into immediate, resonant play in any acute stressful social crisis. It has been discovered that fields of energy on this planet are extensions of the furthest blips picked up on the astronomer's telescope; the molecular structure of human cells vibrates in some way with the vibrations from outer stellar space. Our body is not primarily bounded by skin, but is part of a continuum of geophysical fields. We know the moon affects organic life and the phasing and maturation of organic processes. It affects all the waters of the earth. In the tides, an enormous amount of water moves up and down with the moon. Over eighty percent of our body is made up of water, and it seems inevitable that our fluids are going to be affected by such things as the moon. That's not cranksville, that's perfectly ordinary common sense.

I've gone over Kallman's work in detail and it is scientifically less than worthless. It's a disgrace. In fact, all the major published statistics so far on monozygotic twins and twin family research are, I would say, scientifically inconclusive, though some are great improvements on Kallman. But not a single one of the major studies quoted in textbooks offers scientific evidence to confirm a so-called genetic theory of schizophrenia, nor do they explain even what they mean by "schizophrenia," at least not to my satisfaction.

EVANS: You've said that you don't object to the classification of mental disorders, but you feel that many of the judgments implicit in these classifications are without any real foundation. In your own work and writing you have focused on a particular mental disorder, schizophrenia, which in the traditional classification, of course, is listed as one type of functional psychosis. Classically, schizophrenia has been described as a lacking in affect of the patient, the ultimate in withdrawal. It seems to be characterized by rather specific symptoms with different subtypes relating to paranoia, the basic regressive aspects of the disorder, and so on. To you, schizophrenia would be symptomatic of the limitations of such labelling. I gather you're particularly concerned because this is such a prevalent disorder and this label is so widely used. Is that correct?

LAING: Yes. It illustrates and epitomizes a certain sort of process which is widespread. To be a bit impish about it, we could say that it demonstrates a disorder, generally found all over society, to which some people are subject, many of whom have managed to reinforce their disorder in a socially acceptable way by becoming psychiatrists! They've institutionalized the disorder, which consists of being able to see in certain other people all the things they can't see in themselves. I would certainly think that people who are diagnosed as schizophrenic are often disorganized and disordered, but not in a way that is different from the way many psychiatrists are. A great degree of psychopathology and psychiatric theory is an institutionalized, reciprocally reinforced projection system applied by people to people and that says, in many cases, more about the psychiatrist than it does about the patient. There was an institution during the Inquisition a few hundred years ago, a very highly regarded group of men who were called prickers. They carried around pricks—needles of different calibers—that they used to stick through the skin and into the bone marrow of women who were thought to be witches. They listened to the screams. If they didn't scream, they were probably witches, able to counteract the exquisiteness of the pain. If they did scream, it had to be determined if the screaming was genuine or fake. It's the same sort of mind, the same sorry thing today. It's evil. It is a fundamental error in the original set, if you like, generating all these treatment programs and classifications, streamlining the classifications, then streamlining the treatments into more classifications and on and on.

EVANS: It seems to me that you've used schizophrenia as a test case for challenging this whole matter of classification. As you learned more about it, you began to particularly tie in the family as a factor. You seemed particularly responsive to the work of Gregory Bateson (1956) who used the term "double bind" and you applied this term in a rather broad sense as you explored the family structure of the schizophrenic.

LAING: I use the phrase less frequently now, because in Bateson's sense, it's got a very precise meaning and I think there is something to be said for allowing that precision to remain. It should not be applied to every situation where you might say you can't win. Various internal and external systems play off against each other and neutralize the command system so that one can't move; one is immobilized, actually brought to a standstill by the contradiction. There are many different sorts of contradictions, paradoxes, locks, binds, fangles, tangles, impasses, check-and-checkmate situations for which we haven't got a systematic language. We may very well be developing one. I believe Bateson has begun this. In our environment we have these jams and impasses of an interpersonal and social nature, where there's nothing physically the matter with the essential processing capacities of an individual, but where the person is exposed to such contradictory programs, injunctions, different types of data in different ways that the activating systems of the body boggle, and one gets into classifiable dysfunctional states.

EVANS: Recalling your focus on what you call the double-bind family in the background of the schizophrenic, can you specifically describe what the situation would be like for that member who is the victim of this family?

LAING: Let's say the quotient of truth and deception in a communicational system varies. There may be no metacommunicational system which recognizes this fact; the meta system may be consonant with the deceptive alpha systems. Any questioning of the truth value propositions displayed in the alpha systems may be punished. I can think, right off,

of several cases where I have been presented with a member of a family
—mother, father, son or daughter—not sure who they were, and agonized
by consternation and bewilderment as to what was true and what was
not true. The family tries to be sympathetic, to help. They come to me
and decide they have to level with me. And in an extraordinarily naïve
way, they come out with something in the past which might very well
cause anyone in that situation to pick up cues of such confusion, such
dishonesty and duplicity about his or her identity, as to find oneself in
a state of bewilderment, with no idea why.

EVANS: In the area of psychiatric, psychological and social work
training, supposing you had an ideal situation, and could control it,
what things would you put into the curriculum to increase the probability that the students would develop or grow into this openness
toward people that you obviously consider so important?

LAING: I couldn't just change the curriculum quite like that. When
it comes to the nitty gritty of anyone's particular job, I am not in a position to tell him how he should act better or say, "Here is what you
should do." I can talk about certain considerations, and certain matters
of principle, and certain specific matters of practice. One of my earliest
encounters with institutional psychiatry was as a psychiatrist in the
British Army at the time, not long after World War II, when British
and American psychiatry had been raised to the dignity of a full-time
speciality. This, hopefully, would serve the interests of all parties,
although all interests might not be entirely coincident when it comes
to any one single guy who might want out of the Army, unconditionally.
There might be a lot of people who want to be out that the Army wants
to be in, and when it comes to such an issue, it is very much a matter of
what mood one happens to be in as to how one will inflect the balance
of contending interests. If someone wants out, for instance, it is very
easy just to say that he is emotionally malfunctioning—a personality
disorder, an inadequate personality, psychopathic, etc. If he wants to
take the stigma of being a homosexual, a schizoid personality, or even
psychotic, then he'll probably be out. But he will be picked up by the
computer for life. That is already part of it, you know; all such data is
beginning to be programmed into the world-computer-brain. That's one
extreme of a system that psychiatrists are part of, and there are quite a
lot of psychiatrists who have been among the architects and designers
of this system. In a way I haven't got anything to say about it, except
that I hate it.

EVANS: A good deal of what is going on in training in psychology,
social work and psychiatry programs is designed to equip individuals to
fit into the system and meet a need.

LAING: I'm not saying whether or not I would like to see the system working better, I am just saying that it is a fact of life. In the mental
health field, what is supposed to be bought, to a great extent, is not a
manufactured commodity that can be handled, or even a mere tech-

nique, but a capacity to be openheartedly available to other people. You might say that this puts the mental health professions in a position that is fairly analogous to that of prostitution—what is being paid for is a relationship. What is being paid for has to do with the actual encounter, meeting person-to-person, face-to-face, with people who are called patients. Yet, for whatever reason, for someone's "good," or because he or she become insufferable to those they live with, a child is taken away from its mother, the mother is stripped of her legal rights, or a father is taken away, and whether he wants it or not, he is going to get severe things done to him which will change his mind, his chemistry, his body. Electricity is going to be shot through his brain whether he wants it or not. There are a tremendous number of medical-legal issues there. I think these things are dreadful. They reinforce persecution by more persecution. But we haven't gotten to the thing that I'm particularly interested in, that there is still a domain, an arena in which one human being actually gets into the same place at the same time to meet another human being. This is what all this intrastructure and superstructure should be for. It seems to me that the medical student in this country and in America has been trained only to receive input, to keep it unscrambled and to reproduce it as output in the form of a written communication, or in terms of well-organized, syntactically correct answers to questions in oral examinations. He must be able to examine patients in a clinical setting, make informed judgments, and then be able to express those judgments in a formal manner, in the form of an oral examination. In the course of time, he is going to be very lucky, within the context of his professional life, if he hasn't had *cultured out* of him his capacity to relate to other people in a personal way. I don't see that being a professional need necessarily preclude someone being able to be open-hearted and open-minded, but it seems to happen to many people. What about using the apprenticeship method for training? It has been demonstrated in a series of experiments, that different psychiatrists at different ages, with different personality structures that are measurable, get into different kinds of relationships with people. Some hit it off better than others. When that personal relationship does click, it is the single most important therapeutic factor in the whole thing.

EVANS: As a social psychologist, I am particularly aware of a line of research that appears rather conflicting, triggered off by the Kitty Genovese case in Queens, New York. As you know, a group of bystanders stood by and allowed an individual to be attacked violently, without lifting a finger to help. This has led to a tremendous interest in what we call bystander apathy, and in turn, to the whole area of altruism. Subsequent research into this matter, however, doesn't come up with that clear-cut a picture. It seems to show that there are conditions under which people will help and conditions under which they will not. In terms of your previous statements, how do you feel about these observations of bystander apathy?

LAING: I haven't had much direct relevant experience with this. But before we start talking about bystander apathy as a feature of the alienation of vast urban population complexes and all that, consider that we don't know much about bystander apathy fifty years ago or a hundred years ago. I imagine there was plenty of it. People have always been frightened. Look at the German bystander apathy about the concentration camps. Look at the British apathy when their bomber command destroyed a city like Dresden, just to show the Americans and Russians what the British Air Force could do. What about the bystander apathy that we know of everywhere?

EVANS: You bring up the greater issues. It may not be just a question of the Kitty Genovese case, but something much more basic, such as the way we stood by and watched the Nazi atrocities develop, as you pointed out. But what about the strange apathy of the Jewish people themselves as they were led into these camps to be exterminated? They seemed to just stand by and let it happen. Does that seem to be a curious situation to you?

LAING: From the reports of the survivors of those camps, as you know, one of the most prominent things seemed to be that so many couldn't believe it was happening. I mean, in Germany, in many an ordinary German town, Jews were not seemingly isolate. They were Europeans like everyone else, in a civilized town, living in a civilized manner. The Nazis were at the time, apparently, their neighbors, people they went to school with, shopped with, worked with, played with. It was very difficult, actually, to realize that what was happening, was actually happening. We have a word for someone who feels he is being persecuted when the majority view is that he is not being persecuted: *paranoia*. But there is no word for a situation where one can't bring oneself to realize that one is being persecuted when one is.

EVANS: Dr. Laing, several months ago, you went off to India and Ceylon, to get a better feel of their views of reaching certain conscious states. Some of these practices—yoga, for example—involve meditative qualities that somehow seem to lull us away from the material world and bring us closer, perhaps, to grips with ourselves and our own conscious state. What, exactly, did you learn from your experience there? Do you have a better understanding of where this sort of thing is going, and perhaps why it is suddenly becoming so interesting to a greater proportion of contemporary Western society, even though it has by no means saturated contemporary Indian culture?

LAING: As the world opens up in many different ways, all sorts of spiritual and mental disciplines become visible to everyone, and are nothing like as remote as they once were. We in the West have a type of practice (little practiced, little understood) called psychoanalysis. Within the context of other cultures, different ways developed in which people investigated themselves, together with different ways and methods of actually experiencing the human mind. I'm concerned with the loss of the psyche, of the disintegration of structure of the psyche, without saying we even know what it is. I have been interested in involving myself close up with people who had been in different experiences from my own. I met and stayed for a few weeks with a man who lived up in the Himalayan foothills under a jutting rock, a sort of crag. His only clothing was a loin cloth. He never ate except what was brought to him. This man had been a medical doctor. He was now in his fifties, an orthodox Hindu within one of the primary systems of Hindu orthodoxy, recognized as a Swami. At twenty-nine he had gone off into the wilderness of jungles and mountains and lived there for over seven years without seeing a human being; then he came back and stationed himself about an hour's walk from the nearest village, unapproachable by car. He was there where anyone who wanted to could come to seee him. He grew up in a combination of grass roots Indian culture and Western culture of the most sophisticated kind, but he felt if he didn't get away from human beings for a while he would go completely crazy. Even after recuperating from them for seven years, he still felt that one had to be pretty well grounded to be able to take the normally insane human species for long.

EVANS: You've mentioned that you were seeking a better understanding of the meditative processes that are analogous to psychoanalysis in our culture. Were you able to get into this?

LAING: I wouldn't say that I went to India in order to find their meditational practices. I reckon that I discovered as a child that there are different ways of resting and flexing and employing one's mind. I used to spend a lot of time just sitting, looking into the fireplace. You could call that fire *Kasina*, if you heard someone calling it by the Buddhist name; one could speak about or codify different stages of absorption that the mind goes through, and the phenomenology of that. As one continues to look at the fire, or candle, or any object, without turning away from it for a certain period of time, this particular form of focused attention meditation yields well-documented mental transforms. You can stare at a wall; you can meditate upon a paradox that is impossible to fulfill, you can think the unthinkable. People have different procedures which have been developed in different parts of the world.

EVANS: In this type of meditative process, which is really reacting to a certain kind of stimulus, one is perhaps allowing some sort of increasing impact of a purer conscious state, whatever that means. To what degree can this sort of thing be reproduced with drugs? LSD and other drugs, such as mescaline, have been used both in research and for "trips" among young people.

LAING: I think it's too simplistic to define or characterize this state as a stimulus-induced state. If we do that, we have to talk about the auto-stimulus of the brain, when feedback is part of the stimulus-induced state, because there are many different sorts of meditational practices. The one I was talking about—it's often thought appropriate for "beginners"—is the one in which, with practice, one's complete, undivided attention is brought to bear on one subject.

EVANS: You're talking about an environmental object, now?

LAING: It could be a mental object; it could be a triangle, a dot, a circle.

EVANS: How would that type of state, then, differ from a chemically induced state, as you see it?

LAING: There's no such thing as a chemically induced state of total fixed absorption, as far as I know. One can't take a chemical and achieve instant mental discipline. It might facilitate some things, but everything's chemical. The state we're in right now is chemical. If you put in another chemical, you get another chemical state; so it's one chemical state or another. And you might say that one chemical state is artificial, and the other is like, for example, our stomach and gastro-intestinal-alimentary system without food.

There are very few people in the world, I would say, who have got minds that they can just move into a sustained, twenty-minute, on-cue, fixed attention on any object and out again, with complete effortlessness. The mind goes away from you, you bring it back, it goes away again. When you finally get it settled down to rest itself, as it were, upon an object, then there are nonverbal transformations of mind that occur, absolutely straightforward and continuing. They've been mapped out in extraordinary scholastic detail. In this particular procedure, it's not a question of theory, or what you think about, or what your motivation or intentions are. All that's entirely irrelevant. You just do it. This state of mind, with no discursive thoughts arising, with no conscious processing of sense data, is a very restful state, indeed. But I don't think it proves anything, metaphysically, ontologically, or existentially.

EVANS: Dr. Laing, I think that a number of people in the fields of psychiatry, psychology, and social work have become acutely aware of the circularity of the mental hospital, essentially training so-called mentally ill people to become good mental hospital patients. This criticism is directed not only to the earlier years, when treatment was often abusive and vicious. There are those who say that the patronizing, almost too gentle concern about patients that characterizes some hospitals today is probably equally bad. Both systems seem to be doing the same thing, that is simply training people to adjust to this environment which has nothing to do with rehabilitating them in the sense of resocializing them. I know that one of the answers you had to this type of criticism was a venture in, for want of a better term, what we could call the therapeutic community at Kingsley Hall.

LAING: All that was there still goes on. There are actually seven households like Kingsley Hall in London right now.

EVANS: What are the general patterns of these "Kingsley Halls" that seem to be effective in dealing with some individuals, in contrast to what goes on, perhaps, in a traditional mental hospital?

LAING: I don't want to say in contrast to what goes on in a traditional mental hospital. I've never put down traditional mental hospitals in the blanket condemnation sort of way that some people have. Many people who stay in our households, very often I would say, are people who might well be in mental hospitals, and they're not staying because there's anything special or even particularly pleasant about the households, but for these people, in their own experience almost anywhere is better than a mental hospital.

EVANS: These households have been described as communelike in structure. Would this be a fair statement?

LAING: Yes. All the things that have been happening since we started this specifically, in 1964–1965, are experimental and remain experimental. If I state the principle of it, it can be put very simply. My impression, out of my years of psychiatric practice and experience, is that the main single thing that really makes a difference to people who are in a state of distress is to come across another human being who is really there, as a real presence to him. That is very rare. In our experimental places we've tried to do without roles. I'm not sure that doing without the roles really improves matters or is possible. That's not the essential thing. It's experimenting with social form, so that we can find within the context of our social system the best sanctuary wherein a nexus of relationships can subsist. When one is frightened, to become unfrightened one has got to feel safe at the same depth in one's bone marrow as one was afraid. And the most important thing in an environment, as far as safety goes, is the people in it. So we try to experiment with how we can, in our context, be safe people for other people to meet. When we don't know people, we have to show by our presence that we are not going to do anything to anybody in the name of anything.

EVANS: Dr. Laing, what do you believe to be your most significant contributions?

LAING: I hope that I haven't yet made what might be my most significant contributions. I see myself in the skeptical tradition of Western thought, which is to say, to look at the nature of matter, the nature of man, the nature of the mind, the nature of phenomena, directly, without presuppositions, to suspend judgment, as practiced in the Greek schools. In other words, I think it's a tremendously important thing not to fill the gaps in what I really know from my immediate, direct sight, sound, taste, touch, smell, which is all I have to go on, all that anyone's got to go on—not to fill the gaps with beliefs one then has to defend. That's the beginning of fanaticism, and I attribute a great deal of the world's woes to that propensity, which I recognize in my own mind and that of other people, to become convinced that one is right, that the questions are finally answered. One has seen the final revelation, one has seen the angel, seen God, been redeemed. The water is moved and one has crossed over to the other shore: one has achieved enlightenment. I'm not preaching cynicism, or nihilism, or what else, either.

EVANS: You have been subjected to a great deal of criticism by colleagues in psychiatry, and people in various other fields, and you certainly must be aware of these criticisms. It would be only fair to hear, first, which of these criticisms has troubled you the most, and secondly, what your reaction to some of these specific criticisms might be.

LAING: There are two areas to which I'm particularly sensitive because they are two areas of my own uncertainty and indecision, and there are also areas in which I feel unhappy that I've been attacked. I think some of it is based on misunderstandings on the part of my critics, and a failure to read a bit more accurately what I actually wrote. Some people have felt that I thought it enhanced one's wisdom to take drugs like acid, mescaline, and whatnot, that it was a recommended part of the curriculum of somebody who wished to understand the full human story, that really you couldn't expect to enter into reality, or have much to say, unless you'd taken a trip. There's a great deal of confusion about the psychedelic model of psychosis, and stuff like that. I hope I can manage to get myself around, in the next few months, to writing something in which I at least try to state my own position about that, to disclaim many of the positions that have been attributed to me.

EVANS: You mention the psychedelic model of psychosis. Are you referring here to what some writers have called your psychedelic theory of schizophrenia? That becoming schizophrenic is a type of trip in the same sense that there is a drug trip, and upon returning from this trip, the person will be miraculously cured?

LAING: We'd have to take my answer to that within the context of the way we've dealt with the concept of schizophrenia before. You'd have to move that out of the way. A number of people who have had this type of experience, and who have afterwards taken acid, feel that there is a big overlap. There are many people diagnosed as schizophrenic, who would disagree completely.

EVANS: What are you going to be approaching next that you think will be worthy of your attention and concern?

LAING: Well, what is more worthy of my attention and concern than the self, the human heart, intellect, emotions, and/or physicality?

REFERENCES

Bateson, G. D., Jackson, D., Haley, J., and Weakland, J. 1956. Toward a theory of schizophrenia. *Behav. Sci.* 1: 251–64.

Evans, R. I. 1976a. *Jung on elementary psychology.* New York: Dutton.

Freud, S. 1953. *The standard edition of the complete psychological works.* Ed. J. Strachey. London: Hogarth Press.

Heath, R. G. 1960. A biochemical hypothesis on the etiology of schizophrenia. In *The Etiology of Schizophrenia,* ed. D. D. Jackson. New York: Basic Books.

———, Martens, S., Leach, B. E., Cohen, M., and Angel, C. 1957. Effect on behavior in humans with the administration of taraxein. *Amer. J. Psychiatr.* 114: 14–24.

————, Martens, S., Leach, B. E., Cohen, M., and Feigley, C. A. 1958. Behavioral changes in nonpsychotic volunteers following the administration of taraxein, the substance obtained from the serum of schizophrenic patients. *J. Amer. Psychiatr.* 114: 917–920.

————, Krupp, I. M., Byers, L. W., and Liljukvist, J. I. 1967. Schizophrenia as an immunologic disorder. *Arch. Gen. Psychiatr.* 16: (1) 1–33.

Illich, Ivan. 1975. *Medical nemesis.* London: Calder and Boyars.

Kallman, F. J. 1958. The use of genetics in psychiatry. *J. Ment. Sci.* 104: 542–49.

————. 1953. *Heredity in health and mental disorder.* New York: Norton.

Kraepelin, 1883. *Lehrbuch der psychiatrie.*

Laing, R. D. 1960. *The divided self: a study of sanity and madness.* London: Tavistock Publications.

————. 1967. *The politics of experience.* New York: Pantheon Books.

————. 1970. *Self and others,* 2d ed. New York: Pantheon Books.

————. 1970. *Knots.* New York: Pantheon Books.

————. 1971. *The politics of the family, and other essays.* New York: Pantheon Books.

————, and Cooper, D. G. 1964. *Reason and violence: a decade of Sartre's philosophy, 1950–1960.* New York: Humanities Press.

————, Phillipson, H., and Lee, A. R. 1966. *Interpersonal perception: a theory and a method of research.* London: Tavistock Publications.

————, and Esterson, J. A. 1971. *Sanity, madness and the family: families of schizophrenics.* New York: Basic Books.

Levi-Strauss, C. 1966. *The savage mind.* Chicago: University of Chicago Press.

Albert Bandura

(1925–   )

Albert Bandura graduated from the University of British Columbia in 1949 and received the Ph.D. from the State University of Iowa in 1952. As a clinical psychologist he recognized the need to examine the clinical behavior modification process more precisely. Based on Hullian learning theory, Skinnerian theory, and the concepts of modeling and imitation, his landmark research has resulted in a broader, more socially oriented approach to behavior modification which he calls social learning theory. His work on aggression illustrates the application of these concepts in a particularly clear manner. A recipient of a Guggenheim Fellowship (1972–1973) and a past president of the American Psychological Association (1974), Professor Bandura joined the faculty of Stanford University in 1953 where he is David Jordan Starr Professor of Social Science in Psychology.

Imprinted on an Experimental Model/A Better Empirical Base/More Effective Procedures//Models/Effective Tutors/Inhibitors and Disinhibitors/Cues for Action/Imitation/Identification/Modeling/Observational Learning/A Cognitive Process/Action and Consequence/An Awareness of the Relationship/Directly Observed or Self-Produced Models/The Judgmental Process//Environmental and Personal Determinism/The Reciprocal Influence Model/Generalizing and Maintaining Change/Functional Value/ Environmental Support/Self-Evaluation//Aggression/Three Views/Example/ Experience/Interaction/Controlling Aggression/A Very Contemporary Example//Moral Codes and Moral Conduct/Dissociation and Self-Exonerating Mechanisms/Humanizing and Personalizing/Not a Fixed Regulator But a System//The Worth of a Theory/Translating Theory Into Practice//

As we begin our discussion, Dr. Bandura explains that he was first attracted toward a clinical program with a strong experimental emphasis, and tells of his early interest in developing adequately assessed methods of psychotherapy. He recalls some of the early influences that led to his conceptualization of social learning theory, and to his research in modeling and aggression. He distinguishes between modeling, imitation, and identification, and elaborates on modeling and observational learning, emphasizing the importance of cognitive processes. He then describes the complex range of consequences that affect human behavior and the interrelationship of directly experienced consequences, vicarious or observed consequences, and self-produced consequences. We discuss his reciprocal influence model of behavior control and the contingencies of that control, and he analyzes the conditions under which behavior change is effected and maintained. We then turn to his work on aggression, and after a brief review of the traditional theories, Dr. Bandura presents a concise summary of his theory of aggression, making a particularly relevant connection with the depiction of violence in the mass media. We discuss his work on the social learning view of moral codes, self-exonerating mechanisms, and self-evaluation. In conclusion, he reacts to criticisms generated by his work and emphasizes again his strong interest in converting theory to practice: "The worth of a theory is ultimately judged by the power of the change procedures it produces. Psychologists are skillful at developing theories but rather slow in translating them into practice."

EVANS: Dr. Bandura, your career typifies the diversity of many of our most creative contemporary psychologists. You were trained in clinical psychology; you have demonstrated crucial innovations in the area of learning; you have looked at subtle types of motivational problems relating to aggression, and more recently, you've been looking at aggression defined in terms of morality and moral codes. To begin, what were the things that attracted you to clinical psychology?

BANDURA: Well, I did my graduate work at Iowa where you get imprinted on an experimental model very effectively. I was most interested in seeing how one can begin to provide a better empirical base for clinical practice. I had a strong interest in conceptualizing clinical phenomena in ways that would make them amenable to experimental test, with the view that as practitioners, we have a responsibility for assessing the efficacy of our procedures, so that people are not subjected to treatments before we know their effects. Because there is no evidence that psychotherapy kills or maims people, it is easy to adopt a casual approach of applying methods before they have been adequately assessed. I entertained a three-stage process for the development of psychotherapeutic practices. First, we should try to understand the basic mechanisms by which change is effected; secondly, that knowledge should enable us to devise preliminary treatment methods; and only after we have some evidence of the effects of those procedures, should we apply them on a clinical level. Having that kind of model of practice, I was attracted to a program with a strong experimental emphasis oriented toward the development of more effective psychological procedures.

EVANS: At Iowa, of course, you were influenced by Kenneth Spence (1956), who had worked with Clark Hull (1943, 1951, 1952) at Yale. Neal Miller, who was also influenced by Hull, attempted to conceptualize clinical constructs in more empirical, experimental terms in his work on social learning and imitation. Were you influenced by this line of thinking?

BANDURA: I was very much influenced by the Miller and Dollard writings, and I was intrigued by the book, *Social Learning and Imitation* (Miller and Dollard 1941). That was a stimulus for some of my early work. I became interested in broadening the notion of vicarious experience and the range of phenomena that could be explained through a social learning approach. I distinguish between the diverse effects of exposure to models. Models function as effective tutors in transmitting new forms of behavior. They serve as inhibitors or disinhibitors in that observing the actions of models and the consequences of those actions can increase or reduce restraints in observers. Models can also serve as cues for actions—in the social-facilitation effect, the model's behavior guides the actions of others.

EVANS: Miller used the term *imitation,* and Freud, *identification.* In your use of the term *modeling* you imply distinctions. Could you clarify these terms, which may be confusing to beginning students?

BANDURA: Imitation, in the minds of most people, means response mimicry—the exact duplication of what the model does. This term carries a very narrow connotation. Identification usually implies a wholesale incorporation of patterns of behavior. I use the term modeling because the psychological effects of exposure to models are much broader than the simple response mimicry implied by the term imitation; and the defining characteristics of identification are too diffuse, arbitrary, and empirically questionable either to clarify issues or to aid scientific inquiry. The more interesting effect of modeling is what I call "abstract modeling." From observing examples, people derive general rules and principles of behavior which permit them to go beyond what they see and hear.

EVANS: The ethologists, Lorenz (Evans 1975) and Tinbergen, for example, have observed imitation at an animal level for many years, and find it very apparent there. The distinctions between imitation at the animal level and what you call modeling at the human level are very important, are they not?

BANDURA: Modeling and observational learning involve, in large part, cognitive processes. Cognitive functions become especially important in delayed modeling, because the modeling influence is gone and you have to represent it in some way, then use that representation as a guide for action on later occasions. Most animal research is restricted to instantaneous imitation. The model serves as a direct cue for a simple response that the animal already has in its repertoire. Few animal studies involve delayed imitation. One could conduct a comparative analysis: the higher the species, the more capable it should be of delayed imitation, because wherever you have delay, there is need for symbolic representation. In humans, most observational learning occurs in the absence of performance. We observe a pattern of behavior, and have no opportunity during observation to enact it or experience its consequences. It is only later that we may exhibit what we have learned. Emphasis is placed on the human capacity for symbolization of experience because it is the representation that remains after the model is gone. The symbol serves as the guide for action. In modeling one is dealing with complex cognitive processes. I would conceptualize observational learning as essentially a cognitive process, and our theories of learning are moving in a more cognitive direction. Operant conditioning in humans can be viewed as an instance of observational learning. You observe the consequences of your actions, and on the basis of that information, you get some idea of what behavior is appropriate in what setting. In the case of modeling, the information is derived from example. In operant conditioning, the response information is derived from the pattern of consequences to actions. Some theorists have attempted to reduce observational learning to an operant paradigm. I consider learning through response to consequences as an instance of observational learning.

EVANS: B. F. Skinner (Evans 1968) took what were some of Thorndike's (1932) most fundamental ideas and expanded them in a very brilliant way, introducing this whole concept of operant conditioning. He demonstrated how it operates at the animal level in a very dramatic way, and then demonstrated that these same principles operate at the human level. One of the major criticisms leveled at Skinner is that he took principles designed and tested on lower animals and, almost literally, used them at the human level. But you're saying that in humans you cannot ignore cognition in the sense that Skinner did. Do I understand you correctly?

BANDURA: Yes. The literature on human conditioning indicates that representation of the connection between action and consequence is an important determinant of whether or not a change will occur. If there is no awareness of the relationship, there is very little change effected. Cognition also plays an important role in mediating the effects of consequences where belief is pitted against actual consequences. There can be a tremendous variation in responsiveness under different beliefs, but with the same objective consequences for action. Expanding the range of consequences that affects human behavior adds complexity to the influence process.

EVANS: Would you elaborate on that?

BANDURA: People do not act as isolates. They operate as social beings who see the consequences occurring to others. These observed consequences also provide a standard for judging whether the direct consequences are equitable. Depending on the schedule by which others are reinforced, your own direct experiences can be perceived as punishing, as rewarding, or as neutral. A third source of reinforcement is the capacity of humans for self-reaction. People adopt certain standards of conduct and respond to their own behavior in self-approving or self-disapproving ways, depending on whether their behavior exceeds or falls below their standards. In the analysis of how behavior is regulated by consequences, one must be concerned with the complex interrelationship of directly experienced consequences, vicarious or observed consequences, and self-produced consequences.

EVANS: Can you give us some examples of how these are interrelated?

BANDURA: Consider the complex relationship between directly experienced consequences and self-generated consequences. You might have a situation where a person would be generously rewarded for behavior that produces self-condemning reactions. When one's own self-evaluative reactions outweigh the power of the externally administered ones, the external consequences will not effect a change. If the external consequences are powerful, you get cheerless compliance. Other conflicts arise when external punishment of behavior is a source of self-pride. The conditions under which external consequences are most likely to effect change are when they are compatible with self-reinforcement, when the behavior is socially approved and is a source of self-satisfaction, or when the behavior is externally punished and is self-disapproved. In any formalization of theory, one would need to work on the interrelationships of these three systems rather than focusing solely on how directly experienced consequences influence behavior.

EVANS: I believe you expanded these ideas very effectively in your book, *Principles of Behavior Modification* (Bandura 1969). It would be interesting to hear Skinner's reactions to this. In a very basic way, you're looking at a much broader range of reinforcers, defining consequences in a much more subtle way. You're really challenging his notion that mental processes are irrelevant to a science of behavior. What do you think his reactions would be, or have you had some reactions?

BANDURA: One reaction might be that these are processes that could be externalized. If one subscribes to the view that behavior is governed by external events, one might attempt to externalize these processes and place them in the environment. In the case of observed reinforcement, one might characterize it, from an operant point of view, from the viewpoint that rewards and punishments to others are discriminative stimuli for action. Externalization ignores the judgmental processes involved. I am more interested in setting up experimental procedures to measure these processes, to manipulate them independently, and to see how they govern behavior. In the case of observational learning, we have studied some of these symbolic processes in ways that are manipulated instructionally. We obtain an independent measure of their presence. It turns out that cognitive functions do exercise a powerful control over behavior.

EVANS: Perhaps the strict behavior modifiers—the so-called "behavior modification movement"—have been too literal, more literal than Skinner ever expected, at the human level. They began to effect short-term changes, but in the long run, the modified behavior just didn't continue. For example, we are currently involved in a massive study of smoking behavior, beginning with children who have never started to smoke, rather than working with the confirmed smoker. We have what we believe is an effective behavioral measure, and we're trying to enter this area in such a way that the permanent change we get will be the ability to cope with the pressures to smoke, so that smoking behavior is never started. Our survey of the literature indicates that behavior modification in this case has only a short-term effect; that as long as the person is under the control of the experimenter, the behavior may be controlled, but once that external control is gone, the person regresses. The issue seems to be that of shifting from external to internal control. Essentially, this seems to be a powerful challenge to behavioral science, and it would be interesting to hear how, from your system, we might attempt intervention and move from external to internal control.

BANDURA: I favor a reciprocal influence model. Environmental determinism implies that behavior is governed solely by environmental conditions; therefore, if you produce a change in behavior but fail to alter the environment, the behavior will be short-lived. Personal determinism assumes that the individual is the source of all control of behavior. Both positions are extreme ones. Reciprocal determinism assumes that behavior is controlled both through personal and environmental means. One can therefore designate the conditions under which behavior change will generalize and be sustained over time, and the conditions under which it will not. If the treatment is aimed at producing functional skills, these usually persist because they have value for the individual. Procedures used to instill a pattern of behavior that is of convenience to the reinforcing agent but of no functional value to the recipient of the influence do not usually produce sustained results. I don't see that as a regrettable state of affairs. If change agents could, through brief application of reinforcement procedures, instill patterns of behavior that would persist after those procedures were removed, they could enslave people. I do not view generalization and maintenance necessarily as an unmitigated virtue.

EVANS: That's a very interesting point. You're saying, in a sense, that it's better to allow a few people to be overweight, to keep smoking, to go around with neuroses, that it's better to have these checks and balances to experimental control that's too easy?

BANDURA: In analyzing change processes, one must distinguish between induction of behavior change, its generalization, and its maintenance. One condition under which change is maintained is when that behavior has functional value for the person. A second maintaining condition exists when there are strong environmental supports for behavior, even though it may not have much functional value for the individual. Sometimes society decides to set up contingencies that foster behavior for the common good, even though it may be inconvenient for the individual. One's own self-evaluation also becomes an important reinforcer, particularly in those activities which we engage in for their own sake. Originally, such activities did not hold much interest. For example, blowing a tuba is not intrinsically reinforcing for most people, but to a tuba artist, a skillful tuba performance could be a tremendous source of reinforcement. To develop this kind of reinforcement requires skill acquisition, adoption of standards of excellence of performance, and investment of the activity with self-evaluative significance. Signs of progress then serve as sources of personal satisfaction. Performances that fall short of the standard motivate performance until improvement is achieved. Self-reinforcement for that activity is self-provided. Under such conditions, a self-reinforcement system can sustain a tremendous amount of tuba blowing in the absence of any external reinforcement. So self-reinforcement is another maintenance system. In the more difficult areas where a pattern of behavior is immediately rewarding with delayed detrimental consequences, such as overeating, smoking, etc., one is involved in the difficult task of helping people acquire some capacity to control their own behavior. The research on self-control provides the most promising approach to self-management of detrimental behavior.

EVANS: As a social psychologist, some questions have always bothered me, and your work in some of these areas has been particularly fascinating. What about the social influences that are involved in destructive behavior, not only suicide and war, but in the progressive self-destructive behavior that's involved in ignoring cardiovascular and cancer risk factors in such behavior as smoking, etc., and in alcoholism, which is becoming an increasing problem among our youth? I'm sure you're familiar with all these areas, and others, and I'm wondering if there is some tie-in here to the whole area of aggressive behavior. Was it this kind of thinking that led you into your work on aggression, or was it a logical outgrowth of some of the other things you had been doing?

BANDURA: I originally began studying aggression in children. Dick Walters and I conducted field studies on the familial antecedents of aggression, and we found that the best predictors were not the frustration determinants, but the life styles that the families exemplified and reinforced. The behavior that the parents modeled and the attitudes they exhibited toward the expression of aggression, both in the home and outside it, emerged as important determinants.

These studies suggested that modeling influences and reinforcement patterns were critical determinants in extreme forms of aggression. This led to laboratory studies and the development of modeling paradigms to examine systematically the effects of exposure to aggressive models on children's behavior. In the course of this research, I became more interested in the general issue of observational learning and modeling, but I'm in the habit of working on several different things at the same time—

I find that more interesting and challenging than working only in one area.

EVANS: That's obvious!

BANDURA: I became fascinated with issues of observational learning and the processes and mechanisms by which this occurs. But I never gave up my interest in trying to formulate an alternative view of aggression. There are, essentially, three views. The instinct theory contends that man is innately endowed with aggressive energy.

EVANS: The view Konrad Lorenz took in his controversial book *On Aggression* (1966) when he described man as a dangerous aggressor. In our discussion (Evans 1975) he emphasized this point again, and also talked about his dream of seeing these aggressive forces directed toward socially useful, creative ways. And of course, Freud had a tremendous interest in this area.

BANDURA: Freud, of course. The second view is the reactive drive theory, in which the aggressive drive is instigated by frustrating environmental conditions. Frustration is ever-present; man is burdened by aggressive drives which he must discharge, hopefully in ways that are not interpersonally injurious. The frustration-aggression theory (Dollard, et al. 1939) is still very popular, even though it does not fit well with the cumulative evidence. We know that frustration has diverse effects on behavior. You don't need frustration to aggress. Much human aggression is based on anticipated benefits of the aggression rather than the push of distress. And the term frustration has been stretched to the point where it no longer has any particular meaning. The approach that interests me looks at aggression as a style of behavior that is acquired through observation, through direct experience, and is, to some extent, influenced by structural biological factors. A theory of aggression must explain three things: How is the behavior acquired? What instigates aggressive action? What sustains the behavior over time? In my conceptualization, aggressive behavior is acquired through example, through direct experience, and through interaction with structural factors. People are instigated to aggression by modeling influences, by seeing others aggress. They are instigated through aversive experiences—personal insults, physical assaults, thwarting of goal-directed behavior, adverse reductions in the quality of life. Then there is obedient aggression; people are trained to obey orders, and they are willing to aggress when legitimate authorities who possess coercive power instruct them to aggress. Some aggression, of course, is provoked by bizarre beliefs.

Then there are the regulators of aggressive behavior. Aggression is maintained by many different factors. First it's maintained by external consequences—material rewards, social and status rewards. Some people are reinforced by signs of injury in the victim. Aggression is also reinforced when people alleviate punitive treatment by defensive recourse. Performance of aggression is affected by observed rewards or punishment—vicarious reinforcement. One must also consider the role of punishment in the regulation of behavior. The reason that deterrent procedures often do not work well is because when people have limited options, and the benefits of successful aggression are high, people don't discard aggression under risk of punishment. They simply refine the behavior to increase its chances of success. Self-reinforcement likewise serves as a regulator because aggressors have to contend with themselves as well as with others. This is where the role of moral codes comes in. From the social learning point of view, the origin, instigation, and regulation of aggression is a complex process.

EVANS: Let's discuss, for a moment, the effect of models of aggression—obviously a great concern of society. There are differing points of view, for example, about the effect of aggressive behavior, or violence, as it is depicted in the mass media. One point of view suggests that watching professional football games or violent drama on television allows persons to extinguish aggression vicariously. Another group argues that such viewing tends to instigate aggressive acts. From your rather sophisticated analysis, it seems that such conclusions are too simplistic. It's just not that simple, is it?

BANDURA: The evidence indicates that in general, exposure to aggression tends to increase, rather than to reduce, aggression, but since aggression is controlled by so many different factors, predictions about the effects of modeling must consider all these different determinants. It involves a qualified judgment.

EVANS: You've looked at this problem as intricately as anyone in contemporary psychology, and your book on aggression (Bandura 1973) is rapidly becoming a classic. Suppose you were asked by a government agency, for example, about the advisability of some form of control in depicting violence in the mass media. All things being equal, would you recommend such control?

BANDURA: In the aggression book, I outline four different strategies for trying to reduce commercial modeling of violence on television. The first is congressional control. Congress doesn't have that authority, and to avoid government censorship, few of us would want to grant it that authority. If you go the congressional route, every three or four years a hearing is scheduled. These are like television re-runs—same characters, same plots, same outcomes. The researchers present evidence and the network researchers negate the evidence, and nothing much changes. You have a re-run every few years. Restrictive control is a negative approach. If there is any general principle of behavior change that's well established, it is that change is achieved more effectively through a better alternative than by prohibiting what is disvalued.

EVANS: There has been some attempt at industry self-control. How do you see that?

BANDURA: That's the second approach, industry self-control. That's largely a joke. Television is used to deliver audiences for marketing purposes, and commercial considerations are very powerful. People have been led to believe that viewers are attracted to violent content. If you examine the ratings, the violent programs are usually absent from the top ten. The reason they are so prevalent on television is because the action-adventure format is economical. For a western, all you need is a transient evil-doer, a superhero, a makeshift saloon, and the open range. It's a very attractive proposition economically. Another approach is the development of a system for monitoring the level of violence; the presence of a violence index might reduce excesses. Here you face the tremendous diffusion of responsibility. No one feels personally responsible for what is shown on television. The approach I favor is the development of alternate programming outside the commercial medium, and then using that as a means for influencing commercial television. One improves the quality of programming by providing people with more interesting alternatives, and then influencing commercial television by the tastes developed on noncommercial broadcasting systems.

EVANS: Public broadcasting, by and large, has not received the support that would make such programming possible, but ideally, I think what you're describing makes excellent sense. Moving to another area, now, we have a tremendous amount of evidence that we are, somehow, going to be cruel and aggressive toward our fellow man; that we are involved in a duplicity of roles where in one setting we can be cruel and destructive and in another setting kind and considerate. I'm particularly thinking of the studies of Latané and Darley (1970) on bystander apathy, Milgram's (1974) obedience to authority work, Zimbardo, Haney, and Banks (1973) and the prison-simulation study, and others that seem to emphasize this impersonal, cruel, or vicious side of man. I was very pleased to see that you have moved into this question of moral codes, ethics, the morality of aggression.

BANDURA: I think the issue raises the fundamental question of the relationship between people's moral codes and principles and their moral conduct. Our traditional theories of morality assume that one adopts a set of moral principles and that these serve as built-in regulators of conduct. If we could only instill the proper moral codes, our society would not be burdened with injurious behavior. From a social learning point of view, moral codes and self-evaluative actions do regulate behavior, but under certain conditions, one can dissociate reprehensible actions from self-sanctions. In fact, through self-exonerating mechanisms one can produce radical shifts in behavior at different times and in different settings without altering moral principles. I have been interested in the methods by which this disengagement process operates. One method is to assign high moral purpose to the activities; through appropriate moral justifications, one can transform aggressive behavior into an honorable activity. Much human cruelty has been perpetrated in the name of religious principles and righteous ideologies. Another method is the palliative comparison process. By comparing one's actions against more heinous deeds, the actions take on a benevolent quality. Moral justification and palliative comparison are especially powerful ways to neutralize moral self-reactions because they convert injurious behavior into positive behavior through cognitive restructuring. Another mechanism is the displacement of responsibility, which was studied by Milgram. As long as authorities are willing to assume responsibility for the consequences of culpable behavior, people feel they are not personally responsible. And then, you can dehumanize the victim. If those who are objects of attack are treated as subhumans, one is less likely to generate moral self-reactions. You can't engage morality if the consequences of your actions are distorted or not assessed. You can also attribute blame to the victim. All of these are mechanisms that enable one to behave injuriously with the same moral principles. We have studied in some detail how self-sanctions are acquired. The disengagement of internal control, which has considerable theoretical and social import, is a more intriguing issue. Our current research is directed at that very question. How does one produce marked variations in moral conduct with the same moral principles?

EVANS: You've done research that attempts to move away from the dehumanization that leads to aggression to the opposite end of the spectrum, in the sense that increased humanization would lead to less punishment and aggression. Could you tell us something about that?

BANDURA: Many of our societal conditions are especially conducive to dehumanization—bureaucratization, automation, urbanization, mobility and social practices that separate people into in-groups and out-groups—all of these produce estrangement and depersonalization. One of the instructive findings in the experiments we have been conducting is that it is difficult to aggress toward people who are humanized and personalized without eliciting self-condemning consequences for such actions.

EVANS: The old trick of catching the other driver's eye, when you want to cut in, driving in heavy traffic!

BANDURA: I know exactly what you mean. There is another point that I would emphasize here. We tend to use examples from military and political violence. These same mechanisms operate where people are trapped in activities and occupations requiring them to produce products for profit that have dehumanizing effects. The study of these processes in common practices is important because they affect our everyday life, whereas political and military violence are episodic.

EVANS: You mentioned earlier conditions under which moral codes are and are not activated. Could you describe an example of this?

BANDURA: The most dramatic example would be a general consensus in a country about the morality of a war. Given adequate moral justification, people are willing to kill without having to undergo personality transformations. When they are discharged from the military, they are not put through a resocialization process. After they return to civilian life, their internal control system is reengaged. Self-sanctions do not operate as fixed, internal regulators of conduct. Many external factors exercise control over their activation.

EVANS: The implications of that for such things as prison reform could be extremely interesting, too. Now, Dr. Bandura, in conclusion, certainly your work must have precipitated some criticism. Which of those criticisms have bothered you, if any?

BANDURA: In the early research on aggression, I was criticized for using nonhuman targets for measuring the acquisition of aggressive behavior. Different methodologies are required to assess whether aggressive patterns have been learned and whether these skills will be used for injurious purposes. One does not use live targets to study learning effects. To assess the learning of bombardier skills, one does not bomb New York City. People subscribing to the operant view object to the introduction of cognitive operations into behavioral process. And in the area of aggression, my view differs from the traditional ones. So there's a lot of room for controversy there.

EVANS: Yes, I think you've made that clear. Now, what do you have planned for the future?

BANDURA: I would like to move in at least four directions—I will continue to examine the processes underlying observational learning; because I believe that it is a fundamental mechanism by which human beings learn, I will pursue my research on component process in self-regulation; I plan to continue the study of aggression, especially the processes by which internal control is selectively activated and disengaged. I am involved in research designed to develop the power of modeling for therapeutic purposes. The worth of a theory is ultimately judged by the power of the change procedures it produces. Psychologists are skillful at developing theories, but rather slow in translating them into practice, so I maintain an interest in translating theory and principles into practice.

REFERENCES

Bandura, A., Ross, D., and Ross, S. 1961. Transmission of aggression through imitation of aggressive models. *J. Abnorm. Soc. Psychol.* 63: 575–82.
———. 1969a. *Principles of behavior modification.* New York: Holt.
———. 1969b. Social learning of moral judgments. *J. Pers. Soc. Psychol.* 11: 275–79.
———. 1971. Psychotherapy based upon modeling principles. In *Handbook of psychotherapy and behavior change,* eds. A. Bergin and S. Garfield, pp. 653–708. New York: Wiley.
———. 1971. *Social learning theory.* New York: General Learning Press.
———. 1973. *Aggression: a social learning analysis.* Englewood Cliffs, N.J.: Prentice-Hall.
———. 1973. Institutionally sanctioned violence. *J. Clin. Child Psychol.* 83: 301–03.
Dollard, J., et al. 1939. *Frustration and aggression.* New Haven: Yale University Press.
Evans, R. 1968. *B. F. Skinner: the man and his ideas.* New York: Dutton.

————. 1975. *Konrad Lorenz: the man and his ideas.* New York: Harcourt.

Hull, C. 1943. *Principles of behavior.* New York: Appleton.

————. 1951. *Essentials of behavior.* New Haven: Yale University Press.

————. 1952. *A behavior system: an introduction to behavior theory concerning the individual organism.* New Haven: Yale University Press.

Latané, B., and Darley, J. 1970. *The unresponsive bystander: why doesn't he help?* New York: Appleton.

Lorenz, K. 1966. *On aggression.* New York: Harcourt.

Milgram, S. 1974. *Obedience to authority.* New York: Harper.

Miller, N., and Dollard, J. 1941. *Social learning and imitation.* New Haven: Yale University Press.

Spence, K. 1956. *Behavior theory and conditioning.* New Haven: Yale University Press.

Thorndike, E. 1932. *The fundamentals of learning.* New York: Teachers College.

Zimbardo, P., Haney, G., and Banks, C. 1973. Interpersonal dynamics in a simulated prison. *Int. J. Criminol. Penol.* 1: 69–97.

H. J. Eysenck

(1916–)

Hans Eysenck received both his B.A. (1938) and his Ph.D. (1940) from the University of London. After World War II he joined the faculty of the University of London where he set up the first psychology department in England offering training in clinical psychology. The author of a number of books, several of which have exceeded sales of one million copies, he is currently with the Institute of Psychiatry at the University of London and is senior psychiatrist at Maudsley Hospital and Bethlehem Royal Hospital. Professor Eysenck's significant contributions include the approach he terms behavior therapy as well as important factor analytic approaches to personality measurement.

Freud Set Us Back Fifty Years/A Very Precise Criticism of Psychoanalytic Theory//Behavior Therapy/An Applied Science/Desensitization and Aversion Therapy//The Underlying Pattern/Factor Analysis//Finding the Right Dimension/Typology//Taste and Humor/Some Interesting Connections//Some of the Facts of Life/The Black-White IQ Question// Mental Health Is a Social Creation/Science and Common Sense//

As we begin the discussion, Dr. Eysenck makes some pointed criticisms of the effectiveness of psychoanalytic theory and compares it to behavior therapy, which he believes to be an applied science with measurable results. He particularly emphasizes the results of two types of behavior therapy, desensitization and aversion therapy. He explains the use of factor analysis as a research tool, discussing both its inductive and deductive approaches. He clarifies the concept of typography and outlines research that allowed him to develop a more precise hypothesis. Dr. Eysenck tells about his interest in the fields of humor and taste, and some rather interesting connections he has discovered in this area with the introvert/extravert concept. Reacting to Arthur Jensen's work on the genetic basis for IQ, he feels that we should be concerned with the facts, and makes some suggestions for dealing with those facts. In conclusion, as we discuss mental health techniques, he says, "Mental health is a social creation; what we call mental health is not something objective; it is behavior. You're not dealing with diseases of the medical kind at all. You're dealing with behavior—that's all—full stop!"

EVANS: Dr. Eysenck, to begin our discussion, I thought it might be interesting to get your reactions to some of the basic concepts in psychoanalytic theory. Now, as you know, in Freudian theory, one of the central concepts is the kind of developmental model that centers around the Oedipus complex. Does that make any sense to you?

EYSENCK: I think it is a beautiful story. I don't think it makes any sense, and I don't think there is any evidence for it. I think it's quite typical of most of the psychoanalytic theories. They're semi-interesting, particularly to humanists and people like that. But in a scientific and psychological quantity, no, I don't think they have much value.

EVANS: Of course, Freud (1953) is considered by most people as a fantastic genius. They even go so far as to say that if 1 percent of what he had to say were valid, it would still be an immense contribution. Is there anything in Freudian theory that you think from your standpoint would be acceptable?

EYSENCK: There's not an awful lot now. To my way of thinking, Freud was a great storyteller, a novelist; a maker of myths, if you like, like Marx and people like that—a tremendous influence on people and on society, literature, and so on. But I don't think any of the theories he put forward are defensible or are, in fact, scientific in the sense that they can be classified; they are too vague, too general. To my mind, he really has been a great misfortune to the development of scientific psychology and scientific psychiatry. He set us back about fifty years.

EVANS: You have created really international attention through your very, very precise criticism of psychoanalytic theory (Eysenck 1953). Why have you developed this series of reservations about it? What are the things that led you to feel strongly enough about it that you not only wrote about it in professional journals, but you felt it was important for society in general to know about this?

EYSENCK: Well, essentially, I think my role has been that of the little boy in the story of "The Emperor's New Clothes." He said, "But look, he hasn't got any clothes on." It was becoming fairly obvious, I think, to anyone who looked at the literature that there was really no evidence for the efficacy of psychoanalysis at all. But everybody talked about it as if it were useful and cured people and so on. There was not a single experiment or clinical study with proper control groups and proper evaluation. I think it is an important point to make because so many deeply troubled and unhappy people possess faith in this, pay a lot of money for it, and devote their time to it. I think they have the right to be told what the facts are.

EVANS: Analysts, whether they are more or less orthodox Freudian analysts or those who are following some of the newer traditions, which involve a little greater concern for cultural-social factors, will say that about 60 percent of the patients who complete analysis are helped substantially; although they are willing to admit that a lot of them they can't help. I gather that you feel that this is not valid.

EYSENCK: It isn't valid for three main reasons. In the first place, selection. People treated by psychoanalysts are selected for intelligence, social status, education, and so on. In the second place, the analyst is himself a judge of what he calls improvement. Outside doctors often do not agree and the patient himself often does not agree with this. In the third place, and this is the most important, there is no control group of people who are not treated by psychoanalysts—those who are not treated at all or are treated in some other way. The neurotics tend to get better regardless of what kind of treatment you give them, whether you extract their teeth as they used to do in the 1920s or give them cold baths or hot baths or do nothing at all, give them placebos. They tend to get better roughly in the proportion of two out of three, exactly the proportion as the psychoanalysts claim.

EVANS: Now are you saying that this criticism of Freudian analysis or psychoanalytic therapy would also apply to others as well, or do you think some of them have demonstrated more substantially the validity of their techniques?

EYSENCK: No, my point applies to all the psychotherapies that are currently in use. They all fail to give proof that they work better than no therapy at all. And until you get that proof, the whole movement is unscientific. It doesn't tell you anything.

EVANS: Now, of course, behavior therapy, an area of your own interest, is becoming a very important movement. What can be said about behavior therapy that sets it apart? It seems to me that if you have what you're describing here, a criterion problem, what you say are no controls, how can the behavior therapist fare any better?

EYSENCK: Well, essentially there are two reasons. The first one is that therapy is an applied science, or should be. An applied science means that you are applying facts and theories and so on which are taken from pure science. None of the others do this. They simply erect a structure of their own. Behavior therapy takes its cues from learning theory, conditioning theory, from the laboratory studies and general principles that are derived in that way. And therefore, it immediately is linked with a great body of knowledge which we have as to how conditioned emotional responses grow, how they become extinguished, and so on. And in the second place, of course, right from the beginning when I coined the term behavior therapy, I have insisted that behavior therapists must have control groups with which to compare their own data. I reviewed about twenty studies using behavior therapy where, in fact, there were control groups of various kinds, and I concluded from this comparison that in every single case the behavior therapy groups did considerably better than the control groups where they had psychotherapy or whatever it might be, or at least they didn't do worse. In one or two cases there was no difference. In the great majority, the behavior therapy groups were very much better.

EVANS: Well, perhaps it might be a good idea since you're painting this very optimistic picture about behavior therapy to ask you to describe just what is involved in behavior therapy as you see it.

EYSENCK: Well, behavior therapy is a generic term to denote all types of treatment of neurotic—particularly the neurotic, but also in some cases, psychotic—disorders or behavior disorders that are based on the principles of academic psychology, particularly learning theory. Now, the best known probably is Wolpe's (1958, 1969) method of desensitization. Then there is aversion therapy.

EVANS: What is involved in desensitization?

EYSENCK: Essentially, desensitization is used with people who have very strong feelings of anxiety or fear, whether related to one single object, as in a phobia, or more generalized and intangible.

EVANS: A fear of high places would be an example.

EYSENCK: Yes, or it could be much more widespread, such as a feeling of dread that you can't localize. Essentially, the procedure is one in which you countercondition the person to feelings of relaxation in connection with the stimulus by training him in a method of relaxation through actual muscle relaxation, or in some other way. And you associate that with imagining the stimuli in a very mild form.

EVANS: Let's say we had a patient here with an extremely intense fear of high places. Now, what would be an example of what you would do?

EYSENCK: You would begin by relaxing him and then telling him to imagine he's standing in the street and looking up at a high building, which doesn't worry him very much. Then you would say he's getting nearer to it. And gradually you will get him to walk up to the top and look down, and so on, always making sure that the anxiety produced is less than the relaxation can counterbalance.

EVANS: There is another approach you mentioned a moment ago, aversion therapy.

EYSENCK: This is exactly the opposite and used when a person indulges in a type of conduct which he doesn't want to indulge in, say alcoholism or homosexuality or fetishism or whatever it might be. But he does reinforce it to some degree, and we've found this very difficult. You want to associate this type of activity with anxiety. So you get him to indulge in the activity or imagine it and you give him, say, an electric shock so that he gradually begins to get feelings of anxiety in connection with that kind of activity. That is aversion therapy in its simplest form.

EVANS: The classic so-called "psychodynamic reaction" to what you've said here would be that with these two methods you're dealing with symptoms and not causes. The symptom may appear elsewhere, even in more serious form.

EYSENCK: Well, as always it's a question of proof or disproof. There never was any evidence for that theory. And in all the years that behavior therapy has been done (people have been followed up over quite a number of years now), we have hardly any cases of symptom substitution or relapse of this kind. So it just doesn't happen. And that, of course, puts in jeopardy the whole theory that these are symptoms supported from behind by some complex or some unimaginable event that happened early in life. We have applied a different and much simpler alternative hypothesis, which is that these are all conditioned emotional responses that have grown up according to the simple laws of conditioning.

EVANS: To move to another area, Dr. Eysenck, I think when you first got into the area of typology, it was a very unpopular thing to do. For example, in our introductory psychology classes, we were teaching students that we don't divide people into groups such as introverts and extraverts. You seem to be willing to reexamine the whole question of typology.

EYSENCK: Yes. I think the typical American textbook really does a disservice to the study of personality by essentially coming up with some notions on this which are quite erroneous, to wit that typologies are essentially either-or kinds of classifications, either an extravert or an introvert. But of all the unlikely people, it was Wilhelm Wundt in Germany who, in his textbook, pointed out that some of these categories are rather similar and reduced them all to two independent dimensions, along either of which a person could be placed at any point. One of these he called emotionality against stability, and the other one he called changeability against unchangeability, which we now call extraversion and introversion. This means that people are not either-or; they can be at any point in this two-dimensional framework.

EVANS: Then you yourself would be strongly opposed to the idea of categorization in a sense.

EYSENCK: Completely. I wouldn't go with it for a minute. It has nothing to do with the question of typology. The question of typology is to find the right dimensions and then to produce methods of measuring this.

EVANS: You, of course, are extremely well known for your very imaginative work in the technique we call factor analysis. I wonder if you could very briefly explain what is meant generally by factor analysis as a statistical analysis device.

EYSENCK: Yes. Essentially, it's really a simple kind of thing. Factor analysis is a method for analyzing the whole large table of correlations to reveal the pattern underlying all these interrelationships, sorting out those that are high from those that are low, and so on, and grouping the people or the tests or whatever you are analyzing according to the relations between them. That's all it does. It's very useful, but I think probably of all the factor analysts you may know, I'm the one who thinks least of it. I regard it as a useful kind of adjunct, a technique that was invaluable under certain circumstances, but one which we must leave behind as soon as possible in order to get a proper causal type of understanding of the factors and to know just what they mean.

Why is a person at this particular point of the continuum and not at another one? So I've been trying to link up the factors in the personality field to the causal factors, such as biological heredity. If you find a factor of emotionality characterizing people, some being very emotional and others not, this may be linked with the autonomic system and so on. And at the other end, I ask myself is there any relationship between extraversion and, say, criminal behavior and/or a relationship between introversion and neurotic behavior.

EVANS: As we read your work, we get the impression that your approach to factor analysis is a somewhat atypical departure; that is, we would suspect that factor analysis is really what we might call an inductive technique, which is throwing a lot of data from a lot of personality tests together and trying to find out which of these relate in which way and which types of factors emerge. You would appear to be using not this inductive approach but a more deductive approach where you already have a theory before you go into the factor analysis.

EYSENCK: I wouldn't say it was a departure so much. Thurstone (1947), in his fundamental book on factor analysis, pointed out that the technique could be used in both these ways. It is true, I think, that most factor analysts have probably used it more in the inductive sense, and I've used it in that sense too. My work on social attitudes, for instance, was entirely that. I didn't really know what to expect. But in the majority of cases, I think it is much better if you can start out with a hypothesis and arrange the situation in such a way that it can be supported or disproved as a result of the factor analysis. I think this is a much more scientific approach, if it is possible of course. In a new field it isn't always possible.

EVANS: We talked a moment ago about typologies on a spectrum, or a continuum, like introversion and extraversion.

EYSENCK: The first step was to establish these two: emotionality and extraversion as the two main dimensions.

EVANS: Now what other dimensions did you find?

EYSENCK: Emotionality and neuroticism. The next step was, of course, to show descriptively and by means of experimental studies just how these two dimensions were constituted, what traits belong to each and with each. So we did a large number of studies, mostly of a descriptive kind, taking introverts and extraverts to see how they differed in a great variety of experimental tests, and thus came to understand the nature of the extraversion-introversion dimension better. Finally I thought I was in a position to make a hypothesis as to the underlying psychological-physiological nature of this dimension. This idea is in my book (Eysenck 1967) on the dynamics of anxiety and hysteria—the hypothesis being that extraverts are characterized by cortical inhibition and introverts by cortical excitation. Now I think the theory has been linked up. We have EEG studies and other electrophysiological studies that link up in the predicted direction very satisfactorily.

EVANS: You're almost saying that the personality test is rapidly outliving its usefulness; that we now can make some very important determinations just by neurophysiological measures. Isn't that correct?

EYSENCK: I don't think the psychological personality has outlived its usefulness because it's very much simpler to use than an electrophysiological type of test, which needs great expertise, is very difficult to do, and needs very expensive apparatus. But I think in principle the trend is in that direction. And in due course I think we should investigate the biological background of the person rather than the kind of personality test that we've been used to so far.

EVANS: To move to a different area, I note that some years ago you were very interested in the areas of aesthetics and humor. As a precise quantifier of personality behavior, it seems that these would be the least important to you. How did you get involved in these fields?

EYSENCK: Well, in the first place, I believe that everything that exists, exists in some quantity, and therefore it can be measured. I did this during the war when there was no chance of doing anything else because no equipment was available. It was quite easy to work with aesthetic material—your pictures, your poetry, and so on. In any case, I'm very interested in these areas. Art means a lot to me. When I was young, I was exceptionally interested in poetry, particularly lyric poetry, and as I got older I became interested in painting and finally music. It always seemed to me that psychology should throw some light on this.

EVANS: I believe I understood from an earlier discussion that your father was actually a comedian.

EYSENCK: That's right.

EVANS: What have you come up with in these fields that you think might be useful?

EYSENCK: Well, I don't know that any of it would be particularly useful. I finally arrived at what I think is a reasonable theory which emphasizes three aspects—a sort of three-cornered type of theory. The first aspect is the cognitive one, that in anything that is humorous, you have an element of incongruity, which of course many people had realized before. And then there's what we might call the "affective side" that only works under certain conditions, what we might call "happy emotionality"; in other words, people who are in a happy group atmosphere and so on are much more likely to laugh and find things funny. And there is a certain aspect you might call what Hobbs used to call "triumphant laughter," the kind of conative superiority, the feeling that you are superior to somebody, therefore you laugh at him. Now any individual experience of humor or laughter will fit into that triangle at some point. Some, like jokes, are usually in the incongruity corner. Actual life situations may be quite close to either the emotional or the conative side, and you can have any combination of these factors.

EVANS: In the area of aesthetics, did you come up with some dimensions also?

EYSENCK: Yes. There were essentially two main ones. The first one I called "T," for good taste, which was perhaps not a very good term for it. Essentially I found that some people do have better taste than others in a sense which could be defined in factorial terms, in terms of an analysis of their judgments. And this was not particularly correlated with intelligence, training, upbringing, or anything else. It seems to be something innate. And the other orthogonal dimension that I selected was the preference for simple or complex types of stimuli. Some people seem to go for the simple, colorful kind of stimuli, and others for the complex, less colorful. This seemed to be correlated with extraversion-introversion, the extraverts going for the simple, colorful kind of thing and the introverts for the complex and the less-colorful type of stimulus. We've found similar things in relation to poetry, and so on.

EVANS: I think it would be interesting to hear you express what you consider your most significant contributions.

EYSENCK: Well, I think my most significant contribution has been really in bridge building. As far as I can see, you have two great sides to psychology. One is what we call experimental psychology and physiological psychology, which is usually excellent, high-standard work on relatively small and isolated phenomena that in themselves are of no great interest, like verbal learning and so on. On the other hand you have social psychologists working in a less rarified atmosphere and probably at a less rigorous level with very important problems like criminality, the causation of neuroses, strikes, and so on. What I have tried to do has been to build a bridge between these two and show that in certain fields, at least, you can form a link between the theoretical conceptions of the experimental psychologist and the physiologist and the kinds of behaviors that social psychologists are studying. Now to take a very brief example (it won't be very convincing because it has to be so brief), in my theory, introverts are characterized by high cortical arousal. This leads them to form conditioned responses better. Conditioned responses are responsible in part for the production of neurotic disorders because these are conditioned emotional responses; therefore, introverts are very likely to be found among the neurotics. Conversely, extraverts condition poorly, but socialized behavior is largely due to conditioned responses we acquire under the guise of conscience as young children; therefore, extraverts tend to become criminals. So you have a chain running all the way. This is a very difficult thing to prove.

EVANS: Well, Dr. Eysenck, one of the issues that's facing psychologists in the United States at the moment is how much involved they should become in important problems of the day, that is, social action. There are those who feel that the scientist as a scientist should stay aloof to a certain degree, that in playing the role of a psychologist it's not appropriate for him to become directly involved in issues like war and peace, the racial crisis, and so on. Do you feel that there is a way that the scientist-psychologist can be consistent and still become involved in movements of various sorts?

EYSENCK: Well, he obviously has a duty to remain a scientist. That's a first point; so that whatever he has to say should be based on scientific principles. I'm sure that psychology has a great contribution to make to all these social problems, but that contribution is probably mostly in the future. At the moment, we just don't know enough to really make a genuine contribution to the color problem or peace and war and so on. There's a further point which I think Huxley has always emphasized.

EVANS: Meaning Sir Julian Huxley, the biologist.

EYSENCK: Yes. His point is that it is quite possible that we would have to rethink our system of ethics, to throw away the revered-religion type of ethics, and to build an ethics on biological principles—what is for the good of the species, and so on—and in that, I think, a psychologist would have a contribution to make too—in fact, probably the major contribution. But very few people have really thought about this very much.

EVANS: Another question that I think might be interesting to pursue here relates to a very, very central conflict in the United States today that was generated by an article in the *Harvard Educational Review* by an educational psychologist by the name of Arthur Jensen (1969).

EYSENCK: I know. He was with me for a couple of years.

EVANS: Yes, this is why I'm bringing this up. Jensen was looking at the Headstart Program that we have in the United States and concluded that this program was failing, not because we couldn't overcome deprived environments with enrichment, but because there might be some genetic or biological determinants, that the very makeup of intelligence of the black, or Negro, is genetically different from that of the white; so you're not just fighting a cultural deprivation, but you may actually be fighting a biological deficit in at least one type of intelligence. Of course, this created quite a stir. Immediately many groups began to brand these observations as racist, and Jensen has now had to defend himself repeatedly. I was wondering how you felt about this.

EYSENCK: When Jensen was working with me, he was concerned with personality rather than intelligence. Well now, the number of issues that come into this are difficult to disentangle. The first one is what one would like to be true and what is in fact true. I have always taught that while American Negroes scored lower than whites on intelligence tests, this most probably is due to the deprivation they have suffered. And there was some evidence, I think, for that statement. As the evidence grew to point out that there were some real genetic differences, I became more and more doubtful about this, and then the second edition of Schooy's book on Negro intelligence really brought this to a head. I think now the balance of probability is very much the other way, however much we may dislike it.

Jensen was simply taking this act from Schooy. He didn't create anything new or say anything new. He simply said something that to people who are knowledgeable in this field I think is now commonplace. This is just one of the facts of life. And he pointed out this Headstart deficit, which again is a fact of life. I don't think anybody doubts it. The government has admitted it. Everyone concerned with it has admitted it. He has simply brought out that it was doomed from the start. But because they didn't pay attention to the facts of the case, it was based rather on a sort of pious hope that all men are created equal, which is of course true. They are created equal in the sight of God and as regarding the judicial system, but they are not created equal as far as beauty is concerned, or strength, or intelligence, or a great many other things. It's just one of those things that Americans have always found difficult to believe, for some unknown reason, and the Russians too. Therefore, the first point is that we've got to base judgments about ourselves on facts. The second point is, given that, what is the best method of education? Possibly the same method of education is not suitable for people who are bright and people who are dull. That's a tenable point. Jensen goes on to quote some research of his own, to make certain suggestions as to what methods might be better, and ends up with a plea for more research. This seems to me a very rational and reasonable kind of thing. And I think it's very sad that he was treated the way he was.

EVANS: Well now, just playing devil's advocate for a moment, Dr. Eysenck, the Society for the Psychological Study of Social Issues, as you know, has been one of the divisions of the American Psychological Association. It's been very, very concerned about the problem of social action. Their official feeling on this is something like this: that we are in the middle of an era when knowledge from the behavioral sciences has been made public very quickly. And although you and I sitting here or a group of scientific psychologists could look at what Jensen said or what you just said and recognize that you're just simply talking within the realm of probability—you're not certain, for example, that in some areas of intelligence Negroes are genetically inferior—you'd be the first to admit this . . .

EYSENCK: Of course.

EVANS: Then, nevertheless, by the time this is compressed and digested and integrated and synthesized, it hits the press, just like Jensen's article hit *Time* magazine in the United States. We suddenly have given the idea to the public that, in fact, what Jensen and the others have said is that Negroes are definitely genetically inferior; all the qualifications the scientist makes disappear in the telling. Therefore, the Society for the Psychological Study of Social Issues feels that this is a most unfortunate sort of thing to be publicized; they are afraid that the impact on society will be to reinforce the bigots.

EYSENCK: Well, this is not a scientific problem, of course. It's a social one and an ethical one, and I don't know the answer.

EVANS: What advice could we give society to create good mental health—whatever that is, I might add? Do you think we are ready to communicate to society techniques that could be shared by all?

EYSENCK: I think one can make a number of points which are quite important. I think the first one is that mental health in many of its aspects is a social creation, that what we call mental health is not something objective; it is behavior we like or dislike, and therefore, a much greater variety of behavioral performances can and should be tolerated than are in fact tolerated. The second point would be that mental health is a misnomer anyway because you're not dealing with diseases of the medical kind at all. You're dealing with behavior, that's all, *full stop!* The whole disease concept is an erroneous application of medical history to this field, which doesn't really fit the facts at all. What you're dealing with is essentially conditioned autonomic responses and various other types of learned behavior, partly due to Pavlovian conditioning, partly due to operant conditioning; we know a good deal about how to get rid of the worst of these, which are really debilitating for the child and too annoying for the parents or the teachers to be tolerated.

EVANS: Do you think that these kinds of tools can be handed over, say, to a mother or to a teacher or to society at large, to the boss, to the husband and wife? For example, do you think that you could get on the BBC and describe these and really have an impact on the British citizenry that would help?

EYSENCK: Well, let's face it. The fact is that mothers have for thousands of years used these methods in some way or another—desensitization, for example. The child doesn't want to go in his bath, so his mother sits him on her knee a bit nearer to the water, then coaxes him a bit, and gradually desensitizes him. Furthermore, these methods make sense, common sense in the way that Freudian theories never did. And of course, we do this in actual treatment quite a lot. We could just as well teach it over the BBC, at least the simple cases.

REFERENCES

Eysenck, H. J. 1953. *Uses and abuses of psychology.* Baltimore: Penguin.

———. 1960. *The structure of human personality.* New York: Macmillan.

———. 1966. *The effects of psychotherapy.* New York: International Science Press.

———. 1967. *The biological basis of personality.* Springfield, Ill.: Thomas.

———, and Eysenck, S. B. G. 1963. *The Eysenck personality inventory.* San Diego, Calif.: Educational and Industrial Testing Service.

———, and Rachman, S. 1965. *The causes and cures of neurosis.* San Diego, Calif.: Knapp.

Freud, S. 1953. *The standard edition of the complete psychological works of Sigmund Freud,* ed. J. Strachey. London: Hogarth Press.

Jensen, A. 1969. How much can we boost IQ and scholastic achievement? *Harvard Educational Review* 39: (1) 1–123.

Thurstone, L. 1947. *Multiple-factor analysis.* Chicago: University of Chicago Press.

Wolpe, J. 1958. *Psychotherapy by reciprocal inhibition.* Stanford, Calif.: Stanford University Press.

———. 1969. *The practice of behavior therapy.* New York: Pergamon Press.

Section Five
Personality: Analytic

This section includes a group of contributors whose work in the area of personality psychology is, in one way or another, logically derived from psychoanalysis.

Of course, Ernest Jones, Freud's faithful biographer, represents the most traditional psychoanalytic position. It is interesting to note that in addition to his solid interpretations of Freudian theory, Jones quite independently ventured into the fascinating problem of applying psychoanalytic interpretations to Shakespearean characters such as Hamlet. His urbane perspective on various problems, including child rearing, reveals that he was able to project Freudian constructs in a global fashion.

Carl G. Jung was not convinced that the key to personal growth, or as he called it, individuation, could be found solely in psychosexual development, and became one of the major dissenters from the Freudian view. His interest in the metaphysical and transcendental facets of personality development also exceeded that of Freud. Taking Freud's early idea of phylogenetic inheritance, he developed not only a notion of an individual unconscious, but a race, or collective, unconscious as well. Like Allport, he was interested in the broad, overall problem of religion, believing that virtually all neuroses in the individual from middle age on could be attributed to "religious" conflicts.

One of the most creative of the post-Freudian contributors is Erik Erikson. Not satisfied with what he considered Freud's excessive focus on biological-sexual components of early development, he developed, through intriguing cross-cultural studies, a parallel psychosocial conception of development. He paid far more attention to the ego and personal growth than Freud; his concept of the "identity crisis" dramatically emphasizes the lack of resolution of self and ego, not only in adolescence, but carried through in stages to old age, and apparent in such movements as the women's and minority-group identity strivings. His fascinating analyses of Hitler and Gandhi illustrate this identity-seeking process.

From his intellectual roots in psychoanalytic theory, Erich Fromm fashioned a psychohistorical analysis of the reaction of the individual to Nazism, an approach also utilized by Erik Erikson. He also attempted to embody his particular approach to psychoanalysis in the existential mode of Martin Buber and Jean-Paul Sartre; Sartre, interestingly enough, also influenced Ronald Laing. Fromm has constantly examined the individual's struggle to maintain freedom in a society that constantly attempts to curtail that freedom. Like Freud, Fromm is overwhelmed by the collective destructiveness of individuals in society. In a more positive sense, his examination of the "art of loving" is a classic delineation of love of self, self-love, and love of others.

Although all of the contributors to this section began in the psychoanalytic tradition, each of them interpreted psychoanalytic theory in such a creative manner that new concepts or areas of focus emerged.

Ernest Jones

(1879–1958)

*Ernest Jones received his education and train-
ing at the University of London, the University
of Wales, and Cambridge University. He established a practice in London in the field of neurology, an area in which he made a number of
significant contributions. His observation of
neurotic symptoms in his patients led him to
Freud's writings, and then in 1908 after a period of study with Kraepelin, he went to Vi-
enna where Jung introduced him to Freud. He became a colleague of Freud, and
one of the leading interpreters of Freudian theory. In addition to his contributions to
psychoanalysis and a very interesting analysis of some of Shakespeare's leading characters, Dr. Jones wrote what is considered to be the definitive biography of Sigmund
Freud.*

Man Is an Animal/Biological versus Cultural Factors/The Libidinal Drives//
None of It Is Accidental/Unconscious Motivation//There Has Always Been
Conflict/Conformity versus Individuality/Control: Social or Inborn?//
Psychoanalysis and the Creative Personality/Writer and Critic/Shakespeare's
Examples//The Impact of Genius/Jones and Freud/A Personal View//Some
Social Issues/Children/Frustration/Tolerance/Drug Therapy//

Dr. Jones and I discuss Freud's emphasis on biological factors, and he states,
"I don't see how anyone could overestimate them. Freud took the view, and
I take the view, too, that man is an animal." He elaborates on the interaction
of biological factors with cultural and environmental influences and the effects
of the libidinal drives in terms of Freud's repressed sexuality concepts. We
discuss unconscious motivations, and Dr. Jones comments on the origins of
social control. He then describes his interesting analysis of some of Shakespeare's work, generalizing to the effects of psychoanalysis on both writer and
critic. As one of the individuals closest to Freud and his most noted biographer, Dr. Jones gives us a personal view of the man behind the theory. We
conclude this discussion as Dr. Jones reacts to such issues as child-rearing
practices and the use of tranquilizers in therapeutic practice.

This discussion is an excerpt from the book, *Conversations with Carl Jung and Reactions from Ernest Jones* (1964) by Richard I. Evans. New York: D. Van Nostrand
Company.

EVANS: Dr. Jones, going into your own feelings about Dr. Freud's work and your relationship with Dr. Freud, as we look at psychology, psychoanalysis, and psychiatry today, we are struck by the fact that Dr. Freud's contribution seems to postulate a strong biological pattern which he suggests has a tremendous effect on the early development of the individual. These biological patterns, though they are modifiable by the environment or the culture within which the individual lives, nevertheless continue to direct the individual to a great extent.

Very recently, as you know, there have been a number of people who feel that perhaps Dr. Freud and the psychoanalysis of this period emphasized biological factors a bit too much, that maybe the culture in which we live, our society and environmental surroundings, have as much or more effect in the molding of the individual than do these biological factors. I wonder if you would like to comment on this in terms of whether, first of all, we are unfair in suggesting that Freud was over-emphasizing biological factors; and secondly, about those views emphasizing cultural factors, that stem from the so-called "neo-Freudian" movement. How would Freud have reacted to them?

JONES: No, I don't think for a minute it would be fair to say that he was over-emphasizing the importance of biological factors. I don't see how anybody could over-estimate them. Freud took the view, and I take the view too, that man is an animal. In other words, man is in line biologically with the rest of living creatures and is actuated by instincts and reactions of a similar kind, though certainly of a more elaborate kind. That is in the nature of things, the basis of man's being. You can take another view and say that that is only part of his being, and that there is the spiritual part which came from the sky and was put into him on top of it all; but we don't happen to take that view. There doesn't seem to be any direct evidence for it. I don't see how you can over-estimate the nature of man.

EVANS: What would you say about cultural influences?

JONES: When you come to cultural influences, they too are the produce of the biological motives; so it's really at the next remove, you see. Take for example the Oedipus complex, which we think is very fundamental and possibly even inborn—we don't know exactly about that—but anyhow very fundamental, a fundamental tendency. Well now, you look at a society, say particularly a German society where the father is very important, lays down the law, etc. Very well. You would expect to get an Oedipus complex there. However, what about other societies where that is less so? What about America, where the mother is more important than the father, where the "Mom" is really *the person*? Or what about still more matrilineal societies where the woman ranks very high indeed? What about native societies where the father doesn't live with the mother and only visits her occasionally, where she lives with her brother and the boy is brought up by this brother, his uncle? What about them?

Well now, you are going to call that a cultural, environmental influence. All right, you can, but that causes naturally a shift in the form taken by your biological reactions; it's like a pressure. In the case of that last society, for instance, the boy will react to his uncle with jealousy, rivalry, opposition, hatred, and love as well, as he normally would toward the father. And his real father, who only comes in occasionally, plays with him and is his comrade in games and fun but has no authority over him, will correspond with our uncles or grandparents who spoil the child. In other words, it causes that shift. It doesn't alter the biological pattern; it only alters the form it takes.

EVANS: To refer to the biological pattern in Dr. Freud's concept of libido in which he seems to talk about a broad, psychic sexual energy, there is a question as to how we should interpret the term "sex" here. Are we talking about *narrow* sexuality, or is this broad sexual drive he is talking about merely the total involvement of all biological drives? In other words, are those individuals who have suggested that he tried to explain everything in terms of repressed sexuality unfair to Freud?

JONES: Trying to explain everything in terms of repressed sexuality? I think that's going very wildly astray, don't you? He thought that the libidinal drives were a part of the biological inheritance of man, just as other instincts are, like curiosity or perhaps aggression, etc.; and he found by experience that this often enters into conflict with other aspects of the personality, which we know quite well is true and gets people into trouble in consequence. But I don't quite see—it would be ridiculous to say that some people explained everything in terms of sex, because if it were as simple as that, what would happen to his whole theory of conflict? There are two sides.

EVANS: Would this be a fair statement of the situation? With his patients in the repressed culture of Vienna, Dr. Freud very often saw conflicts centered around sexuality. Therefore, in these particular patients he saw sexual conflicts as fundamental to their neuroses, which could account, at least in part, for the great emphasis on sexuality as a causative factor to be seen in his reporting. He might actually have been willing to see other underlying causes if they had been visible.

JONES: Yes, I think he would have been willing to see anything that was there.

EVANS: This, of course, has been one of the bases for much criticism of Dr. Freud.

JONES: Yes, you would expect that, because by his theory there is a great deal of repression of sexuality; and naturally, if you point that out, you are bound to run into the repression, aren't you? This would illustrate what we call resistance, or opposition, or criticism, or anything you like.

EVANS: To go further, Freud's interesting paper on psychopathology in everyday life revealed how Dr. Freud rather ingeniously and brilliantly could analyze any number of specific situations in just day-today living, seeing into the operation of the unconscious. Would Freud have said that everything we do is determined in this way? Would Dr Freud have said that things which would appear to have been accidental really were not? Does one assume that there is always some unconscious involvement?

JONES: It is quite simple. Freud says all our spontaneous activity is motivated, broadly speaking. That's what you mean; none of it is accidental. No, it would be very unscientific to think it could be.

EVANS: Moving along to quite a different area, Dr. Jones, one of the problems that interests us a great deal today in the United States is the one of man's over-conformity. We are asking ourselves such questions as: Are we losing individual identity? Is the individual more or less becoming, as one American writer has said, "other-directed"? Are we worried so much about what the other person thinks that we don't develop truly individual personalities?

JONES: Well, I don't know what he is "becoming," but it seems to me that the state of affairs you point to is universal and eternal; that is to say, there always must have been conflict between the individual's desire to act freely without taking into regard anybody else, and the necessity he recognizes to take other people into consideration. Obviously a community would be impossible if everybody did exactly whatever he liked.

EVANS: We need some order, of course, some organization.

JONES: Yes, and that is how civilization clearly evolves. Then you say, "Is man becoming more conforming?" Well now, I think we are getting freer and freer in that way. We are certainly allowed to do many things that we couldn't in the middle ages, for instance, or say 120 years ago.

Of course, the extent to which free development of individuality can take place must vary in different cultures and in different periods, and that raises the very interesting problem as to why. It is generally thought that in France there is more individual development and less conformity; they don't even pay their taxes very often there. They can't get a stable government. Everyone wants to act on their own. That has its advantages, no doubt, in that it allows freer development of the individual, but it leads to practical troubles from a social point of view.

In America, I don't really know. I suppose in the small town places, places like Sinclair Lewis describes in *Main Street* and *Babbitt*, there must be a good deal of conformity. I should think the obvious factor in determining on which side the accent is placed, say in the French way of life versus the American, is probably a matter of social penalty. Now, if a man in France doesn't conform, does anything very awful happen to him? Not really. However, if a man doesn't conform in America, a lot of very awful things do happen to him. He loses his job and is not allowed to get another; or he is thrown out of the university. A whole lot of things can happen to him, and that increases the necessity to conform.

EVANS: In a sense, then, you feel that immediate social pressures are forcing the individual to conform, but in the long-range, historical perspective, man is actually becoming freer and freer, more of an individual. These particular pressures to which man is subject are only momentarily relevant.

JONES: Yes, and so all over Europe in the same way. I suppose the freest place was Russia in tsarist times, provided you didn't talk about politics. Now that is all changed. In another hundred years, however, we'll round-about again. In other words, there are constant shifts, about every fifty years or so in different countries.

EVANS: Would you say that the process of undergoing psychoanalysis in a very broad sense bears on this? In other words, would you say that an individual who has sort of lost his identity by over-conforming and being too afraid of social pressures, who is disturbed and unhappy, through analysis might come to realize individual trends in himself more and perhaps become a more productive, creative individual?

JONES: Bound to. That's the aim of analysis, isn't it? The aim of analysis is to make the person more himself; that is to say, to make him the whole of "himself," not only the visible part, but the repressed part, the hidden part, the part in conflict. They should all come into play and be under a unified control so that he would be a bigger, fuller, more complete personality.

EVANS: Doesn't this unified control of which you speak necessarily imply control which is social in origin?

JONES: No. I'm talking about his own conscience, and his own conscience is a thing that develops only partly from social sources, social control, etc. As you know, he begins very much earlier in life, and his conscience goes back at least to the first year of life. You can trace the beginning of it.

EVANS: The first impact of the small family structure on the neophyte.

JONES: Yes, and possibly even inborn tendencies.

EVANS: What exactly is the nature of these inborn tendencies bearing on social morality to which Freud referred as the super-ego? Are we to believe that man is already born with built-in prohibitions on his social existence?

JONES: It is hard to prove or demonstrate things of that sort. I should think myself it is very likely, because I don't think that all of the super-ego comes from the outside pressure. I think some comes from inside. The child is born with much wilder impulses than we have when we are grown up. He not only has to learn to control them and guide them in certain directions for social reasons, but also for personal reasons, because some of them are very harmful to himself, very destructive to himself, or destructive to somebody he loves. In other words, there are dangers coming from within as well as from without; so there is a necessity to control or repress, or to do something about those internal dangers. It seems very likely to me that that control is inborn, for biological reasons of survival.

EVANS: We have read with great interest your analyses of literary figures such as Hamlet in Shakespeare. There has been a very interesting tendency in literary circles to apply psychoanalytic theory to an understanding or evaluation of great literature. Does it follow that the young writer should study psychoanalytic theory? Would this be of help to him? Should the critic become thoroughly acquainted with these ideas also?

JONES: I think there is a sharp distinction between the writer and the critic. I would say "no" for one and "yes" for the other. I think the writer would be harmed if he tried to benefit by psychoanalytic knowledge, because he would be harmed if he tried to benefit by any knowledge from outside himself and how he personally feels about things, say political knowledge or what not; it would take away from his own spontaneous impulses. The more spontaneous the writer, the greater the writer. The creation must come from within. I'm quite definite about that. On the other hand, when it comes to the critic, this internal aspect of the problem is not really important.

EVANS: With repect to the use of psychoanalytic theory and understanding, you have commented that with the author it may actually be a stifling thing. It may not allow him to free his individuality adequately. On the other hand, you suggested that with a critic this may be a different matter.

JONES: Quite different. But let me be quite clear in what I mean about the writer before we discuss the critic. I didn't mean to say that being analyzed would be harmful to the writer, but rather that reading about it would be harmful. I meant that if a writer should be analyzed, he would be a freer, fuller writer; he would be clearer and more spontaneous.

With the critic, however, it's different again, because I think all the way around psychoanalytic knowledge can be helpful to the critic. The critic's job is to assess both the aesthetic side of the work that he is reviewing or criticizing, and also the intellectual content. The aesthetic evaluation depends, of course, upon the critic's sensibility, which implies the need for freedom of his feelings; and where the intellectual analysis of the content is concerned, I think a knowledge of psychoanalysis is very helpful, enabling the person to more accurately estimate how consistent the production is. Now take the case of "Hamlet"; that was a play that was relevant on many different levels. It probably had a current political reference, perhaps forgotten now. There were all sorts of social allusions at that time, peculiar to the specific period of the play, which people then could understand; there were particular jokes maybe, different layers, until you got deeper and deeper, and the whole thing became unified. Now if any production is a really great work of art, it is consistent all the way through; and when I say consistent, I mean it's true all the way through. That, I think, a critic ought to be able to evaluate.

EVANS: A certain intrinsic unity in the over-all analysis.

JONES: Yes.

EVANS: Dr. Jones, a very interesting question, one brought to mind by your biography of Dr. Freud (1957), concerns the impact of a genius's own personal life on what he produces. For example, there has been much research in recent years in which there has been some attempt to study the basic personality of individuals in the hope that what leads them into various professions or into various productive efforts can be ascertained. In fact, Freud himself with his analysis of DaVinci suggests that we can in a very deterministic type of analysis understand how an individual may produce, the basic foundation upon which production rests. Now in the case of Freud's own personal life, in what way do you feel his life may have influenced the direction of his psychoanalytic theories and the formulations therein?

JONES: Well, there again we've got to distinguish. I think the main direction in which he was influenced was from the point of view of interest; certain things led him to take an interest in this, that, and the other. That's one thing. Now another consideration inherent in your question concerns the actual formulation of his various scientific theories. And then there is also a third thing; that is, to what extent his personal penchant, his own general outlook on life, served as an influence on him. Those are three quite different things. Which shall we take first now?

I should think that there must be ultimately some form of curiosity, surely. Why curiosity should take that particular direction would depend probably on more delicate infantile influences than are easy to put your finger on now. But as regards any personal influences acting on his theories, I am really not aware of that. I should say that his theories were objective and originated as a result of his experience. He came across certain facts, and he tried to group them as every scientist does; he tried to provide a unifying hypothesis for them. Of course, it is obvious that his personal experiences must have influenced him a great deal in his general outlook on life. For instance, he was an atheist. That must have been due to something in his early life. He was never brought up with a strong religious influence, so it may have been easy for him to do without it. What other things can we say?

EVANS: Well, for example, let us take the fact that his father was so much older than his mother. Do you think it possible that this age differential might be discernible in some of his formulations?

JONES: I think that made it harder for him to recognize the Oedipus situation. He was very fond of his father, and they got along very well, being of similar types of mind. His father was a free-thinking, humorous, witty, liberal-minded type of man, just like Freud. Freud had an extraordinary sense of humor, and was very fond of jokes, etc. Most of this, he got from his father. Thus, to discover that there was within him a secret hatred of his father must have been very difficult.

EVANS: I know that in some of his later work he became, in the opinion of some, more speculative than scientific with his discussions of such things as religion and war. Do you think that Freud's work could be better understood if we could separate this type of speculation from his more fundamental observations?

JONES: Yes, very definitely.

EVANS: When can we say that Freud's work became more a reflection of personal ideology, as opposed to an earlier time when it can be described as more scientific and objective?

JONES: I think that there is a very sharp point at which we can make this distinction, the year after the end of the First War, the year 1919, when he was writing the book, *Beyond the Pleasure Principle* (Freud, 1922). In this book he was getting into philosophy over his conception of the death instinct. You see, the death instinct was supposed to be not only a human thing, but a concept that applied to all living matter. There was an inherent tendency toward self-destruction, not only in all animals, but in vegetables as well. Now one has to say that that is not a biological conception, and one also has to say, strictly speaking, that it is not a scientific one. It's an idea like any other philosophical idea. I think that period in Freud's career marks the beginning of the ideological tone to which you referred. You can trace several things after that probably, but they are always all mixed up, aren't they? I mean, he was a rationalist, which means he tried to take an objective stand in viewing this, that, and the other, rather than depending on intuition or emotion. So with respect to his books on group psychology, even those which fell in that period, I think you've got to take into account the rational aspect, which is really the scientific part, as well as his personal outlook. It's not all personal.

EVANS: In some of his later works on mental telepathy, clairvoyance, and so on, could their contents be classified under the realm of his genuinely empirical research?

JONES: No, not a bit. That's purely personal. I mean, he considered, or it was his opinion, that there was sufficient evidence to hold such and such a belief. Very well. Whether or not one considers the evidence sufficient in a given case to draw conclusions cannot, in the final analysis, be entirely objective. You nearly always are influenced for or against by some prejudice or emotional element stemming from your background. In Freud's case, there was a tendency to believe, and also a tendency to doubt. It is very interesting that in his different statements one could see certain alternations. There was both a sort of credulous attitude and a skeptical attitude. Undoubtedly, he had both.

EVANS: A question that is very much the center of controversy, particularly in the United States and to some extent in England, is one of the amount of freedom our children should be allowed as they grow up. We have some extremes on this issue. We have one extreme which follows the disciplinarian approach that historically has been part of most of our cultures. Utilizing this approach, we control the child almost completely and give him very little freedom. Then, of course, the other extreme has been a very permissive approach where we allow the child to develop his individuality, attempting to force upon him absolutely no restrictions or frustrating demands whatsoever. As a result of this approach, we have seen in many of our households children behaving in a destructive and antisocial manner with parents who tolerate this poor behavior because they fear they may frustrate their children. Unfortunately, particularly in the United States, many individuals have blamed psychoanalysis—

JONES: For both of them?

EVANS: For suggesting the unrestrained view. In fact, many laymen have referred to the psychological approach as a product of Freud's work. I wonder if you might comment upon how Freud actually viewed this problem.

JONES: He would recognize that frustrations are an inevitable part of living in a community. There must be frustrations. Nobody can do absolutely everything he likes. He can't go and defecate in the street, and limitations such as that begin as early in life as infancy. Now the extent to which he experiences difficulty with these social frustrations we think depends upon the varying ease or difficulty he has in tolerating them. The point is that abolishing frustrations isn't the answer; you must learn to tolerate them.

EVANS: So it was Freud's psychoanalytic view, and certainly it is your view, that in order to develop frustration tolerance, the developing child must be exposed to some frustrations.

JONES: Well, you are exposed to them anyway, and you are overlooking that when you talk about freedom.

EVANS: Now, let us address ourselves to the problem of the treatment of mental disorders. In addition to the pioneer technique of psychoanalysis, various other types of techniques for treatment of these disorders have been developed. Among these are shock therapy, psychosurgery, variations of the original psychoanalytic approach, and so on. One of the most recent developments has been the use of tranquilizing drugs. In fact, the first one, chlorpromazine, was first used here in France. Since then, many milder tranquilizers have been developed which are being dispensed by physicians on quite a large scale. How do you view this practice?

JONES: It's like sitting on a steam safety valve. Of course you can dampen it down. If you want to, you can give a drug that will make a person unconscious; give enough opium and you can dampen anything down. The same principle is involved in lowering the degree of tension with barbituates, or what not. You can lower the degree of tension in the individual, but you aren't changing anything. Whatever caused the tension is still there. If you take away the drug, it comes back again. I don't think there is any evidence to show that any drug can change either the personality or the content of particular conflicts or ideas which may be disturbing the individual.

EVANS: One view has been that certain types of seriously ill psychotic patients, such as the schizophrenic with whom the psychotherapist is simply unable to communicate, become more amenable to therapy through use of drugs. Under these conditions do you think the use of drugs is in order?

JONES: No, I don't think it is very helpful. Is there value in the patient becoming more amenable, let us say, to psychoanalytic therapy? No, I don't think so, because when you dampen the emotions in that way, you're making them less accessible to change; and, of course, changing them is your aim. You have to get hold of a thing before you can handle it, before you can change it. By temporarily abolishing it, you are no further along.

EVANS: In other words, although it may appear to be a way of making the patient more accessible, it really is making him less so?

JONES: That's correct; it makes him less accessible.

EVANS: Now, of course, all of this reflects new developments in treating much more seriously disturbed patients, such as the psychotic.

JONES: It then becomes a practical matter, just like strait jackets in the old days—a practical matter, tie them up.

REFERENCES

Evans, R. I. 1964. *Conversations with Carl Jung and reactions from Ernest Jones.* New York: Van Nostrand.

Freud, S. 1922. *Beyond the pleasure principle.* London: International Psychoanalytical Press.

Jones, E. 1957. *The life and work of Sigmund Freud,* vol. 3. New York: Basic Books.

C. G. Jung

(1875–1961)

C. G. Jung received his medical degree from the University of Basel in 1900. He studied with Pierre Janet in Paris and worked for a period of time with Eugene Bleuler, who developed the concept of schizophrenia. In 1913 he gave up his position at the University of Zurich to allow more time for private practice, research, and writing. A colleague of Freud, he eventually broke with Freud on a number of important issues, including the psychosexual theory of development which Jung found too restrictive. Acknowledged as one of the century's great thinkers and the founder of analytic psychology, Jung's contributions to psychology include such basic concepts as introvert and extrovert, the word association test, the collective unconscious, and the more controversial notion of archetypes. Much of his writing also reflects his intense interest in the broad problems of religion in the development and individuation of the person.

Jung and Freud: Interaction and Reaction/The First Point of Difference/ The Unconscious Is *Really* Unconscious/The Constantly Building Ego/The Eternal Truths in Man//Jung: Definitions, Explanations, and Examples/ Archetypes/The Collective Unconscious/Mythology/Religion/Alchemy/ *Anima/Animus/Persona*/Self/The Square in the Circle/Mandala//Introvert/ Extrovert/Thinking/Feeling/Sensation/Intuition//Therapy: Where to Begin/ The Word Association Test/Psychosomatic Illnesses/Drug Therapy//

Dr. Jung and I begin our discussion with his reactions to Freud's theory, and he describes the first point of difference that led him to eventually break with Freud. He elaborates on his concepts of the unconscious, the id, ego, and superego, and the ways in which his thinking differs from traditional Freudian theory. He then gives a fascinating explanation of archetypes and the collective unconscious, with its underlying patterns of mythology, religion, and alchemy. He defines the terms anima, animus, and persona, clarifies his use of the term self, and traces the mandala, the circle in the square image so per-

---

This discussion is an excerpt from the book, *Jung on elementary psychology: a discussion between C. G. Jung and Richard I. Evans*. New York: E. P. Dutton. Copyright © 1976 by Richard I. Evans. Reprinted by permission of E. P. Dutton. Originally published as *Conversations with Carl Jung and Reactions from Ernest Jones* (1964) by Richard I. Evans. New York: D. Van Nostrand Company.

vasive in his work, through its historical and symbolic meanings. As the originator of the concept of introvert and extravert, he explains his development of this notion and the relationships to thinking, feeling, sensation, and intuition. In a rather charming confession he describes the development of the Word Association Test: "In the beginning . . . I was completely disoriented with patients. I didn't know where to begin or what to say, and the association experiment has given me access to their unconscious." Concluding our discussion, Dr. Jung reacts to my questions about psychosomatic illness and the effects of tranquilizing drugs in therapy.

EVANS: Dr. Jung, going into the development of Freud's theory, which you acknowledge as a significant factor in the development of many of your own early ideas, Dr. Freud talked a great deal about the unconscious.

JUNG: As soon as research comes to a question of the unconscious, things become necessarily blurred, because the unconscious is something which is really unconscious! So you have no object—nothing. You only can make inferences because you can't see it; and so you have to create a model of this possible structure of the unconscious. Now Freud came to the concept of the unconscious chiefly on the basis of the same experience I have had in the association experiment; namely, that people reacted—they said things—they did things—without knowing that they had done it or had said it. There is a certain depotentiation of consciousness; it sinks below the level of consciousness and thus becomes unconscious. That is Freud's view too, but he says it sinks down because it is helped; it is repressed from above. That was my first point of difference with Freud. I think there have been cases in my observations where there was no repression from above; those contents that became unconscious had withdrawn all by themselves, and not because they were repressed. On the contrary, they have a certain autonomy. They have discovered the concept of autonomy in that these contents that disappear have the power to move independently from my will. Either they appear when I want to say something definite; they interfere and speak themselves instead of helping me to say what I want to say; they make me do something which I don't want to do at all; or they withdraw in the moment that I want to use them. They certainly disappear!

EVANS: Dr. Freud suggested that the individual is born under the influence of what he called the id, which is unconscious and undeveloped, a collection of animal drives. It is not very easily understood where all these primitive drives, all these instincts, come from.

JUNG: Nobody knows where instincts come from. They are there and you find them. It is a story that was played millions of years ago. It is quite ridiculous, you know, to speculate about such an impossibility. So the question is only, Where do those cases come from where instinct does not function? That is something within our reach, because we can study the cases where instinct does not function.

EVANS: To continue, another part of Dr. Freud's theory, of course, that became very important, to which we have already alluded, was the idea of the conscious; that is, out of this unconscious, instinctual "structure," the id, an ego emerges. Freud suggested that this ego resulted from the organism's contact with reality, perhaps a product of frustration as reality is imposed on the individual. Do you accept this conception of the ego?

JUNG: If man has an ego at all, that is your question. Ah, that is again such a case as before; I wasn't there when it was invented. However, in this case, you see, you can observe it to a certain extent with a child. A child definitely begins in a state where there is no ego, and about the fourth year or before, the child develops a sense of ego—"I, myself." The identity with the body is one of the first things which makes an ego; it is the spatial separateness that induces, apparently, the concept of an ego. Later on there are mental differences and other personal differences of all sorts. You see, the ego is continuously building up; it is not ever a finished product—it builds up.

EVANS: In his later writing, in addition to the ego, Freud introduced a term to describe a particular function of the ego. That term was the super-ego. Broadly speaking, the super-ego was to account for the "moral restrictive" function of the ego.

JUNG: Yes, that is the super-ego, namely that codex of what you can do and what you cannot do.

EVANS: Built-in prohibitions which Freud thought might be partly acquired and partly "built-in."

JUNG: Yes. However, Freud doesn't see the difference between the built-in and the acquired. You see, he must have it almost entirely within himself; otherwise, there could be no balance in the individual. And who in Hell would have invented the Decalogue [the Ten Commandments]? That is not invented by Moses, but that is the eternal truth in man himself, because he checks himself.

EVANS: At this time would you please elaborate on the concept, archetype?

JUNG: Well, you know what a behavior pattern is, the way in which a weaver bird builds its nest. That is an inherited form in him. It is quite certain that man is born with a certain functioning, a certain way of functioning, a certain pattern of behavior which is expressed in the form of archetypal images, or archetypal forms. For instance, the way in which a man should behave is expressed by an archetype. Therefore, you see, the primitives tell such stories. A great deal of education goes through story-telling. For instance, they call together the young men, and two older men act out before the eyes of the younger all the things they should not do. Another way is they tell them all of the things they should not do, like the Decalogue, "Thou shalt not," and that is always supported by mythological tales. That, of course, gave me a motive to study the archetypes, because I began to see that the structure of what I then called the collective unconscious was really a sort of agglomeration of such typical images, each of which had a unique quality. The archetypes are, at the same time, dynamic. They are instinctual images that are not intellectually invented. They are always there and they produce certain processes in the unconscious that one could best compare with myths. That's the origin of mythology. So the statements of every religion, of many poets, etc., are statements about the inner mythological process, which is a necessity because man is not complete if he is not conscious of that aspect of things.

And the next question I asked myself was, "Now, where in the world has anybody been busy with that problem?" I found that nobody had except a peculiar spiritual movement that went together with the beginning of Christianity—the Gnostics. They were concerned with the problem of archetypes, and made a peculiar philosophy of it. Everybody makes a peculiar philosophy of it when he comes across it naïvely, and doesn't know that those are structural elements of the unconscious psyche. The Gnostics lived in the first, second, and third centuries; and I wanted to know what was in between that time and today, when we suddenly are confronted by the problems of the collective unconscious which were the same two thousand years ago, though we are not prepared to admit that problem. I found to my amazement that it was alchemy, that which is understood to be a history of chemistry. It was a peculiar spiritual movement or a philosophical movement. They called themselves philosophers, like Gnosticism. Of course, I cannot tell you in detail about alchemy. It is the basis of our modern way of conceiving things, and therefore, it is as if it were right under the threshold of consciousness.

So you see, in our days we have such and such a view of the world, a particular philosophy, but in the unconscious we have a different one. That we can see through the example of the alchemistic philosophy that behaves to the medieval consciousness exactly like the unconscious behaves to ourselves. And we can construct or even predict the unconscious of our days when we know what it has been yesterday.

EVANS: Could this action of the archetype be described as spontaneous?

JUNG: Quite spontaneous. You are seized with a certain spell and you do a thing that is unexpected. You see, the archetype is a force. It has an autonomy, and it can suddenly seize you. So, for instance, falling in love at first sight, that is such a case. You have a certain image in yourself, without knowing it, of the woman—of any woman. You see that girl, or at least a good imitation of your type, and instantly you get the seizure; you are caught. And afterward you may discover that it was a hell of a mistake. He sees that she is no good at all, that she is a hell of a business, and he tells me so. He says, "For God's sake, doctor, help me to get rid of that woman." He can't though, and he is like clay in her fingers. That is the archetype. It has all happened because of the archetype of the anima, though he thinks it is all his soul, you know. It is like the girl—any girl. When a man sings very high, for instance, sings a high C, she thinks he must have a wonderful spiritual character, and she is badly disappointed when she marries that particular "letter." Well, that's the archetype of the animus.

EVANS: To recapitulate then, the archetype is just a higher order of an instinctual pattern, such as your earlier example of a bird building a nest. Is that how you intended to describe it?

JUNG: It is a biological order of our mental functioning, as, for instance, our biological-physiological function follows a pattern. We are only deeply unconscious of these facts because we live by all our senses and outside of ourselves. If a man could look into himself, he could discover it. When a man discovers it in our days, he thinks he is crazy—really crazy.

EVANS: Now would you say the number of such archetypes is limited or predetermined, or can the number be increased?

JUNG: Well, I don't know what I do know about it; it is so blurred. You see, we have no means of comparison. We know and we see that there is a behavior, say like incest; or there is a behavior of violence, a certain kind of violence; or there is a behavior of panic, of power, etc. Those are areas, as it were, in which there are many variations. It can be expressed in this way or that way, you know. And they overlap, and often you cannot say where the one form begins or ends. It is nothing concise, because the archetype in itself is completely unconscious and you only can see the effects of it. You can see, for instance, when you know a person is possessed by an archetype; then you can divine and even prognosticate possible developments.

EVANS: To be more specific, Dr. Jung, you have used the concepts, anima and animus, which you are now identifying in terms of sex, male or female. I wonder if you could elaborate perhaps even more specifically on these terms? Take the term "anima" first. Is this again part of the inherited nature of the individual?

JUNG: Well, this is a bit complicated, you know. The anima is an archetypal form, expressing the fact that a man has a minority of feminine or female genes. That is something that doesn't appear or disappear in him, that is constantly present, and works as a female in a man. As early as the sixteenth century, the humanists had discovered that man had an anima, and that each man carried female within himself. They said it; it is not a modern invention. The same is the case with the animus. It is a masculine image in a woman's mind which is sometimes quite conscious, sometimes not quite conscious; but it is called into life the moment that woman meets a man who says the right things.

Then because he says it, it is all true and he is *the* fellow, no matter what he is. Those are particularly well-founded archetypes, those two. And you can lay hands on their bases.

EVANS: Dr. Jung, to pursue our discussion of the unconscious further, let us take the particular situation of a dream and its interpretation. It is my understanding that, in your view of the unconscious, what you would find in the dream would not necessarily be an image or symbol of what has happened in the past to the individual.

JUNG: Oh, no! It is the manifestation of the situation of the unconscious, looked at from the unconscious.

EVANS: Now if the unconscious acts on the present situation, looking at this in broad motivational terms, this effect of the unconscious is not something which is a result of repression in the way the orthodox psychoanalyst looks at it at all.

JUNG: It may be, you know, that what the unconscious has to say is so disagreeable that one prefers not to listen, and in most cases people would be probably less neurotic if they could admit the things. But these things are always a bit difficult or disagreeable, inconvenient, or something of the sort; so there is always a certain amount of repression. But that is not the main thing.

EVANS: Would there be quite a lot of equivalence between the unconscious of a particular individual who was raised in one culture, and another individual who was raised in an entirely different culture?

JUNG: Well, that question is also complicated because when we speak of the unconscious, Jung would say, "Which unconscious?" We say, "Is it that personal unconsciousness which is characteristic for a certain person, for a certain individual?"

EVANS: You have talked in your writings about a personal unconsciousness as being one kind of unconscious.

JUNG: Yes. In treatment, for instance, the treatment of neuroses, you have to do with that personal unconsciousness for quite a while, and then only when dreams come that show the collective unconscious can it be touched upon.

EVANS: Now the distinction between the personal unconscious and the collective unconscious, then, is that the personal could be more involved with the immediate life of the individual, and the collective would be universal—the unconscious realm composed of elements which are the same in all men?

JUNG: Yes, collective. For instance, the psyche has collective problems, collective convictions, etc. We are very much influenced by them, and there are examples to prove it. You belong to a certain political party, or to a certain confession; that can be a serious determinant of your behavior. Now if there arises a matter of personal conflict, the collective unconscious isn't touched upon. But the moment you transcend your personal sphere and come to your unpersonal determinant—say you respond to a political question, or to any other social question which really matters to you—then you are confronted with a collective problem; then you have collective dreams.

EVANS: Another very interesting concept or idea in your work is the "persona." This seems to be highly relevant to the daily living of the individual. I wonder if you would mind elaborating a bit more about how you construe this term, "persona."

JUNG: It is a practical concept we need in elucidating people's relations. I noticed with my patients, particularly with people that are in public life, that they have a certain way of presenting themselves. The persona is partially the result of the demands society has. On the other side, it is a compromise with what one likes to be, or as one likes to appear. So the persona is a certain complicated system of behavior which is partially dictated by society and partially dictated by the expectations or the wishes one nurses oneself. Now this is not the real personality. In spite of the fact that people will assure you that this is all quite real and quite honest, yet it is not. Such a performance of the persona is quite all right, as long as you know that you are not identical to the way in which you appear; but if you are unconscious of this fact, then you get into sometimes very disagreeable conflicts. It is a question of Jekyll and Hyde. Occasionally there is such a difference that we would almost be able to speak of a double personality, and the more that it is pronounced, the more people are neurotic. They get neurotic because they have two different ways; they contradict themselves all the time, and inasmuch as they are unconscious of themselves, they don't know it. They think they're all one, but everybody sees that they are two.

EVANS: Actually, would you say that the individual may even have more than two personae?

JUNG: We can't afford very well to play more than two roles, but there are cases where people have up to five different personalities. In ordinary cases, it's just an ordinary dissociation of personality. One calls that a systematic dissociation, in contradistinction to the chaotic or unsystematic dissociation you find in schizophrenia.

EVANS: You also use the term "self." Now the word "self"—does it have a different meaning than "ego" or "persona"?

JUNG: Yes. When I say "self," then you mustn't think of "I, myself," because that is only your empirical self, and that is covered by the term "ego"; but when it is a matter of "self," then it is a matter of personality and is more complete than the ego, because the ego only consists of what you are conscious of, what you know to be yourself. Now you see, while I am talking, I am conscious of what I say; I am conscious of myself, yet only to a certain extent. Quite a lot of things happen. When I make gestures I'm not conscious of them. I may say or use words and can't remember at all having used those words, or even at the moment I am not conscious of them. Or say when I am writing a paper, I am continuing to write that paper in my mind without knowing it. You can discover these things, say in dreams; or if you are clever, in the immediate observation of the individual. Then you see in the gestures or in the expression in the face that there is what one calls "*une arriere pensée*," something behind consciousness. There are, of course, great individual differences. There are individuals who have an amazing knowledge of themselves, of the things that go on in themselves. But even those people wouldn't be capable of knowing what is going on in their unconscious. For instance, they are not conscious of the fact that while they live a conscious life, all the time a myth is played in the unconscious, a myth that extends over centuries, namely, archetypal ideas. Really it is like a continuous stream, one that comes into daylight in the great movements, say in political movements or in spiritual movements.

If somebody is clever enough to see what is going on in people's minds, in their unconscious minds, he will be able to predict. For instance, I could have predicted the Nazi rising in Germany through the observation of my German patients. They had dreams in which the whole thing was anticipated, and with considerable detail. And I was absolutely certain—in the years before Hitler, before Hitler came in the beginning—I was sure that something was threatening in Germany, something very big, very catastrophic. I only knew it through the observation of the unconscious.

There is something very particular in the different nations. It is a peculiar fact that the archetype of the anima plays a very great role in Western literature, French and Anglo-Saxon. But in Germany, there are exceedingly few examples in German literature where the anima plays a role. . . . She must have a title; otherwise she hasn't existed. And so it is just as if—now mind you, this is a bit drastic, but it illustrates my point—in Germany there really are no women. There is Frau Doctor, Frau Professor, Frau the grandmother, the mother-in-law, the daughter, the sister. Now that is an enormously important fact which shows that in the German mind there is going on a particular myth, something very particular.

EVANS: This is of course a very interesting and remarkable set of statements here. How would you look at Hitler in this light? Would you see him as a personification, as a symbol of "father"?

JUNG: No, not at all. I couldn't possibly explain that very complicated fact that Hitler represents. It is too complicated. He was a hero in the German myth, mind you, a religious hero. He was a savior; he was meant to be a savior.

EVANS: To get back specifically to the idea of the self. . . .

JUNG: The self is merely a term that designates the whole personality. The whole personality of man is indescribable. His consciousness can be described; his unconsciousness cannot be described, because the unconscious—and I repeat myself—is always unconscious.

EVANS: What seems to be a very fundamental part of your writing and one of your main ideas is reflected in the term "mandala." How does this fit into the context of our discussion of the self?

JUNG: Mandala. . . . Well, it is just one typical archetypal form. It is what is called *ultimo exquadra circulae*, the square in the circle, or the circle in the square. It is an age-old symbol that goes right back to the pre-history of man. It is all over the earth and it either expresses the deity or the self; and these two terms are psychologically very much related, which doesn't mean that I believe that God is the self or that the self is God. I made the statement that there is a psychological relation, and there is plenty of evidence for that. It is a very important archetype. It is the archetype of inner order; and it is always used in that sense, either to make arrangements of the many, many aspects of the universe, a world scheme, or to arrange the complicated aspects of our psyche into a scheme. It expresses the fact that there is a center and a periphery, and it tries to embrace the whole. It is the symbol of wholeness. A mandala spontaneously appears as a compensatory archetype during times of disorder. It appears, bringing order, showing the possibility of order and centralness. It is, we should say, the main archetype.

EVANS: Dr. Jung, another set of ideas, original with you and very well known to the world, center around the terms "introversion" and "extroversion." They have become probably the psychological concepts most often used by the layman today.

JUNG: There are certain people who definitely are more influenced by their surroundings than by their own intentions, while other people are more influenced by the subjective factor. The psyche has two conditions, two important conditions. The one is environmental influence and the other is the given fact of the psyche as it is born. The psyche is by no means *tabula rasa* here, but a definite mixture and combination of genes, which are there from the very first moment of our life; and they give a definite character, even to the little child. That is a subjective factor, looked at from the outside. But when you observe yourself within, you see moving images, a world of images generally known as fantasies. Yet these fantasies are facts. These houses were all fantasies. Everything you do here, all this, everything, was fantasy to begin with, and fantasy has a proper reality. Fantasy is, you see, a form of energy, despite the fact that we can't measure it. And so psychical events are facts, are realities. And when you observe the stream of images within, you observe an aspect of the world, of the world within, because the psyche, if you understand it as a phenomenon that takes place in so-called living bodies, is a quality of matter, as our bodies consist of matter.

EVANS: Of course, one of the very common misconceptions, at least in my opinion, about your work among some of the writers in America is that they have characterized your discussion of introversion and extroversion as suggesting that the world is made up of only two kinds of people, introverts and extroverts. I'm sure you have been aware of this. Would you like to comment on it?

JUNG: Bismarck once said, "God may protect me against my friends; with my enemies I can deal myself alone." You know how people are. They have a catchword, and then everything is schematized along that word. There is no such thing as a pure extrovert or a pure introvert. Such a man would be in the lunatic asylum.

EVANS: Of course, tied in with your typology of introversion-extroversion, we know of your four functions of thinking, feeling, sensation, and intuition. It would be very interesting to hear some expansion of the meaning of these particular terms as related to the introvert-extrovert orientations.

JUNG: Well, there is a quite simple explanation of these terms, and it shows at the same time how I arrived at such a typology. Namely sensation tells you that there is something. Thinking, roughly speaking, tells you what it is. Feeling tells you whether it is agreeable or not, to be accepted or not, accepted or rejected. And intuition—there is a difficulty because you don't know ordinarily how intuition works. When a man has a hunch, you can't tell exactly how he got that hunch, or where that hunch came from. It is something funny about intuition. My definition then is that intuition is a perception, beyond ways or means, of the unconscious. That is near as I can get it. This is a very important function, because when you live under primitive conditions, a lot of unpredictable things are likely to happen. For instance, you are walking in primeval forests. You can only see a few steps ahead, and perhaps you go by the compass. You don't know what there is ahead; it is uncharted country. If you use your intuition, then you have hunches; and when you live under such primitive conditions, you instantly are aware of hunches.

EVANS: We American psychologists do a great deal of testing, utilizing "projective tests." You certainly played a major role in developing projective testing with your word association method. What led you to develop the Word Association Test?

JUNG: Well you see, in the beginning when I was a young man, I was competely disoriented with patients. I didn't know where to begin or what to say; and the association experiment has given me access to their unconscious. I learned about the things they did not tell me, and I got a deep insight into things of which they were not aware. I discovered many things.

EVANS: In other words, from such association responses you discovered complexes or areas of emotional blocks in the patient. Of course, the word "complex," which originated with you, is used very widely now. Are you familiar with Rorschach's test which uses inkblots?

JUNG: Yes, but I never applied it, because later on I didn't even apply the Word Association Test anymore. It just wasn't necessary. I learned what I had to learn from the exact examinations of psychic reactions, and that, I think, is a very excellent means.

EVANS: But would you recommend that other psychiatrists, clinical psychologists, and psychoanalysts use these projective tests, such as your Word Association Test or Rorschach's test?

JUNG: Well, perhaps. For the education of psychologists who intend to do actual work with people, I think it is an excellent means to learn how the unconscious works. I think I don't over-rate the didactic value of projective tests. I think very highly of them in this capacity, that is, for educating young psychologists. And sometimes, of course, they are useful to any psychologist. If I have a case who doesn't want to talk, I can make an experiment and find out a lot of things through the experiment. I have, for instance, discovered a murder.

EVANS: Is that right? Would you like to tell us how this was done?

JUNG: You see, you have that lie detector in the United States, and that's like an association test I have worked out with the psycho-galvanic phenomenon. Also, we have done a lot of work on the pneumograph which will show the decrease of volume of breathing under the influence of a complex. You know, one of the reasons for tuberculosis is the manifestation of a complex. People have very shallow breathing, don't ventilate the apices of their lungs anymore, and get tuberculosis. Half of tuberculosis cases are psychic.

EVANS: An interesting area which is being discussed a lot in the United States today, and I'm sure is of interest to you as well, is that of psychosomatic medicine, an area dealing with the way in which emotional components of personality can affect bodily functions. Of course, the classic example in the literature is the peptic ulcer. It is believed that this is a case where emotional factors have actually created pathology. These ideas have been extended into many other areas. It is felt, for example, that where there already is pathology, these emotional factors can intensify it. Speaking of such psychosomatic disturbances, as for instance, your experiences and studies into tuberculosis, do you have any ideas as to why the patient selects this type of symptom?

JUNG: He doesn't select; they happen to him.

EVANS: Perhaps one of the most radical suggestions in the area of psychosomatic medicine has been the suggestion that some forms of cancer may have psychosomatic components as causal factors. Would this surprise you?

JUNG: Not at all. We've known about these a long time, you know. Fifty years ago we already had these cases: ulcer of the stomach, tuberculosis, chronic arthritis, skin diseases. All are psychogenic under certain conditions. You can have an infectious disease in a certain moment—that is, a physical ailment or predicament—because you are particularly accessible to an infection, maybe sometimes because of a psychological attitude. When the disease has been established and there is a high fever and an abscess, you cannot cure it by psychology. Yet it is quite possible that you can avoid it by a proper psychological attitude.

EVANS: Another development that falls right in line with this whole discussion of psychosomatic medicine has been the use of drugs to deal with psychological problems. Of course, historically drugs have been used a great deal by people to try to forget their troubles, to relieve pain, etc. However, a particular development has been the so-called non-addictive tranquilizing drugs. They are now being administered very freely to patients by general practitioners and internists.

JUNG: This practice is very dangerous.

EVANS: Why do you think this is dangerous? These drugs are supposed to be nonaddictive.

JUNG: It's just like the compulsion that is caused by morphine or heroin. It becomes a habit. You don't know what you do, you see, when you use such drugs. It is like the abuse of narcotics.

EVANS: Have you actually seen any patients or had any contact with individuals who have been taking these particular drugs, these tranquilizers?

JUNG: I can't say. You see, with us there are very few. In America there are all the little powders and the tablets. Happily enough, we are not yet so far. You see, American life is in a subtle way so one-sided and so uprooted that you must have something with which to compensate the real nature of man. You have to pacify your unconscious all along the line because it is in absolute uproar; so at the slightest provocation you have a big moral rebellion in America. Look at the rebellion of modern youth in America, the sexual rebellion, and all that. These rebellions occur because the real, natural man is just in open rebellion against the utterly inhuman form of American life.

REFERENCES

Evans, R. I. 1976a. *Jung on elementary psychology.* New York: Dutton.

Jung, C. G. 1956. *Symbols of transformation,* vol. 5. New York: Pantheon Press.

————. 1963. *Memories, dreams, reflections.* Rec. and ed. Aniela Jaffé; transl. R. C. Winston. New York: Pantheon Books.

Erik Erikson

(1902–   )

Trained as an artist, Erik Erikson was encouraged by Freud to study psychoanalysis, and graduated from the Vienna Psychoanalytic Institute in 1933. He began his clinical work in the United States that same year, and has been a training analyst in Institutes of the American Psychoanalytic Association since 1942. His career has included posts at Harvard and Yale schools of medicine, the University of California, and the Austin Riggs Clinic. He was professor of human development and lecturer in psychiatry at Harvard University, from which he retired as professor emeritus. Moving away from Freud's emphasis on the biological-sexual components of early development, his work has focused brilliantly on the critical and creative stages of personal development, the resolution of various identity crises, and the continued development of personality throughout life, a concept he has studied in a variety of cultural and social settings.

Each Period Offers New Insights/The Eight Stages of Man//We Learn to Take in/The Oral-Sensory Stage: Trust versus Mistrust/Hope//Just Think of Swear Words/Muscular-Anal Stage: Autonomy versus Shame and Doubt/ Will Power//Thinking Big/Locomotor-Genital Stage: Initiative versus Guilt/Purpose//A Wish to Learn and Know/Latency Stage: Industry versus Inferiority/Competence//An Instinct for Fidelity/Adolescent Stage: Identity versus Role Diffusion/Fidelity//The Range of One's Excitements and Commitments/Young Adulthood Stage: Intimacy versus Isolation/Love// Everything that Is Generated/Adulthood Stage: Generativity versus Stagnation/Care//Some Wisdom Must Mature/Old Age and Maturity Stage: Ego Integrity versus Despair/Wisdom//Gandhi and Hitler/A Psychohistorical Analysis and Comparison//

Using Freud's theories as background and as a basis for comparison, Professor Erikson and I discuss his conceptions of "the eight stages of man," with their parallel psychosocial traits and emerging virtues or capacities such as hope, purpose, and competence. He traces his developmental model from the in-

---

fant's experience of trust and mistrust and the beginning of hope, through the adolescent's groping for identity, the young adult's search for intimacy, to the crisis resolvement of old age. At each stage, Professor Erikson explains his choice of focus, and allows us to follow the thinking that led to the conceptualization of this model. In comparing his concepts with those of Freud, he says, "I realized gradually that any original observation already implies a change in theory. Normality and pathology change with cultures and each period offers new insights." He elaborates particularly on the "identity crisis" period as it affects adolescents, women in today's culture, and as it applies to later life. Professor Erikson concludes our discussion with a psychohistorical comparative analysis of Hitler in Nazi Germany and Gandhi in India.

EVANS: Professor Erikson, to begin our dialogue it might be interesting to explore your provocative analysis of the eight stages of man (1963a). Although these formulations admittedly have their roots in Freud's (1953) work, you have added various innovative dimensions. For example, as we all know, Freud presented a very important model of psychosexual development. He felt that during the first five years of life, in the biological unfolding of the individual, he was confronted with a series of conflicts which he resolved with varying degrees of success. Through what he called a repetition compulsion, reflections of these early patterns of the first five years continue to be operative later in life. Freud did not emphasize to the same extent development in periods after these first five years. It seems that you not only try to conceptualize these later periods in more detail, but have developed an analysis of man's over-all development in these eight stages of man.

The very first stage Freud talked about was a narcissistic or self-love level of development, which included a preoccupation with the oral zone. You also speak of an oral-sensory level. Throughout your eight stages, you have some character dimension in a psychosocial development parallel to Freud's psychosexual development. At this first stage, you talk about basic trust versus basic mistrust being related to this oral-sensory level.

ERIKSON: When I started to write extensively about twenty-five years ago, I really thought I was merely providing new illustrations for what I had learned from Sigmund and Anna Freud. I realized only gradually that any original observation already implies a change in theory. The scientific climate has changed so much that older and newer theories cannot really be compared. One knows only that without the older ones, newer ones could not have emerged. Freud's original formulations were based on the imagery of a transformation of energy.

EVANS: This would reflect the effects of nineteenth-century physics.

ERIKSON: That's right. Today we are guided by concepts such as relativity and complementarity, even where we don't know it. Sexuality seemed to Freud to be the most likely area in which quantities of excitation could be found which rise out of body chemistry. And here, the theoretical configuration fits both the data and the job, because there was something almost palpably quantitative that had become excessive or repressed or both in the patients of his time. He became aware of the possibility that the "oral stage" contributes instinctual energy to normal sexual activities as well as to perverted ones, and to neurotic inhibitions as well as to character formation. He realized that psychopathology could make a fundamental contribution to "normal psychology." But normality and pathology change with cultures and each period contributes new insights. So we are interested here in what orality may contribute to the child's psychosocial development, and now I am ready to answer you. Orality—that is, a complex of experiences centered in the mouth—develops in relations with the mother who feeds, who reassures, who cuddles, and keeps warm; and that is why I refer to this first stage as the oral-sensory and kinesthetic one. The first thing we learn in life is to take in. Now, the basic psychosocial attitude to be learned at this stage is that you can trust the world in the form of your mother. Moreover, mothers in different cultures and classes and races must teach this trusting in different ways, so it will fit their cultural version of the universe. But to learn to mistrust is just as important.

EVANS: It's interesting that such aspects of psychosocial development are at the basis of some of the fundamental virtues which you schematized.

ERIKSON: Yes, this is true. I tried to formulate what I thought were the basic human strengths. Somewhat challengingly, I called them basic "virtues," in order to point to an evolutionary basis of man's lofty moralisms. You see, hope is a very basic human strength without which we couldn't stay alive, and not something invented by theologians or philosophers.

EVANS: The first stage then for man would be the development of hope emanating from a favorable ratio of trust versus mistrust. As you have referred to the second stage of development, we see the emergence of the muscular-anal stage, which is likewise related to the Freudian narcissistic level of development. You are referring to a psychosocial trait which will develop in parallel terms with this anal level; you have described these traits as autonomy versus shame and doubt.

ERIKSON: That's right. We have to consider that the anal musculature is part of musculature in general, so that the child entering this phase of his development must learn not only to manage his sphincters, but his muscles and what he can "will" with them. Now the urinary and anal organs are, of course, tied in physiologically with psychosexual development, and also with aggression. Just think of swear words! It would, of course, only be in cultures in which cleanliness and punctuality are overemphasized for technological and sanitary reasons that the problem of anal control might develop into a major issue in childhood. But the shift from the first to the second stage also marks one of those difficult human "crises." For just when a child has learned to trust his mother and to trust the world, he must become self-willed and must take chances with his trust in order to see what he, as a trustworthy individual, can will. Cultures have different ways of cultivating or breaking this will. Some use shame, which can be a terrible form of self-estrangement for the human.

EVANS: So, autonomy will result from constructive resolutions of feelings of shame and doubt that develop during this muscular-anal level?

ERIKSON: Yes. Again, a ratio is necessary to development here.

EVANS: I think we should underline the point you made earlier. In considering this polarity, you're not saying that ideally one quality should be produced and the other not at all. Both must emerge out of this developmental stage.

ERIKSON: Yes, but the ratio, of course, should be in favor of autonomy. If in some respects you have relatively more shame than autonomy, then you feel or act inferior all your life—or consistently counteract that feeling.

EVANS: At this point we might look at the use of the phrase "epigenetic diagram." You called these eight stages epigenesis, which is an interesting way to describe your developmental model.

ERIKSON: "Epi" means "upon"; and "genesis," "emergence." So epigenesis means that one item develops on top of another in space and in time, and this seemed to me a simple enough configuration to be adopted for our purposes. But, of course, I extended it to include a hierarchy of stages, not just a sequence.

EVANS: The third stage, which would probably occur in our culture somewhere about two, three, or four years of age is the locomotor-genital stage. Here you talk about the characteristics of initiative versus guilt emerging from this level. The phallic stage in Freudian theory introduced the so-called Oedipal situation where the male child falls in love with the mother and the female child falls in love with the father and out of this, ideally for ego growth, the male child should identify with the father and develop a strong ego. When you talk about initiative versus guilt, you are saying that these are outgrowths of the Oedipal situations, are you not?

ERIKSON: Obviously we would not agree today with all the generalizations which have been made with regard to the Oedipus complex, least of all the female Oedipus complex. If you say that the little boy falls in love with his mother, and that later on he has trouble falling out of love with her, we must remember that from the beginning she was everything to the child. The problem is that the mother becomes naturally involved in the boy's first genital fantasies at a time when his whole initiative has to be and is ready to be deflected from the home and must find new goals. Immense new faculties develop in him at this time, and if his potentialities are permitted to develop fully, the child will be in much less danger of developing a severe complex. But I would think the Oedipus complex is more and less than what Freud made of it. From an evolutionary point of view, it is the ontogenetic way in which the human individual first experiences the inexorable sequence of generations, of growth, and of death.

EVANS: The particular virtue you see coming forth from all this is "purpose." Out of initiative, then, would develop some goal-directedness for the individual?

ERIKSON: Yes. The child begins to envisage goals for which his locomotion and cognition have prepared him. The child also begins to think of being big and to identify with people whose work or whose personality he can understand and appreciate. "Purpose" involves this whole complex of elements. It is during this period that it becomes incumbent upon the child to repress or redirect many fantasies which developed earlier in his life. Paradoxically, he continues to feel guilty for his fantasies.

EVANS: Let us discuss the next period, which you have termed latency. This period in the child's life loosely parallels the period Freud also termed latency, but you have departed somewhat from the Freudian notion by introducing the parallel psychosocial traits, industry and inferiority.

ERIKSON: Well, once you speak of the whole child, and not only of libido and defense, you have to consider that in each stage the child becomes a very different person, a person with increased cognitive capacities and a much greater ability to interact with a much wider range of people in whom he is interested, whom he understands, and who react to him. It would not be fair, in a way, to say that Freud did not consider this, because he was only concerned with the question of what happens to sexual energy during that time. To him, latency meant only that certain passionate and imaginative qualities of life are then relatively subdued, and the child is free to concentrate and learn. The further psychoanalysis has changed its focus from an id psychology to an ego psychology, the clearer it has become that the ego can only remain strong in interaction with cultural institutions and can also only remain strong when the child's inborn capacities and potentials are developed. There is an enormous curiosity during this stage of life—a wish to learn, a wish to know.

EVANS: During the latency period, then, the polarities of industry versus inferiority are operating and the virtue of competence emerges. When inferiority develops, it is because the child's attempts toward mastery have failed?

ERIKSON: Yes, his attempts toward specialized competence.

EVANS: Then, moving on to the period which you call puberty or adolescence, around thirteen or fourteen years, you introduce the important psychosocial mechanisms of identity versus role diffusion. I think these concepts have given rise to some of the most intriguing observations in your work. Would you comment on these constructs generally and on how you see this development through puberty and adolescence in particular?

ERIKSON: Since we first described identity as a relatively unconscious conflict, there has been something of an identity explosion. "Identity" and more surprisingly "identity crisis" are words used all over the world. Even where a person can adjust sexually in a technical sense and may at least superficially develop what Freud called genital maturity, he may still be weakened by the identity problems of our era. I would, in fact, add that he cannot develop without the development of a firm identity at the conclusion of adolescence.

EVANS: The virtue which is developed at this stage is fidelity, is it not?

ERIKSON: Many people are dubious of the attempt to tie anything which sounds like virtue or strength to an evolutionary process. But I'm not speaking of values; I only speak of a developing capacity to perceive and to abide by values established by a particular living system. When I say fidelity, I don't mean faith in a particular ideology, just as in using the word hope I don't mean a particular religious form of hope. I believe that these virtues are as necessary in human adaptation as instincts are among the animals. I would go further and claim that we have almost an instinct for fidelity—meaning that when you reach a certain age you can and must learn to be faithful to some ideological view. Speaking psychiatrically, without the development of a capacity for fidelity the individual will either have what we call a weak ego, or look for a deviant group to be faithful to.

EVANS: The point you are making here is that adolescence is the phase specific to which identity or role confusion emerges, and that these are the basic ingredients of ego strength and development.

ERIKSON: I think the potential for the development of ego strength comes out of the successful completion of all the earlier developmental processes. I would say that you could speak of a fully mature ego only after adolescence, which means, after all, becoming an adult.

I feel that our sense of identity is composed of both positive and negative elements. There are some things which we want to become, and we know we are supposed to be, and which—given good sociohistorical situations—we can fulfill. Then there are things which we do not want to be or which we know we are not supposed to be.

EVANS: You speak about the negative and positive aspects of ego identity, and you have indicated that this is related to ideology, and since this seems to be a central aspect of your theory, I wonder if you would elaborate on that notion a bit.

ERIKSON: The phenomenon has evolutionary as well as historical aspects. I would put it this way: Man has become divided into pseudo-species, and in the present era he is trying to overcome one of the last forms of pseudospecieshood, namely nationalism. The tribal animal is on the defensive, just because more inclusive ideologies are being formed. But how to form a wider identity—that now becomes the problem of youth. As I see it, the adolescent is driven and often disturbed by a new quantitive pressure of conflicting drives. So the ontogenetic aspect of adolescence is really representative of what each individual's ego strength must tackle at one and the same time, namely inner unruliness and changing conditions. A person whose potentialities as a person have no place in the historical trends of his time simply is more upset about what drives him amorphously, more inclined to regress and thus also more bothered with infantile remnants in his sexuality. You can see in any number of young people that they can take sexuality in their stride, can weather crises, and absorb some severe mistakes. So identity has that developmental importance. But then it also has its societal side, which is what makes it psychosocial. On the basis of cognitive development the young person is looking for an ideological framework by which to envisage a future of vast possibilities. It's very important to see that ideologies, by definition, cannot consist of mature values. Adolescents are easily seduced by totalitarian regimes and all kinds of totalistic fads which offer some transitory fake values. While the adolescent is vulnerable to fake ideas, he can put an enormous amount of energy and loyalty at the disposal of any convincing system. This is what makes it so tragic and gives all creators of new values such responsibilities. We in the West pretend that we want to uphold only a way of life, while in fact we too are creating and exporting technological and scientific ideologies, which have their own ways of enforcing conformity. These are two great sources of contemporary identity and identity confusion: faith in technology and a reassertion of a kind of humanism. Both are apt to be dated in their utopianism and inadequate for the gigantic struggle for man's mastery of his own powers.

EVANS: You seem to refer here to two levels of identity—one emerging in the biological developmental sequence, and the other tied to the psychosocial realm. In the latter case, you would say that an ideology then becomes a basis for identity.

ERIKSON: It doesn't have to be an ideology in the political sense, but an ideological framework, which is tuned to the need for new and more inclusive identities. Now, the problem of identity is that it must establish a continuity between society's past and future and that adolescence in all its vulnerability and power is the critical transformer of both. Mixed in with the positive identity, there is a negative identity which is composed of what he has been shamed for, what he has been punished for, and what he feels guilty about: his failures in competency and goodness. Identity means an integration of all previous identifications and self-images, including the negative ones. Much of this goes on in the unconscious, of course, and it occurs to me that we have simply taken the unconscious for granted here. Let me pause to make this retroactive for everything we have said. Very important is the fact that the young (consciously or unconsciously) recognize their own negative identity in their parents, and begin to doubt whether earlier identifications with them are altogether as useful and admirable as previously thought. In other words, identity formation is really a restructuring of all previous identifications in the light of an anticipated future. In primitive cultures there are puberty rites which rather forcefully inform the growing youth where he belongs. He learns that he belongs to a particular tribe or a particular clan, and must pay the price of conformity for a sense of belongingness. Of course, the more a culture gives free choices and decisions as to who one is going to be, the more open conflict is aroused. But, of course, it also means that wherever the identity is so preordained that you have fewer choices, there are fewer provisions for being somebody special or deviant or both.

EVANS: Could you discuss in a bit more detail how you feel the identity crisis relates to positive and negative identity, and to the existentialist orientation?

ERIKSON: One could almost say that adolescents are transitory existentialists by nature because they become suddenly capable of realizing a separate identity. They therefore can feel not only involved in acute conflict but also very much isolated, a feeling which they are apt to totalize to the point of being preoccupied with premature wisdom and death or of being willing to sacrifice themselves for a cause, and sometimes for any escape from isolation and sense of restriction. The integration of infantile part-identities and fragmentary roles can be interfered with by early frustration, by a schizoid sickness latent in the young person, by tragedies in the family, or by rapid social evolution or technological change. Given a quantity of sudden drives that becomes unmanageable, any combination of these can become critical. The adolescent may then take pride in being delinquent.

EVANS: When one looks at this from the point of view of social psychology, it sometimes appears as if a delinquent youngster, in rebelling against the conformist pressure of so-called conventional society, has become a conformist in a delinquent subculture.

ERIKSON: For the longest time we have failed to see that the delinquent adolescent, too, is looking for the chance to conform to some subculture, to be loyal to some leader, and to display and develop some kind of fidelity. There are very few really bad people in the world, and I think they can be found rather among those who misuse youth. Those who become delinquent have simply been sidetracked because we failed them, and if we fail to recognize this fact, we lose them.

EVANS: I wonder if you might have some observations on the notion of positive and negative identity as a recurring problem for the person as he moves through adolescence toward maturity and old age.

ERIKSON: I am glad that you lead me beyond the adolescent stage and our culture's fixation on it. You are right that even though one has resolved his identity crisis, later changes in life can precipitate renewal of the crisis. Maybe as an immigrant I faced one of those very important redefinitions that a man has to make who has lost his landscape and his language, and with it all the "references" on which his first sensory and sensual impressions, and thus also some of his conceptual images, were based. Migration can do that. As you have said, old age can do it too, because the person who has not adequately solved his identity problem earlier will frantically try to see whether he can still develop another identity. His life is not quite acceptable to him as the only life he will ever have.

EVANS: Another current area of discussion relating to the problem of identity in a broad sense deals with the female in our culture. Freud, of course, reflecting the difficulties of the female child in resolving the Oedipal situation, seemed to view the female as being destined to a basic immaturity throughout her life. We might raise the question of whether Freud's analysis remains valid or whether it was another example of his alleged culture-bound perception, possibly influenced by the female of his era.

ERIKSON: My feeling is that Freud's general judgment of the identity of women was probably the weakest part of his theory. Exactly what is to blame for that I don't know, except that he was a Victorian man, a patriarchal man. He may have missed the whole substratum of matriarchy in man. Also, he was a doctor, and he obviously saw in his women patients what you first get in the free association of any patients, namely, the story of deprivation and resentment. And finally, it probably took a certain development of the field, including the participation of women doctors, to help men to empathize with women—a dangerous undertaking for a man if your public role, your preferred method, and your masculine identity all depend on each other. The point is not to deny what Freud saw and generalized. For there can be no doubt that women in many ways envy masculinity deeply. Any little girl growing up at that time, or for that matter throughout the patriarchal era of mankind, could see that a boy just because of his anatomical appendage was considered more important. That behind man's insistence on male superiority there is an age-old envy of women who are sure of their motherhood while man can be sure of his fatherhood only by restricting the female, that is another matter. At any rate, psychoanalytic literature tends to describe woman as an essentially passive and masochistic creature, who not only accepts the roles or identity assigned to her submissively, but needs all the masochism she can muster to appreciate the phallic male.

EVANS: And you don't accept that view?

ERIKSON: I would think that passive and masochistic are relative terms. Basically, the female anatomy suggests different modes of activity within which a woman can be very active indeed, or very passive, and even very active in playing passive. Freud's perception might also have been colored by the sexual mores of his time, which could not admit at first that an upper-class woman could have passionate and active sexual

wishes and yet be refined and intelligent. At the same time, the evaluation of childbearing in the culture of Freud's era was slanted toward
considering it a more animalistic activity, one that needed less brains,
and could be less easily sublimated into higher strivings. All of this most
women had, in fact, accepted. So you are right: women could not help
harboring that inner rage which comes from having to identify with your
exploiters' negative image of you.

EVANS: Do you think we may eventually get to greater unity and
look at the individual as an individual regardless of whether the person
is male or female, thus allowing for greater individual development of
identity?

ERIKSON: I would think that what we need is a hierarchy of differences. For example, I think that in problems of individuality and self-
hood a man and a woman are much more alike than in anything else,
though of course never the same, for individuality is tied to a body. On the
other hand, there are aspects of the body—as I mentioned earlier—in
which women are basically so different from men that the feminine ego has
a very specific task to perform in integrating body, role, and individuality.
For example, it may be that woman has a finer touch, a finer sense of
texture, finer discrimination for certain noises, a better memory for most
immediate experience, a greater capacity to empathize immediately and
emotionally, while the man may rate less in all of that. The point is: in a
man, all of this would make him more aesthetic than most men; in a
woman such aesthetic giftedness may be part of a total configuration
which makes her a better mother of a number of children, one of whom
may be a baby and one an adolescent, not to mention her husband. She
has to empathize, in one day, with totally different joys and calamities,
needs and sicknesses. Or the man may be more muscular than the woman
and therefore judged to be stronger, while she has the hips to bear twins
and later to carry one on each hip.

EVANS: Now, moving to the next stage in your epigenetic cycle
which you refer to as young adulthood, here you introduce intimacy
versus isolation. This would appear to refer to the individual who having
grown beyond the beginnings of dealing with his identity problem can
move toward the issue of relationships with others.

ERIKSON: Of course, I mean something more—I mean intimate relationships, such as friendship, love, sexual intimacy, even intimacy with
oneself, one's inner resources, the range of one's excitements and com-
mitments. Intimacy is really the ability to fuse your identity with somebody else's without fear that you're going to lose something yourself. It
is this development of intimacy which makes marriage possible as a
chosen bond. When this has not developed, marriage is meaningless. But,
of course, sometimes the inner development waits for the formal bond.

EVANS: The traits you stress in connection with the young adult
stage which comes after adolescence are intimacy versus isolation and
the virtue here is love. This is really the beginning of what we call the
mature, unselfish kind of love. And in the next stage, which is adulthood,

you say that adulthood begins to deal with generativity versus stagnation. The individual presumably takes his place in society-at-large.

ERIKSON: Yes. At this stage one begins to take one's place in society, and to help in the development and perfection of whatever it produces. And one takes responsibility for that. I know that generativity is not an elegant word, but it means to generate in the most inclusive sense. If I would call this strength creativity, I would put too much emphasis on the particular creativity which we ascribe to particular people. I use the word "generativity" because I mean everything that is generated from generation to generation: children, products, ideas, *and* works of art.

EVANS: The virtue which you propose to accompany the notion of generativity versus self-absorption in adulthood is care. Superficially, the productive connotation of this dichotomy is clear, but the concept of care seems to be somewhat inconsistent with the model of creativity. Would you clarify for us what you mean by the term "care" in this regard?

ERIKSON: I needed one word and of all the words that I considered, I thought "care" was the strongest. Care originally meant an anxious kind of solicitude, but I think it has taken on more positive connotations. I use "care" in a sense which includes "to care to do" something, to "care for" somebody or something, to "take care of" that which needs protection and attention, and "to take care not to" do something destructive.

EVANS: Your final stage is old age and maturity. You have counterposed ego integrity versus despair, with wisdom being the virtue of this period.

ERIKSON: I'm not satisfied with the term "wisdom," because to some it seems to mean a too strenuous achievement for each and every old person. It is also perfectly obvious that if we live long enough, we all face a renewal of infantile tendencies—a certain childlike quality, if we're lucky, and senile childishness, if we're not. The main point is again a developmental one: only in old age can true wisdom develop in those who are thus gifted. And in old age, some wisdom must mature, if only in the sense that the old person comes to appreciate and to represent something of the wisdom of the ages, or plain folk wit.

EVANS: Perhaps we can conclude this portion of our discussion of your eight stages of man by asking you to respond briefly to some questions which I believe represent a particularly difficult challenge. The most difficult application of any developmental model is to relate symptoms of emotional disturbance appearing later in the life of an individual to earlier stages represented in the model.

ERIKSON: We do find in potentially psychotic people that the very first relationships in earliest childhood seem to have been severely disturbed. We could speak here of a psychosocial weakness which consists of a readiness to mistrust and to lose hope in rather fundamental ways. I do see the aggravation of basic mistrust as one of the conditions which induces the psychotic to break off with reality. But I would think that another useful way of employing my developmental model would be an attempt to specify for each stage what seemingly malignant kinds of disturbance may be treatable as an aggravated development crisis rather than as lastingly malignant. This is very important clinically. For it might keep us from confirming a patient as a psychotic who has transitory psychoticlike symptoms during an acute crisis.

EVANS: As you studied the human development cycle of different cultures in an attempt to find data bearing on your theoretical framework, you have explored historically and written about the German culture (1963a), the Sioux Indians (1963a), India (1966), and the Gorky pattern (1963a). You also analyzed historical influences which manifested themselves in Martin Luther (1958). I wonder if you might share with us a few of the insights you have gained from these various analyses and observations.

ERIKSON: I was in Vienna when Hitler came to power in Germany. Luckily (in every way) I had married an American girl, and we had already decided to move to this country. My original purpose was really to explain this phenomenon to myself. I had gone to school in Germany. I myself was born a Dane, but the German language had become my language and the German countryside my first milieu as an artist. These German youths had turned Nazi and were in fact killing off some of my Jewish friends. I felt then, and feel strongly now, what Hannah Arendt (1963) pointed out, that one has no right to consider this simply a criminal interlude in history, the criminals always being the others. That the potentialities for such destruction are in decent and cultured people is something we have to account for. Or rather, we have to study it, psychohistorically, as I would say today. Hitler was a young man with much stored-up rage within him because of his unfulfilled potentials. So was Luther. Some of my friends have not forgiven me for writing about young Hitler as one who at one time, too, wanted to rebuild, as a young person with potentialities that might have gone in a number of directions. The main object of psychohistorical investigations is to try to relate the particular identity-needs of a given leader to the typical identity-needs of his historical time. The solution he finds for himself becomes prototypical of the solution for the young people of his time. If criminality on a large scale results, then the whole adult generation must take the responsibility for not having provided other viable opportunities for the young. Post-World War I was such a period in Germany. Everything that the world had always criticized as German, the Nazis made to appear positive and pretended that it was what they really wanted to be.

EVANS: Are you saying that the national character, the existing stereotype of the German, became incorporated in the feelings of the people, and became in fact a sort of self-fulfilling prophecy?

ERIKSON: More than that. Hitler would go so far as to say, "Conscience is a blemish like circumcision." In other words, traditional

Judaeo-Christian values now became negative self-images and were projected onto the Jews. I call this phenomenon a totalistic split which happens in world history when a group or nation cannot fulfill its positive potentials. It happens in delinquents, as we discussed earlier.

EVANS: Can we say that the leader emerges as an embodiment of the character of a nation, and is positively or negatively shaped according to its national character?

ERIKSON: I think I would have to differentiate here between ideological rebels and innovators and leaders who are more like the caretakers of their nation's existing development. With the group whom I call ideological innovators, the personal life history and personal conflicts are more determining. But to stay within our discourse: the best leader is the one who realizes what potentials can be activated in those led, and most of all, what more inclusive identities can be realized.

EVANS: I imagine the manner in which a leader rises to power is related to this.

ERIKSON: Yes. There are some leaders who surprise us totally because they appear suddenly out of nowhere or what we thought was nowhere. Hitler for years was absolutely nobody. Two years of his life are altogether unaccounted for. Gandhi always insisted that he wanted to be zero, and he deliberately identified himself with the lowest strata of the Indian population. Then he became a leader without assuming any kind of conventional power. But he was a master in molding existing potentialities together. That they fell apart again, and literally with a vengeance, that must be studied, too. The difference between a Hitler and a Gandhi is (in this context) that Hitler's violent methods were tied to a totalistic reinforcement of a pseudospecies (the German race), the fiction of which could only be maintained by vilifying and annihilating another pseudosubspecies, the Jews. Gandhi's nonviolent technique, on the contrary, was not only tied to the political realities of his day, but also revived the more inclusive identity promised in the world religions.

Gandhi seemed to me to exemplify in word and deed what I had come to perceive as a modern version of the golden rule. To put it briefly, this version suggests that wherever one has a choice one should choose to act so as to enhance the potentials of one's counterplayer's development as well as one's own. This ethical principle was, of course, entirely embedded in economic problems: Gandhi never divorced lofty matters from the most concrete ones, including dirty politics.

EVANS: Comparing the techniques of violence which emerged under Hitler in Germany and those of nonviolence in Gandhi's India, there must be some profound cultural differences which account for the emergence of such dramatic differences in the techniques of leadership which the people will tolerate.

ERIKSON: No doubt, there is a long cultural development which makes it historically plausible that nonviolence first was systematized in India. But then the historical problem is the convergence of a life history like Gandhi's with an historical trend, and the resulting actualization of a new direction.

EVANS: Then you feel that the decision to use nonviolence was not necessarily a reflection of passivity at all, but rather represents an active inner process, the nature of which you want to determine. Is it possible that Gandhi was a brilliant master of strategy and that nonviolence, rather than being merely a reflection of faith as many people saw it, reflected a definite strategy as well? In other words, is it possible that Gandhi's appearance of being simply a pious and austere man clouded our perception of his capabilities as an effective strategist?

ERIKSON: Yes, very much so. In fact, Gandhi was never as pious and austere about himself as his followers and his translators make him appear. In studying the details of his personal life as they are reported to me now, I'm very much impressed to see what a marvelous sense of humor he had and how frankly conscious he was of being crafty and cunning as well as saintly, never seeing any contradiction between these qualities. It is both pleasant and important to describe that side of him, for it balances the often deeply neurotic implications of his inner conflicts and of his public contradictions.

EVANS: I imagine that as you began to examine in depth the sources, cultural context, application, and relative effectiveness of the so-called nonviolent techniques of social protest, you realized that you were dealing with an incredibly complex phenomenon, did you not?

ERIKSON: Very much so. Incidentally, we prejudice the whole matter by calling it nonviolence or likening it to passive resistance, which it isn't. Gandhi in many ways was one of the least passive persons you can imagine, and he carefully searched for a better name for nonviolence. He called it Satyagraha, which means truth force. The only passive thing about it was that he exacted a pledge from his people that they would not fight back if they were physically attacked, and not even swear back. But again, this demands (as some of our civil rights fighters know) a most active inner state as compared with the submissive, passive, and masochistic state which most Westerners would think it is. I am studying Gandhi's personal development and his exact technique in a given instant because I believe he may be both the last representative of a great trend in human history, and yet also the first in a new trend. In the past, religious man put himself in total opposition to political and technological man and strove for inner peace through noninvolvement, sacrifice, and faith. On the other hand, political and technological man has cultivated aggressive and expansive systems and has tried to build certain safeguards into them which would keep the peace in a limited area. Now, I think that Gandhi quite consciously established a new trend in combining politics and religion, and this at least temporarily with great psychological acumen. I do not know yet what I will come out with but I do feel that armament has developed to a point where man cannot indulge himself any further in technological vaingloriousness. The new situation challenges man's whole consciousness of his position in the universe on a grand new scale. And here Gandhi has a lasting message, beyond his moment in history, and beyond his ascetic philosophy.

REFERENCES

Arendt, H. 1963. *Eichmann in Jerusalem*. New York: Viking Press.

Erikson, E. H. 1958. *Young man Luther: a study in psychoanalysis and history*. New York: W. W. Norton.

———. 1961. The roots of virtue. In *The Humanist Frame*, pp. 145–166 ed. J. Huxley. New York: Harper.

———. 1950. *Childhood and Society*. New York: Norton.

———. 1963a. *Childhood and Society*. 2nd ed. New York: Norton.

———. 1963b. The golden rule and the cycle of life. In *The study of lives*, ed. R. W. White. New York: Appleton.

———. 1964. *Insight and responsibility*. New York: Norton.

———. 1966. Gandhi's autobiography: the leader as a child. *The American Scholar*, Autumn, 1966.

———. 1966. The ontogeny of ritualization in man. *Philosophical Transactions of the Royal Society of London*. 251 (Series B): 337–349.

Evans, R. I. 1969. *Dialogue with Erik Erikson*. New York: Dutton.

Freud, S. 1953. *The standard edition of the complete psychological works of Sigmund Freud*, ed. James Strachey. London: Hogarth Press.

Erich Fromm

(1900–   )

After completing his Ph.D. in psychology at the University of Heidelberg in 1922, Erich Fromm trained at the Berlin Psychoanalytic Institute. After coming to the United States, Dr. Fromm held positions at Columbia University, Yale University, New York University, Bennington College, and Michigan State University. He established a psychoanalytic practice in New York and began to divide his time between New York, where he was professor of psychology at New York University, and Mexico City where he set up a department of psychoanalytic training at the Medical School of the National University of Mexico. He was also instrumental in establishing the William Alanson White Institute of Psychiatry, Psychoanalysis and Psychology. Professor Fromm's work has effectively explored the concept of freedom in society, the capacity for collective destructiveness, and in a classic study, the concept of love— love of self, self-love and love of others.

The Possibilities of Man/Nonproductive/Receptive/Hoarding/Exploitive/ Marketing/Necrophilic/Productive//The Illúsion That He Is Free/ Automaton Conformity/Destructiveness/Authoritarianism//The Capacity to Love/Authenticity versus Facade/Love of Self and Self-Love//The Significance of Dreams/Accidental/Universal Symbols/Jung's Archetypes// Therapy—A Sense of Responsibility/Group versus Individual/The Therapist's Unconscious/The Science of Psychotherapy//The Significant Problems/Alienation/Alternativism/The "Real Possibilities"/A Conflict of Conscious/Caesar and God//

Dr. Fromm and I discuss the development of his character types, relating nonproductive and productive man to Freudian theory, and he emphasizes the differences and the similarities. We explore the effects of society's influence on the development of these characteristics and the ways in which individuals react to these influences in the responsibilities which they accept or the escape mechanisms they employ. Dr. Fromm talks about man's capacity to love and the important difference between love of self and self-love. As we

---

discuss the significance of dream interpretation in therapy, he explains his concept of accidental and universal symbols and compares these to Jung's archetypes. Dr. Fromm evaluates group therapy and individual therapy and emphasizes the responsibility of the therapist. He argues strongly for the scientific nature of psychoanalytic theory, pointing out to its critics that, "Perhaps some psychologists are so concerned with rigorous proof because what they are trying to prove is not too significant." We conclude the discussion with Dr. Fromm's concern for what he considers the significant problems: alienation and conflict of conscience, offering what he feels are the real possibilities and alternatives for man today.

EVANS: To begin our dialogue, Dr. Fromm, it might be interesting to discuss one of the areas that particularly brought your work to the attention of many of us in the field of psychology. Like Freud, you examined not only the concept of fixation [that is, becoming arrested at an earlier point in development] but also the ways such fixations manifest themselves in later character types. For example, you apparently have taken very seriously Freud's work on the relationship between fixation and later character, and even expanded such concepts as oral and anal character patterns. Beyond that you have developed other character orientations or typologies of your own (Fromm, 1947). One group of these character orientations you called "non-productive," the Freudian parallel being termed "pre-genital." And one mode of the non-productive orientations you labeled "receptive." Do you still find that the receptive orientation is an important one in your culture?

FROMM: Yes, I do. I think it is more important in the twentieth century than in the nineteenth century. The nineteenth-century European middle class was characterized by hoarding; the twentieth-century man is the eternal suckling, taking in cigarettes, drinks, lectures, knowledge. Everything is taken in, in a receptive way. And I find, indeed, that the Freudian concepts of character are of immeasurable value. In fact, I think the scientific study of character begins with the day when Freud published his short paper on the anal character (Freud, 1938). There is a vast difference, however, between perceiving the validity of this entity which Freud has described and explaining it theoretically. Although my theoretical explanation disagrees with Freud's, that doesn't alter the fact that I believe what he saw is a picture which nobody saw before him; and the matter of theoretical explanation is of somewhat secondary importance.

EVANS: So you see the receptive orientation as being more broadly based than Freud's "oral character." However, you have conceptualized the "hoarding orientation" as stemming from a fixation at the anal level, as Freud postulated was the case with the "anal character type." It would be interesting to see how you have explained Freud's hypothesis that early anal and oral fixations are directly related to character type.

FROMM: As you have stated, Freud's concept was that the genesis of any particular kind of character orientation, whether oral or anal, receptive or sadistic, lies in the fixation of the libido [simply defined, a broad psychosexual energy] on one of the erogenous zones in the libido development, helped by certain events, such as toilet training, overfeeding, underfeeding, and so on. In other words, here is the libido fixated at some erogenous zone by the particular fate of this libido in the course of development. The resultant character trait is either the sublimation of or the reaction-formation against this libidinal desire. Such desires manifest themselves in drinking, retaining feces, and so forth.

I believe that it is not a fixation on some primary erogenous zone; for in the process of assimilating the world, man has only a few possibilities. I can get things by receiving them passively; I can get things by taking them by force; I can get things by hoarding them. There is another possibility which I mentioned in my writings; namely, that I can get things by exchanging. And I can get things by producing them. There are no other possibilities. I think it depends primarily upon the nature of the society, of the culture, and secondarily upon the character of the parents, as to which of these modes of assimilation will be primary in a person. Then, and only secondarily, whatever is true of the erogenous zones might appear as a consequence rather than as a cause.

EVANS: It would be interesting here to discuss more specifically the exploitative character to see exactly how it differs from the hoarding, receptive, and productive orientations.

FROMM: First of all, let me explain that the exploitative character is a person whose whole sense of life is based on one conviction: that he cannot produce. He thinks that all he can get is what he takes from somebody else, but because this somebody else will not give it to him voluntarily, he must take it by force. His concept of living becomes robbing and stealing, and this is essentially cannibalistic. The exploitative orientation of a cannibal is the orientation in which I take from others what I need for myself. In the receptive orientation, I expect others to feed me if I'm nice to them. In the hoarding orientation, I don't expect anything from anyone else because I'm sitting here in my castle, guarding my treasures. In the productive orientation, I feel I can get what I need by working and producing. What I get is the result of my own efforts.

EVANS: There seems to be one point here which could be misunderstood. You describe the exploitative orientation as robbing, taking by force, etc. Now, it needn't be as overtly aggressive as it might have been, say, in primitive man. Can it not be a more subtle kind of thing in civilized society?

FROMM: Indeed. A man who always falls in love with a married woman is usually the exploitative character, because for him value lies only in what can be taken from somebody else. It's just like someone who likes cherries only if he can pick them from a tree that isn't his; it's like an intellectual who can write only what is stolen from somebody else. Now, this can be more or less rationalized; it can be more or less intense. If you observe the subtlety with which the exploitative character is expressed, then you will find that we have indeed a great sector of our modern population not only in the West, but in all civilized countries, in which the way of getting something is to take it from somebody else.

EVANS: Your concept of the marketing orientation particularly intrigues those of us in social psychology. Here you talk of the individual seemingly selling himself to the highest bidder. Do you still believe that the marketing character is one of the most disturbing products of our contemporary culture?

FROMM: Yes, I think so, because the marketing orientation is really a specifically modern one. The person with a marketing orientation is neither productive nor exploitative nor hoarding nor receptive. His whole idea is that the only way to create is to exchange. The market becomes really the judge of values. The market refers not to the local market, but to the market in which things, labor, and personality are for sale. The market is a central feature of our economy.

EVANS: How, then, did you derive the conception of a marketing character?

FROMM: Well, I derived it not from the development of the libido, but from the character of the parents and from what I called the social character, that is to say, that type of character which is specific to every society. To put it simply, society needs men who want to do what they have to do.

EVANS: Here you are saying that Freud's anal and oral characters are not directly parallel to your hoarding and receptive orientations, and that you actually have other culturally determined and historically appropriate bases to account for them.

FROMM: I would say that they are parallel in terms of description of the syndrome. They are not parallel in terms of their generic explanations. I appreciate your raising this issue, because I may not have made it clear enough in my writing just where my concepts are parallel to Freud's and where they are not. Actually, this distinction has grown clearer in my own mind over the last few years.

EVANS: Might there be a parallel between the marketing orientation and what David Riesman (1961) has called the "other-directed" individual or what you have referred to as the "alienated" individual?

FROMM: Oh, yes, very definitely. I think Riesman described it very well and gave it an interesting name. Essentially, other-directedness is closely related to what I call the marketing orientation and the alienated personality. You see, Freud also was concerned with cultural determinants. But there is a difference. For Freud, culture was a quantitative entity in which civilization was more or less the determinant of the degree or intensity of repression of instincts. I look at culture not in a quantitative sense which determines the amount of repression, but as something qualitative which structures man to conform to the social mold. In other words, I assume we are what we have to be, in accordance with the necessities of the society in which we live; therefore for me it is terribly important to analyze the particular structure of any given society, whether feudalism or nineteenth-century capitalism or Greek slave society.

EVANS:　Dr. Fromm, you have been working recently on the delineation of a fifth character type within the nonproductive orientations; and as I understand it, you have termed this the "necrophilic" mode, descriptive of the person who is preoccupied with death. Would you elaborate on this mode for us?

FROMM:　Now, usually "necrophilic" refers to a specific and relatively rare sexual perversion. What I mean by "necrophilic" is the kind of person whose full orientation is to be attracted to death, decay, illness, to all that is not alive, to the inorganic as against the organic. Now, the necrophilous character is a malignant derivative of what would be anal —to use Freud's typology—in a less malignant form; in Freudian terminology, it would be the extreme form of a person almost completely directed by the death instinct.

EVANS:　Do we see people like this in society? Would we recognize such people by the things that they do?

FROMM:　Yes, you can recognize them very easily if you keep your eyes open. Perhaps the best-known example is Hitler. He was a typical necrophilous character, a man obsessed with destruction. There is a story that in the first world war he was found in a trancelike state gazing at the decayed corpse of a soldier, and they had great trouble getting him away from it. Hitler's end, his *Götterdämmerung*, the end of himself, of his friends, of their children, and of all of Germany, was really what he had been working for. Consciously he persuaded himself—and many Germans—that he wanted to save Germany; but in effect he was working for its destruction. The needless cruelty and the murder of millions of people were the manifestations of a necrophilic person.

EVANS:　Over the years, you have continued to develop the characteristics of the constructive alternative to these nonproductive orientations: the "productive character" (Fromm, 1947). I wonder if you would expand a little on how you describe what you consider to be the productive orientation for the individual.

FROMM:　In the context of what I said before about nonproductive characters, I mean by "productive character" the person who can produce. He is capable of producing on his own what he needs. This is not a Robinson Crusoe kind of producing, in the sense of literally being isolated from society; rather, the productive individual is able to be relatively independent of others in producing what he needs as he functions within society. The productive character is an active person, not only in physical work but also in feeling, in thinking, in his relationships with people. He approaches the world as the possessor in an active manner, and all the expressions of his being are authentic; that is, they are genuinely his, and are not put into him by an outside influence, such as a newspaper or a movie.

EVANS: So you're saying, then, that Americans tend to be more nonproductive than productive?

FROMM: I'm afraid that is so. Today we obey by signal, whereas a hundred years ago we obeyed because we were told what to do and were warned of the consequences of not doing so. It was a much cruder but more healthy method.

EVANS: It's the same basic authoritarian system today, only more subtle.

FROMM: Yes, more subtle, and therefore worse, because we operate today at a more unconscious level.

EVANS: You are saying that the socialization process, rather than developing individuality in a constructive sense, creates through social conditioning individuals who function as automatons. In fact, one of your mechanisms of escape is called "automaton conformity"; and you have described in your writings the process we have just been discussing (Fromm 1941). This mechanism could distinguish nonproductive from productive orientations, could it not?

FROMM: Yes, it does indeed. And, after all, quite a few books have been written about the organization man (Whyte 1956), the hidden persuaders (Packard 1957), and so forth. They show how far we have already developed in our bureaucratic society a system of subtle signals by which we test and discern our acceptability or nonacceptability, and by which we learn to do the right things. Today we refer more to the concept of individuality. Private initiative was a notion of the nineteenth century, where it applied mainly to economic endeavors. Today, however, in the age of big corporations, private initiative is no longer relevant either to economic endeavor or to private existence, and the concept of individuality by and large has been relegated to the realm of ideals which bear scant relation to practice.

EVANS: You are implying that to be truly productive one must be free. But inherent in that freedom is responsibility. By becoming an automaton—the kind of individual who operates on the "signal system" —he escapes from this freedom of choice and its concomitant responsibility.

FROMM: Yes . . . and, I may add, with the illusion that he is free.

EVANS: Now that we have described one of your mechanisms of escaping from freedom—automaton conformity—perhaps we could discuss at least briefly the other two. One of these you have mentioned is the escape mechanism of destructiveness. Would you comment a bit on this syndrome?

FROMM: To elaborate on that concept, I would like to take the opportunity to say something which I have not formerly stated. Briefly, I regard man as a freak of nature, because although he is an animal, he is the only case of a living organism having awareness of itself. The situation of self-awareness incorporated into the body of an animal creates a tremendous sense of separateness and fright. Therefore man has to look for some unity, for some meaning, and he can do so either by progressing or by regressing. By regressing, I mean that he can try to become a nonreflective animal again and thus do away with awareness and reason. But by progressing, on the other hand, I mean that he can try to develop his human powers to such an extent that he finds new unity. The person who cannot live productively, who cannot create at all, nevertheless does not wish to be a passive person, like a die thrown out of a cup. He wants to transcend life; he wants to be a man; he wants to make an imprint on the world. If he cannot create, he can transcend his creature status also by destroying. To destroy life is as transcendent as to create it; to create requires conditions of interest, of capacity, etc.; to destroy means only one thing—a pistol or a strong arm. In the process of destruction, I also fulfill the desire to transcend my passive-creature status and triumph over life. You might say this is a vengeance against life for not permitting me to be oriented to it productively. For this reason, I feel destructiveness is one of the deepest forms of mental pathology.

EVANS: We've discussed automaton conformity and the destructive mechanisms of escape from the standpoint of freedom and the responsibility it involves. A classic contribution in this area is your development of the mechanism of authoritarianism. Do you feel as strongly about the effects of authoritarianism today?

FROMM: No, not quite. When I wrote about authoritarianism, I was under the influence of the two great events of modern history, namely, the systems of Hitler and Stalin, both of whom had built up authoritarian regimes.

EVANS: In your earlier discussion of authoritarianism, you analyzed it in terms of such Freudian concepts as sadism and masochism. Would you say the sado-masochistic dimension is still as important in understanding authoritarianism?

FROMM: Masochistic and sadistic elements are still pertinent to the overt form of authoritarianism. But I see overt authoritarianism yielding more and more to covert authoritarianism, which as I indicated earlier, is manifested by the manipulation of people through signals.

EVANS: What you're saying, then, is that the authoritarian mechanism of escape is gradually becoming an automaton conformity mechanism.

FROMM: That's right. I want this to be very clear. This development is likely to take place in the Soviet Union, but it is also happening here.

EVANS: In *The Art of Loving* (1956) you distinguish between the concepts of love of self and self-love.

FROMM: What we call selfishness, egotism, or "self-love" is really one form of greediness. Greediness in itself is one of the most fundamental human vices, and most of us have it. Buddhism and Christianity both teach that true freedom is the overcoming of greediness. Now, what I have termed love of self in *The Art of Loving* is something quite different. It is a loving, friendly, affirmative attitude toward himself; he will have it also toward others; that love is something indivisible.

EVANS: Another way, then, that you would distinguish between the productive and the nonproductive orientations is by saying that the productive person is capable of a genuine love of self, while the nonproductive individual shows greediness, or self-love.

FROMM: Yes, indeed. One of the elements of the productive orientation is the capacity of a person to love that which is other than himself. A secondary factor is the capacity to use his reason. Together these constitute what I call authenticity, and this constitutes another aspect of the productive orientation. Much has been said by Sartre (1956) and other existentialists about the really authentic experience, and I feel the concept is an important one.

EVANS: Dr. Fromm, you have done some writing that deals with the area of dream interpretation—most notably in *The Forgotten Language* (1951). It would be interesting here to see how this fits into your approach to the therapeutic process.

FROMM: Dream interpretation is about the most important instrument we have in psychoanalytic therapy. There is nothing more significant or revealing of the patient's behavior than dreams. I agree with Freud that dream interpretation is really the royal road to understanding the unconscious. I should say I stand neither with Freud nor with Jung in my orientation to dream interpretation. In my book to which you referred, I distinguished between accidental symbols and universal symbols. If a patient dreams about a city, a house, or some particular time, then we deal with an accidental symbol, and only by the association of the patient can I really know what this means.

EVANS: Jung (Evans 1976a) felt that an almost infinite number of behavioral propensities, often reflected in symbolic form, could be inherited from past cultures. Could not your conception of universal symbols in dreams be similar to archetypes as Jung conceived of them?

FROMM: Yes. In many ways what I call universal symbols are the same as Jung's archetypes. It's often difficult to talk meaningfully about Jung because his way of expressing himself, although brilliant, is sometimes not too clear. I feel, however, that the concept of archetypes is a fruitful one. From the humanistic standpoint, we see that man always shares a basic condition of existence in that he not only is determined by his animal nature but also has an awareness of himself. This split in his basic nature leaves man with few solutions to the questions posed to him by life. It follows therefore that the number of symbols which represent these answers is also limited. They are universal, however, because there is only one ontological structure of the nature of man.

EVANS: An innovation which challenges traditional concepts of individual therapy is the growing use of group therapy. Those who advocate it claim that individual therapy creates a somewhat artificial atmosphere from which the patient finds it difficult to extricate himself in order to cope with the society at large, out of which his problems arose in the first place. Group therapy, they feel, maintains a more nearly normal social setting in which the patient can more effectively work out his problems. How do you feel about this idea?

FROMM: I'm very suspicious of it, but I must also say that I have never done any group therapy precisely because I dislike it. The idea of one person talking intimately about himself in front of ten other people is one which would make me most uneasy. I cannot but suspect that this is psychoanalysis for the man who cannot pay twenty-five dollars. Group therapy might be useful with a group of adolescents if they are not very sick and because they have similar problems: it might relieve their anxiety to learn that others share their particular problems. With good teaching and advice, some superficial basis for relief could be possible. However, I do not feel that this is in any way a substitute for individual psychoanalysis, because that deals with problems which are highly individualized and so personal that I don't think they lend themselves to the procedure of group therapy.

I'm an individualist, and I'm old-fashioned. I feel that the atmosphere of privacy is being continually eroded, reflecting an antihumanist attitude which is not conducive to any good therapy. I am afraid some of this atmosphere exists also in group therapy.

EVANS: Adler developed a prototype of the first five years of life, asserting that a style of life was established within that time which would determine the behavior of the individual for the remainder of his life. Freud said somewhat the same thing. Do you feel that this concept of the origins of man's life style is viable?

FROMM: Adler asks the patient in the first hour to recount the most important memories of his childhood, and I find this a good idea. Often what really is very relevant material emerges through this procedure. I am convinced that a great deal happens in the first five years which really is very important in the individual's development, but I feel that later events are equally capable of effecting changes within him.

Freud's concept that the individual continually repeats behavioral responses born out of emotional responses to events which occurred in the first five years is to me too mechanistic. This notion makes things very easy for the patient. All he does is put the blame on the people around him.

EVANS: This represents a way of denying or fleeing independence through rationalizing behavior and possibly contributes to the maintenance of often antisocial response patterns.

FROMM: Exactly, and I think that's wrong. Successful therapy depends upon both the constitutional factors and the patient's ability to mobilize his own sense of responsibility and activity. To effect change, the patient must have a strong will and impulse to bring it about.

EVANS: Some research in psychotherapy has suggested that the particular theoretical persuasion of the therapist—be it Freudian, Rogerian, Adlerian, etc.—is not the truly important factor in psychotherapy; rather, the extent of the actual therapeutic *experience* of the therapist, regardless of his theoretical orientation, is the principal factor which pervades the therapeutic relationship. Experience seems to cause therapists of different backgrounds to behave more and more alike. How do you feel about these findings?

FROMM: I would essentially agree with them. What matters first is that analysis makes sense in a theoretical frame of reference. Some theories are better than others, but the most important thing is the analyst's experience and his personal qualities which permit him to understand another human being. However, there is a pitfall into which many analysts fall. Many persons become analysts because they feel inhibited in reaching other human beings, and the role of the analyst affords them a degree of protection—particularly those who sit behind the couch. The primary consideration is that the analyst not be afraid of his *own* unconscious, for then he will not be afraid or embarrassed by opening up the *patient's* unconscious.

EVANS: There is in the behavioral and social sciences today a situation which tends to create conflicting ideologies. In American psychology, for example, there are varieties of determinism, most of which present a psychology modeled after the natural sciences. On the other hand, there are many thinkers in the field who are not bound by these models and who seek instead a more humanistic approach. Do you believe that there is room for both frames of reference within psychology?

FROMM: My answer to that question must be a qualified yes, although the dynamic orientation of which I am a proponent limits my ability to speak authoritatively about the more static mechanistic viewpoint. I'm certain that there are many studies in the behavioristic field and the Pavlovian field which are sound and which enrich the science of psychology. I have nothing to say against them as long as they remain in the field of science, do not make claims which they cannot substantiate, and do not attack psychoanalysis or the dynamic view without adequately understanding it.

I would say, from my standpoint, that psychoanalysis is the most scientific form of psychology. What is the essence of psychoanalytic procedure? It is observing facts. Nobody is as minutely observed as is a patient during hundreds of hours of psychoanalytic interviews. The procedure of psychoanalysis is to draw inferences from the observed facts, to form hypotheses, to compare the hypotheses with further facts which one finds, and eventually to coalesce a body of material sufficient to recognize the possibility of the hypotheses, if not their verification.

Now, to speak on the question of the cure of the patient as proof of the correctness of the hypothesis . . . I am rather skeptical of that "proof." Is the nature of the cure really to be explained by the correctness of the findings, or is it something else again? That's a much more difficult problem, really.

EVANS: Of course a typical criticism directed both to the work of Freud and to that of dynamic psychologists and psychiatrists in general is that many of the hypotheses involved in their theoretical models simply are not subject to empirical testing. In many cases some would classify dynamic theories as speculation in spite of the possible inclusion of a few rather sophisticated empirical observations. To formulate theories which by their very nature preclude empirical testing, they feel, is not equivalent to rigorously investigating a hypothesis on the basis of empirical research. Neither would they accept a view which denies the necessity of employing a more or less deductive approach in addressing a problem.

FROMM: Well, Dr. Evans, it all depends on what we call "rigorous." I definitely do not believe it is correct to assert that psychoanalysis does not lend itself to empirical tests. Let us say I have listened to a patient for thirty hours. I have heard some of his dreams. I form a hypothesis. I get more material, and eventually whatever further information comes forth from him will or will not make sense in terms of my hypothesis. I consider this a rather empirical test. The person who wants to have some conviction of whether or not my theory makes sense has to share with me the observations and the knowledge about the patient and the mechanisms.

EVANS: I have on occasion met very creative biologists, chemists, and physicists who talk the same way. In fact, they contend that psychologists demand more "rigor" in an experimental situation than might a "hard science" researcher.

FROMM: Exactly. In fact, I'm afraid our psychological colleagues sometimes are a little old-fashioned in their conception of science. I think I could explain the scientific character of the psychoanalytical method more easily to a theoretical physicist or biologist than to many psychologists, because the theoretical physicist or biologist today is much more aware that what he is studying is not just simple facts which can be counted or weighed, and for which there can be so-called rigorous proof. No one in theoretical physics speaks much about rigorous and strict proofs of anything, and the same thing is true very often in biology. Perhaps some psychologists are so concerned with rigorous proof because what they are trying to prove is not too significant.

EVANS: A question which concerns social psychologists is the overpreoccupation with classifying categories of mental illness when there are other problems of probably greater importance to society than the number of potential mental-hospital patients. For example, your writings have reflected a concern for such matters as prejudice, authoritarianism, and misanthropy. Of particular interest to many is your conception of "alienation."

FROMM: I am glad you raised this problem, because I think it's one of the most serious. I use "alienation" as it was used by Hegel (1960) and later by Marx (1932): instead of experiencing his own human powers—for example, love or wisdom, thought or reason, acting justly—a person transfers these powers to some idol, to a force or forces outside himself. In order, then, to get in touch with his own human power, he must submit completely to this idol. This often happens in religion. God or some idol in a pagan image is endowed with a human power. The individual impoverishes himself, gives all his power to the figure outside, and then is in touch with himself only by submitting to and worshipping that figure. That was not, of course, the concept of biblical monotheism or of Christianity, but it is what religion often becomes.

And how do we know people are becoming more and more alienated? That is why *Führer* figures develop; why people have little sense of self, little sense of their own creative powers; why they worship the state; why they worship idols in every field—film stars, successful businessmen. They have a sense of their own creative powers only by worshiping symbols to which they have transferred their own human power.

I have to say something here about the role of dynamic psychology in our time. For a hundred years the term "alienation" has been the property of philosophy; indeed, it is still a philosophical term. But alienation actually refers to specific concrete behaviors which may be investigated by empirical methods. Until now the two worlds of philosophical conceptualizing and psychological research have never come together. A concept like alienation, to be meaningful beyond a relatively speculative level of description, must be studied empirically by dynamic psychology, and is a good example of how philosophical speculation or description can supply appropriate avenues for psychological research. Attitudes which in the past were used only in politics—"liberal," "socialist," "progressive," etc.—but which have no meaning in terms of character must be studied by psychology in order to define their meaning accurately. Freudian dynamic psychology—especially the work on character—has given us the basis for studying all these religious, philosophical, and political phenomena in concrete terms. I think there is a tremendous field for social psychological research based on dynamic psychological theory.

EVANS: It may be interesting at this point to pursue the overall question of free will and determinism. One frequent approach to this issue is to consider the question of what constitutes legal responsibility for one's acts. The question of the limits of self-responsibility is a problem not only for the legal profession but also for the social scientist and psychiatrist—particularly when he is called upon to testify in these cases.

FROMM: The question of determinism versus free will is a crucial one; but at the same time, as it is proposed by many theologians, by a number of philosophers, and recently by the existentialists, it presents an untenable position. In fact, I find it a cruel and inhuman position (Fromm, 1947).

Consider a boy who has grown up in an environment of alcoholism, who has had no schooling, who has been on the streets, who was in prison at an early age, and who at the age of twenty is confronted with the possibility of stealing something in order to get money—and society says that he was free to do whatever he liked! I think this is unrealistic and cruel. He was not free. On the other hand, the position of determinism also is not quite convincing to me. Quite often we see in ourselves and in others a choice being made which is not expected, which is different from previous behavior, and which is not just a religious or an ethical conversion. I'm much inclined to formulate the problem in a different way and to talk about what one might call "alternativism." I mean that it follows from the nature of every constellation of choices that there are only certain limited real possibilities in the first place. There is not a choice of endless possibilities; there is only a choice between two or three "real possibilities," as Hegel called them. Second, even the freedom I have changes with every act I perform. Every action produces a result which either increases or limits our freedom. Therefore we cannot speak of the freedom we have even in terms of what I call alternativism. But we also must say that this freedom we have is something which changes all the time, and there is a point at which we have no more freedom to do right.

EVANS: Psychology today seems to be shifting toward a greater concern with this problem of free will. How can we develop a consistent psychological system that shows man as being "driven about," yet within this system retain the possibility that man is, in a sense, himself doing the driving?

FROMM: Often Spinoza is quoted as a determinist; Freud and Marx have been also. The allegation is to some extent true; but the essential part is often ignored, and that is that all thinkers have said, "Yes, man is determined. But the task of life is to overcome this determinism, either of economic forces or of the irrational passions in oneself, and to reach an optimum of freedom." Only by being aware of the forces which act upon me can I achieve optimal freedom as a human being. As long as I am not aware of the forces which drive me, I am irresponsible; I am shoved around by forces which act behind my back. Yet I live under the illusion that I am the one who determines my fate.

What, then, was the nature of Freud's therapy? He believed that you can change determinism through awareness of forces which pull you behind your back. This is the essence of psychoanalytic therapy.

EVANS: On the source of the ethics of a society: Are ethics essentially a question of expediency, or are they a spiritual given? How can this question be resolved in a system of individual analysis? How does an ethic develop, and how does it affect the individuals within the range of its influence?

FROMM: This is an empirical matter. In the first place, if we examine social ethics in a given society, we find that they are the norms of that society. Such ethics reflect cultural expediency or natural law. Or one could consider ethics as derived from and based on a concept of divine revelation. In *Man for Himself* I have also tried to define ethics in terms of norms, but these norms are those which present the best answers to the problem of being human. We can raise the questions, What is existence for man? What are his possibilities, and what are the conflicts with which he must cope? We would then consider ethical behavior that behavior which is most appropriate to unify, harmonize, and strengthen the individual, given his human constitution. Most humanistic religions have come to this interpretation of man and essentially agree with the psychological point of view.

EVANS: Then what one might call a transcendental point of view must emerge from the very behavior of man?

FROMM: Yes. The simple fact is that in all societies there is a conflict between the interests of that society to survive in its own form and the general human interest in the development and salvation of man (using theological terminology) or the full unfolding of man (using humanistic terminology). This conflict is very old, and is symbolized by the conflict between Caesar and God. It is a conflict of conscience, and the sad fact is that in most societies the expedient social ethics have been stronger than the universal, humanistic, or religious ethics. But there have always been some people who have been at least able to see the difference.

REFERENCES

Evans, Richard I. 1976a. *Jung on elementary psychology.* New York: Dutton.
Freud, Sigmund. 1938. *Basic writings of Sigmund Freud.* New York: Modern Library.
Fromm, Erich. 1941. *Escape from freedom.* New York: Farrar & Rinehart.
———. 1947. *Man for himself.* New York: Rinehart.
———. 1951. *The forgotten language.* New York: Rinehart.
———. 1956. *The art of loving.* New York: Harper.
———. 1959. *Sigmund Freud's mission: an analysis of his personality and influence.* New York: Harper.
———. 1961. *May man prevail?* Garden City, N.Y.: Doubleday.
Hegel, Georg W. F. 1960. *Hegel highlights: an annotated selection,* ed. Wanda Orynski. New York: Philosophical Library.
Marx, Karl. 1932. *Capital,* ed. Max Eastman. New York: Modern Library.
Packard, Vance. 1957. *The hidden persuaders.* New York: David McKay.
Riesman, David. 1961. *The lonely crowd,* ed. Seymour Martin Lipset. New York: Free Press.
Sartre, Jean-Paul. 1956. *Being and nothingness,* tr. Hazel E. Barnes. New York: Philosophical Library.
Whyte, William H., Jr. 1956. *The organization man.* New York: Simon and Schuster.

Section Six
Social
Behavior

The final section of this book includes a group of individuals who can be broadly described as social psychologists. Social psychology has, in recent years, accepted the serious challenge to leave the laboratory and address the meaningful problems of human existence. However, certain significant theoretical constructs, or paradigms, must be employed as the social psychologist attempts to deal with such problems.

Leon Festinger illustrates this notion through the development of his theory of cognitive dissonance, which evolved from small group research in the tradition of Kurt Lewin. Beginning with a series of experiments that explored the dissonance-resolving process in the individual and the influence of society on that process, he approached broader social problems. After a distinguished career as a social psychologist, Festinger has moved effectively into the area of physiological psychology, attempting to explore perception in a sensory modality.

Milton Rokeach worked originally with the group who developed the concept of the authoritarian personality; he extended his interest into the area of ideology and personality with his work on dogmatism, moving finally into an intensive examination of values and how they affect behavior. Since Gordon Allport posited the importance of the study of values to psychology, no social psychologist has approached this difficult problem more systematically than Rokeach.

Stanley Milgram, in a more experimental sense, began to explore conformity pressures and the effects of authoritarianism and demonstrated how blind obedience to authority can lead to punishment of supposedly innocent, anonymous human beings. Milgram's highly creative examination of significant social problems has also taken him into the cities and has led to his particularly penetrating analysis of the numbing alienation that congested city life can induce.

Philip Zimbardo has also examined the effects of authoritarian roles, including authoritarian social systems, both on the individual and on his behavior toward others. He simulated prison conditions for a group of student subjects and demonstrated how such systems can envelop the human being. He is presently involved in working out a model of madness, with far-reaching implications.

The effects of the work of such innovative researchers as Milgram and Zimbardo are so dramatic that they are in part responsible for much soul searching by psychologists over the rights of human subjects in experiments, which in turn has led to specific statements of such rights in an ethical code.

In the discussions in this book, each contributor has described various aspects of his own work and its implications as he perceives it. The reader is allowed to follow the development of major constructs and theories in psychology as they emerge, develop, are criticized and accepted or rejected. It is interesting to observe that in most instances, these notions generate more creative research. If the criteria for creativity remain elusive, the results of that creativity are obvious in the work of these individuals, in that of the men who inspired them, and in the work of any number of other highly creative contributors to psychology who, but for space limitations, could easily be included here.

Leon Festinger

(1919–   )

Leon Festinger received his B.S. in psychology at the College of the City of New York in 1939, and his M.A. and PhD. from the State University of Iowa in 1942. He has held positions at the University of Rochester, Massachusetts Institute of Technology, and was program director of the Research Center for Group Dynamics of the University of Michigan. He was professor of psychology at Stanford University before moving to his present position as Distinguished Professor of Psychology at the New School for Social Research. The American Psychological Association awarded him its Distinguished Scientific Contribution Award in 1959, citing in particular his group dynamics work. Professor Festinger's cognitive dissonance theory has generated a vast amount of creative research. Moving away from the social psychological field, he is now exploring perception from a physiological stance.

I Was with It When It Opened Up/The Evolvement of the Small Group Studies//Simply a Nonfitting Relationship/A Definition of Cognitive Dissonance/With Some Contemporary Examples//Behavior Commits You to Something/The Cognitive Components of Feelings and Attitudes//Looking at the Question Behind It/The Shift from Social to Physiological Psychology//Criticism/Validity/A Look at the Future//

Dr. Festinger and I discuss his early work in the area of small groups, and he describes some of the studies that opened up this field, recalling his work as a graduate student with Kurt Lewin. He traces the thinking that led up to the publication in 1957 of A THEORY OF COGNITIVE DISSONANCE, and then applies the theory to some real-life situations, including smoking and health and contemporary politics in the United States. We discuss the relationship between attitudes and behavior and the effects of rewards in reducing dissonance. He reiterates his strong feeling that changing behavior can change attitudes and values. He describes his shift from research in social psychology to the perceptual-sensory work in which he is currently engaged. Reacting to questions about criticisms of his work, he comments, "I have never been bothered by any of the criticisms of my work. There should be criticism in science. One hopes that the criticism will be constructive, leading to improvement."

EVANS: Dr. Festinger, an intriguing thing about your career is that you became well known, and deservedly so, for your contributions to social psychology and to psychological theory in general. Then you began to look at the effects of certain physiological factors on behavior. Had you become disenchanted with social psychology?

FESTINGER: It's probably more accurate to say that I became somewhat disenchanted with the rut I was in. I felt I wasn't making any significant contributions to social psychology any longer.

EVANS: You did your graduate work with Kurt Lewin, who in my opinion is one of the truly creative and profound thinkers in the history of psychology. It would be very interesting to hear how working with him might have affected your own career as you went into social psychology.

FESTINGER: Of course, I was very much influenced by him. There was a very good group of people working with him at the University of Iowa at that time—Ronald Lippitt, Dorwin Cartwright, and quite a number of others. I mention those two because they were also with me later at MIT at the Research Center for Group Dynamics. One of the things about Kurt Lewin was that he really understood the role of theory in science, and even more than that, had a superb understanding of the relationship between theory and data in the empirical world. Those, in particular, are the things I learned from him.

EVANS: There's a very profound paper that Lewin wrote on the distinctions between Aristotelian and Galilean modes of thought (Lewin 1935) that seems, at a highly sophisticated level, to look at the core of one of psychology's problems: the historical versus the contemporaneous examination of phenomena. Did working with a man of this philosophical sophistication present any problems for his students? Did his exposure to the European tradition of philosophical training give him a different slant than most psychologists?

FESTINGER: I'm not sure of the different slant. There was a trend in American psychology at one point toward a highly empirical orientation. They used to call it "dust-bowl empiricism." But that trend was on the wane then. People like Hull, Tolman, and Spence were all theoretical people. Some of Lewin's theoretical contributions were, indeed, on a much more philosophical level—what you might call describing a framework within which theory could be built. But a lot of his contributions at a theoretical level were very precise hypotheses about the empirical world. Lewin's (1951) work on tension systems, satiation, and resumption of interrupted tasks all involved very specific theory. I don't think there is a great gap.

EVANS: With your knowledge of Lewin, what do you consider to be his most important contribution, aside from his tremendously interesting general perspective?

FESTINGER: I don't think the general framework of topological psychology ends up as a very important contribution because it has waned without really influencing psychological theory, although for him, it was a fruitful, heuristic framework within which to think and in which to work. His major contributions are specific theories about tension systems and their effects, the new areas he opened up for investigation, such as level of aspiration, and the psychological effects of interrupted tasks; the whole experimental approach to social psychology.

EVANS: As you began to develop your interests as a social psychologist, you first worked with small groups—group dynamics—and some of this work was included in a book that you did with Schachter and Back, *Social Pressures in Informal Groups* (Festinger, Schachter, and Back 1950). What were some of the key findings you reported that you still consider to be of some importance?

FESTINGER: I would say, mainly, the conclusions about how groups generate pressures toward uniformity, how groups react to deviance, and the whole notion of the variable of cohesiveness of a group as affecting the strength of those pressures. The theories that we developed explaining those results led to a whole series of laboratory experiments attempting to test and develop them further. Most of that work is embodied in my article on informal social communication (Festinger 1950).

EVANS: That article appeared in the *Psychological Review* in 1950. What were some of those findings that you still consider to be significant? That's a big test.

FESTINGER: That article is entirely theoretical, and it attempted to explain and account for the data concerning pressures toward uniformity in groups, the variable of cohesiveness as it affected those pressures, reactions to deviance, and the implications of this whole process for interpersonal communication within a group.

EVANS: The whole area of group dynamics continues to be important, yet there is no doubt that as a field, group dynamics has been somewhat replaced by exotic applications of small group theory, such as sensitivity training and encounter groups. This seems to be a tremendous jump from the set of theoretical principles that you formulated to attempts to solve an array of complicated human problems. How do you feel about this?

FESTINGER: Forgive me a little bit of skepticism. I think sensitivity groups and training groups represent a big jump, but I don't think they jumped off from any theory that I developed, or that anybody else developed that was based on empirical evidence. They took off on a big jump out of ideology, and they may or may not be worthwhile, but I don't see any scientific evidence for these procedures. It doesn't mean that they are not valuable. Science may learn something from them, but so far I don't see the connection.

EVANS: Even though some of the people in these groups talk about some of the same constructs that you talk about—group pressures, dealing with deviance, etc.—you don't feel that it is really theory-based? You think it has evolved at a more pragmatic level.

FESTINGER: I think so, but then my particular talents don't seem to include the application of scientific knowledge to practical problems. Other people may see firmer connections than I do.

EVANS: Perhaps one of the few constructs in contemporary psychology that has really become a part of the concurrency of thinking at almost all levels is your notion of cognitive dissonance. Your book, *A Theory of Cognitive Dissonance* (Festinger 1957), in which you brought together a group of papers expanding this notion, is obviously considered a classic in the field, still much referred to and widely circulated. It would be interesting for our students to have you trace the development of dissonance theory. One widely held belief is that it might have begun out of a homeostatic model—the physiological notion that many psychologists have adopted in their motivational theories—that the organism seeks balance and that much of the function of the organism can be understood as a process of balance and imbalance. Would that be a fair asumption, that dissonance theory might have been rooted in a homeostatic model?

FESTINGER: No, I don't think so. In the introduction to that book, I really state very specifically and accurately how it arose, but I guess nobody believes it. Or else nobody reads introductions to books! I had been going through the literature on rumor transmission, and was interested in the problem of how rumors spread. It's a question of whether somebody feels strongly enough about the rumor so that he has to communicate it to others. I came across an article on rumors (Prasad 1950) that I really had difficulty understanding. This study was done in India after a big earthquake, and the rumors were collected among people outside the area of destruction. Most of the rumors predicted even more catastrophic things to come in the future, and it was just difficult for me to understand at the time why people would be spreading and believing frightening things like that. Generally, we don't go around frightening ourselves. One possible explanation that occurred to me was that these people had felt this enormous quake and were frightened and couldn't turn the fear off. Since they were outside the area of destruction, looking around, they didn't see anything different. There was nothing to justify that fear, so they invented things to justify it. It is the idea of cognitive invention, cognitive distortion, cognitive change to make your view of the world fit with how you feel or what you are doing; that was the basic idea out of which the formulation of dissonance theory developed.

EVANS: How would this idea that you're describing differ from the Freudian defense mechanisms, such as rationalization?

FESTINGER: That's an impossible question for me to answer directly, but let me answer it tangentially. There are all kinds of mechanisms and techniques available to the human being, and any of these that are in his repertoire can be used in the service of many different things. Assuming that Freud is correct, and in some areas I am sure he is, people use these mechanisms to protect themselves from such things as guilt. They also use these mechanisms to get rid of dissonance. The mechanisms may be identical, but the basic theories involved are about different processes.

EVANS: That's an interesting point. To put it another way, you're giving more specificity to a general concept, and not necessarily relating it to more generic defense mechanisms, such as rationalization.

FESTINGER: Dissonance is highly specific; it is something that one can define with reasonable specificity. Mechanisms can be used for the purpose of reducing dissonance as well as for many other purposes.

EVANS: There's a paper in your 1957 book that has been receiving attention again because of the current concern for smoking and public health. You were reporting a state-wide study that had to do with the effects of the surgeon-general's report on smoking, and how heavy smokers, moderate smokers, and nonsmokers perceived that information. There were two aspects to it: whether or not people were aware of the message on the relationship between smoking and health; and secondly, if they were aware of it, how likely were they to believe it. It clearly showed that heavy smokers were less aware of the message; but if they were aware of it, they were less likely to believe it. As I recall, you used this study to illustrate dissonance theory.

FESTINGER: That's right. The main thing was the relationship between how much people smoked and the extent to which they believed this information. Heavy smokers tended not to believe it.

EVANS: A number of studies have shown that almost everybody now believes that smoking is bad for health, heavy smokers and nonsmokers alike. There are very few people who don't believe these data. Now the data, as I see it, are probability data—they don't say that if you smoke, you will definitely get these diseases and die young—we're talking about probabilities, risk-taking. You're taking more of a risk if you're a heavy smoker, but there is no certainty. It's very clear that handling dissonance by simply not believing the data is almost impossible now. How would dissonance theory deal with continued smoking, even heavy smoking, on the part of the individual, given this type of information?

FESTINGER: It's no trouble to specify all the ways you can deal with this dissonance, even though you can't deny the harmful effects of smoking any longer without being unrealistic. But you can persuade yourself that your life expectancy reduction is really relatively small, that it's really a choice of how you want to die, that after all, lung cancer is a relatively painless death. You can persuade yourself that you can equalize your life expectancy by avoiding other situations, like driving a car. If you don't drive a car and you do smoke, your life expectancy is longer than if you don't smoke and do drive a car. And you can persuade yourself that if you avoid all the things that are just as dangerous as smoking, you can end up just lying in bed, and that's dangerous too. And who wants to live to the age of ninety-eight anyhow?

EVANS: Another interesting aspect of dissonance theory deals with doing something that is at odds with one's convictions. For example, let's take the people around Nixon. We could argue that some of these individuals started out as bright young lawyers, with the idealism that bright young lawyers often have, and surely many in that group, by their own testimony, were idealistic. As they begin to carry out orders that are discrepant with these idealistic beliefs, the question becomes how the dissonance-resolution process is involved in terms of the rewards that may or may not be present. I believe that it's historically rather important that we analyze things like this, because we see so much of this in our society today.

FESTINGER: The question you're asking is not why they did these acts, but what would dissonance theory say about the subsequent effects on their behavior, on their attitudinal structure, from having committed these acts.

EVANS: Exactly.

FESTINGER: The consequent effects of these actions would depend, according to dissonance theory, on how much pressure there was on these people to do those things. If there were huge pressures, so that the actions could be justified in their own minds in terms of this pressure, I don't think there would be any subsequent changes in ideology or in attitudinal structure. But what probably happens is that there is relatively little pressure applied to do these things, and the first things that are done are not so horribly dissonant with prior ideology. Dissonance is created because the actions are dissonant with existing ideology and the pressure to engage in those actions was relatively weak. Then they persuade themselves (or try to persuade themselves) that what they did wasn't really very bad, and that the purposes for which they were doing it were very, very important. Once that process starts, it can go on and on, to end up with their believing that they didn't do anything wrong, that what they did was for national security. Very gradually and subtly their attitudes change. On the surface, their ideology may have remained the same, but there are all kinds of exceptions in their minds for national security, and there are all kinds of redefinitions of what represents national security.

EVANS: It seems to me that dissonance theory can be useful in describing the corruption process. Moving into another area now, *When Prophecy Fails* (Festinger, Riecken, and Schachter 1956) is still a very interesting study. Could you tell us how you happened to get involved in this particular study?

FESTINGER: That occurred very early in the period where we were developing dissonance theory. If you start with the notion that if a person has two beliefs or two cognitive items that don't fit together, there will be a process going on that tries to change one or the other of them so that they fit together better. It's easy to ask the question, what happens if both pieces of information that are in a dissonant relationship with each other are very, very resistant to change? It occurred to us at the time that some lovely instances of this kind of thing were available in historical movements where groups of people were predicting the end of the world and the second coming of Christ. If you really believe the second coming is going to occur and the world as it exists today is going to vanish, you don't go about your life in a normal manner. Material possessions don't mean anything, jobs don't mean anything. You just prepare for the second coming. We started looking into these historical movements. Many of these movements predict a specific day for the end, and when the event doesn't occur, these people are left with a very large dissonance between their belief system and their behavior on the one hand, and the fact that the prediction didn't come true on the other. They have incontrovertible evidence that their belief system was wrong. Yet it is very difficult for them to change their belief system because they are committed to it by all their behavioral acts, which can't be undone. One way to lessen the dissonance would be to go out and persuade more people that your belief system is correct—perhaps this one little prediction was somewhat erroneous—but the general belief system is correct. So these discomfirmations of the belief system could lead to greater proselytizing efforts. And in all the historical movements that we could find, that seems to have occurred. Then we ran across this small newspaper article about a group that was predicting a specific date and time for the end of the world—not a millennial group in the traditional sense—but they were predicting that the world would be destroyed by flood on a specific date. In the hope that this would not occur, we thought we could have a live study and see whether there was an increase in proselytizing after this discomfirmation. That's why we did the study, and indeed, that is what happened.

EVANS: You were actually able to study this right in the field, you were able to follow it up right after the predicted event failed to occur.

FESTINGER: Oh, yes, we were right there.

EVANS: From the standpoint of a naturalistic study it was really beautiful. Now let me recall a paper that you presented at the American Psychological Association several years ago in which you challenged the field of psychology to think carefully about the relationship between attitudes and behavior. You were saying that there isn't much evidence that changing attitudes will change behavior. This led to a lot of thinking about whether we should be involved in attitude-change research at all if changing attitudes doesn't change behavior. On the other hand, dissonance theory seems to suggest that if we change behavior, a change in attitude will follow. This was the model that was demonstrated in the historic 1954 Supreme Court decision, *Brown* versus *Board of Education*, that implied if we developed laws to change our segregation practices, the attitude changes would follow. How do you feel about this theory?

FESTINGER: There are two different things that are embodied in your question. One is the relationship between behavior and attitudes, and the other is the relationship between attitude change and behavior change. By and large, I'm sure you will find a relationship between the attitude that is held and the relevant behavior that is overtly exhibited. The question is, if you change the attitude, will you then change the behavior or will that attitude simply slip back? At the time I could find no evidence in the literature to support the idea that if you could change the attitude, the behavior would change and stay changed. Whatever evidence existed, and it was very little, seemed to say that the attitude would just slip back. I would still maintain that if you change attitudes with the idea of wanting to change behavior, you'd better get some commitment about the attitudinal change so that the dissonance-reduction processes will drag the behavior into line with it. Usually, if you want to create a change to which a person is committed, it's much easier to get that person committed to a behavioral change, and if you do that, without too much pressure, I think you will find that attitudes will slide into line with the behavior.

EVANS: Now the people involved with the behavior-modification movement have increasingly focused on behavior, on modifying or arranging the contingencies in the environment to increase the probability that the desired behavior will occur. For their purposes, cognitive processes involved in attitudes are more-or-less irrelevant. That is, of course, an extreme view, but do you feel that it is sufficiently sophisticated to be adopted generally by psychology? Would we be losing a lot to ignore cognitive constructs, such as attitudes, altogether?

FESTINGER: As a practical mechanism for creating certain kinds of changes, perhaps we could look at behavior and nothing else. But from the point of view of understanding humans, if you look at nothing but behavior, you're ignoring a vast world that exists for human beings.

EVANS: You mention something very interesting here—the point of view of understanding. Characteristically, we talk about three different areas psychologists are concerned with—understanding, prediction, and control. With behavior modification, we're talking about controlling behavior, possibly predicting it, but we're not really concerned with understanding behavior. In other words, behavior modification says that we should go where the action is. But you're saying that we shouldn't ignore understanding. Do you think that progress would be seriously thwarted in psychology if we focused primarily on controlling and/or predicting behavior, forgetting about the understanding?

FESTINGER: It's very easy to control behavior. I can point a gun at you, and if you believe I'm ready to use it, you will do what I tell you to do. That's not what you really mean by controlling behavior. You're concerned with creating a change in behavior that lasts and endures in the absence of supervision. That means that something has to have gone on inside the person. You may find a technique for doing that in some limited area, but unless you understand the processes that are involved, unless you have a good theory about it, you don't know where it is going to work and where it isn't going to work. You aren't going to make progress. It's a little like the economic indicators. Every time they don't work, they post hoc create another economic index.

EVANS: That's very well put. And if we look at what's happening in the behavior-modification movement, we can take the very interesting work of Albert Bandura (1973), who has introduced the concept of modeling and who is talking about such things as vicarious cognitive dimensions in modifying behavior. Some of the behavior-modification people are talking about "intraceptive conditioning," which introduces some form of cognitive component (imagination) into behavior change. I think what is happening in this movement bears out what you're saying, that you have to enrich what you're doing beyond the simpler delineation of behavior in its own right.

FESTINGER: The history of science is filled with demonstrations that the more you understand about the dynamics of a process, the better your prediction is, and the better your control of relevant events is.

EVANS: One facet of your work in dissonance theory involves the concept of public commitment—a tool used quite often by propagandists —that if you make a public commitment to a point of view that is essentially at odds with your "real" point of view, this commitment can have an effect on altering your "real" point of view.

FESTINGER: That's from the point of view that once a dissonance is created, how can you reduce it? If you have a public commitment or any other kind of commitment to something, changing that cognitively will be very difficult. The person will attempt to reduce the dissonance by trying to work on those cognitions, those aspects of the situation that are less resistant to change. By creating a commitment, making the cognition about that behavior very resistant to change, the dissonance-reduction processes will be oriented toward the other, less-resistant items.

EVANS: In your more recent work, you have shifted rather radically to research at the physiological level in the area of vision. What got you interested in studying the properties of vision?

FESTINGER: It's a rather long story. It emerged primarily out of the fact that I didn't feel I was making much progress, theoretically, with dissonance. And without making progress and having new ideas, I became dissatisfied with myself. So I returned to the old question of what happens if there's a dissonance between two pieces of information, both of which are highly resistant to change. It occurred to me that one of the things that makes a piece of information resistant to change is to have that information come to you through your own sense experience. If I see something is white, it's very hard for me to persuade myself that it's red. If you put wedge-prism spectacles on a person and he looks at a straight, vertical line or edge, that line appears curved. If he rubs his hand up and down that edge, the information from his arm tells him that it's straight. There would be two pieces of information, both from direct sense experience, that would be dissonant with each other. We tried that, and it turned out to be a very bad way to study dissonance reduction because no dissonance was created. What happens is that the arm feels it is moving in a curved pattern. I later discovered that Gibson (1933) had pointed this out in an article in 1933! But the attempt to understand that led me into the study of vision, and I was willingly trapped by all of the fascinating problems about vision and the visual system.

EVANS: Briefly, could you describe the gist of your present work in vision? I know this work is very intriguing to a number of people who are familiar with it.

FESTINGER: I can tell you briefly what I'm working on currently, although how I got there, and why I'm working on it, and why I find it fascinating, I cannot tell you briefly. That would take time. But the visual system is a relatively peculiar system in that the perceptual system does not get any information about eye movement or eye position based on feedback information from the muscles that move the eye. If you move your arm, for example, there is feedback, primarily from the joint receptors, that tells the central nervous system something about the position of the arm. There is no such information fed back to the perceptual system from the extraocular muscles, the muscles that move the eye. Any information that the perceptual system has about eye position or eye movement is based on monitoring of the efferent output to the eye muscles. The perceptual system knows the position of the eye only insofar as it knows where the eye was told to go. Because of that situation, anything the perceptual system knows about eye position and eye movement has to be information that was contained in the efferent command at the point at which it was monitored by the perceptual system. Because of that, the visual system becomes a window onto the workings of the efferent output system, which you can't get as cleanly with any other system. What I'm working on primarily is trying to understand and pin down the information contained in those efferent output commands to the eyes at various stages in the transmission chain.

EVANS: In looking over your great number of contributions, both in social psychology and in vision, what criticisms of your work have bothered you?

FESTINGER: I have never been bothered by any of the criticisms of my work. I have felt that some of them were rather useless, but that is the prerogative of other people. There should be criticism in science. When something is published, one imagines that it is not perfect; one imagines that others will criticize it; one hopes that the criticism will be constructive, leading to improvement.

REFERENCES

Bandura, A. 1973. *Aggression: a social learning analysis.* Englewood Cliffs, N.J.: Prentice-Hall.

Brehm, J., and Cohen, A. 1962. *Explorations in cognitive dissonance.* New York: Wiley.

Festinger, 1950. Informal social communication. *Psychol. Rev.* 57: 271–82.

————. 1957. *A theory of cognitive dissonance*. Stanford, Calif.: Stanford University Press.

————. 1964. Behavioral support for opinion change. *Pub. Opin. Quart.* 28: 404–17.

————, Schachter, S., and Back, K. 1950. *Social pressures in informal groups: a study of human factors in housing*. New York: Harper.

————, Riecken, H., and Schachter, S. 1956. *When prophecy fails*. Minneapolis: University of Minnesota Press.

Gibson, J. 1933. Adaption aftereffect and contrast in the perception of curved lines. *J. Exper. Psychol.* 16: 1–31.

Lewin, K. 1935. *Dynamic theory of personality*. New York: McGraw-Hill.

————. 1951. Selected papers by K. Lewin in *Field theory in social sciences: selected theoretical papers,* ed. D. Cartwright. New York: Harper.

Prasad, J. 1950. A comparative study of rumours and reports in earthquakes. *Brit. J. Psychol.* 41: 129–44.

Milton Rokeach

(1918–   )

Milton Rokeach took his B.A. at Brooklyn College and his M.A. in 1941 from the University of California. He received a Ph.D. in psychology in 1947 from the University of California at Berkeley where he was a member of the authoritarian personality research group. He has held positions as professor of psychology at Michigan State University and the University of Western Ontario, and he is presently professor of psychology and sociology at Washington State University. Professor Rokeach has extended authoritarian study into the broader field of ideology and personality in his work on dogmatism, and his current research involves an intensive examination of human values as they affect behavior.

Trapped into a Concrete Mode of Thought/Rigidity and Ethnocentrism/
A Phenomenon That Pervades All Areas of Human Life/The Authoritarian
Personality/Not Left or Right/A Structural Analysis/The "And Besides"
Syndrome/Isolation/Only a Simple-Minded Fool/The Opinionation Test/
Race versus Belief/Two Kinds of Prejudice or One?/Opinionation/
Dogmatism/Ethnocentrism/Authoritarianism//The Three Christs of Ypsilanti/
Self-Confrontation/Values/Beliefs/Attitudes/Opinions/No Correct Way/
Only Fruitful Ways/Value Has a Transcendental Quality/Terminal Values/
End States/Instrumental Values/Behavior/Changing Values Changes
Attitudes/The Possibility of Genuine Long-term Change//

Dr. Rokeach was involved with the group that did the seminal work on the
authoritarian personality. His doctoral dissertation was a study of the relationship between rigidity in thinking and ethnocentrism. The authoritarian-
personality work evoked criticisms of a nature that persuaded Dr. Rokeach to
try and build a structural foundation for such concepts, which would be
broader, more basic and nonideological. In testing qualities such as prejudice
with questions designed to elicit the quality no matter what its manifestations, he collected some surprising results, results that are still difficult for
some of his critics to accept. Pursuing his interest in belief systems as they
relate to human dissonance, he brought together three mental patients, all of
whom thought they were Jesus Christ. A great deal of Dr. Rokeach's later work
has been in the area of human values, with an extensive effort to define terms

and with experiments conducted in efforts to change values and thus to modify behavior. He outlines these findings, and I ask him some of the questions his critics have asked about this work. We end our discussion on the subject of ethics, which, when it comes to the manipulation of human values, is crucial. Reacting to the possibility that value change could be negative as well as positive, Dr. Rokeach is optimistic: "I believe that the self is so constructed that it is willing to allow itself to be changed in one direction, but not the opposite. I can influence you to grow, but I cannot influence your values in the direction of retrogression; I think there is a built-in protection."

EVANS: Dr. Rokeach, looking at your impressive career, one recalls that your significant contributions really began while you were completing your doctorate at the University of California at Berkeley. It is well known that that was a very exciting period in the social psychology group there. Out of that group of innovative behavioral scientists came the classic work on the authoritarian personality (Adorno, et al. 1950). Your doctoral dissertation became one of the significant investigations during this period. Could you tell us a little bit about that early research? It had to do with the matter of rigidity and ethnocentrism, is that not correct?

ROKEACH: Yes, it did. It was an attempt to relate an ideological or attitudinal variable, ethnocentrism—or in plainer English, prejudice toward outgroups—on the one hand, and a variable that could be called a purely cognitive variable, a variable that had to do with the ability to solve problems. I thought that I saw a connection that had something to do with rigidity or structural rigidity of thinking. And to study it, I picked a problem that was well known to me as a result of my studies with Solomon Asch, the Gestalt psychologist, and that was the problem of *Einstellung*, worked over extensively by Luchins (1942), Wertheimer (1945), and others. It attempted to find out whether people who are rigid in solving problems involving the development of sets, or *Einstellung*, are also more likely to be prejudiced. I remember vividly as an undergraduate student at Brooklyn College first learning about *Einstellung* and its influence from Solomon Asch, who argued that the conditions that led to a person being rigid had to do only with the field conditions and that personality had nothing to do with it. I myself couldn't believe that personality counted for nothing.

EVANS: As I recall, in one of your particularly intriguing experiments you had a group of individuals given an opportunity to solve arithmetic problems that were really simple enough so that they could do them in their heads. They were given scratch paper and pencil, and one of the measures you used was the amount of scratch paper they actually used, which related to what might be called "concreteness," or what the authoritarian-personality group called "extraceptiveness."

You found that those who are prejudiced are likely to use more scratch paper than those who are not. How did you conceptualize that?

ROKEACH: They seem to be related to two very different things, but in my reading of the literature on the determinants of rigidity, I discovered that one of the major determinants of rigidity in problem solving is the inability to think abstractly, or being trapped into a concrete mode of thought.

EVANS: You were in a rather unusual position to react to this entire authoritarian-personality study. In fact, you did your doctorate under Nevitt Sanford (Adorno, et al. 1950), one of the original coauthors of the volume, and you had the privilege of working with people like Else Frenkel-Brunswik (1945). They started out studying anti-Semitism, then proceeded to study ethnocentrism. Interrelationships among such concepts suggested to them a "prefascist" or "authoritarian" personality. They drew a picture of the high authoritarian as being very rigid, black-white overly conventional, an individual who is likely to stereotype, and to think in concrete dichotomies.

ROKEACH: Who is intolerant of ambiguity.

EVANS: Yes. The picture one gets is of a rather distasteful individual. Now, Dr. Shils (1954) at the University of Chicago, reacting to this work on the authoritarian personality, felt that the background of the investigators might have led them to a kind of self-fulfilling prophecy. They hated nazism; some of them had escaped from Nazi Germany. They hated authoritarianism, and so they were almost bound to find the authoritarian personality a bad guy rather than a good guy. A lot of people, therefore, questioned this study on the grounds that it might have reflected more the values of the investigators than genuine scientific findings. Do you think those criticisms were justified?

ROKEACH: Well, yes, I think they were justified, but I also felt that the Shils criticism that the workers on the authoritarian personality had neglected the authoritarianism of the left was just as self-serving and just as ideologically motivated as the original workers contending that it was the Fascist who was the bad guy. I felt that there was something tremendously self-righteous about the proposition that it's those guys, the "theys," who are the authoritarians and bigots. I felt that the phenomena of authoritarianism, of bigotry if you like, were phenomena that pervade all areas of human life. I saw these phenomena to be manifest at all points along the political spectrum and in the academic world as well. I noticed that psychoanalysts were intolerant of behaviorists, Gestalt psychologists were intolerant of psychoanalysts; they were all anti–anti-Semitic. Those people who read my work from secondary sources, not from my own work, are under the impression that all I've done was to insist that authoritarianism exists on the left as well as on the right. I would vigorously deny it. What I was saying was that this is a phenomena that has to be studied independently of the left-right continuum. And for this reason, I launched into what I called a structural analysis, a study of the structural properties of authoritarianism that would allow us to make statements about it regardless of ideological content. I came up with such Lewian properties as the "degree of isolation" of belief-disbelief systems, "degree of differentiation," "time perspective," and the like.

EVANS: I wonder if you could elaborate on those concepts. They were very central to your thinking at that time.

ROKEACH: Well, take the concept of isolation. That refers to two ideas coexisting in two adjacent regions but with no communication between them. They are in a state of isolation, or what is more commonly known, of compartmentalization. One might believe two logically opposite things but not realize that they are opposite because of isolated boundaries. Whenever a person uses too many arguments that have a certain form, like, "No, that's not so, and besides, . . ." which I call the "And Besides Syndrome," that tips me off to a condition of isolation. A good illustration of that is my coming home one day and seeing my son, Marty, who was then five, hitting a kid smaller than he was. I bawled him out, and he answered me, "Dad, I didn't hit him, and besides, he hit me first, and besides, I didn't hit him very hard." Well, that suggests a condition of isolation between three cognitions, each of which contradicted each of the others. So in my own work on the authoritarian, on dogmatism, I tried to reformulate the concept so that it structured the properties of authoritarianism as it might exist in any area of human endeavor. Whether I succeeded is another matter, but that's what I tried to do.

EVANS: There was a test developed called the F-Scale, which was supposed to measure the authoritarian personality in a broad sense; as a matter of fact, it's still being widely used. Take a test like the F-Scale, even there authoritarianism principally seems to be related to something like the right and left on the political spectrum. You feel there is the need for something a little less value-loaded; perhaps the term, dogmatism. Would that be a fair statement?

ROKEACH: Yes. Let me illustrate. One of the items in the F-Scale, the scale for the measure of predisposition toward fascism, states, "There are two kinds of people in this world, the weak and the strong." Now, to agree with it is to agree with a fascist idea, but it only captures an authoritarianism of the extreme right. Hoping to measure the same trait, but at all points along the continuum, I reworded it to read: "There are two kinds of people in this world, those who are for the truth and those who are against the truth." Now notice that agreeing with that idea doesn't instruct us on what the person thinks is the truth, but whether he is a Freudian, a Leninist, a Hitlerian, a Nietzscheian, or a whatever, he would still agree with it if he were authoritarian. So I think that that insight allowed me to proceed from the very specific concept of fascist authoritarianism to the more general, but in so doing, I had to get rid of the content.

EVANS: At this point, however, you now found it more valuable to begin calling this dogmatism, or open- and closed-mindedness rather than using a word that was somewhat more value-laden like authoritarianism. Is that correct?

ROKEACH: Sure, but this is not to say that open-mindedness is not value laden. I'd be the last one to deny that it is. But even so, it is not ideologically value-laden. I found that the fundamental way of defining prejudice was equally objectionable. The traditional way that social scientists have developed for measuring prejudice is to find out how people feel about this or that ethnic or racial group, how they like Jews, blacks, Chicanos, Japanese. The more you say you dislike them, the more prejudiced you are. And yet, I found phenomena of prejudice among people who wouldn't be caught dead with an anti-Semitic statement, or with an antiblack statement; it was another form of bigotry that simply escaped attention. I therefore conceptualized this phenomenon of bigotry, not in terms of how much you like or dislike ethnic or racial groups, but in terms of how much you like people who agree with you or disagree with you, whatever they may be. And liking somebody because they agree with you is no less a manifestation of prejudice because it has a qualificational string attached to it than disliking people because they disagree with you. So I invented this test I called the "Opinionation Test" that had phrases like, "Only a simple-minded fool would say that there is a God," and "Only a simple-minded fool would say there is no God." And what I expected from the tolerant person was to disagree vehemently with both of these things in order to qualify as tolerant; if he agreed with either one of them, I considered this a manifestation of prejudice. This was the same structural strategy of getting at prejudice regardless of the content of prejudice. From there, of course, I moved to the whole question of whether there are two kinds of prejudice or one. You are the coauthor with me on that research (Rokeach, Smith, and Evans 1960), and there the question was, What happens if you pit a racial variable against a belief variable? How do you feel about a white person who is an atheist and a black person who is an atheist or a white person who believes in God and a black person who believes in God? By systematic design of studies of that kind, we were able to begin to ask, How much do people like other people on grounds of belief similarity rather than on grounds of racial similarity? That has led to some interesting research controversies.

EVANS: Right. That study, among several others, was the culmination of approximately ten years of work; *The Open and Closed Mind* (Rokeach 1960) was published in 1960. What were some of the reactions to that book, which is now certainly regarded as very significant?

ROKEACH: Well, there were some fairly interesting reactions. When I first mentioned the work on race versus belief to a very prominent social psychologist, I explained to him that this work was done at Michigan State University, and I asked him if he would take a look at the results.

He believed that the results would show that people would like a person of their own race who disagreed with them more than a person of the opposite race who agreed with them about something important, because everybody knows how important race is. When I told him that the vast majority of the subjects do exactly the opposite, he said, "Oh, the reason why you got these results is because the subjects are at a liberal midwestern university, and you brainwashed them. They know what answers you wanted. If you were to repeat this study in a southern university, you wouldn't get this sort of thing." Whereupon I told him the study had also been done at a southern university; then I mentioned your work, Dick (Rokeach, Smith, and Evans 1960), and pointed out that the results were no different at the University of Houston than they were at Michigan State University.

EVANS: I would have completely agreed with him and was probably just as surprised as he with what we found down here.

ROKEACH: His next reaction was, "Oh, I know what's happening. This is all at the verbal level, but at the behavioral level, you wouldn't get this sort of thing." Well, I had no answer for him, there. But it did lead to further work, the work that I did with Mezei (Rokeach and Mezei 1966) that was eventually published in *Science*. That work required us to do field experiments. In one case it involved unemployed workers who didn't even know they were in an experiment. They were asked to make choices between persons they wanted to work with, whether they wanted to work with two people of the same race as they, or two people who agreed with them on a particular issue. So we replicated the work on race versus belief in a natural behavioral field condition, and we found the same thing. Whereupon the criticism shifts once more and this time it's, "But work isn't all that important. They're not marrying each other." And so, as each point was responded to with the next experiment, the criticism shifted to a new level. Rather than concerning themselves with the theoretical, political, social, and economic implications of these findings, the critics are rather preoccupied with thinking up alternative interpretations designed to deny and to trivialize the results. I guess the only response that I have left is to say that as far as I can tell, the belief principle works up to and including marriage, as evidenced, for example, by the fact that belief congruence is found to be more important than race as a determinant of marriage, say, in Hawaii where the social constraints against interracial marriage are considerably weaker than they are in the United States.

EVANS: You mentioned the use of the Opinionation Scale. Of course, a widely used scale in psychology is also the Dogmatism Scale, the D-Scale. Do you see any difference between what you were measuring in the Opinionation Scale and the Dogmatism Scale?

ROKEACH: Yes, I think the relationship between opinionation and dogmatism is the same as the relationship in the authoritarian personality research between ethnocentrism and F. Ethnocentrism is the attitudinal correlate of bigotry that is supposed to be somehow causally related to that which underlies it—authoritarianism. Opinionation, similarly, is the intolerance variable that is supposedly causally related to the dogmatism that supposedly underlies it.

EVANS: One of the most unique research efforts by a social psychologist is reflected in your book, *The Three Christs of Ypsilanti* (Rokeach 1964). Could you tell us a little bit about what this is all about and some of the things you found?

ROKEACH: Well, basically, it's a clinical study. I had lots of quantitative data, but I deliberately left them out. It's a story of three paranoid schizophrenics, each of whom believes that he is Jesus Christ. I brought these three people together.

EVANS: They were all in the hospital?

ROKEACH: Two of them were in different parts of the same mental hospital, and one was in a different hospital. I brought them together and put them to work in the same laundry room; they ate at the same dining table; they slept on three adjacent cots. Every day, day in and day out, for a period of two years, they were living in each other's environment. The purpose of this confrontation was to create the maximum human dissonance that I could imagine; each one had to live with two other people who constantly thought they were he. I was motivated by my interest in balance and dissonance and by my lifelong interest in the structure of belief systems. I wanted to find out, in this clinical context, what happens when the most fundamental of all beliefs that I can imagine was constantly being challenged in a way that it could not possibly be challenged in our daily lives. It's much too complicated to discuss here, but in my book, *The Three Christs of Ypsilanti*, I tried to describe the sequence of changes of beliefs that took place in these three people over a period of two years. I think I learned what it is to confront other people with contradictions, and I also think I learned something about what it means to confront one's self. Basically, this work laid the groundwork for the work that I'm now doing on changing values, and with it, changing behavior by what I call the method of self-confrontation.

EVANS: By and large, the term "conflict of values" has been anathema to experimenters in psychology, because values are something that are considered almost in the spiritual realm, not subject to scientific investigation. As Skinner (Evans 1968) says, we can arrange the contingencies in the environment, reinforce the right response; so why worry about values, attitudes, beliefs? Even non-Skinnerians argue, What is a value? What is an attitude? What is a mood? How do all these things tend to differ? So maybe we ought to start right there. What is the difference between a value, a belief, and an attitude?

ROKEACH: Well, it was about 1964 that Gardner Lindzey invited me to write the article on attitudes for the *International Encyclopedia of Social Sciences* and after much thought, I decided I would. Then I spent approximately six months reading the literature on what the social sciences—sociology, psychology, and other areas, but mainly those two— have to say about attitudes. And I became acutely aware that these social sciences seemed to be using that word interchangeably with other words—opinion, value, value system, ideology. What began to grate on me was that the specialists in the field had only the dimmest perception of what the difference was, if any. The field was in chaos. Now intuitively I knew there had to be some very profound distinction between attitudes and values. I was forced to face up to the question, How shall I tell myself and others what it is that makes a thing a value, and that question led to my current interest in values.

EVANS: You use the words *belief* and *belief systems*; you use the term *value* and the term *attitude*; and in fact, you use the word *opinion* (Rokeach 1968).

ROKEACH: First of all, I must say that there is no correct way of defining concepts. There are only fruitful ways. The question is, Is it a difference that makes a difference or is it a difference that makes no difference? So having said this, I can only say that I've attempted to make certain distinctions on the assumption that such distinctions make an important difference. What's the difference between an attitude and an opinion? To me, an opinion is nothing more than a verbal expression. An attitude is that which underlies the opinion; it may be exactly the opposite of the opinion expressed. For me, an attitude is a hypothetical construct that I can only infer from all the things a person says or does, and I've got to take my chances on being wrong. Perhaps more important, in my thinking, is the difference between an attitude and a belief. For me, an attitude is a set of beliefs that are focused on a particular object or a particular situation. For instance, a Likert Scale is a set of statements, each of which has the same subject, Jew, or black, or church, or God. A Likert Scale measures attitudes toward God through a set of statements, each of which asks the person to agree or disagree with a belief that he has about the properties or attributes of God.

EVANS: And how do you define values?

ROKEACH: Value has a transcendental quality. It is not focused; it's across objects, across situations. I distinguish two kinds of values. One kind of value concerns a desired end-state of existence, a state of equality, a state of happiness, a state of inner harmony. I prefer to call these terminal values. The other kind of a value is what I call an instrumental value, an idealized way of behaving, cutting across objects and situations—honesty, for example. You're never taught to behave honestly only with respect to whites and not with respect to blacks. Honesty, responsibility, courage, helpfulness, cleanliness, politeness, obedience— these would be instrumental values. So one set of values, terminal values, relates to prescribed end-states, and the other set of values, instrumental values, relates to idealized behavior.

Defining values and attitudes this way, one can immediately infer that there must be thousands of attitudes, but only a small number of values. You can't have thousands of end-states, or thousands of ideal modes of behavior, but there are thousands of objects toward which we have attitudes. To me this was a very important distinction.

EVANS: What are the implications of this, as you see it?

ROKEACH: Distinctions aren't worth making just to be made, at least not in science. Science is an activity that leads to theoretical constructions, which lead to predictions of behavioral effects that will take us beyond what we know. So what I was really after in distinguishing the concepts of value from attitude was to try to conceptualize why people have the attitudes they do, and beyond that, with what are the behavioral consequences of these attitudes? Beyond this, there is the question, Is it possible to change values, and if so, can we thus change attitudes, and with it, behavior? So, I began to move away from where my colleagues in the field were focused—I might almost use the word fixated—the concepts of attitude change and the theories of persuasive communication designed to change attitudes. I moved to theories of value organization and value change, to a consideration of the consequences of value change for attitude and behavioral change.

We are now looking through the literature on attitude change in the *Journal of Personality and Social Psychology* to determine how long after the experimental treatment the posttest is administered. I am reasonably sure, intuitively, from my reading of the literature of the past quarter of a century, that this literature is a literature of short-term attitude change. By short-term I mean changes taking place a few minutes after an experimental treatment, sometimes a day or so afterward, rarely a week or more. This literature doesn't tell us anything about the changes we look for in therapy or in education and reeducation. It's a literature of the things that would be more useful to Madison Avenue and propagandists rather than to educators, therapists, and counselors. Moreover, the closer the posttest is to the experimental treatment, the more it is suspect because the more it is vulnerable to alternative interpretations.

EVANS: Dr. Leon Festinger (1964) reviewed the literature on attitude change to see if there was a relationship between attitude changes and behavior changes. He found that the relationship was rarely, if ever, demonstrated. Do I understand you correctly, that your research on values introduces the possibility that modifying values can affect behavior? In your book *The Nature of Human Values* (Rokeach 1973) you do incorporate studies that report actual behavior and demonstrate that a change in values will affect behavior, not only for a short period of time but for a long period of time. As I recall, there was a study that had to do with joining the NAACP that illustrated this? Is that correct?

ROKEACH: Yes. It involved attempting to change the values that underlie civil rights behavior. What we did, by feedback to the subjects about their own and others' values, was to increase experimentally their own values for equality and freedom. One hundred days later and again four hundred and sixty-five days later, the NAACP solicited them to join. The experimental findings are very clear on the point. They showed that approximately two and a half times as many experimental subjects joined the NAACP as control subjects. And in my book, *The Nature of Human Values*, I report other independently obtained behavioral effects of the experimental treatment that had changed values, for example, actual enrollments in courses on race relations obtained from official registration figures of the university, or changes of majors from physical science or natural science to social science. When we look at all the results from all these studies, it is unlikely that you can explain away the behavioral differences between experimental and control groups on the purely methodological grounds.

EVANS: There is probably no doubt that there are certain types of behavior that have a strong compulsive component, like smoking, over-eating, or alcoholism. That's a class of behavior that we sometimes call addictive, and that we find extremely difficult to change. The relative complexity and really compulsive nature of this type of behavior is a factor that obviously has to be dealt with. Isn't it a lot more difficult, even with your approach, to change a compulsive behavior than one that is not compulsive?

ROKEACH: Well, I can respond very briefly by saying I'm sure that compulsive behavior is going to be more difficult to change than non-compulsive behavior, but in principle, I see no theoretical reason why it would be impossible to change. In any case, presently known empirical findings show that both compulsive types of behavior, namely smoking, and noncompulsive types of behavior, namely joining a political organi-zation, and others that I haven't mentioned, can be changed on a rela-tively long-term basis by first changing the values that underlie such behavior.

EVANS: Of course, this is very exciting and could be a significant breakthrough for those interested in behavior modification. However, Skinnerian theory of behavior modification (Evans 1968) is obviously extremely attractive because of its simplicity. It doesn't require compli-cated value constructs; it suggests that by simply controlling the contin-gencies of the environment the probability that certain behavior will occur is increased. So the Skinnerian would say that consideration of values is irrelevant and needlessly complicated.

ROKEACH: All you're really saying is that the Skinnerians offer an alternative interpretation of the known facts. We need to examine this alternative interpretation in order to ascertain whether it will indeed account for the known facts. Well now, Skinnerian behavior modification requires that a change of the contingencies of reinforcement would involve at least several treatments, so that behavior can be shaped grad-ually. No Skinnerian study that I've ever heard of claims to change the contingencies of reinforcement over a long-term period by a single-shot experimental treatment. I would then ask, How would one account for a change observed twenty-one months after a single experimental treatment? And if the observed behavioral consequences are remote, and if there are demonstrable cognitive mediators of those consequences, you have to account for all the cognitive changes that are observed to occur three weeks later, three months later, fifteen months later, all as a result of a single experimental intervention. That's why I don't believe that a Skinnerian interpretation is a viable alternative interpretation of the known empirical facts.

EVANS: Dr. Rokeach, I've already mentioned a few criticisms of your work; are there others that bother you?

ROKEACH: I naturally anticipated that if a psychologist claims behavioral change as remote in time as I have claimed, as the result of a single experimental treatment, it will be regarded with the gravest skepticism. I know that I myself would regard it with great skepticism because all of our training tells us that this is beyond what is presently known. In my book, one of my chapters is entitled, "Some Alternative Interpretations." I felt especially obligated to consider all the conceivable alternative interpretations of the data. I raise statistical arguments, methodological arguments, alternative substantive arguments; in all, perhaps ten different types of alternative interpretations that might represent threats to validity. I've done the best job I possibly could in considering fairly all these alternatives. After doing so, I'm forced to the conclusion that any one of them can reasonably account for some of my experimental findings, but that none of them could account for all of them. Therefore, I am left with the interpretation that a single experimental self-confrontation, one that demonstrates a contradiction between a person's values and his self-conceptions, can create an effective state of self-dissatisfaction that has long-term cognitive and behavioral consequences that cannot be accounted for in any other way except to assume they are results of genuine, long-term value changes.

EVANS: I would like to ask you about an issue that plagues social psychology, perhaps all of psychology, now more than ever before in history. This was generated partly by applications of Skinnerian notions, which appears to control behavior, but also in experiments such as Milgram's (1974) and Zimbardo's (Zimbardo, et al. 1973) that expose subjects to certain kinds of conditions that may be aversive or uncomfortable, even though they are operating with informed consent. There are charges that we are not operating ethically. What right do we have, as social scientists, to control behavior or to engage in experiments that disturb human subjects?

ROKEACH: Well, you're really raising the question of ethics. What right have I got to decide which values to change in which direction? For a long time I worried about it because I genuinely felt that if we could change behavior in one direction, we could change it in the other. I no longer think so. I believe that the self is so constructed that it is willing to allow itself to be changed in one direction, but not the opposite. Thus, I think I would have a good chance of persuading you, or anyone else, to increase your value for a world at peace, but under no circumstances do I think I could persuade you to decrease it. Similarly, I believe I could persuade you to increase your value for wisdom, but not to decrease it, to increase your value for a world of beauty, but not to decrease it. Self-conceptions are learned by human beings in the context of a society that socializes each person; it teaches the individual how to obtain mileage for himself, how to increase or maintain his self-conception as moral and competent, and that mileage can be obtained by changing in one direction but not the other. So, for this reason I no longer worry about whether I could manipulate a person arbitrarily, to change him in a direction opposite to his own need to self-actualize. My theory is really a theory of self-actualization. I can influence you to grow, but I doubt that I can influence your values in a retrogressive direction; so I think there is built-in ethical protection against arbitrary value manipulation.

EVANS: Can you demonstrate the validity of what you're saying?

ROKEACH: Yes, we're about to embark on some actual research designed to demonstrate the "unidirectionality hypothesis," namely, that values can be changed in one direction for any one person, but not in both directions.

REFERENCES

Adorno, T., et al. 1950. *The authoritarian personality*. New York: Harper.

Conroy, W., Katkin, E., and Barnette, W. 1973. Modification of smoking behavior by Rokeach's self-confrontation technique. Paper presented at the annual meeting of the Southeastern Psychological Association in New Orleans, April 7, 1973.

Festinger, L. 1964. Behavioral support for opinion change. *Pub. Opin. Quart.* 28: 404–17.

Frenkel-Brunswik, E., and Sanford, N. 1945. Some personality factors in anti-Semitism. *J. Psychol.* 20: 271–91.

Luchins, A. 1942. Mechanization in problem solving. *Psychol. Monogr.* 54: 6.

Milgram, S. 1974. *Obedience to authority*. New York: Harper.

Rokeach, M. 1960. *The open and closed mind*. New York: Basic Books.

———. 1964. *The three Christs of Ypsilanti*. New York: Knopf.

———. 1968. The nature of attitudes. In *International Encyclopedia of the Social Sciences*, ed. E. Sills. New York: Macmillan.

———. 1968. *Beliefs, attitudes and values*. San Francisco: Jossey-Bass.

———. 1973. *The nature of human values*. New York: Free Press.

———, and Mezei, L. 1966. Race and shared belief as factors in social choice. *Science* 151: 167–72.

———, Smith, P., and Evans, R. 1960. Two kinds of prejudice or one? In *The open and closed mind*, ed. M. Rokeach, pp. 132–68. New York: Basic Books.

Shils, E. 1954. Authoritarianism: "Right" and "Left." In *Studies in the scope and method of "the authoritarian personality,"* eds. R. Christie and M. Jahoda. New York: Free Press.

Wertheimer, M. 1945. *Productive thinking*. New York: Harper.

Zimbardo, P., et al. 1973. The mind is a formidable jailer: A Pirandellian prison. *New York Times*, p. 38, April 8, 1973.

Stanley Milgram

(1933–   )

Stanley Milgram completed his work for the Ph.D. at Harvard University in 1960 and became an assistant professor of psychology at Yale University for several years before returning to Harvard where in the department of social relations he joined the faculty in experimental social psychology. Since 1967 he has directed doctoral studies in social psychology at the Graduate Center of the City University of New York. Dr. Milgram began to explore conformity pressures and the effects of authoritarianism, a study which led to his highly controversial demonstration of blind obedience to authority. His research has consistently evolved out of creative approaches to such social problems as the effects of life in large cities, and the American Association for the Advancement of Science awarded him its Prize for Research in Social Psychology in 1964. His innovative approaches have included an award-winning film, The City and the Self.

Just How Far Will a Person Go?/Obedience to Authority//Better/Worse/
The Same as Me/Conformity or Obedience with Some Social Implications//
You Don't Know There Will Be Stress/Ethics in Psychological Research//
The Experience of Living in Cities//

Dr. Milgram and I begin our talk with the widely discussed experiment on obedience to authority. He describes the development of this study and the way in which it was carried out, and he reacts to some of the criticisms that have been directed toward it. "I'm convinced much of the criticism," he states, "whether people know it or not, stems from the results of the experiment. If everyone had broken off at slight shock or even moderate shock, this would be a very reassuring finding and who would protest?" He distinguishes between the concepts of conformity and obedience and points out their significance for society. We discuss the problem of ethics in psychological research, and particularly the issues raised by the obedience-to-authority study and Philip Zimbardo's Stanford prison simulation. Dr. Milgram then moves to his research involving the experience of living in the city and why he thinks this work is so important. In conclusion, he describes the studies that have been most meaningful to him, and some of his plans for the future.

EVANS: Dr. Milgram, in looking over your very interesting career in social psychology, one can't help but be impressed by the apparently high regard that you had for the eminent, innovative, social psychologist Solomon Asch, how he influenced you, and how, in fact, his work on conformity to group pressure (Asch 1958) obviously had a marked effect on some of your own work. One of your experiments has received particularly wide attention. It was a kind of outgrowth of the group-pressure study, testing just exactly what people will do under pressure from an experimenter, a scientist in a kind of laboratory setting. How did you happen to begin thinking in terms of this type of experiment? Maybe you would describe it briefly for us.

MILGRAM: Very often, when there's an idea, there are several points of origin to it. It doesn't necessarily develop in linear fashion from what one has been working on previously. I was working for Asch in Princeton, New Jersey, in 1959 and 1960. I was thinking about his group-pressure experiment. One of the criticisms that has been made of his experiments is that they lack a surface significance, because after all, an experiment with people making judgments of lines has a manifestly trivial content. So the question I asked myself is, How can this be made into a more humanly significant experiment? And it seemed to me that if, instead of having a group exerting pressure on judgments about lines, the group could somehow induce something more significant from the person, then that might be a step in giving a greater face significance to the behavior induced by the group. Could a group, I asked myself, induce a person to act with severity against another person? And since my natural inclination is to get right to the bottom line of things, I envisioned a situation very much like Asch's experiment in which there would be a number of confederates and one naive subject, and instead of confronting the lines on a card, each one of them would have a shock generator. In other words, I transformed Asch's experiment into one in which the group would administer increasingly higher levels of shock to a person, and the question would be to what degree an individual would follow along with the group. That's not yet the obedience experiment, but it's a mental step in that direction. Then I wondered how one would actually set it up. What would constitute the experimental control in this situation? In Asch's experiment, there is a control—the proportion of correct judgments the person makes in the absence of group pressure. So I said to myself, Well, I guess I would have to study a person in this situation in the absence of any group pressure. But then how would one get the person to increase the shocks? I mean, what would be the force that would get him to increase the shocks? And then the thought occurred that the experimenter would have to tell him to give higher and higher shocks. Just how far will a person go when an experimenter instructs him to give increasingly severe shocks? Immediately I knew that that was the problem I would investigate. It was a very excited moment for me, because I realized that although it was a very simple question, it would admit itself to measurement, precise investigation. One could see the variables to be studied, with dependent measure being how far a person would go in administering shocks.

EVANS: Well, let's be a little bit more specific. We could talk about authority in the form of the experimenter, or we could talk about group pressure, acquiescence to the group. There's a very interesting distinction here.

MILGRAM: There are both features in common and features that are different. What we have in common is, in both instances, the abdication of individual judgment in the face of some external social pressure. But there are also factors that are quite different. I would like to call what happens to Asch's subjects "conformity," and I would like to call what happens in my experiment "obedience." In conformity, as illustrated by Asch's experiment, there is no explicit requirement on the part of the group members for a person to go along with them. Indeed, the presence of an explicit requirement might even eliminate the person's yielding. The individual members of Asch's group give their judgments; there's pressure to comply with them, but there's no explicit demand to do so. In the obedience situation, the experimenter explicitly prescribes certain behavior. That's one difference. A second very important difference is that in conformity, as illustrated in Asch's experiment, you're dealing basically with a process in which the end product is the homogenization of behavior. The pressure is not that you be better than me or worse than me, but that you be the same as me. Obedience arises out of differentiation of social structure. You don't start from the assumption that we are the same; one person starts with a higher status. You don't repeat his action; you execute his order. And it doesn't lead to homogenization of behavior, but rather to some kind of division of labor. There's another distinction that's quite important psychologically. After subjects have been in Asch's experiment and they are questioned by the experimenter, they almost invariably deny that they gave in to the group. Even if errors in judgment are pointed out, they will tend to ascribe them to their own deficiencies. But in the obedience experiment, the result is the opposite. The subjects disclaim any responsibility for their action. So I think there are factors in common, certainly. We're dealing in both cases with what I would call the abdication of individual initiative in the face of some external social pressure. But there are also these distinguishing aspects to it. And in a broader philosophic way they're quite different also. I would say that conformity—I say it about 175 years after de Tocqueville said it—conformity is a natural source of social control in democracy because it leads to this homogenization. But obedience in its extreme forms is the natural expression of fascistic systems because it starts with the assumption of differences in the rights of people. It's no accident that in Nazi Germany, the virtues of obedience were extolled and at the same time an inherent part of the philosophy was the idea of inferior and superior groups; I mean, the two go together.

EVANS: As an example, let me just take a current piece of research that we are involved in dealing with a very fascinating phenomenon in our culture—smoking. Now we have some pretty good evidence, and this is one of the things we're going to be looking at, that perhaps smoking begins as a reaction to peer pressure. On the other hand, we have the very interesting fact that authorities stress that this type of behavior is going to lead to cardiovascular disease, cancer, etc. Here you have at once peer and authority pressure. In terms of this distinction you made, how could you resolve this type of situation?

MILGRAM: I'll try. First, the word authority is used in many different ways. When we talk about a medical authority, we're talking about someone with expertise. That's not quite the same as the kind of authority I was studying, which is someone perceived to have the right to control one's behavior. When a teenager hears an authority on television saying he shouldn't smoke, he doesn't accept the fact that that person has the right to control behavior. Secondly, you still have these conflicts between peer pressure and authority pressure. In one of the experiments I carried out, it was shown that when peers in my experimental situation rebelled against the experimenter, they tremendously undercut his power. I think the same thing is operating here; you have pressures from an authority, but you have pressures from peers that sometimes neutralize this. It's only when you have, as you have in my experiment, an authority who operates in a free field without countervailing pressures other than the victim's protests that you get the purest response to authority. In real life, of course, you're confronted with a great many countervailing pressures that cancel each other out.

EVANS: One of the things, of course, that you're acutely aware of is that, partly because of congressional pressure, partly because of some —what would we say—some second looks at our consciences in the behavioral sciences, we are beginning to get increasingly concerned now about the whole matter of what rights we have with respect to our subjects. When you were doing that earlier obedience-to-authority study, it's very clear that you were operating completely within the ethical framework of psychologists in those days. You debriefed the subjects, and there was really no harm done to the victims and so on. However, in the present utilization of subjects, we are very hung up on the phrase, "informed consent," and this raises a very tough problem for the investigator. For example, do you think you could have done that experiment if you followed the present ethical standards of "informed consent"? Let's say that you were about to engage in an experiment where the subjects were going to be exposed to a certain amount of stress. One type of stress might be the fact that you're going to be ordering somebody to get shocked.

MILGRAM: Well first of all, before you do the experiment, you don't know there will be stress.

EVANS: All right, that's a good point.

MILGRAM: The subject must make a decision, but we don't know if it's going to be accompanied by stress. Many of the most interesting things we find out in experimentation you don't learn until you carry it out. So to talk about "informed consent" presumes that you know the fundamental consequences of your experiment, and that just isn't the case for my investigations. That's one aspect of the problem; it's not the entire problem, however. There is the fact that misinformation is used in these experiments, that illusions are used. For example, in my obedience experiment the victim does not actually get the shocks, although the subject is told that the victim is getting the shocks. Furthermore, it's an experiment on obedience in which the subject is the focus of the experiment, rather than the other person, but a cover story attempts to deflect attention from that. Now could the experiment be run if we told people beforehand that this was going to be the case? Not in its particulars. It is possible that one could develop a system whereby people are told generally that they're asked to be in a psychology experiment, and that in psychology experiments illusions are sometimes used. Sometimes stress arises. Perhaps a subject pool of such persons who are not necessarily used immediately could be created. They would then be invited to an experiment, having been given the general instruction that these things may, but don't necessarily, happen in psychology exeprimentation. That would be one way of handling the problem.

EVANS: Well, if I may get a bit personal here, since we are talking about the whole area of ethics in psychological research, at the last American Psychological Association meeting, I chaired a symposium in which Philip Zimbardo participated. He took this opportunity to present his Stanford prison experiment (Zimbardo, et al. 1973). He talked in great detail, including slides, and presented the entire picture of what happened to the "guard" students as they increasingly began to assume roles of authority. In fact, this role playing soon led to surprising reality. The persons playing prisoners began to feel this. A reporter from *Newsweek* was there and asked me afterwards how it was that of the hundreds of psychologists sitting there in the audience very few were protesting the horrible things that were happening to the subjects. Now, as a matter of fact Dr. Zimbardo's experiments, and yours, have been singled out in terms of having particularly, shall we say, captured the imagination of those who are concerned about violating the rights of human subjects. So it's only fair, in this total context, to hear you react a little bit to Zimbardo's experiment and whether or not it's fair to group his and yours together. Perhaps neither one of them should be, as you see it, the object of this concern.

MILGRAM: Well, it's hard to know whether to call the Zimbardo prison study an experiment. An experiment ordinarily calls for many trials; this was a one-shot run through. It was a reenactment of sorts. Many psychologists have said recently that role playing, simulation, is the answer to the ethical problems of deception. Some psychologists, for example, have suggested that my kind of work could be done without any ethical problems through simulation.

EVANS: For example, Herbert Kellman at Harvard.

MILGRAM: Exactly. Well, now we have Zimbardo who does the simulation. After all, he's simulating a prison situation, and what we get is a reaction against that effort. People ought to put these two facts together—that on the one hand, they've been calling for simulation, and on the other, Zimbardo has done a simulation and he now becomes the focus of criticism. One of the points worth making, therefore, is that simulation doesn't seem to be the answer psychologists have sought. The fact of the matter is that in the degree to which the simulation approaches reality, it gives one the psychological substance one wants to deal with. In the degree to which it's a pallid imitation of reality, it becomes ethically unobjectionable, but it also removes you from the phenomenon you want to study. There's one essential detail in Zimbardo's experiment that I don't know about, and that is under what circumstances could the person involved leave prison. Could you tell me that?

EVANS: Yes, as I understand it, they really had the option to get out any time they wanted to.

MILGRAM: Well, I would say that that is a very serious scientific difficulty in the study, because the essence of being a prisoner is precisely that you cannot get out when you want to. Now, there's another question. Didn't Zimbardo give them a fairly detailed account of the experiment beforehand?

EVANS: Yes, yes he did.

MILGRAM: So he also met the requirement of informed consent. Now, is it simply going to be the case that whenever there's something exciting and real in psychology it evokes ethical criticism? He seems to have met two of the requirements that psychologists have called for: informed consent and simulation.

EVANS: Of course one of the points that has been made about informed consent is that we're often dealing with a purely phenomenological situation. How can you give informed consent in advance as a human subject in an experiment when the total mass of feelings and experiences and sensitivities, even pain, cannot really be verbalized?

MILGRAM: Well, I think to some extent that's true, added to the fact that one is very often ignorant of what will happen before an experiment. Reactions to such situations can be diverse. Ninety percent of the subjects can react in a perfectly calm way; others can become agitated. But then we must know whether psychology is excluding stress and agitation from its domain of study. Do we really want to say that any of these aversive emotions are to be excluded from psychological inquiry? I think that's a question that's yet to be resolved, but my personal vote is "no." I don't want to be put in the position of saying that I'm *for* any kind of experimentation.

EVANS: Were you surprised by the reaction to your obedience experiment?

MILGRAM: I must say that I was totally astonished by the criticism that my experiment engendered. I thought that what I was doing was posing a very legitimate question: How far would people proceed if they were asked to give increasingly severe shocks to another person? I thought that the decision rested with the subject. Perhaps that was too naive an assumption from which to start an investigation. It is true that technical illusions were used in the experiment. I would not call them deceptions because that already implies some base motivation. After all, the major illusion used was that the person did not receive shocks. One might have imitated the investigators who have done studies in traumatic-avoidance conditioning, where human beings are, in fact, shocked to near-tetanizing levels. I chose not to. I thought that the illusion was used for a benign purpose. I'm convinced that much of the criticism, whether people know it or not, stems from the results of the experiment. If everyone had broken off at slight shock or moderate shock, this would be a very reassuring finding and who would protest? Indeed, I would say that there's a tendency these days to make inferences about the experimenter's motives on the basis of the results of his investigations, and I think that's a very pernicious tendency. Personally and even professionally I would have been very pleased if people had broken off at mild shock.

EVANS: Were you surprised that they went so far?

MILGRAM: I was, but even if they had not been so obedient, it would not have prevented my research program. I would simply have studied the variables leading to an increase or diminution in the amount of obedience. And in fact, one could say that the results that I got threw a wrench into the program in that many variables were washed out because too many people obeyed. One didn't have that distribution of responses—that bell-shaped distribution—that would have been most convenient for studying the effect of specific variables.

EVANS: There have been statements made by people about both the work of Zimbardo and yourself that I think it's only fair to hear you react to. Some people have suggested, some journalists particularly, that both you and Dr. Zimbardo got involved in experiments that were exciting, interesting, unique, and that because of the uproar about the ethics, you have begun to rationalize by trying to extrapolate from your findings something relating to a bigger picture. For example, in the case of Zimbardo, he has now become a strong advocate for prison reform, arguing that this little experiment will teach mankind how horrible prisons are. In your case, you have, more or less, extrapolated the whole question of the dangers of authoritarian rule in American culture. In your book *On Obedience to Authority* (Milgram 1974a) you go into this. Now, Dr. Zimbardo is not here to speak for himself, but what about your reaction to this?

MILGRAM: The very first article that I wrote on obedience, "Behavioral Study of Obedience" (Milgram 1963), before anyone had really reacted to the experiments, discussed the societal problem. So it's not true that trying to find the larger application of the issue is motivated by ethical criticism. Beyond that, what disturbs me somewhat is the absence of any assumption of good will and good faith. I believe that a certain amount of good will is necessary on the part of society for the conduct of any enterprise. Criticisms of that sort seem to me to start from some assumption of bad faith on the part of the investigators, which I don't believe has anything to do with the truth, in my case or in Zimbardo's case.

EVANS: Were there any criticisms of this particular effort that have troubled you that perhaps we haven't mentioned?

MILGRAM: Well, I think the question of the limits of experimentation is a real one. I believe that there are many experiments that should not be carried out. I don't oppose criticism because I think there's a societal function served by it. The investigator wants to study things. Society, in the form of certain critics, will establish limits. I think the net outcome will be a kind of equilibrium between scientific values and other values, but I don't believe that most investigators, certainly myself, are limited to scientific values. There are thousands of experiments that could be very useful from the standpoint of increasing knowledge that one would never carry out because in one's own estimation they would violate strong moral principles. It doesn't mean that one doesn't think of them. For example, an experiment in which neonates are deposited onto a deserted island and their development watched over three generations, assuming they survived, would be stupendously informative but grossly immoral.

EVANS: Well now, moving to another area of your work that is extremely intriguing, we have the research dealing with the experience of living in cities. While in your earlier experiment you were studying obedience to authority and the resulting cruelty, at the same time, beginning to become noticeable were cases like the famous Kitty Genovese case, where we had another kind of, shall we say, horrendous reaction to a fellow man. But in this case, rather than the administering of shock under experimental conditions, the apathy was what was cruel. The work of Latané and Darley (1970) and a great deal of subsequent work has very carefully gone into trying to understand something about the nature of bystander apathy, and also asks: Is there any real altruism in man? The findings of this line of research suggest that there's some cause for optimism. It seems to me that in your analysis of living in the cities (Milgram 1970a, 1970b), in a very broad and fascinating way, you extend some of these interpretations, and so, it might be interesting to hear what led you in this particular direction.

MILGRAM: May I, before doing that, try to draw some connections between the bystander work and the work on authority?

EVANS: Oh yes, certainly.

MILGRAM: To some extent, a lot of bystander work shows that when society becomes complicated, there are specialized organizations set up, such as the police, which have authority in particular domains, and then people abdicate responsibility to them. After all, in the Genovese case, people thought it was not their responsibility; it was the responsibility of those in authority—that is, the police—to do something about this matter. The particular tragedy in the Genovese case was that no one even notified the police. There's another thing that comes out in some of the other Latané and Darley studies—I'm thinking particularly of the smoke experiment; they showed that a group of people is less likely to respond to an emergency than a single individual. That really shows how ineffectively people function in the absence of authority. When there's no group structure, when there's no predesignated leadership, it can lead to enormous inefficiency. You see, none of these issues is really one-sided. Under certain circumstances, authority is very useful. It wouldn't exist in human society, I assure you, if it did not perform important adaptive functions.

EVANS: You might be a little bit more specific about the experience of living in cities.

MILGRAM: I guess my underlying view is that people are adaptive creatures. To some extent I accept the tone and insight of the Darwinian interpretation. Now I don't want to apply it with a naive directness to the issues I study, but in a general way, I see people as very adaptive. If you live in a town with two hundred people, you can say hello to every one of them as you're walking along a country road. If you live in a town with five million people, you find that it's simply not possible to do that, and so certain standards of behavior develop in response to these demographic realities. Think what it would mean to walk up Fifth Avenue and nod your head, smiling, and saying hello to every one of the people you pass in the course of a half hour; there might be five thousand people. You would be reduced to a robotlike creature who would immediately be shipped off to the nearest mental institution. I think people adapt to realities, and that norms, standards of behavior, in some way reflect these adaptations. I think this is a thought that underlines any explanation of both obedience to authority and the response to the city. Why do we have authority? It must be that it performs some useful function. An organized group of people can deal more effectively with the input from the environment than those who are planless, without direction. Some people think I am implying that there's something wrong in the city, and life is much better elsewhere—say in the small town—but that's not what I'm saying. I'm saying that given any set of demographic realities, there's a certain optimal level of adaptation that has its advantages and disadvantages. In the city, you have the possibility of choice, the possibility of much greater communication than you have in small towns. On the other hand, you can't have the pleasure of saying hello to everyone you meet on a road. In a small town, the possibilities for choice are more limited. On the other hand, there's a closer feeling of community and solidarity. Every set of demographic facts will give rise to an optimal social adaptation. That is all one is speaking about when he's talking about adapting to these realities. But this then comes to create the characteristic feeling and tone of city life. It's true that I can walk up the street and not see anybody I know in New York City, and that's one of the characteristics of the city. It's true that there are norms against intrusion on people, so that if you see two people arguing, it's very unlikely that you will intrude in the situation. But that seems almost to be a requirement of living in the midst of millions of other people.

EVANS: In many of your experiments, illustrated by your film "The City and the Self" (Milgram 1974), where you are on location, say, in a subway, you are really studying life on the city streets. But actually, life in the city is, well, we're living in the city right now, sitting here in your office talking. Life in the city is in your home, at a party. Perhaps what happens to be happening on the streets is not even very important. Even as a stranger, I could find social climates in many places in this city that are entirely different from what I would find out here on Forty-second Street.

MILGRAM: I think you're quite right, but I am dealing with the public life. I think it is important. It's the only aspect of the city to which the traveler has access. It has an importance in itself because it reflects something about the city, and the public lives of different places are enormously different. You're quite right, though, that almost all the work I've done deals with the atmosphere, the street ambience. I notice enormous differences in the ambience of different public settings when going through different cities and towns. You can sense differences in the friendliness, unfriendliness, hostility, suspicion, liveliness, and I thought that these were worthy of investigation. Sometimes psychology becomes so academic and removed from the ordinary nature of things that it has to be balanced by turning attention to them.

EVANS: It would be interesting at this point to hear what you consider to be your most important contributions to psychology. You're a relatively young man; you've already become very well known.

MILGRAM: Well, I'll list some papers that I personally like the best. One would be "Some Conditions to Obedience and Disobedience to Authority" (Milgram 1965), which I think tells the authority story quite well. Another is "The Small World Problem," (Milgram 1967; Travers and Milgram 1969; Korte and Milgram 1970) which social psychologists are not very much aware of, but in certain ways, it was a very exciting study—the idea you could take two people in any part of the country out of two hundred million and you could find an acquaintance network linking the two. It seemed to me a problem with potentially vast technical difficulties that were surmounted by rather simple means. And then I think I would choose "The Experience of Living in Cities." (Milgram 1970). One article that I think expresses my methodological viewpoint very well is not known at all. It's called "Interpreting Obedience," (Milgram 1972) and it's a response to a criticism by Martin Orne. It appeared in Arthur Miller's book, *The Social Psychology of Psychological Research.*

EVANS: What are you working on now, Dr. Milgram?

MILGRAM: I spent last year in France trying to study the mental maps of Paris held by the residents of that city. I interviewed over two hundred Parisians coming from all parts of the city and was interested in the parts of the city they knew and those they didn't. As you know, the mental map may not correspond to the geographic reality, as Kevin Lynch showed in his seminal book *The Image of the City* (Lynch 1960). I want to know what kind of emotional overlay there is on the city of Paris. Are there parts that attract, parts that repel? That is my current area of interest.

REFERENCES

Asch, S. 1958. Effects of group pressure upon modification and distortion of judgments. In *Readings in social psychology*, 3rd ed., eds. E. E. Maccoby, T. M. Newcomb, and E. L. Hartley. New York: Holt.

Korte, C., and Milgram, S. 1970. Acquaintance networks between racial groups: application of the small world method. *J. Pers. Soc. Psychol.* 15: (2) 101–8.

Latané B., and Darley, J. 1970. *The unresponsive bystander: why doesn't he help?* New York: Appleton.

Lynch, K. 1960. *The image of the city.* Cambridge, Mass.: M.I.T. Press and Harvard University Press.

Milgram, S. 1963. Behavioral study of obedience. *J. Abnorm. Soc. Psychol.* 67: 371–78.

———. 1965. Some conditions to obedience and disobedience to authority. *Hum. Rel.* 18: (1) 57–76.

———. 1967. The small world problem. *Psychol. Today* 1: (1) 60–67.

———. 1970a. The experience of living in cities. *Science* 167: 1461–68.

———. 1970b. The experience of living in cities: a psychological analysis. In *Psychology and the problems of society*, eds. F. F. Korten, S. W. Cook, and J. I. Lacey. Washington, D.C.: American Psychological Association.

———. 1972. Interpreting obedience. In *The social psychology of psychological research*, ed. A. Miller. New York: Free Press.

———. 1974a. *Obedience to authority.* New York: Harper.

———. 1974b. The city and the self. Time-Life Films: Time-Life Building, Rockefeller Center, New York, N.Y. 10020.

Travers, J., and Milgram, S. 1969. An experimental study of the small world problem. *Sociometry* 32: (4) 425–43.

Zimbardo, P., et al. 1973. The mind is a formidable jailer: a Pirandellian prison. *The New York Times*, p. 38, April 8, 1973.

Philip Zimbardo

(1933–   )

Philip Zimbardo received his B.A. from Brooklyn College in 1954 and his M.S. and Ph.D. from Yale University in 1959. He held positions at Yale University and New York University before moving to Stanford University in 1968. Dr. Zimbardo has examined the effects of authoritarianism including the relation of authoritarian social systems to the individual and his role in society. To demonstrate in an impressive manner some of his conceptualizations, he simulated prison conditions for a group of volunteer student subjects with far-reaching consequences and significant results. He has generalized the effects of this study to a number of other authoritarian systems. His current research involves a diversified range of ideas, including studies on the effects of shyness on the individual and a model of madness.

Full Circle Back/Moving from Experimental to Social Behavior/
Transcending the Limits of Biology and Environment/Cognitive Control of
Motivation/Some Practical Examples/Becoming an Active Controlling
Agent/The Individual and the Social Institution/In Order to Change Society
You Have to Change Both//Broader Classes of Variables/Time Perspective/
The Single Most Important Determinant/The Implications for Society/
Some Very Obvious Examples//The Dynamics of Human Choice/
Individuation/Deindividuation/The Ultimate Deindividuating
Circumstance/Simulating the Experience/The Stanford Prison Simulation/
The Relationship Between Research and Social Change/Knowledge and
Political Activity//The Process of Becoming Mad/Discontinuities/
A Model of Madness//

As we begin our discussion, Dr. Zimbardo describes how his career has come
full circle. He entered Yale with the intention of studying social psychology,
became intrigued by the behavioristic model then prevalent, and gradually,
through research based on Festinger's cognitive dissonance theory, moved into
social psychology. He tells about his research in the cognitive control of motivation, its implications and practical applications. We discuss the individual
and the effects of the psychotherapeutic model, and he contrasts individual
and social pathology, concluding that the most effective means of change can
come through approaching problems on a societal basis. Dr. Zimbardo pre-

sents his very interesting view of time perspective and tells why he thinks it may be the most important single determinant of human behavior. A discussion of his ideas about individuation and deindividuation leads to a description of his well-known Stanford prison simulation, which he believes made a compelling point because it focused attention on a particular problem. "My feeling is," he explains, "that if you believe in your research and in your discipline, then you have to go beyond being a researcher and a theorist; you actually have to go out and bring your results to the people in question because they don't read our journals." In conclusion, Dr. Zimbardo elaborates on his recent work in developing a model of madness and speculates on its implications.

EVANS: Dr. Zimbardo, in your work you demonstrate an interesting pattern. You seem to have moved from what we would call fairly hard, experimental training into broader problems dealing with society and the individual. Does that analysis make any sense to you?

ZIMBARDO: I think, Dick, that in one sense, I've come full circle back to where I was before I got my training as a graduate student at Yale. That training was very rigorous and, I think, very sound, not only in research methodology, but in a kind of Hullian, rational behaviorism. But having grown up in a lower-class, southeast Bronx ghetto, a neighborhood of changing minority groups—Italian, black, Puerto Rican, Jewish—I have always been interested in intergroup relations. I went to Yale with the intention of studying social psychology, particularly race relations. However, when I got there, I was told to begin training rats. I worked with Professor K. C. Montgomery (Montgomery and Zimbardo 1957) for the next several years on research in exploratory behavior in the male albino rat. And after a while, I began to think of doing that as "my thing"—being a laboratory psychologist, running rats, doing rigorous research. Then two things happened that changed my orientation. The first occurred when my mother came up to Yale for a weekend. I proudly brought her into this rat lab where I had several hundred rats I had bred, housed, watered, and nourished from infancy to maturity. Aghast, she said, "What are you doing?" And I told her that we were teaching them all these wonderful responses, to which she replied, "You're not supposed to be making them smart; you're supposed to be exterminating them!" Suddenly I realized that for a person from a ghetto neighborhood, rats are the enemy, not the Hullian prophylaxis against anthropomorphic subjectivism. The other thing that I think moved me out of that orientation more toward what could be called a social humanism is my contact with the late Professor Arthur R. Cohen. He pointed out to me that here were all these people in the world who were complex and interesting, who often acted in mysterious ways, who had conflicts and problems, and didn't I think that would be more interesting, spending my life trying to understand, and perhaps even help them, rather than just building a better mouse cage and Y-maze? Ultimately, I saw the light in his wisdom.

EVANS: And so you really began to move into the kinds of inquiries that led to your career as a social psychologist. You wrote a very provocative book dealing with the cognitive control of motivation (Zimbardo 1969a). As I understand it, you had been looking at the area of dissonance theory, and that led to some thoughts about the way people may be cognitively rationalizing their behavior, or cognitively rationalizing ambiguities and inconsistencies and discrepancies. I wonder if you'd tell us how you viewed this field, and the direction you took in your own research.

ZIMBARDO: I guess one of the most interesting and important events that occurred early in my career was meeting Leon Festinger just before the theory of cognitive dissonance was published (Festinger 1957). Festinger came to Yale to give a colloquium, and one of the basic, new aspects of his approach was his consideration of the ways in which behavior affected thinking, attitudes, and values. Until that time my whole training in a behavioristic approach assumed that behavior was the end product, and we looked at all the things that influenced behavior. But he opened up a whole new realm of speculation by turning the causal relationship around. Over time, as I began to do research in that area, I began to see that there was a whole other dimension of significance inherent in the dissonance theory approach. Traditional models of human behavior were models that subjugated the integrity of human beings to the demands of external stimulus conditions and dictates of internal biological conditions. My work on extending dissonance theory into the realm of cognitive control of motivation was important in making me realize that it is through our cognitive intervention that human beings transcend the limits of their biology and the confines of their environment. And so I saw in the implications of the cognitive control of motivation a very different kind of humanism than the humanistic therapists were talking about at the time. I began to see that the way an individual defines reality may be the most important dimension of reality; that is, the cognitive, social reality may in fact determine not only how people perceive the world, but whether or not they are physiologically aroused, whether or not a given event is seen as a reward or a bribe, whether they are motivated to approach or withdraw, and whether a stimulant is painful or irrelevant.

EVANS: I believe you put a lot of this together in your book, which I mentioned earlier, *The Cognitive Control of Motivation* (Zimbardo 1969a).

ZIMBARDO: What it was, essentially, was an edited book of experiments. The experiments themselves are largely rigorous laboratory experiments stimulated by Jack Brehm's original research. The experiment I'm most personally pleased about is the one in which we show the extent to which there can be cognitive control over pain. The methodology is sound and the results powerful. We used paradigms borrowed from the behavioristic approach to show that when people have to justify a commitment to a certain kind of decision, they will come to control the impact that a painful stimulus has on them. They can do so to the same extent as occurs when a pain stimulus, electric shock, is physically lowered by twenty-five volts. The power of perceived environmental control has not yet been fully appreciated by psychologists, teachers, and parents.

EVANS: Let's take a practical example of the control of pain. Suppose someone goes to the dentist.

ZIMBARDO: Well, all of my early experiences with dentists were very painful, but each time I went back, I always told myself that it wouldn't hurt so much this time, and it turned out it hurt as much or more. Once I began dealing with cognitive control of motivation, I also got interested in hypnosis, because for me, hypnosis is little more than cognitive control of behavior. Hypnosis uses techniques that enable you to believe in yourself; you come to believe that when you say, "It will not hurt as much," you believe in the reality of that statement. When I now go back to the dentist, I believe in what I tell myself, that it won't hurt me so much, and it doesn't. What has really changed is my belief that *I can* control the pain. I may not be able to cut it off altogether, but I can minimize it, and I can do it in a variety of ways. I can distract myself, or I can reconceptualize the experience. I think for a variety of reasons each of us is programmed (at home, at school, and other training sites) not to believe in ourselves. What applying cognitive control would involve is specific training from the time we're very young to believe in the control we have over our physiology and stimulus inputs. This involves thinking of ourselves, not as pawns of fate, not as passive information processors where stimuli come in and responses go out, but as active, controlling agents. We also need to develop confidence so that when we say positive things about ourselves, we believe them.

EVANS: How far removed from this is Julian Rotter's (1962) concept of the internal and external locus of control? For example, Rotter argues that the person who is internal sees himself as actually being master of his own destiny, and the person who is external feels like a feather in the wind, a victim of environmental determinants.

ZIMBARDO: I think to some extent those ideas are overlapping. I see in Rotter's work more of a description of existing differences between people, and what has been coming out of my work is more prescription, that is, ways to improve the quality of an individual's life. In my current work, I'm also moving into an analysis of the social institutions and in our basic socialization training, so that we can come to have a greater sense of control over our own lives. That is not to disparage or make light of the effects of the economic, political, or social forces. My feeling is that all levels exert significant influences; in order to   change society, you have to change the psychology of the individual as well as the broader situational forces that exist in any given society.

EVANS: Let's look, for example, at the kind of therapeutic process described by Carl Rogers (Evans 1975) and to some degree by Victor Frankl (1962) and others as well. They would also say that what they're trying to do is shift responsibility to the self. Starting from an experimental base, how are you really approaching this problem differently than, say, the self-actualizing humanistic kinds of therapists?

ZIMBARDO: The therapeutic model, whether it's the humanistic model of self-actualization or a more traditional model, has a basic flaw from my orientation, and that is that it is too individualistic. It deals only with a limited number of people who recognize "their problem" to begin with, and even if any therapy were 100 percent effective, if every single person who went to see Carl Rogers were "cured" and left feeling actualized, it would still have a minimal effect on changing society. What we have to do is to look not at individual pathology, but at social pathology, where we now have "epidemics" of violence, alienation, helplessness, shyness, free-floating paranoia, and the like. Whether it is being promoted by religion, by certain socialization practices, by things happening in school, or business, we must approach the problem as a social problem, not an individual one.

EVANS: Kurt Lewin was very interested in what he called time perspective—the idea that a person can be preoccupied with the past, the present, or the future—and even argued that the time perspective would have a lot to do with survival in certain situations. Lewin's ideas were pretty well supported by the work of both Bruno Bettelheim (1943) and Victor Frankl (1962) that discussed concentration camps, where they demonstrated that those who survived had to keep thinking of the future. In your experiments you pursue a similar idea in a very interesting way. I wonder if you could expand on this.

ZIMBARDO: In my own intellectual development, I've been looking at broader and broader classes of psychological variables, those that, if they do make a difference, will make a big difference. As you move toward concerns like time perspective, you're moving away from problems that are tightly prescribed, that can be approached with rigorous methodology. You begin to move into the area of philosophical speculation, basic values, and political change. For myself, I am beginning to feel comfortable doing that. The thinking I've been doing about time, very briefly, begins with the assumption that time perspective is the single most important determinant of human behavior, and that it is one of the major aspects of the socialization process, perhaps second only to learning our native language or maybe it is equally important. For me, the concepts of past and future are logical human constructs, not empirical ones, that are invented and promoted by society in a variety of ways; it is upon these conceptions that all mechanisms of the social control of human behavior rely. For example, the young child has only one reality, the immediate and present. Such a child is at the mercy of the immediate stimulus situation.

EVANS: The child is incapable of delay of gratification.

ZIMBARDO: There is no concept of "delay" for the young child who has no sense of the future. The concept of delay requires knowing that if I don't delay, I will be punished; if I do delay, I'll get a reward. But you first have to learn the concepts of future and past. We've been so imbued with belief in the reality of past and future that for many of us the least important part of our life is the present moment. We're insensitive to the fact that time perspective is an independent variable that influences our thinking, our feelings, and much of our daily behavior. For example, you could not have meaningful concepts of guilt, fear, incentive, deterrence, of commitment, liability, responsibility, obligation, unless you had the foundation of past and future. Therefore, it is incumbent on society to program into us concepts of referring present behavior to future consequences as well as to past contracts. What I've been doing in my research, with Christine Maslach, is using hypnosis as a technique for altering time perspective. You take college students who have been programmed to be very future oriented, to delay gratification, and put them in an expanded-present orientation, and they switch from being reflective and analytical to being reactive, impulsive, emotional, spontaneous, and sensual. They get totally involved in action for its own sake; they're not concerned with consequences or products, only process and belief.

EVANS: Won't certain drugs do this?

ZIMBARDO: I think one of the attractions of not only mind-expanding drugs, but a lot of the tranquilizers, as well as alcohol, is that they perform a similar kind of function for us. They stop you from being concerned about past and future, and your behavior becomes "uninhibited," that is, liberated from time-bound controls.

EVANS: Aren't anxiety, fear, depression, most of the "ills" of our times, wrapped up in this concept?

ZIMBARDO: Precisely. Now in any technologically oriented, productive society, people have to plan ahead; they have to delay gratification, "save for a rainy day," and we couldn't have stronger people attacking weaker people just because they felt like it at any given moment. So we have to have some mechanisms of social control.

EVANS: This is the idea with the prisoners "doing time."

ZIMBARDO: I was just going to raise that point, in fact. Think of the effect of the concept of deterrence on a criminal. Middle-class people make the laws and enforce them. They say that they wouldn't commit a certain crime because it would get them fired or get them five years in jail. They may act on this knowledge but those laws are most likely to be really applied to lower-class people. Even so, they are not as likely to be deterred by a future-time perspective as the middle class. This argument goes on to suggest that lower-class people have a vague or nonfunctional sense of the future. To have a sense of the future, you have to have faith in the future—that is, when you plan ahead, the rewards will be waiting—and further, you have to have a relatively stable environment. Lower-class people learn to cope with an environment that is neither stable nor benign, one that discourages faith. Consider the classic studies done by Mischel (1958, 1962) and others on delay of gratification. You tell a young child that he can have a candy bar immediately, but if he waits ten minutes, he can have two. At a very young age, when the experimenter leaves the room, the kid will eat the candy bar immediately. He hasn't learned the concept of "future" so the temptation of now wins out over the promise of later. At some older age, the middle-class child will wait and reap the reward of the two candy bars. Now think of the same experiment done in the ghetto. The experimenter tells a lower-class nine-year-old, "You can have one candy bar now, but if you wait ten minutes, I'll give you two." The kid waits ten minutes, and the experimenter says, "Sorry, but they were stolen from me (or I lost my job, etc.) so I can't give you any." You continue this type of training in faith-violation until at some point the kid will behave in a way that looks totally irrational to an observer when he says, "I want the little slice now. I'm not going to wait for pie-in-the-sky." His belief that the future will pay off has been extinguished. What happens then is that you get this terrible negative feedback cycle. One of the reasons you're poor, or in a ghetto, is that you have not learned to delay gratification; you have not learned to plan ahead, to sacrifice pleasure for progress. Unless you do, you can't break out.

EVANS: So you have been looking at time perspective as a not frequently enough observed factor that contributes to making a person a victim. And being a victim deindividuates a person; he loses his individuality. You set up one of the most intriguing and controversial social psychological experiments in the last forty or fifty years, when you took some of these ideas into a simulation. I emphasize *simulation* because I think that's one of the areas of misunderstanding about your "prison experiment."

ZIMBARDO: Actually, there are two threads of thought that merged to become this Stanford prison simulation—one purely theoretical, the other social and pragmatic. In an article called "The Human Choice" (Zimbardo 1969*b*), I speculated quite freely about the dynamics of human choice. We are each aware of our individuality, of our mortality, of our degree of social fit, of our concern for what others think about us. Those are the forces of individuation, reason, and order; we see ourselves as consistent over time and situation. We are constantly evaluating our own behavior so that behavior is under the control of our past and our future conceptions, under the control of rules, of laws, of norms, of social expectations. On the other hand, there is in each of us, I believe, the deindividuated self, the child who takes what he or she wants. There is not the concern for past and future, but concern for the present, enjoying life to the fullest right at this very moment. It's what you experience when you get drunk or when you get stoned. In a sense, it's "stepping out of yourself." Your behavior is totally responsive to the forces in the immediate physical and social environment, so you can become part of a lynch mob or part of a sexual orgy with equal facility. From thinking like this, I began speculating on what the constraints on human behavior are, and what kinds of things liberate behavior from these typical constraints. So I began doing research on deindividuation, and one aspect of deindividuation is anonymity. If no one knows who you are, or no one cares, then one of the main constraining influences on doing what is "good," "proper," "appropriate" is eliminated. We began doing research on the effects of anonymity on aggression, and we demonstrated in laboratory and field studies that conditions that make people feel anonymous facilitate antisocial behavior.

EVANS: What kinds of antisocial behavior specifically?

ZIMBARDO: Cheating, lying, cursing, physical and verbal aggression, and vandalism, all are shown to be facilitated by conditions of perceived anonymity. In this deindividuated state, as it relates to time, there's also a sense of expanded present; behavior is not as much controlled by the past and future. You can get this deindividuation where social responsibility is diffused in a group, where you're in an altered state of consciousness, where you're physically involved in an action, a process, and not in producing a product. This kind of research led me to wonder what happens when the social environment makes everyone anonymous. Well, I then began thinking about prison as the ultimate deindividuating circumstance. I decided that it was important to me to understand more about prison experience. I tried to gain access to some of the local prisons, but was denied for various reasons. So we decided to simulate a prison environment, maximizing the deindividuating properties of it—taking away people's names and identities, giving them numbers, substituting role and function for identity and human values, and putting people in an environment where we took away their sense of time and their liberty to avoid or escape one another.

EVANS: So this was a functional simulation of a prison?

ZIMBARDO: We did not try to create a literal translation of a prison. We had some of the mundane realities of a prison; there were bars on the doors, there were guards with billy clubs and prisoners in uniforms, as well as visiting hours from parents and friends. The important thing was that we had previously done a social-psychological analysis of the nature of imprisonment, and we tried to recreate that cognitive aspect, that phenomenology in our subjects. For example, we had learned through talking to a number of prisoners and guards and reading much of the available literature that one of the things that a prison environment does is try to emasculate male prisoners. To be masculine and antisocial means to be very dangerous, because then you are aggressive, assertive, independent. By emasculating you in a variety of ways—by promoting homosexuality, by making you dependent, by making you behave in regressive ways, by giving you no control over any aspect of your life—it's easier to run a prison. So we put our prisoners in smocks, with no underclothes. In real prisons they don't do that, but by doing this we immediately created a psychological set in which young, virile males felt more like a woman than a man.

EVANS: Now, what kind of people populated your prison?

ZIMBARDO: We put an ad in both the student newspaper and the city newspaper that simply said, "Wanted: Volunteers for an experiment on prison life—$15 a day. The experiment will last two weeks." We got about one hundred callers. We screened about twenty-five over the phone; we didn't want anybody with prior prison experience. Craig Haney and a long clinical interview and gave them a battery of a dozen psycholog-Curt Banks personally interviewed each of the remaining seventy-five in a long clinical interview and gave them a battery of a dozen psycholog-ical tests. Then we picked out twenty-four of the applicants, who, on all dimensions, we felt were most average, most normal, most representa-tive of middle-class, intelligent youth. We randomly assigned half of them to be guards and half of them to be prisoners—and they knew the basis of choice in that assignment. None of them were there because they wanted to experience what it meant to be a prisoner—they were there simply to make the fifteen dollars a day. We didn't tell the prisoners they were going to be prisoners; we simply told them to wait at home, and we'd call them when the study was going to begin. However, we made arrangements with the Palo Alto Police Department to arrest them. And so, each one was picked up on a Sunday morning, brought to the police station in a police car, handcuffed, and put through a very formal, very realistic booking. The purpose of that was to deprive them abruptly of their freedom, which is a critical element in becoming a prisoner. The guards were called earlier to come down and help set up the prison.

EVANS: Did you give either group any training for their roles?

ZIMBARDO: No, and once the experiment began, we, as experi-menters, had very little input into the guard-prisoner interaction. At that point, we were simply videotaping and observing the drama unfold. We had intended it to last for two weeks, but the pathology we observed was so extreme, we ended the study after only six days. By "pathology" I mean that half the students who were prisoners had emotional break-downs in less than five days. On the other hand, the guards behaved brutally, sadistically; the only difference among them was their fre-quency of brutal, sadistic, dehumanizing behavior. But they all did it to some degree. What we had done was put good people in an evil situ-ation, and the situation won. My feeling is that the evil situation will always win unless we begin to train people in our society in very different ways than we now do. My argument is that *society* did the training of our subjects to be guards or prisoners, just as society trained Milgram's (1974) subjects to be obedient to authority.

EVANS: Of course, you're referring to Stanley Milgram's study on blind obedience to authority, where people thought they were shocking other people and were willing to give higher and higher voltage on instruction of the experimenter, despite the cruelty.

ZIMBARDO: The argument that I'm making is that in both Milgram's study and our study, the training took place not in the experiment, but in society. In school and at home, they learned the meaning of power and blind obedience to authority and witnessed guard-prisoner roles in their various forms (teacher-student, parent-child, doctor-patient).

EVANS: Currently, there is great concern in the behavioral sciences over the problem of ethics. One of the most difficult issues has been that of "informed consent." Now, as I understand it, both you and Milgram got, in effect, what amounted to signed contracts from subjects that involved obtaining their informed consent to participate in these studies.

ZIMBARDO: In fact, it's even more extreme than that. The informed-consent contracts I had drawn up by the legal staff of Stanford University had a statement that said, in effect, "If you are a prisoner, you can expect to have some of your civil rights violated, loss of freedom, harassment, and for this you will get fifteen dollars a day, a minimally adequate diet, and health care." There were no deceptions during the experiment. We told them it was going to be a prison, and in fact it was, but before doing it, we had no idea how extreme it could be. There is no question that people suffered in this. But we and the legal staff and the subjects all made the same assumption, namely, how bad could it be, if we all know it's an experiment, if we all know it's role playing, and obviously they could leave at any time. What happened is that we all were insensitive to the power of social situational forces, and too certain of dispositional power, thus, within a very short time, identity was totally overwhelmed by role. In terms of the ethics, I'm very much concerned because people did suffer, even with "informed consent" contracts.

EVANS: You're studying means of trying to alleviate human suffering and here you're causing some of it. For a humanistic person such as yourself, it must have been pretty traumatic.

ZIMBARDO: Well, it was traumatic. You could argue why not end the experiment after a prisoner broke down. But we kept assuming they were faking. We began to have long discussions about whether our personality tests didn't really pick out the pathology that was there; we kept blaming it on the person, not the situation. I should mention something else that people are unaware of: parents of those kids came down and saw them in that situation, so did friends, a Catholic priest who was a former prison chaplain, and a public defender. Twenty or thirty psychologists and some of their wives came down and looked in through our observation screens. Not one of these people said we ought to end the experiment because they, too, were playing roles. They came down as my "guests," and we were in a guest-host relationship, and in a sense, they were more bound by that role relationship than by, say, their filial relationship with their child, or their social relationship with people suffering.

EVANS: And in the informed-consent contract, they were given the option of withdrawing at any time. Is that correct?

ZIMBARDO: Yes, they could have withdrawn at any time; instead of doing so, they asked for a doctor, a lawyer, a priest, etc., and we accommodated these requests. We had a parole board meeting, and the first question we asked was, "Are you willing to forfeit the fifteen dollars a day you've earned for your prison labor if we parole you?" And most of the prisoners said, "Yes." So we said, "O.K. Go back to your cell and we'll think about it." And every one of them did. It wasn't until two days later that we wondered why. When they had reached the point at which they said, "We don't want your money," they should have just gotten up and walked out. I mean there were no guns. We were still playing the game—not consciously—to keep them in, but that was the verbal reality that began to govern all our relationships.

EVANS: On the subject of informed consent, you can't really project what subjects are going to experience, can you?

ZIMBARDO: I would think that what is important in overseeing research on human beings is that there is foremost a concern for any possible danger to the subjects. Informed consent helps minimize that, but especially where it's a new area, you can never be certain in advance. I think where an experiment is judged to be of social significance—there are clear benefits to be gained, but there are also clear risks—approval should be provisional, the human subjects research committee should put a detached, dispassionate monitor onto the study. That person would observe the experiment in progress and have the authority to terminate it at any time.

EVANS: You have paid a personal price for this experiment in terms of some of the reactions of the public and of fellow psychologists. On the other hand, you have done something that may have a tremendously important social significance. I know for a fact that you have been invited to testify before Senate and House committees. You've been called in to various prisons as a consultant to share your views. Would you say that your work has been more important in persuading individuals to favor prison reform than efforts that have come out of first-hand reports by participant observers in actual prisons?

ZIMBARDO: I think that for me that is the most critical question of all. It's really a question of relationship between research and social change, and it gets into the whole question of where research ends and advocacy begins. In one sense, we didn't discover anything new from this experiment. But we've used the fundamental characteristics of the scientific method to produce a truth which is compelling. By preselecting subjects who had normal personalities, who had never behaved antisocially, we picked people who were similar to the lawmakers, criminal justice people, and law enforcement personnel. Then by randomly assigning the prisoner and guard roles, we eliminated all of the so-called dispositional explanations of prison pathology, namely, antisocial prisoners and psychopathic guards. We peopled our prison with middle-class people who had never committed crimes nor abused power and found that such an institution has within itself powerful forces that will overwhelm years of socialization, personality traits, and deeply ingrained values. And on the basis of that message, we have been able to get prison officials, as well as legislators, and judges, and lawyers, looking more closely at conditions in their prisons. My feeling is that if you really believe in your research and in your discipline then you have to go beyond being a researcher and a theorist; you actually have to go out and bring your results to the people in question because they don't read our journals. Social change never comes merely from knowledge; it comes from the political activity that knowledge of injustice generates.

EVANS: Recently you have been doing work in the area of madness. It would seem that "madness" has been looked at in so many ways—what else is new? How are you approaching it?

ZIMBARDO: I think I have an interesting perspective in trying to understand the process by which normal people become mad. The basic approach I've been taking is that the process of going mad is essentially a very normal, rational search for explanation for an experience an individual has which is anomalous, some perceived discontinuity. For me, the basic process begins with awareness of source of discontinuity. For example, you suddenly notice that your heart is pounding; there's a sinking feeling in your stomach; you're perspiring; your head is aching; that's a discontinuity because you weren't feeling that a few moments ago. There are other types. One is in your performance. Perhaps one day a man can't get an erection in a situation where he normally does, making love to a woman he cares for. That's a discontinuity from previous performance although there seems to be nothing in the environment that has changed. There are also discontinuities in the natural environment, like an eclipse of the sun or a drought. Life is filled with discontinuities—birth, sickness, failure, death—and for each one that seems significant, human beings come up with an explanation. My research focuses upon the many things that make that search for these explanations into a *biased* search, so that we end up with explanations that other people in society define as "crazy" or "mad." Often, the society provides an explanation or a pseudoexplanation for us, like telling a child he has had a "nightmare" when at some point in his life he is suddenly being chased by lions and tigers, and he wakes up screaming. Where there is no apparent explanation, or no one provides you with one, you are already socially isolated in some way. Sometimes we don't want to acknowledge the "true" cause of a discontinuity, especially if it is a chronic, apparently nonmodifiable state, such as being "ugly," "stupid," "incompetent," "unloved," etc. Then we generate motivational explanations that appear to be more modifiable, such as being impotent or frigid, distracted, hostile, and so on. When the cause occurs infrequently or randomly, or is transient, then any explanation is an "effective" one. The ultimate test of such explanations is whether others with more social power than the person in question accept it as "rational." Because in the final analysis, madness is always an attribution of social inappropriateness of one person by others in his or her society. Some explanations that we come up with are in terms of unseen causes. Explaining observed discontinuities, such as eclipses, lightning, famine, and so on, by saying God, or the gods, were the cause, was probably the way religion started. Now, when you say, "I'm having headaches because there are cosmic forces from outer space causing them," that explanation is not approved in our society, and you would be judged as crazy. But if you say, "God is making me suffer for my sins," there is a large class of people who would accept that explanation as reasonable.

EVANS: How are you going about testing this?

ZIMBARDO: We've been using hypnosis to create states of unexplained arousal to create the experience of discontinuity. A person, under hypnosis, is told that later when he sees a certain object he will experience a sinking feeling in his stomach, his heart will pound, he will have difficulty breathing, and he won't know why. Then we have also told him that it's important for him to find out why, and we've programmed in classes of explanations. My feeling is that different societies and different subgroups in a society give higher priority to certain classes of explanations than to others. So to some subjects we will say, "The explanation will have something to do with your physical health." To others, we say the explanation will have something to do with other people. A third explanation is to search the physical environment. And also, we tell others the explanation may be in their past experience. What we think we've done is produce analogs or models for different kinds of pathology. Thus, a paranoid person is one who sees people as central to the explanation for a series of discontinuous events. For the phobic person, anxiety is channelled into explanations that point to external stimuli in the physical environment. Hypochondriacal persons center explanations for their discontinuities on physical health issues. People who search for explanations in the past, I think, are people who become depressed, who stimulate in themselves guilt and feelings of helplessness. After this posthypnotic suggestion, we run through a standard interview, and what we've been able to show is that normal people come up with explanations that are limited or biased by the categories we gave them. Many of the explanations are very reasonable and rational, but some of them turn out, in fact, to be mad—"mad" judged by logical standards. It is the explanation that becomes the symptom, and the symptom is the madness.

EVANS: The experience, then, has got to be discontinuous; no one else in the group has it, and they can find no social confirmation for it?

ZIMBARDO: Well, suppose you experience a discontinuity, and you search for some explanation of it, but nobody else present is reacting the way you are. One of the things you can do is actually proselytize, getting other people to believe in your explanation. If you can convince two people to believe in your madness, then nobody judges you mad because it's the start of a social movement. Other people can think you're crazy, but nobody's going to hospitalize you because you have "followers," "true believers." So I guess my model says: At an individual level, if the person does not have the power of the social resources to get at least two other converts, then he or she is more likely to be judged by other people as mad, and possibly institutionalized. But that same process of trying to explain a perceived discontinuity, I think, is the process that starts social movements and gives rise to intellectual, "disciplined" searches for discontinuities in physics, astronomy, history, medicine, religion, and psychology. Once again, I believe, it is essential for psychologists to deal with such phenomena on both the personal and societal levels if we want to understand the dynamics of human behavior and also to improve the quality of human life.

REFERENCES

Bettelheim, B. 1943. Individual and mass behavior in extreme situations. *J. Abnorm. Soc. Psychol.* 38: 417–52.

Evans, R. I. 1975. *Carl Rogers: the man and his ideas.* New York: Dutton.

Festinger, L. 1957. *A theory of cognitive dissonance.* Stanford, Calif.: Stanford University Press.

Frankl, V. 1962. *Man's search for meaning.* Boston: Beacon.

Milgram, S. 1974. *Obedience to authority.* New York: Harper.

Mischel, W. 1958. Preference for delayed reinforcement: an experimental study of a cultural observation. *J. Abnorm. Soc. Psychol.* 56: 57–61.

———, and Metzner, R. 1962. Preference for delayed reward as a function of age, intelligence, and length of delay interval. *J. Abnorm. Soc. Psychol.* 64: 425–31.

Montgomery, K. C., and Zimbardo, P. G. 1957. The effects of sensory and behavioral deprivation of exploratory behavior. *J. Percept. Motor Skills* 7: 223–29.

Rotter, J. 1962. An analysis of Adlerian psychology from a research orientation. *J. Indiv. Psychol.* 18: 3–11.

Zimbardo, P. G. 1969a. The cognitive control of motivation: the consequences of choice and dissonance. Glenview, Ill.: Scott, Foresman.

———. 1969b. The human choice: individuation, reason and order versus deindividuation, impulse, and chaos. In *Nebraska Symposium on Motivation*, eds. W. J. Arnold and D. Levine. Lincoln, Neb.: University of Nebraska Press.

———, et al. 1973. The mind is a formidable jailer: a Pirandellian prison. *The New York Times*, p. 38, April 8, 1973.

———, Marshall, G., and Maslach, C. 1971. Liberating behavior from time-bound control: expanding the present through hypnosis. *J. Appl. Soc. Psychol.* 4: 305–23.

Subject Index

Ablation, 139–40

Acetylcholinesterase, 140, 141

Achievement: measurement of, 148, 149; need for, 149

Achievement motivation, 147–57; cross-cultural studies, 153–4; and power, 151–2

Acid, *see* LSD

Adolescence: delinquency in, 298; Erikson's theories on, 295–8; rebellion in, 209

Adrenaline, 143, 156, 166, 167

Adulthood, Erikson's theories on, 300–1

Aesthetics, 261–2

Affectivity, 43

Affiliation, 159–61

Aggression: and anonymity, 364; Bandura's studies of, 248–53; frustration-aggression hypothesis, 173–4, 249; Lorenz on, 10–15, 174; in operant conditioning, 9, 10; and social stress, 28; and territorial behavior, 11, 23

Aging, 206; Erikson's theories on, 301; and identity, 299

Alchemy, 282

Alcohol, 362

Alcoholic psychosis, 231

Alcoholism, 248; and power motivation, 152, 155–6

Alienation, 206, 309, 317

Alpha rhythm, 122–8

American character: Fromm on, 311; Jones on, 272; Jung on, 290

American Medical Association, 81

American Psychiatric Association, 230, 264

Anal stage of development, 293, 307–8, 309

"And Besides Syndrome," 337

Anima, 283–4, 286

Animals: aggression, 11, 13–14, 23; communication, 25; courtship, 13; extrasensory perception, 115; homosexuality, 4–5; man compared with, 21–2, 31, 32; modeling, 244; and overpopulation, 5–7; sexual dominance, 4, 24; social interaction, 24–5; territorial behavior, 6, 23, 25; Tinbergen's studies of, 18–26

Animus, 283–4

Anonymity, 364

Anthropomorphism, 31

Anti-Semitism, *see* Jews

Anxiety, 12, 206, 362; and affiliation, 161; and behavior therapy, 258; and crime, 167; and smoking, 165

Apathy of bystanders, *see* bystanders

Archetypes, 229–30, 281–3, 286, 287, 313

Attitudes, 340–2; and behavior, 329–30; changing, 342

Authoritarianism, 152, 311; F-Scale test, 337; Fromm's ideas on, 312; in Milgram's experiments, 352–3; Rokeach's studies of, 335–7, 340

Authority pressure, 349

Autistic children, 27–8

Name Index

ABOUT THE AUTHOR

Richard I. Evans received his Ph.D. from Michigan State University and is currently professor of psychology at the University of Houston and a principal investigator at the National Heart and Blood Vessel Research and Demonstration Center. A National Science Foundation grant has enabled him to film interviews with some of the world's foremost psychologists, including Carl Jung, Erich Fromm, Erik Erikson, Gordon Allport, Carl Rogers, Jean Piaget, and Konrad Lorenz. He is a pioneer in educational television and in the social psychology of communication, and has published a number of professional articles in the area of social psychology. His most recent books include *Resistance to Innovation in Higher Education, Social Psychology in Life* (with Richard Rozelle), *Jung on Elementary Psychology,* and volumes on B. F. Skinner, Jean Piaget, Carl Rogers, Konrad Lorenz, and R. D. Laing. His recent honors include the American Psychological Foundation Media Awards for the book, *Gordon Allport: The Man and His Ideas,* and the film, *A Psychology of Creativity.* He and his colleagues received the American Psychological Association Division 13 Research Excellence Award for a research paper in the area of social psychology of communication.

A NOTE ON THE TYPE

The text of this book is set in CALEDONIA, a Linotype face designed by W. A. Dwiggins. It belongs to the family of printing types called "modern face" by printers —a term used to mark the change in style of type-letters that occurred about 1800. Caledonia borders on the general design of Scotch Modern, but is more freely drawn than that letter.
The book was composed by Cherry Hill Composition, Pennsauken, N.J. Printed and bound by R. R. Donnelley & Sons Company, Crawfordsville, Indiana.